DATA ANALYSIS WORKSHOP

Solve business problems with state-of-the-art data analysis models, developing expert data analysis skills along the way

Gururajan Govindan, Shubhangi Hora, and Konstantin Palagachev

THE DATA ANALYSIS WORKSHOP

Authors: Gururajan Govindan, Shubhangi Hora, and Konstantin Palagachev

Reviewers: Brent Broadnax, John Wesley Doyle, Ashish Jain, Robert Thas John, Ravi Ranjan Prasad Karn, Ashish Patel, and Pritesh Tiwari

Managing Editor: Snehal Tambe

Acquisitions Editors: Manuraj Nair, Royluis Rodrigues, Kunal Sawant, Archie Vankar, and Karan Wadekar

Production Editor: Salma Patel

Editorial Board: Megan Carlisle, Samuel Christa, Mahesh Dhyani, Heather Gopsill, Manasa Kumar, Alex Mazonowicz, Monesh Mirpuri, Bridget Neale, Dominic Pereira, Shiny Poojary, Abhishek Rane, Brendan Rodrigues, Erol Staveley, Ankita Thakur, Nitesh Thakur, and Jonathan Wray

First published: July 2020

Production reference: 2040820

ISBN: 978-1-83921-138-6

Published by Packt Publishing Ltd.

Livery Place, 35 Livery Street

Birmingham B3 2PB, UK

EXPERIENCE THE WORKSHOP ONLINE

Thank you for purchasing the print edition of *The Data Analysis Workshop*. Every physical print copy includes free online access to the premium interactive edition. There are no extra costs or hidden charges.

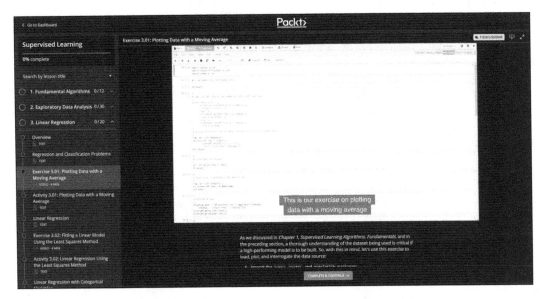

Figure A: An example of the companion video in the Workshop course player (dark mode)

With the interactive edition you'll unlock:

- **Screencasts**: Supercharge your progress with screencasts of all exercises and activities.

- **Built-In Discussions**: Engage in discussions where you can ask questions, share notes and interact. Tap straight into insight from expert instructors and editorial teams.

- **Skill Verification**: Complete the course online to earn a Packt credential that is easy to share and unique to you. All authenticated on the public Bitcoin blockchain.

- **Download PDF and EPUB**: Download a digital version of the course to read offline. Available as PDF or EPUB, and always DRM-free.

To redeem your free digital copy of *The Data Analysis Workshop* you'll need to follow these simple steps:

1. Visit us at https://courses.packtpub.com/pages/redeem.

2. Login with your Packt account, or register as a new Packt user.

3. Select your course from the list, making a note of the three page numbers for your product. Your unique redemption code needs to match the order of the pages specified.

4. Open up your print copy and find the codes at the bottom of the pages specified. They'll always be in the same place:

EXERCISE 4.02: PERFORMING MISSING VALUE ANALYSIS FOR THE DATAFRAMES

In this section, we will be implementing a missing value analysis on the first DataFrame to find the missing values. This exercise is a continuation of *Exercise 4.01, Importing Data into DataFrames*. Follow these steps to complete this exercise:

1. Import the **missingno** package:

```
# To analyze the missing data
!pip install missingno
import missingno as msno
```

2. Find the missing values in the first DataFrame and visualize the missing values in a plot:

```
# Missing Values in the first DataFrame
msno.bar(dataframes[0],color='red',labels=True,sort="ascending")
```

A B 2 1 C

**Figure B: Example code in the bottom-right corner, to be used
for free digital redemption of a print workshop**

5. Merge the codes together (without spaces), ensuring they are in the correct order.

6. At checkout, click **Have a redemption code?** and enter your unique product string. Click **Apply**, and the price should be free!

Finally, we'd like to thank you for purchasing the print edition of *The Data Analysis Workshop*! We hope that you finish the course feeling capable of tackling challenges in the real world. Remember that we're here to help if you ever feel like you're not making progress.

If you run into issues during redemption (or have any other feedback) you can reach us at workshops@packt.com.

Table of Contents

Chapter 5: Analyzing the Online Shopper's Purchasing Intention   233

Chapter 7: Analyzing the Heart Disease Dataset   319

Chapter 10: Analyzing Air Quality   441

Appendix   489

Index   601

PREFACE

ABOUT THE BOOK

Businesses today operate online and generate data almost continuously. While not all data in its raw form may seem useful, if processed and analyzed correctly, it can provide you with valuable hidden insights. *The Data Analysis Workshop* will help you learn how to discover these hidden patterns in your data, to analyze them and leverage the results to help transform your business.

The book begins by taking you through the use case of a bike rental shop. You'll be shown how to correlate data, plot histograms, and analyze temporal features. As you progress, you'll learn how to plot data for a hydraulic system using the Seaborn and Matplotlib libraries, and explore a variety of use cases that show you how to join and merge databases, prepare data for analysis, and handle imbalanced data.

By the end of the book, you'll have learned different data analysis techniques, including hypothesis testing, correlation, and null-value imputation, and will have become a confident data analyst.

AUDIENCE

The Data Analysis Workshop is for programmers who already know how to code in Python and want to use it to perform data analysis. If you are looking to gain practical experience in data science with Python, this book is for you.

ABOUT THE CHAPTERS

Chapter 1, Bike Sharing Analysis, teaches you how to analyze data from bike-sharing services and identify usage patterns, depending on time features and weather conditions.

Chapter 2, Absenteeism at Work, teaches you how to perform standard data analysis techniques, such as estimating conditional probabilities, Bayes' theorem, and the Kolmogorov-Smirnov test for distribution comparison.

Chapter 3, Analyzing Bank Marketing Campaign Data, teaches you how to analyze marketing campaign data related to new financial products and model the relationships between the different features in the data and their impact on the final outcome of the campaign.

Chapter 4, Tackling Company Bankruptcy, prepares you to perform exploratory data analysis using pandas profiling and how to handle imbalances in the data using the oversampling technique.

Chapter 5, Analyzing the Online Shopper's Purchasing Intention, teaches you how to perform univariate and bivariate analysis, implement clustering, and make recommendations based on the predictions.

Chapter 6, Analysis of Credit Card Defaulters, teaches you how to analyze the characteristics and build the persona of the customer who is most likely to default on their credit card payments.

Chapter 7, Analyzing the Heart Disease Dataset, prepares you to execute various data analysis techniques, such as searching for missing values and outliers, and plot visualizations to observe trends and patterns that exist in the data.

Chapter 8, Analyzing Online Retail II Dataset, prepares you to analyze data retrieved from an online retail company to observe patterns and correlations, and to evaluate the business more accurately and in more depth.

Chapter 9, Analysis of the Energy Consumed by Appliances, teaches you how to perform feature engineering by creating new features from existing ones, conducting exploratory data analysis, and designing informative visualizations.

Chapter 10, Analyzing Air Quality, instructs you how to implement data analysis techniques pertaining to a specific dataset—the Beijing Multi-Site Air-Quality Dataset.

CONVENTIONS

Code words in text, database table names, folder names, filenames, file extensions, pathnames, dummy URLs, user input, and Twitter handles are shown as follows: "For this reason, use the **np.issubdtype()** function, which checks if the type of the first argument is equal to or a subtype of the second one."

Words that you see onscreen (for example, in menus or dialog boxes) also appear in the text like this: "Then, set the title as **Distribution of Presence of Heart Disease by Number of Vessels Colored by Fluoroscopy**."

A block of code is set as follows:

```
d.set_title('Distribution of Presence of Heart Disease by Number of Major Vessels Coloured by Fluoroscopy')
plt.show()
```

New terms and important words are shown like this: "An **ARFF (Attribute-Relation File Format)** file is an ASCII text file. It essentially explains a list of instances that commonly share an attribute set."

CODE PRESENTATION

Lines of code that span multiple lines are split using a backslash (\ ). When the code is executed, Python will ignore the backslash, and treat the code on the next line as a direct continuation of the current line.

For example:

```
history = model.fit(X, y, epochs=100, batch_size=5, verbose=1, \
                    validation_split=0.2, shuffle=False)
```

Comments are added into code to help explain specific bits of logic. Single-line comments are denoted using the # symbol, as follows:

```
# Print the sizes of the dataset
print("Number of Examples in the Dataset = ", X.shape[0])
print("Number of Features for each example = ", X.shape[1])
```

Multi-line comments are enclosed by triple quotes, as shown below:

```
"""
Define a seed for the random number generator to ensure the
result will be reproducible
"""
seed = 1
np.random.seed(seed)
random.set_seed(seed)
```

SETTING UP YOUR ENVIRONMENT

Before we explore the book in detail, we need to set up specific software and tools. In the following section, we shall see how to do that.

INSTALLATION AND SETUP

Jupyter notebooks are available once you install Anaconda on your system. Anaconda can be installed for Windows systems using the steps available at https://docs. anaconda.com/anaconda/install/windows/.

For other systems, navigate to the respective installation guide from https://docs. anaconda.com/anaconda/install/.

These installations will be executed in the C drive of your system. You can choose to change the destination.

INSTALLING LIBRARIES

`pip` comes pre-installed with Anaconda. Once Anaconda is installed on your machine, all the required libraries can be installed using `pip`, for example, `pip install numpy`. Alternatively, you can install all the required libraries using `pip install -r requirements.txt`. You can find the `requirements.txt` file at https://packt.live/2N6PPZv.

The exercises and activities will be executed in Jupyter Notebooks. Jupyter is a Python library and can be installed in the same way as the other Python libraries – that is, with `pip install jupyter`, but fortunately, it comes pre-installed with Anaconda. To open a notebook, simply run the command `jupyter notebook` in the Terminal or Command Prompt.

ACCESSING THE CODE FILES

You can find the complete code files of this book at https://packt.live/34iiLFK. You can also run many activities and exercises directly in your web browser by using the interactive lab environment at https://packt.live/2UWecgN.

We've tried to support interactive versions of all activities and exercises, but we recommend a local installation as well for instances where this support isn't available.

> **NOTE**
>
> It is imperative that you use a single notebook for each chapter and follow all the practical elements in the order that they appear in the book to avoid errors.

If you have any issues or questions about installation, please email us at workshops@packt.com.

1

BIKE SHARING ANALYSIS

OVERVIEW

This chapter will teach you how to analyze data from bike sharing services and how to identify usage patterns depending on time features and weather conditions. Furthermore, you will apply concepts such as visual analysis, hypothesis testing, and time series analysis to the available data. By the end of this chapter, you should be able to work with time series data and apply some of the main data analysis techniques to business scenarios.

INTRODUCTION

Data analysis is becoming one of the most in-demand skills of the 21st century. The exponential growth of data, the increase of computation power, and the reduced costs for cloud and high-performance computing allow both companies and individuals to analyze large amounts of data that were intractable 20 years ago. This type of analysis unlocks new business opportunities for companies that have decided to adopt data analytics in their business.

Integrating data analytics into the core business of a company is not an easy task. A well-established team of software engineers, data engineers, and data scientists is required, in which the team members not only have a broad experience of algorithms, software architecture, and machine learning, but also a good understanding of the business of the company. While the first three skills are easily transferable from one type of business to another, understanding the business itself takes time.

In this book, we provide an introduction on how to apply analytical skills to various business problems, aiming, in this way, to reduce the gap between theoretical knowledge and practical experience.

We have decided to adopt Python as the only language for the analyses in this book. There are several reasons for this: first, Python is a general-purpose language, with a large community constantly working to improve its features and functionalities. Second, it is also one of the easiest languages to start with, even with no prior experience of programming. Third, there is a broad variety of excellent scientific computing and machine learning libraries written in Python, and, finally, all of these libraries are open source.

Since an introduction to Python is beyond the scope of this book, we assume that the reader has some prior knowledge of it. Furthermore, we assume some basic knowledge of the standard Python packages for data analysis (such as **pandas**, **numpy**, and **scipy**). Although we do not provide a rigorous introduction to these libraries, explanations of the used functions and modules are given where necessary.

We start our first chapter with a relatively easy problem, involving bike sharing data.

Bike sharing is a fundamental service, commonly used in the urban mobility sector. It is easily accessible (as no driving license is required to ride a bike), is cheaper than normal car sharing services (since bike maintenance and insurance are substantially cheaper than automobile ones), and, finally, is often a fast way to commute within the city. Therefore, understanding the driving factors of bike sharing requests is essential for both companies and users.

From a company's perspective, identifying the expected bike demand in a specific area, within a specific time frame, can significantly increase revenue and customer satisfaction. Moreover, bike relocation can be optimized to further reduce operational costs. From a user's perspective, probably the most important factor is bike availability in the shortest wait time, which we can easily see aligning with the company's interests.

In this chapter, we will analyze bike sharing data from Capital Bikeshare in Washington, D.C., USA, for the period between January 1, 2011, and December 31, 2012. The data is aggregated on an hourly basis. This means that no initial and final locations of the individual rides are available, but only the total number of rides per hour. Nevertheless, additional meteorological information is available in the data, which could serve as a driving factor for identifying the total number of requests for a specific time frame (bad weather conditions could have a substantial impact on bike sharing demand).

> **NOTE**
>
> The original dataset is available at https://archive.ics.uci.edu/ml/datasets/Bike+Sharing+Dataset#.
>
> For further information on this topic, check out the following journal article: Fanaee-T, Hadi, and Gama, Joao, '*Event labeling combining ensemble detectors and background knowledge*', Progress in Artificial Intelligence (2013): pp. 1-15, Springer Berlin Heidelberg.

Note that although the conducted analysis is related to bike sharing, the provided techniques could be easily transferred to other types of sharing business models, such as car or scooter sharing.

UNDERSTANDING THE DATA

In this first part, we load the data and perform an initial exploration of it.

> **NOTE**
>
> You can download the data either from the original source (https://archive.ics.uci.edu/ml/datasets/Bike+Sharing+Dataset#) or from the GitHub repository of this book (https://packt.live/2XpHW81).

The main goal of the presented steps is to acquire some basic knowledge about the data, how the various features are distributed, and whether there are missing values in it.

First import the relevant Python libraries and the data itself for the analysis. Note that we are using Python 3.7. Furthermore, we directly load the data from the GitHub repository of the book:

```
# imports
import pandas as pd
import seaborn as sns
import matplotlib.pyplot as plt
import numpy as np
%matplotlib inline


# load hourly data
hourly_data = pd.read_csv('https://raw.githubusercontent.com/'\
                    'PacktWorkshops/'\
                    'The-Data-Analysis-Workshop/'\
                    'master/Chapter01/data/hour.csv')
```

> **NOTE**
>
> The # symbol in the code snippet above denotes a code comment. Comments are added into code to help explain specific bits of logic. Also, watch out for the slashes in the string above. The backslashes (\ ) are used to split the code across multiple lines, while the forward slashes (/) are part of the URL.

A good practice is to check the size of the data we are loading, the number of missing values of each column, and some general statistics about the numerical columns:

```
# print some generic statistics about the data
print(f"Shape of data: {hourly_data.shape}")
print(f"Number of missing values in the data:\
{hourly_data.isnull().sum().sum()}")
```

> **NOTE**
>
> The code snippet shown here uses a backslash (\ ) to split the logic across multiple lines. When the code is executed, Python will ignore the backslash, and treat the code on the next line as a direct continuation of the current line.

The output is as follows:

```
Shape of data: (17379, 17)
Number of missing values in the data: 0
```

In order to get some simple statistics on the numerical columns, such as the mean, standard deviation, minimum and maximum values, and their percentiles, we can use the **describe()** function directly on a **pandas.Dataset** object:

```
# get statistics on the numerical columns
hourly_data.describe().T
```

The output should be as follows:

	count	mean	std	min	25%	50%	75%	max
instant	17379.0	8690.000000	5017.029500	1.00	4345.5000	8690.0000	13034.5000	17379.0000
season	17379.0	2.501640	1.106918	1.00	2.0000	3.0000	3.0000	4.0000
yr	17379.0	0.502561	0.500008	0.00	0.0000	1.0000	1.0000	1.0000
mnth	17379.0	6.537775	3.438776	1.00	4.0000	7.0000	10.0000	12.0000
hr	17379.0	11.546752	6.914405	0.00	6.0000	12.0000	18.0000	23.0000
holiday	17379.0	0.028770	0.167165	0.00	0.0000	0.0000	0.0000	1.0000
weekday	17379.0	3.003683	2.005771	0.00	1.0000	3.0000	5.0000	6.0000
workingday	17379.0	0.682721	0.465431	0.00	0.0000	1.0000	1.0000	1.0000
weathersit	17379.0	1.425283	0.639357	1.00	1.0000	1.0000	2.0000	4.0000
temp	17379.0	0.496987	0.192556	0.02	0.3400	0.5000	0.6600	1.0000
atemp	17379.0	0.475775	0.171850	0.00	0.3333	0.4848	0.6212	1.0000
hum	17379.0	0.627229	0.192930	0.00	0.4800	0.6300	0.7800	1.0000
windspeed	17379.0	0.190098	0.122340	0.00	0.1045	0.1940	0.2537	0.8507
casual	17379.0	35.676218	49.305030	0.00	4.0000	17.0000	48.0000	367.0000
registered	17379.0	153.786869	151.357286	0.00	34.0000	115.0000	220.0000	886.0000
cnt	17379.0	189.463088	181.387599	1.00	40.0000	142.0000	281.0000	977.0000

Figure 1.1: Output of the describe() method

Note that the **T** character after the **describe()** method gets the transpose of the resulting dataset, hence the columns become rows and vice versa.

According to the description of the original data, provided in the **Readme.txt** file, we can split the columns into three main groups:

- **temporal features**: This contains information about the time at which the record was registered. This group contains the **dteday**, **season**, **yr**, **mnth**, **hr**, **holiday**, **weekday**, and **workingday** columns.

- **weather related features**: This contains information about the weather conditions. The **weathersit**, **temp**, **atemp**, **hum**, and **windspeed** columns are included in this group.

- **record related features**: This contains information about the number of records for the specific hour and date. This group includes the **casual**, **registered**, and **cnt** columns.

Note that we did not include the first column, **instant**, in any of the previously mentioned groups. The reason for this is that it is an index column and will be excluded from our analysis, as it does not contain any relevant information for our analysis.

DATA PREPROCESSING

In this section, we perform some preprocessing steps, which will allow us to transform the data into a more human-readable format. Note that data preprocessing and wrangling is one of the most important parts of data analysis. In fact, a lot of hidden patterns and relationships might arise when data is transformed in the correct way.

Furthermore, some machine learning algorithms might not even converge, or they may provide an erroneous result when fed with badly preprocessed data (a typical example of this is not scaling data in deep learning). In other cases, deriving insights from normalized data might be difficult for a human; therefore, it is good practice to transform the data before presenting the results.

In this use case, the data is already normalized and ready for analysis; nevertheless, some of its columns are hard to interpret from a human perspective. Before proceeding further, we will perform some basic transformations on the columns, which will result in a more easy-to-understand analysis at a later stage.

EXERCISE 1.01: PREPROCESSING TEMPORAL AND WEATHER FEATURES

In the first part of this exercise, we are going to encode the temporal features into a more human-readable format. The **seasons** column contains values from 1 to 4, which encode, respectively, the **Winter**, **Spring**, **Summer**, and **Fall** seasons. The **yr** column contains the values **0** and **1** representing 2011 and 2012, while the **weekday** column contains values from 0 to 6, with each one representing a day of the week (0: **Sunday**, 1: **Monday**, through to 6: **Saturday**). Furthermore, we scale the **hum** column to values between 0 and 100 (as it represents the humidity percentage), and the **windspeed** column to values between 0 and 67 (as those are the registered minimum and maximum wind speed):

1. As a first step, create a copy of the original dataset. This is done as we do not want a specific transformation to affect our initial data:

```
# create a copy of the original data
preprocessed_data = hourly_data.copy()
```

2. In the next step, map the **season** variable from a numerical to a nicely encoded categorical one. In order to do that, we create a Python dictionary, which contains the encoding, and then exploit the **apply** and **lambda** functions:

```
# transform seasons
seasons_mapping = {1: 'winter', 2: 'spring', \
                   3: 'summer', 4: 'fall'}
preprocessed_data['season'] = preprocessed_data['season']\
                        .apply(lambda x: seasons_mapping[x])
```

3. Create a Python dictionary for the **yr** column as well:

```
# transform yr
yr_mapping = {0: 2011, 1: 2012}
preprocessed_data['yr'] = preprocessed_data['yr']\
                     .apply(lambda x: yr_mapping[x])
```

4. Create a Python dictionary for the **weekday** column:

```
# transform weekday
weekday_mapping = {0: 'Sunday', 1: 'Monday', 2: 'Tuesday', \
                   3: 'Wednesday', 4: 'Thursday', 5: 'Friday', \
                   6: 'Saturday'}
preprocessed_data['weekday'] = preprocessed_data['weekday']\
                        .apply(lambda x: weekday_mapping[x])
```

Let's now proceed with encoding the weather-related columns (**weathersit**, **hum**, and **windspeed**). According to the information provided by the data, the **weathersit** column represents the current weather conditions, where **1** stands for clear weather with a few clouds, **2** represents cloudy weather, **3** relates to light snow or rain, and **4** stands for heavy snow or rain. The **hum** column stands for the current normalized air humidity, with values from 0 to 1 (hence, we will multiply the values of this column by 100, in order to obtain percentages). Finally, the **windspeed** column represents the windspeed, which is again normalized to values between 0 and 67 m/s.

5. Encode the **weathersit** values:

```
# transform weathersit
weather_mapping = {1: 'clear', 2: 'cloudy', \
                   3: 'light_rain_snow', 4: 'heavy_rain_snow'}
preprocessed_data['weathersit'] = preprocessed_data['weathersit']\
                             .apply(lambda x: \
                             weather_mapping[x])
```

6. Finally, rescale the **hum** and **windspeed** columns:

```
# transform hum and windspeed
preprocessed_data['hum'] = preprocessed_data['hum']*100
preprocessed_data['windspeed'] = preprocessed_data['windspeed']\
                        *67
```

7. We can visualize the results from our transformation by calling the **sample()** method on the newly created dataset:

```
# visualize preprocessed columns
cols = ['season', 'yr', 'weekday', \
        'weathersit', 'hum', 'windspeed']
preprocessed_data[cols].sample(10, random_state=123)
```

The output should be as follows:

	season	yr	weekday	weathersit	hum	windspeed
5792	summer	2011	Saturday	clear	74.0	8.9981
7823	fall	2011	Sunday	clear	43.0	31.0009
15426	fall	2012	Tuesday	cloudy	77.0	6.0032
15028	fall	2012	Sunday	clear	51.0	22.0028
12290	spring	2012	Friday	cloudy	89.0	12.9980
3262	spring	2011	Friday	clear	64.0	7.0015
10763	spring	2012	Thursday	clear	42.0	23.9994
12384	spring	2012	Tuesday	light_rain_snow	82.0	11.0014
6051	summer	2011	Wednesday	clear	52.0	19.0012
948	winter	2011	Saturday	clear	80.0	0.0000

Figure 1.2: Result from the transformed variables

> **NOTE**
>
> To access the source code for this specific section, please refer to https://packt.live/2AFELjq.
>
> You can also run this example online at https://packt.live/3e6xesx. You must execute the entire Notebook in order to get the desired result.

As you can see from the output, the transformed features have categorial values instead of numerical ones. This makes the data more readable and allows certain **pandas** functions to correctly plot the data (as will be demonstrated later).

Note that, in this exercise, we did not transform the **temp** and **atemp** columns (that is, the true and perceived temperatures, respectively). The reason for this is that they assume only positive values in the original dataset (hence, we do not know when the negative temperatures occurred). Furthermore, as their scales are different (the maximum value registered in the true temperature is 41 degrees, while the perceived one is 67), we do not want to modify their relations (that is, the hours at which the true temperature is greater than the perceived one and vice versa).

REGISTERED VERSUS CASUAL USE ANALYSIS

We begin our analysis of the single features by focusing on the two main ones: the number of rides performed by registered users versus the number of rides performed by non-registered (or casual) ones. These numbers are represented in the **registered** and **casual** columns, respectively, with the **cnt** column representing the sum of the registered and casual rides. We can easily verify the last statement for each entry in the dataset by using the **assert** statement:

```
"""
assert that total number of rides is equal to the sum of registered and
casual ones
"""
assert (preprocessed_data.casual \
        + preprocessed_data.registered \
        == preprocessed_data.cnt).all(), \
       'Sum of casual and registered rides not equal '\
       'to total number of rides'
```

> **NOTE**
>
> The triple-quotes (""") shown in the code snippet above are used to denote the start and end points of a multi-line code comment. Comments are added into code to help explain specific bits of logic.

The first step in analyzing the two columns is to look at their distributions. A useful Python package that we will use extensively in this book is **seaborn**. It is a data visualization library built on top of the standard **matplotlib** package, which provides a high-level interface for various statistical plots. In this way, the plots we present later will be both nicer and easier to produce. Let's start by visualizing the distribution of the **registered** and **casual** rides:

```
# plot distributions of registered vs casual rides
sns.distplot(preprocessed_data['registered'], label='registered')
sns.distplot(preprocessed_data['casual'], label='casual')
plt.legend()
plt.xlabel('rides')
plt.title("Rides distributions")
plt.savefig('figs/rides_distributions.png', format='png')
```

The output should be as follows:

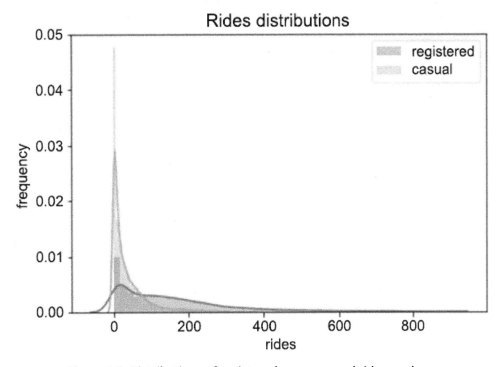

Figure 1.3: Distributions of registered versus casual rides per hour

From *Figure 1.3*, we can easily see that registered users perform way more rides than casual ones. Furthermore, we can see that the two distributions are skewed to the right, meaning that, for most of the entries in the data, zero or a small number of rides were registered (think, for example, of overnight rides). Finally, every entry in the data has quite a large number of rides (that is, higher than 800).

Let's now focus on the evolution of rides over time. We can analyze the number of rides each day with the following piece of code:

```
# plot evolution of rides over time
plot_data = preprocessed_data[['registered', 'casual', 'dteday']]
ax = plot_data.groupby('dteday').sum().plot(figsize=(10,6))
ax.set_xlabel("time");
ax.set_ylabel("number of rides per day");
plt.savefig('figs/rides_daily.png', format='png')
```

Here, we first take a subset of the original **preprocessed_data** dataset. Afterward, we compute the total number of rides for each day by first grouping the data by the **dteday** column, and then summing the single entries for the **casual** and **registered** columns. The result of the code snippet is given in the following figure:

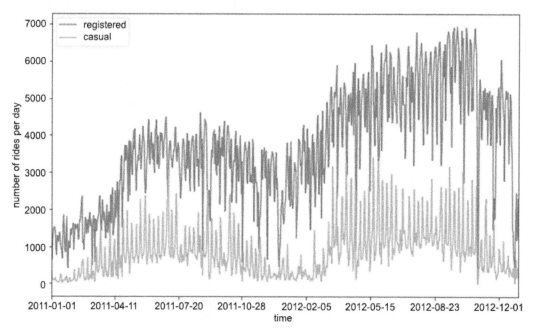

Figure 1.4: Evolution of the number of rides per day for registered and casual customers

As you can see from the preceding figure, the number of registered rides is always above and significantly higher than the number of casual rides per day. Furthermore, we can observe that during winter, the overall number of rides decreases (which is totally in line with our expectations, as bad weather and low temperatures have a negative impact on ride sharing services). Note that there is quite a lot of variance in the time series of the rides in *Figure 1.4*. One way to smooth out the curves is to take the rolling mean and standard deviation of the two time series and plot those instead. In this way, we can visualize not only the average number of rides for a specific time period (also known as a **window**) but also the expected deviation from the mean:

```python
"""
Create new dataframe with necessary for plotting columns, and obtain
number of rides per day, by grouping over each day
"""
plot_data = preprocessed_data[['registered', 'casual', 'dteday']]
plot_data = plot_data.groupby('dteday').sum()
"""
define window for computing the rolling mean and standard deviation
"""
window = 7
rolling_means = plot_data.rolling(window).mean()
rolling_deviations = plot_data.rolling(window).std()
"""
Create a plot of the series, where we first plot the series of rolling
means, then we color the zone between the series of rolling means +- 2
rolling standard deviations
"""
ax = rolling_means.plot(figsize=(10,6))
ax.fill_between(rolling_means.index, rolling_means['registered'] \
                + 2*rolling_deviations['registered'], \
                rolling_means['registered'] \
                - 2*rolling_deviations['registered'], \
                alpha = 0.2)
ax.fill_between(rolling_means.index, rolling_means['casual'] \
                + 2*rolling_deviations['casual'], \
                rolling_means['casual'] \
                - 2*rolling_deviations['casual'], \
                alpha = 0.2)
ax.set_xlabel("time");
ax.set_ylabel("number of rides per day");
plt.savefig('figs/rides_aggregated.png', format='png')
```

The preceding code snippet produces the following figure:

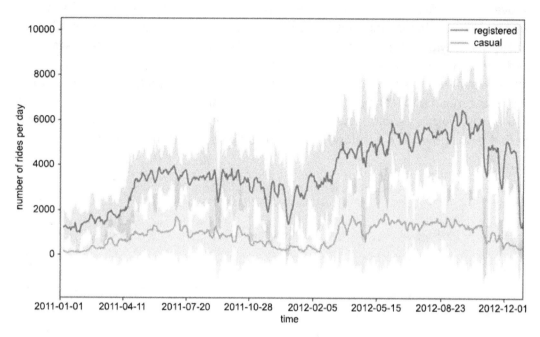

Figure 1.5: The rolling mean and standard deviation of rides

In order to compute the rolling statistics (that is, the mean and standard deviation), we use the **rolling()** function, in which we use **mean()** and **std()** to compute the rolling mean and standard deviation, respectively. This is a handy way to compute rolling statistics on time series, in which only recent entries account for computing them. In other words, the value of the rolling mean (or the standard deviation) at a certain time instance is only computed from the last *window* entries in the time series (in our case, this is 7), and not from the entries of the whole series.

Let's now focus on the distributions of the requests over separate hours and days of the week. We would expect certain time patterns to arise, as bike requests should be more frequent during certain hours of the day, depending on the day of the week. This analysis can be easily done by leveraging various functions from the **seaborn** package, as shown in the following code snippet:

```
# select relevant columns
plot_data = preprocessed_data[['hr', 'weekday', 'registered', 'casual']]
"""
transform the data into a format, in number of entries are computed as
count,
for each distinct hr, weekday and type (registered or casual)
"""
```

```
plot_data = plot_data.melt(id_vars=['hr', 'weekday'], \
                           var_name='type', value_name='count')
"""
create FacetGrid object, in which a grid plot is produced.
As columns, we have the various days of the week,
as rows, the different types (registered and casual)
"""
grid = sns.FacetGrid(plot_data, row='weekday', \
                     col='type', height=2.5, aspect=2.5, \
                     row_order=['Monday', 'Tuesday', \
                                'Wednesday', 'Thursday', \
                                'Friday', 'Saturday', 'Sunday'])
# populate the FacetGrid with the specific plots
grid.map(sns.barplot, 'hr', 'count', alpha=0.5)
grid.savefig('figs/weekday_hour_distributions.png', format='png')
```

Let's focus on the **melt()** function, applied on a **pandas** dataset. It will create a new dataset, in which values are grouped by the **hr** and **weekday** columns, while creating two new columns: **type** (containing the **casual** and **registered** values) and **count** (containing the respective counts for the **casual** and **registered** types).

The **seaborn.FacetGrid()** function will create a new grid of plots, with rows corresponding to the different days of the week and columns corresponding to the types. Finally, the **map()** function is applied to each element of the grid, creating the respective plots. The produced plot is shown in *Figure 1.6*. We can immediately note that on working days, the highest number of rides for registered users takes place around 8 AM and at 6 PM. This is totally in line with our expectations, as it is likely that most registered users use the bike sharing service for commuting. On the other hand, the casual usage of bike sharing services on working days is quite limited, as the plot shows.

During the weekend, we can see that ride distributions change for both casual and registered users. Still, registered rides are more frequent than casual ones, but both the distributions have the same shape, almost uniformly distributed between the time interval of 11 AM to 6 PM.

As a conclusion, we could claim that most of the usage of bike sharing services occurs during working days, right before and right after the standard working time (that is, 9 to 5):

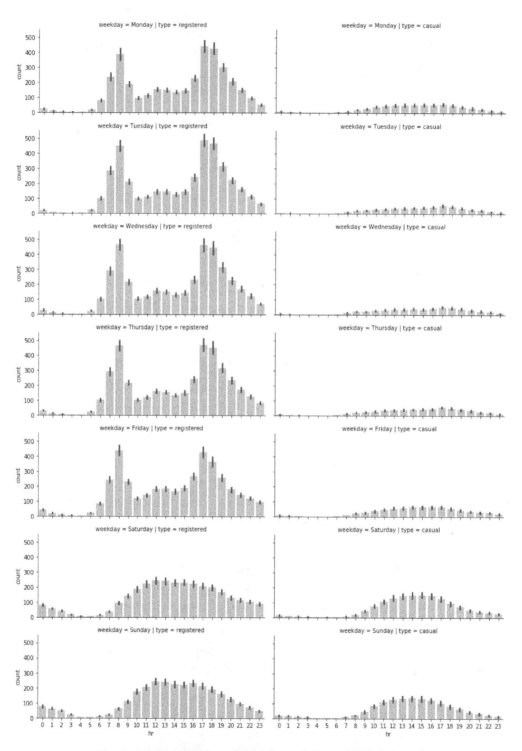

Figure 1.6: Distribution of rides on a daily and hourly basis

EXERCISE 1.02: ANALYZING SEASONAL IMPACT ON RIDES

In this exercise, we will investigate the impact of the different seasons on the total number of rides. Our goal is to create grid plots, similar to the one in *Figure 1.6*, in which the number of rides will be distributed over hours and weekdays, based on the current season. This exercise is a continuation of *Exercise 1.01, Preprocessing Temporal and Weather Features*:

1. Start by combining the hours and seasons. Create a subset of the initial data by selecting the **hr**, **season**, **registered**, and **casual** columns:

```
# select subset of the data
plot_data = preprocessed_data[['hr', 'season', \
                               'registered', 'casual']]
```

2. Next, unpivot the data from wide to long format:

```
# unpivot data from wide to long format
plot_data = plot_data.melt(id_vars=['hr', 'season'], \
                           var_name='type', value_name='count')
```

3. Define the seaborn **FacetGrid** object, in which rows represent the different seasons:

```
# define FacetGrid
grid = sns.FacetGrid(plot_data, row='season', \
                     col='type', height=2.5, \
                     aspect=2.5, \
                     row_order=['winter', 'spring', \
                                'summer', 'fall'])
```

Note that we are also specifying the desired order of rows here. We do this as we want the rows to appear in a certain order.

4. Finally, apply the **seaborn.barplot()** function to each of the **FacetGrid** elements:

```
# apply plotting function to each element in the grid
grid.map(sns.barplot, 'hr', 'count', alpha=0.5)

# save figure
grid.savefig('figs/exercise_1_02_a.png', format='png')
```

The resulting plot is shown in *Figure 1.7*:

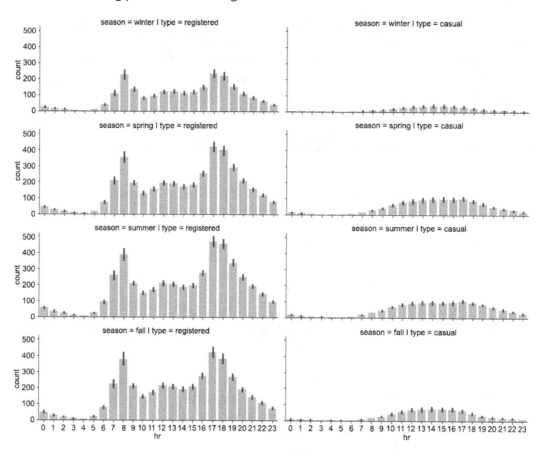

Figure 1.7: The distribution of rides on a seasonal level

As can be seen in the plot, while each season has a similar graph shape, the count is lower for the winter graph. So there are fewer rides (registered and casual) during winter. This makes sense, as fewer rides are likely to occur when the weather conditions are poor.

For the second part of the exercise (the distribution of rides on a weekday basis), we proceed just as we did in the first part.

5. First, create a subset of the initial preprocessed data, containing only the relevant columns (**weekday**, **season**, **registered**, and **casual**):

```
plot_data = preprocessed_data[['weekday', 'season', \
                               'registered', 'casual']]
```

6. Again unpivot the data from wide to long format, but this time use **weekday** and **season** as grouping variables:

```
plot_data = plot_data.melt(id_vars=['weekday', 'season'], \
                           var_name='type', value_name='count')
```

7. The **FacetGrid** object is created using the **seaborn.FacetGrid()** function:

```
grid = sns.FacetGrid(plot_data, row='season', col='type', \
                     height=2.5, aspect=2.5, \
                     row_order=['winter', 'spring', \
                                'summer', 'fall'])
```

8. Finally, apply the **seaborn.barplot()** function to each of the elements in the **FacetGrid** object:

```
grid.map(sns.barplot, 'weekday', 'count', alpha=0.5, \
         order=['Monday', 'Tuesday', 'Wednesday', 'Thursday', \
                'Friday', 'Saturday', 'Sunday'])
```

Note that we are also specifying the order of the days of the week, which is passed as a parameter to the **seaborn.barplot()** function. The resulting plot is shown in the following figure:

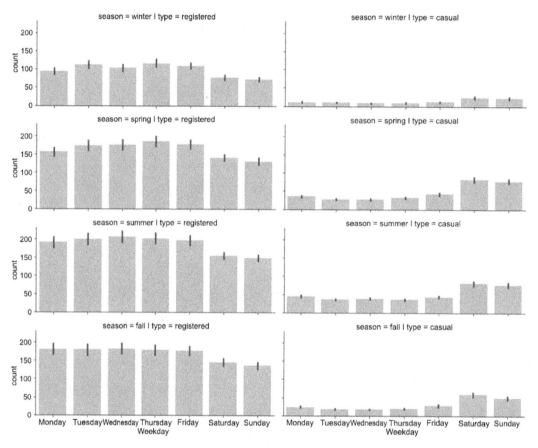

Figure 1.8: The distribution of rides over the days of the week

> **NOTE**
>
> To access the source code for this specific section, please refer to https://packt.live/2Y43Kpx.
>
> You can also run this example online at https://packt.live/30hgeda. You must execute the entire Notebook in order to get the desired result.

An interesting pattern occurs from the analysis conducted in *Exercise 1.02, Analyzing Seasonal Impact on Rides*. There is a decreasing number of registered rides over the weekend (compared to the rest of the week), while the number of casual rides increases. This could enforce our initial hypothesis, that is, that registered customers mostly use the bike sharing service for commuting (which could be the reason for the decreasing number of registered rides over the weekend), while casual customers use the service occasionally over the weekend. Of course, such a conclusion cannot be based solely on plot observations but has to be backed by statistical tests, which is the topic of our next section.

HYPOTHESIS TESTS

Hypothesis testing is a branch of inferential statistics, that is, a part of the statistics field in which a general conclusion can be done about a large group (a population) based on the analysis and measurements performed on a smaller group (a sample). A typical example could be making an estimation of the average height of a country's citizens (in this case, the population) based on measurements performed on a thousand people (the sample). Hypothesis testing tries to address the question, "Is a certain hypothetical value in line with the value obtained by direct measurements or not?"

Although various statistical tests are known in the literature and in practice, the general idea can be summarized in the following steps:

- **Definition of null and alternative hypotheses**: In this first step, a null hypothesis (denoted as H_0) is defined (let's say H_0 is 'the average country's population height is 175 cm'). This is the hypothesis that is going to be tested by the statistical test. The alternative hypothesis (denoted as H_a) consists of the complement statement of the null hypothesis (in our example, the alternative hypothesis, H_a, is 'the average height is not 175 cm'). The null and alternative hypotheses always complement one another.

- **Identifying the appropriate test statistic**: A test statistic is a quantity whose calculation is based on the sample, and whose value is the basis for accepting or rejecting the null hypothesis. In most of these cases, it can be computed by the following formula:

$$\text{test statistic} = \frac{\text{sample statistic} - \text{value under null hypothesis}}{\text{standard error of sample statistic}}$$

Figure 1.9: The formula for the test statistic

Here, the sample statistic is the statistic value computed on the sample (in our case, the average height of a thousand people); the value under null hypothesis is the value, assuming that the null hypothesis holds (in this case, 175 cm); and the standard error of the sample statistic is the standard error in the measurement of the sample. Once the test statistic is identified and computed, we have to decide what type of probability distribution it follows. In most of the cases, the following probability distributions will be used: Student's t-distribution (for t-tests); Standard normal or z-distribution (for z-tests); Chi-squared distribution (for a chi-squared test) and F-distribution (for F-tests).

> **NOTE**
>
> Because exploring probability distributions in more detail is beyond the scope of this book, we refer the reader to the excellent book by Charles Grinstead and Laurie Snell, *Introduction to Probability*. Take a look at the following link: https://math.dartmouth.edu/~prob/prob/prob.pdf.

Choosing which distribution to use depends on the sample size and the type of test. As a rule of thumb, if the sample size is greater than 30, we can expect that the assumptions of the central limit theorem hold and that the test statistic follows a normal distribution (hence, use a z-test). For a more conservative approach, or for samples with less than 30 entries, a t-test should be used (with a test statistic following Student's t-distribution).

- **Specifying the significance level**: Once the test statistic has been calculated, we have to decide whether we can reject the null hypothesis or not. In order to do that, we specify a significance level, which is the probability of rejecting a true null hypothesis. A general approach is to specify a level of significance of 5%. This means that we accept that there is a 5% probability that we reject the null hypothesis while being true (for a more conservative approach, we could always use 1% or even 0.5%). Once a significance level is specified, we have to compute the rejection points, which are the values with which the test statistic is compared. If it is larger than the specified rejection point(s), we can reject the null hypothesis and assume that the alternative hypothesis is true. We can distinguish two separate cases here.

- **Two-sided tests**: These are tests in which the null hypothesis assumes that the value "is equal to" a predefined value. For example, the average height of the population is equal to 175 cm. In this case, if we specify a significance level of 5%, then we have two critical values (one positive and one negative), with the probability of the two tails summing up to 5%. In order to compute the critical values, we have to find the two percentiles of a normal distribution, such that the probability within those two values is equal to 1 minus the significance level. For example, if we assume that the sample mean of the height follows a normal distribution, with a level of significance for our test of 5%, then we need to find the two percentiles, with the probability that a value drawn from a normal distribution falls outside of those values, equal to 0.05. As the probability is split between the two tails, the percentiles that we are looking at are the 2.5 and 97.5 percentiles, corresponding to the values -1.96 and 1.96 for a normal distribution. Hence, we will not reject the null hypothesis if the following holds true:

$$- 1.96 \leq \text{test statistic} \leq 1.96$$

Figure 1.10: Test statistic limit for a two-sided test

If the preceding formula does not hold true, that is, the **test statistic** is greater than **1.96** or less than -1.96, we will reject the null hypothesis.

- **One-sided tests**: These are tests in which the null hypothesis assumes that the value is "greater than" or "less than" a predefined value (for example, the average height is greater than 175 cm). In that case, if we specify a significance level of 5%, we will have only one critical value, with a probability at the tail equal to 5%. In order to find the critical value, we have to find the percentile of a normal distribution, corresponding to a probability of **0.05** at the tail. For tests of the "greater than" type, the critical value will correspond to the 5-th percentile, or **-1.645** (for tests following a normal distribution), while for tests of the "less than" type, the critical value will correspond to the 95-th percentile, or 1.645. In this way, we will reject the null hypothesis for tests "greater than" if the following holds true:

$$\text{test statistic} < - 1.645$$

Figure 1.11: Test statistic limit for a one-sided test

Whereas, for tests of the "less than" type, we reject the null hypothesis if the following is the case:

$$\text{test statistic} > 1.645$$

Figure 1.12: Test statistic limit for a one-sided test

Note that, quite often, instead of computing the critical values of a certain significance level, we refer to the **p-value** of the test. The p-value is the smallest level of significance at which the null hypothesis can be rejected. The p-value also provides the probability of obtaining the observed sample statistic, assuming that the null hypothesis is correct. If the obtained p-value is less than the specified significance level, we can reject the null hypothesis, hence the p-value approach is, in practice, an alternative (and, most of the time, a more convenient) way to perform hypothesis testing.

Let's now provide a practical example of performing hypothesis testing with Python.

EXERCISE 1.03: ESTIMATING AVERAGE REGISTERED RIDES

In this exercise, we will show how to perform hypothesis testing on our bike sharing dataset. This exercise is a continuation of *Exercise 1.02, Analyzing Seasonal Impact on Rides*:

1. Start with computing the average number of registered rides per hour. Note that this value will serve in formulating the null hypothesis because, here, you are explicitly computing the population statistic—that is, the average number of rides. In most of the cases, such quantities are not directly observable and, in general, you only have an estimation for the population statistics:

```
# compute population mean of registered rides
population_mean = preprocessed_data.registered.mean()
```

2. Suppose now that you perform certain measurements, trying to estimate the true average number of rides performed by registered users. For example, register all the rides during the summer of 2011 (this is going to be your sample):

```
# get sample of the data (summer 2011)
sample = preprocessed_data[(preprocessed_data.season \
                == "summer") \
                & (preprocessed_data.yr \
                == 2011)].registered
```

3. Specify the significance level. A standard value is 0.05 (that is, when performing the statistical test), if the p-value obtained by the statistical test is less than 0.05, you can reject the null hypothesis by at least 95%. The following code snippet shows you how to do that:

```
# perform t-test and compute p-value
from scipy.stats import ttest_1samp
test_result = ttest_1samp(sample, population_mean)
print(f"Test statistic: {test_result[0]}, \
p-value: {test_result[1]}")
```

The output should be as follows:

```
Test statistic: -3.492, p-value: 0.000
```

The result of the previous test returns a p-value smaller than 0.001, which is less than the predefined critical value. Therefore, you can reject the null hypothesis and assume that the alternative hypothesis is correct.

Note that you have to make an important observation here: You computed the average number of rides on the true population; therefore, the value computed by the statistical test should be the same. So why have you rejected the null hypothesis? The answer to that question lies in the fact that your sample is not a true representation of the population, but rather a biased one. In fact, you selected only entries from the summer of 2011. Therefore, neither data from the full year is present, nor entries from 2012.

4. In order to show how such mistakes can compromise the results of statistical tests, perform the test again, but this time taking as a sample 5% of the registered rides (selected randomly). The following code snippet performs that:

```
# get sample as 5% of the full data
import random
random.seed(111)
sample_unbiased = preprocessed_data.registered.sample(frac=0.05)
test_result_unbiased = ttest_1samp(sample_unbiased, \
                                   population_mean)
print(f"Unbiased test statistic: {test_result_unbiased[0]}, \
p-value: {test_result_unbiased[1]}")
```

The output should be as follows:

```
Unbiased test statistic: -2.008, p-value: 0.045
```

This time, the computed p-value is equal to 0.45, which is much larger than the critical 0.05, and so, you cannot reject the null hypothesis.

> **NOTE**
>
> To access the source code for this specific section, please refer to https://packt.live/2N3W1la.
>
> You can also run this example online at https://packt.live/3fxDYjt. You must execute the entire Notebook in order to get the desired result.

In this exercise, we performed hypothesis testing with Python on the bike sharing dataset. Furthermore, we saw the importance of having an unbiased sample of the data, as test results can be easily compromised if working with biased data.

Quite often, when performing statistical tests, we want to compare certain statistics on two different groups (for example, the average height between women and men) and estimate whether there is a statistically significant difference between the values obtained in the two groups. Let's denote, with μ_1 and μ_2, the hypothetical means of the two groups, where we will have:

- A null hypothesis: $H_0 : \mu_1 - \mu_2 \neq 0$

- An alternative hypothesis: $H_a : \mu_1 - \mu_2 \neq 0$

Let's denote, with $\bar{X}_1$ and $\bar{X}_2$, the sample means (that is, the means obtained from the two groups), where the test statistic takes the following form:

$$\text{test statistic} = \frac{(\bar{X}_1 - \bar{X}_2) - (\mu_1 - \mu_2)}{\sqrt{\dfrac{s_p^2}{n_1} + \dfrac{s_p^2}{n_2}}}$$

Figure 1.13: Test statistic with the sample means

Here, n_1 and n_2 are the number of samples in the two groups, while s_p^2 is the pooled estimator of the common variance, computed as follows:

$$s_p^2 = \frac{(n_1 - 1)s_1^2 + (n_2 - 1)s_2^2}{n_1 + n_2 - 2}$$

Figure 1.14: Pooled estimator of the common variance

Here, s_1^2 and s_2^2 are the variances of the two groups. Note that the test statistic, in this case, follows Student's t-distribution with $\mathbf{n_1 + n_2 - 2}$ degrees of freedom.

As in the previous case, most of the time, we don't have to compute the test statistics by ourselves, as Python already provides handy functions for that, plus the alternative approach of accepting or rejecting the null hypothesis using the p-value is still valid.

Let's now focus on a practical example of how to perform a statistical test between two different groups. In the previous section, we observed, graphically, that registered users tend to perform more rides during working days than the weekend. In order to assess this statement, we will perform a hypothesis test in which we will test whether the mean of registered rides during working days is the same as during the weekend. This is done in the following exercise.

EXERCISE 1.04: HYPOTHESIS TESTING ON REGISTERED RIDES

In this exercise, we will be performing a hypothesis on registered rides. This exercise is a continuation of *Exercise 1.03, Estimating Average Registered Rides*:

1. First, formulate the null hypothesis. As mentioned earlier, you are interested in identifying whether there is a statistically significant difference between registered rides during working days and the weekend. Therefore, our null hypothesis is that the average number of rides for registered users during working days is the same as the average number of rides during the weekend. In other words:

    H_0 : average registered rides over weekdays-average registered rides over weekend=0

    and

    H_a : average registered rides over weekdays-average registered rides over weekend≠0

2. Once the null hypothesis is established, collect data for the two groups. This is done with the following code snippet:

```
# define mask, indicating if the day is weekend or work day
weekend_days = ['Saturday', 'Sunday']
weekend_mask = preprocessed_data.weekday.isin(weekend_days)
workingdays_mask = ~preprocessed_data.weekday.isin(weekend_days)

# select registered rides for the weekend and working days
weekend_data = preprocessed_data.registered[weekend_mask]
workingdays_data = preprocessed_data.registered[workingdays_mask]
```

3. Perform the two-sample t-tests by using the **scipy.stats. ttest_ind** function:

```
# perform ttest
from scipy.stats import ttest_ind
test_res = ttest_ind(weekend_data, workingdays_data)
print(f"Statistic value: {test_res[0]:.03f}, \
p-value: {test_res[1]:.03f}")
```

The output should be as follows:

```
Statistic value: -16.004, p-value: 0.000
```

The resulting p-value from this test is less than 0.0001, which is far below the standard critical 0.05 value. As a conclusion, we can reject the null hypothesis and confirm that our initial observation is correct: that is, there is a statistically significant difference between the number of rides performed during working days and the weekend.

4. Plot the distributions of the two samples:

```
"""
plot distributions of registered rides for working vs weekend days
"""
sns.distplot(weekend_data, label='weekend days')
sns.distplot(workingdays_data, label='working days')
plt.legend()
plt.xlabel('rides')
plt.ylabel('frequency')
plt.title("Registered rides distributions")
plt.savefig('figs/exercise_1_04_a.png', format='png')
```

The output should be as follows:

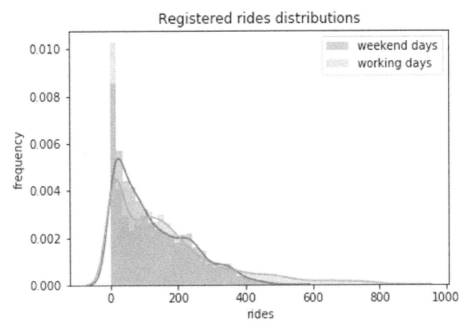

Figure 1.15: The distribution of registered rides: working days versus the weekend

5. Perform the same type of hypothesis testing to validate the second assumption from the last section— that is, casual users perform more rides during the weekend. In this case, the null hypothesis is that the average number of rides during working days is the same as the average number of rides during the weekend, both performed only by casual customers. The alternative hypothesis will then result in a statistically significant difference in the average number of rides between the two groups:

```
# select casual rides for the weekend and working days
weekend_data = preprocessed_data.casual[weekend_mask]
workingdays_data = preprocessed_data.casual[workingdays_mask]


# perform ttest
test_res = ttest_ind(weekend_data, workingdays_data)
print(f"Statistic value: {test_res[0]:.03f}, \
p-value: {test_res[1]:.03f}")


# plot distributions of casual rides for working vs weekend days
sns.distplot(weekend_data, label='weekend days')
sns.distplot(workingdays_data, label='working days')
```

```
plt.legend()
plt.xlabel('rides')
plt.ylabel('frequency')
plt.title("Casual rides distributions")
plt.savefig('figs/exercise_1_04_b.png', format='png')
```

The output should be as follows:

```
Statistic value: 41.077, p-value: 0.000
```

The p-value returned from the previous code snippet is 0, which is strong evidence against the null hypothesis. Hence, we can conclude that casual customers also behave differently over the weekend (in this case, they tend to use the bike sharing service more) as seen in the following figure:

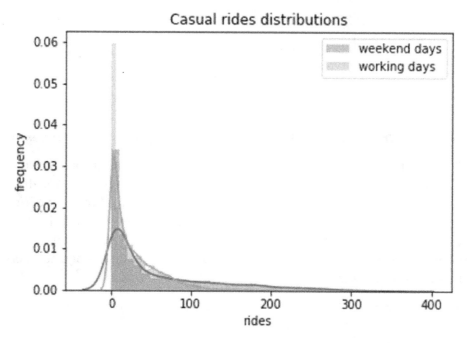

Figure 1.16: Distribution of casual rides: working days versus the weekend

---

NOTE

To access the source code for this specific section, please refer to https://packt.live/3fxe7rY.

You can also run this example online at https://packt.live/2C9V0pf. You must execute the entire Notebook in order to get the desired result.

In conclusion, we can say that there is a statistically significant difference between the number of rides on working days and weekend days for both casual and registered customers.

ANALYSIS OF WEATHER-RELATED FEATURES

Let's now focus on an analysis of the group of features representing the weather conditions. Our expectation is to observe a strong dependency of those features on the current number of rides, as bad weather can significantly influence bike sharing services.

The weather features we identified earlier are the following:

- **weathersit**: This is a categorical variable representing the current weather situation. We encoded this variable with the following four values:

Value	Description
Clear	Representing clear weather or a few clouds
cloudy	Representing mist or cloudy weather
light_rain_snow	Light rain or snow is present
heavy_rain_snow	Heavy rain or snow is present

Figure 1.17: Description of weather features

- **temp**: This is the normalized temperature in Celsius. Values are divided by 41, which means that the highest registered temperature in the data is 41°C (corresponding to 1 in our dataset).

- **atemp**: The normalized feeling temperature in Celsius. Values are divided by 50, which means that the highest registered temperature in the data is 50°C (corresponding to 1 in our dataset).

- **hum**: The humidity level as a percentage.

- **windspeed**: The wind speed in m/s.

From the provided descriptions, we can see that most of the weather-related features assume continuous values (except for **weathersit**). Furthermore, as both our variables of interest (the **casual** and **registered** number of rides) are also continuously distributed, the first and most common way to measure the relationship between two different continuous variables is to measure their correlation.

Correlation (also known as Pearson's correlation) is a statistic that measures the degree to which two random variables move in relation to each other. In practice, it provides a numerical measure (scaled between -1 and 1), through which we can identify how much one of the variables would move in one direction, assuming that the other one moves. Let's denote, with **X** and **Y**, the two random variables. The correlation coefficient between **X** and **Y** is denoted with $\rho(X,Y)$ and is computed by the formula:

$$\rho(X,Y) = \frac{\Sigma_i(X_i - \overline{X})(Y_i - \overline{Y})}{\sqrt{\Sigma_i(X_i - \overline{X})^2}\sqrt{\Sigma_i(Y_i - \overline{Y})^2}}$$

Figure 1.18: The correlation coefficient between X and Y

Here, $\overline{X}$ and $\overline{Y}$ denote the mean of the two variables, and X_i and Y_i represent the individual data points in set **X** and set **Y**. A positive correlation between **X** and **Y** means that increasing one of the values will increase also the other one, while a negative correlation means that increasing one of the values will decrease the other one.

Let's provide a practical example on computing the correlation between two variables. As we want to compare several variables, it makes sense to define a function that performs the analysis between the variables, as we want to follow the *Don't Repeat Yourself* principle (commonly known as *DRY*):

```
def plot_correlations(data, col):
# get correlation between col and registered rides
    corr_r = np.corrcoef(data[col], data["registered"])[0,1]
    ax = sns.regplot(x=col, y="registered", data=data, \
                     scatter_kws={"alpha":0.05}, \
                     label=f"Registered rides \
                     (correlation: {corr_r:.3f})")
# get correlation between col and casual rides
    corr_c = np.corrcoef(data[col], data["casual"])[0,1]
    ax = sns.regplot(x=col, y='casual', data=data, \
                     scatter_kws={"alpha":0.05}, \
                     label=f"Casual rides (correlation: {corr_c:.3f})")
    #adjust legend alpha
    legend = ax.legend()
    for lh in legend.legendHandles:
        lh.set_alpha(0.5)
```

```
      ax.set_ylabel("rides")
      ax.set_title(f"Correlation between rides and {col}")
      return ax
```

Applying the previously defined function to the four columns (**temp**, **atemp**, **hum**, and **windspeed**) returns the following figure:

```
plt.figure(figsize=(10,8))
ax = plot_correlations(preprocessed_data, 'temp')
plt.savefig('figs/correlation_temp.png', format='png')

plt.figure(figsize=(10,8))
ax = plot_correlations(preprocessed_data, 'atemp')
plt.savefig('figs/correlation_atemp.png', format='png')
```

The output should be as follows:

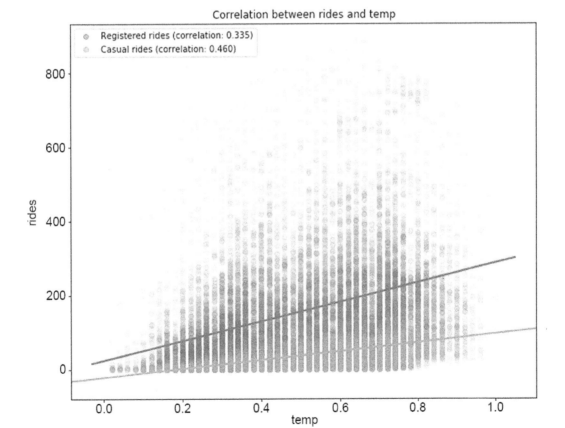

Figure 1.19: The correlation between rides and temp

The plot for correlation between rides and **atemp** would be as follows:

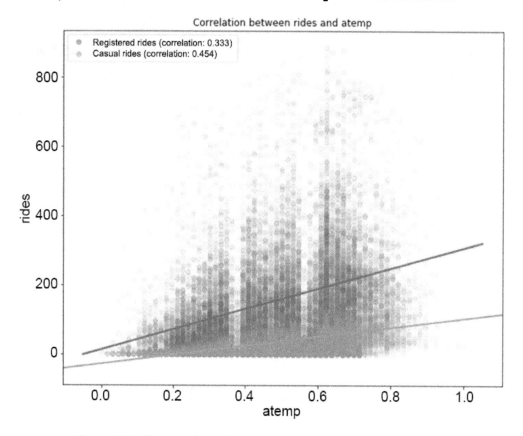

Figure 1.20: The correlation between the rides and atemp features

Now plot the correlation between the rides and **hum, windspeed** features separately:

```
plt.figure(figsize=(10,8))
ax = plot_correlations(preprocessed_data, 'hum')
plt.savefig('figs/correlation_hum.png', format='png')

plt.figure(figsize=(10,8))
ax = plot_correlations(preprocessed_data, 'windspeed')
plt.savefig('figs/correlation_windspeed.png', format='png')
```

The output should be as follows:

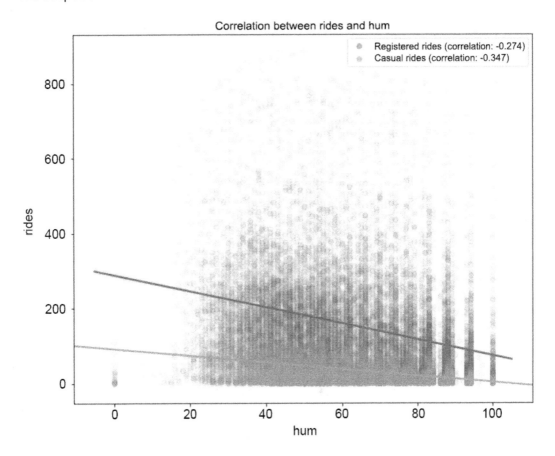

Figure 1.21: The correlation between rides and hum

The correlation between rides and **windspeed** can be visualized as follows:

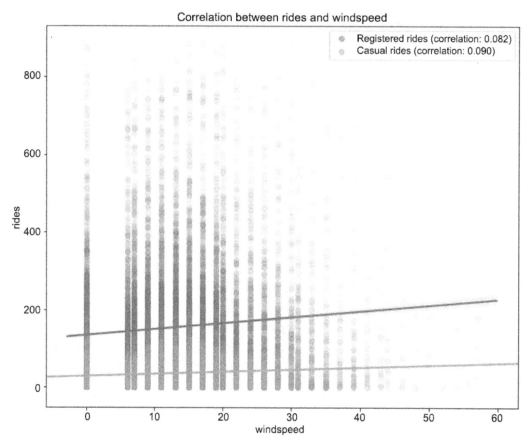

Figure 1.22: The correlation between the rides and windspeed features

From *Figure 1.19*, we can observe that higher temperatures have a positive impact on the number of rides (the correlation between registered/casual rides and **temp** is 0.335 and 0.46, respectively, and it's a similar case for **atemp**). Note that as the values in the **registered** column are widely spread with respect to the different values in **temp**, we have a lower correlation compared to the **casual** column. The same pattern can be observed in *Figure 1.21*, in which the humidity level has a negative correlation with both types of rides (-0.274 for **registered** and -0.347 for **casual**). This means that with a high level of humidity (mist or rain), customers will tend not to use the bike sharing service. From *Figure 1.22*, we can see that there is minimal correlation between the number of rides and the wind speed (a weak positive correlation).

One of the major drawbacks of the correlation coefficient is its assumption of a linear relationship between the two random variables. This is quite a strong assumption as, most of the time, relationships in nature are not linear. A measure that generalizes the Pearson's correlation to monotonic relationships between two variables is the Spearman rank correlation.

Let's illustrate the difference between the two measures in the following example.

EXERCISE 1.05: EVALUATING THE DIFFERENCE BETWEEN THE PEARSON AND SPEARMAN CORRELATIONS

In this exercise, you will investigate the difference between the Pearson correlation (in which a linear relationship between the two variables is assumed) and the Spearman correlation (in which only a monotonic relationship is required). This will help you to understand the difference between the two types of correlations, especially when the data does not satisfy the linear assumption. To better present the difference between the two measures, you will create synthetic data that will serve your purpose:

1. Start by defining your random variables. Create an **X** variable, which will represent your independent variable, and two dependent ones, **Y**$_{lin}$ and **Y**$_{mon}$, which can be expressed as follows:

$$Y_{lin} = 0.5 \cdot X + \varepsilon$$

Figure 1.23: Expression for the dependent variable Y_{lin}

$$Y_t = T_t + S_t + R_t$$

Figure 1.24: Expression for the dependent variable Y_{mon}

Here, ε represents a noise component, which is normally distributed with a mean of 0 and a standard deviation of 0.1:

```
# define random variables
x = np.linspace(0,5, 100)
y_lin = 0.5*x + 0.1*np.random.randn(100)
y_mon = np.exp(x) + 0.1*np.random.randn(100)
```

2. Compute the Pearson and Spearman correlations using the **pearsonr()** and **spearmanr()** functions in the **scipy.stats** module:

```
# compute correlations
from scipy.stats import pearsonr, spearmanr
corr_lin_pearson = pearsonr(x, y_lin)[0]
corr_lin_spearman = spearmanr(x, y_lin)[0]
corr_mon_pearson = pearsonr(x, y_mon)[0]
corr_mon_spearman = spearmanr(x, y_mon)[0]
```

Note that both the **pearsonr()** and **spearmanr()** functions return a two-dimensional array in which the first value is the respective correlation, while the second one is the p-value of a hypothesis test in which the null hypothesis assumes that the computed correlation is equal to zero. This is quite handy at times, as you not only compute the correlation, but also test its statistical significance against being zero.

3. Visualize both the data and the computed correlations:

```
# visualize variables
fig, (ax1, ax2) = plt.subplots(1, 2, figsize=(10,5))
ax1.scatter(x, y_lin)
ax1.set_title(f"Linear relationship\n \
Pearson: {corr_lin_pearson:.3f}, \
Spearman: {corr_lin_spearman:.3f}")
ax2.scatter(x, y_mon)
ax2.set_title(f"Monotonic relationship\n \
Pearson: {corr_mon_pearson:.3f}, \
Spearman: {corr_mon_spearman:.3f}")
fig.savefig('figs/exercise_1_05.png', format='png')
```

The output should be as follows:

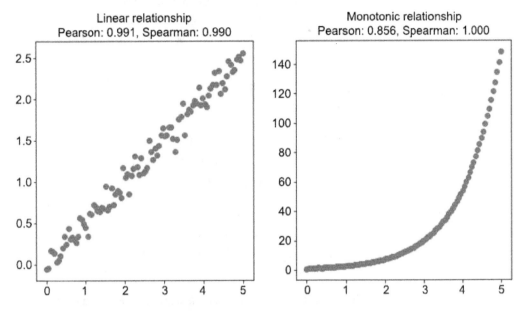

Figure 1.25: The difference between the Pearson and Spearman correlations

As you can see from the preceding figure, when the relationship between the two variables is linear (the figure on the left), the two correlation coefficients are very similar. In the monotonic relationship (the figure on the right), the linear assumption of the Pearson correlation fails, and, although the correlation coefficient is still quite high (0.856), it is not capable of capturing the perfect relationship between the two variables. On the other hand, the Spearman correlation coefficient is 1, which means that it succeeds in capturing the almost perfect relationship between the two variables.

4. Now return to the bike sharing data and investigate the relationship between the different variables in light of the difference between the two correlation measures. Define a function that, on the provided data and column, computes the Pearson and Spearman correlation coefficients with the **registered** and **casual** rides:

```
# define function for computing correlations
def compute_correlations(data, col):

    pearson_reg = pearsonr(data[col], data["registered"])[0]
    pearson_cas = pearsonr(data[col], data["casual"])[0]
    spearman_reg = spearmanr(data[col], data["registered"])[0]
    spearman_cas = spearmanr(data[col], data["casual"])[0]
    return pd.Series({"Pearson (registered)": pearson_reg,\
                "Spearman (registered)": spearman_reg,\
                "Pearson (casual)": pearson_cas,\
                "Spearman (casual)": spearman_cas})
```

Note that the previously defined function returns a **pandas.Series()** object, which will be used to create a new dataset containing the different correlations:

```
# compute correlation measures between different features
cols = ["temp", "atemp", "hum", "windspeed"]
corr_data = pd.DataFrame(index=["Pearson (registered)", \
                    "Spearman (registered)",\
                    "Pearson (casual)", \
                    "Spearman (casual)"])
for col in cols:
    corr_data[col]=compute_correlations(preprocessed_data, col)
corr_data.T
```

The output should be as follows:

	Pearson (registered)	Spearman (registered)	Pearson (casual)	Spearman (casual)
temp	0.335361	0.373196	0.459616	0.570989
atemp	0.332559	0.373014	0.454080	0.570419
hum	-0.273933	-0.338480	-0.347028	-0.388213
windspeed	0.082321	0.122936	0.090287	0.122920

Figure 1.26: The Pearson and Spearman correlation coefficients

> **NOTE**
>
> To access the source code for this specific section, please refer to https://packt.live/30OlyGW.
>
> You can also run this example online at https://packt.live/3e7SmP2. You must execute the entire Notebook in order to get the desired result.

As we can observe, for most of the variables, the Pearson and Spearman correlation coefficient are close enough (some non-linearity is to be expected). The most striking difference between the two coefficients occurs when comparing the **temp** (and **atemp**) and **casual** columns. More precisely, the Spearman correlation is quite high, meaning that there is significant evidence for a nonlinear, relatively strong and positive relationship.

An interpretation of this result is that casual customers are far keener on using the bike sharing service when temperatures are higher. We have already seen from our previous analysis that casual customers ride mostly during the weekend, and they do not rely on bike sharing services for commuting to work. This conclusion is again confirmed by the strong relationship with temperature, as opposed to registered customers, whose rides have a weaker correlation with temperature.

CORRELATION MATRIX PLOT

A useful technique when performing a comparison between different continuous features is the correlation matrix plot. It allows the analyst to quickly visualize any possible relationships between the different features and identify potential clusters with highly correlated features.

The next code snippet does that:

```
# plot correlation matrix
cols = ["temp", "atemp", "hum", "windspeed", \
        "registered", "casual"]
plot_data = preprocessed_data[cols]
corr = plot_data.corr()

fig = plt.figure(figsize=(10,8))
plt.matshow(corr, fignum=fig.number)
```

```
plt.xticks(range(len(plot_data.columns)), plot_data.columns)
plt.yticks(range(len(plot_data.columns)), plot_data.columns)
plt.colorbar()
plt.ylim([5.5, -0.5])
fig.savefig('figs/correlations.png', format='png')
```

The output should be as follows:

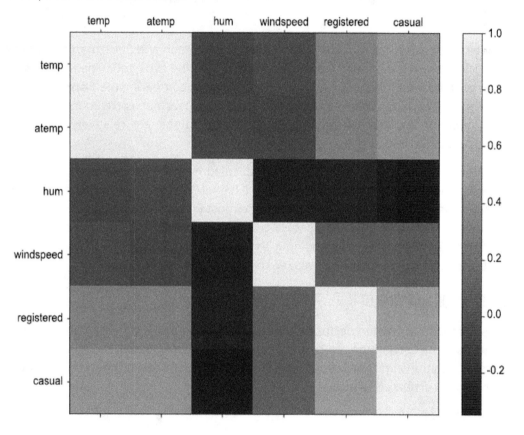

Figure 1.27: Correlation matrix between continuous weather features and rides

This concludes our analysis of the weather columns and their impact on the number of rides. In the next section, we will exploit more advanced techniques for time-dependent features, known as time series analysis.

TIME SERIES ANALYSIS

In this section, we perform a time series analysis on the rides columns (**registered** and **casual**) in the bike sharing dataset.

A time series is a sequence of observations equally spaced in time and in chronological order. Typical examples of time series are stock prices, yearly rainfall, or the number of customers using a specific transportation service every day. When observing time series their fluctuation might result in random values, but, often, they exhibit certain patterns (for example, the highs and lows of ocean tides or hotel prices in the proximity of fares).

When studying time series, an important concept is the notion of stationarity. A time series is said to be *strongly stationary* if all aspects of its behavior do not change in time. In other words, given a time series, $\{Y_t\}_{(t\geq 0)}$, for each **m** and **n**, the distributions of $Y_1, \dots, Y_n$ and $Y_{(m+1)}, \dots, Y_{(m+n)}$ are the same. In practice, strong stationarity is quite a restrictive assumption and, in most of the cases, not satisfied. Furthermore, for most of the methods illustrated later in this section to work, it is enough to have a time series that is *weakly stationary*, that is, its mean, standard deviation, and covariance are stationary with respect to time. More precisely, given $\{Y_t\}_{(t \geq 0)}$, we can observe:

- $E(Y_i)=\mu$ (a constant) for every i

- $Var(Y_i)=\sigma^2$ (a constant) for every i

- $Corr(Y_i, Y_j)=\rho(i-j)$ for every i and j and some function $\rho(h)$

In order to check stationarity in practice, we can rely on two different techniques for identifying time series stationarity: **rolling statistics** and **augmented Dickey-Fuller stationarity test** (in most cases, we consider both of them).

Rolling statistics is a practical method in which we plot the rolling mean and standard deviation of a time series and visually identify whether those values fluctuate around a constant one, without large deviations. We have to inform the reader that this is more a rule-of-thumb approach and not a rigorous statistical test for stationarity.

Augmented Dickey-Fuller stationarity test is a statistical test in which the null hypothesis is that the time series is nonstationary. Hence, when performing the test, a small p-value would be strong evidence against the time series being nonstationary.

> **NOTE**
>
> Since providing a detailed introduction to the augmented Dickey-Fuller test is out of the scope of this book, we refer the interested reader to the original book, *Fuller, W. A. (1976). Introduction to Statistical Time Series. New York: John Wiley and Sons. ISBN 0-471-28715-6.*

In practice, we rely on both of the techniques, as plotting the rolling statistics is not a rigorous approach. Let's define a utility function, which will perform both tests for us:

```
"""
define function for plotting rolling statistics and ADF test for time
series
"""
from statsmodels.tsa.stattools import adfuller
def test_stationarity(ts, window=10, **kwargs):
# create dataframe for plotting
    plot_data = pd.DataFrame(ts)
    plot_data['rolling_mean'] = ts.rolling(window).mean()
    plot_data['rolling_std'] = ts.rolling(window).std()
    # compute p-value of Dickey-Fuller test
    p_val = adfuller(ts)[1]
    ax = plot_data.plot(**kwargs)
    ax.set_title(f"Dickey-Fuller p-value: {p_val:.3f}")
```

We also need to extract the daily **registered** and **casual** rides from our preprocessed data:

```
# get daily rides
daily_rides = preprocessed_data[["dteday", "registered", \
                                 "casual"]]
daily_rides = daily_rides.groupby("dteday").sum()

# convert index to DateTime object
daily_rides.index = pd.to_datetime(daily_rides.index)
```

Applying the previously defined **test_stationarity()** function to the daily rides produces the following plots:

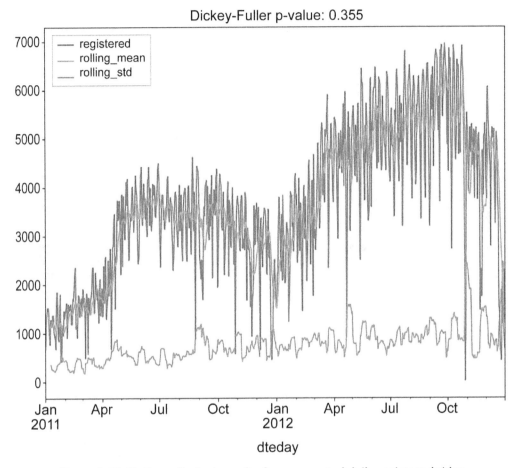

Figure 1.28: Stationarity test results for aggregated daily registered rides

The output for daily casual rides can be as follows:

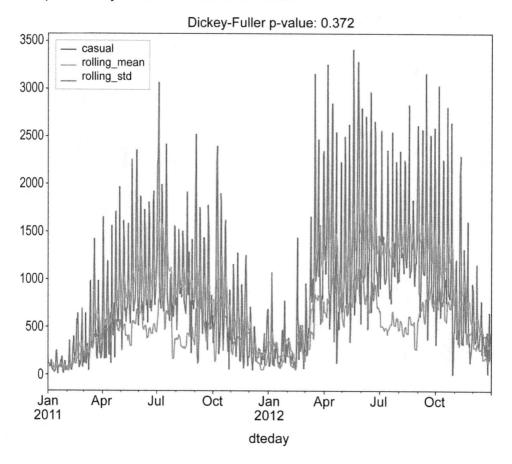

Figure 1.29: Stationarity test results for aggregated daily casual rides

From the performed tests, we can see that neither the moving average nor standard deviations are stationary. Furthermore, the Dickey-Fuller test returns values of 0.355 and 0.372 for the **registered** and **casual** columns, respectively. This is strong evidence that the time series is not stationary, and we need to process them in order to obtain a stationary one.

A common way to detrend a time series and make it stationary is to subtract either its rolling mean or its last value, or to decompose it into a component that will contain its trend, seasonality, and residual components. Let's first check whether the time series is stationary by subtracting their rolling means and last values:

```
# subtract rolling mean
registered = daily_rides["registered"]
registered_ma = registered.rolling(10).mean()
```

```
registered_ma_diff = registered - registered_ma
registered_ma_diff.dropna(inplace=True)

casual = daily_rides["casual"]
casual_ma = casual.rolling(10).mean()
casual_ma_diff = casual - casual_ma
casual_ma_diff.dropna(inplace=True)
```

The resulting time series are tested for stationarity, and the results are shown in the following figures:

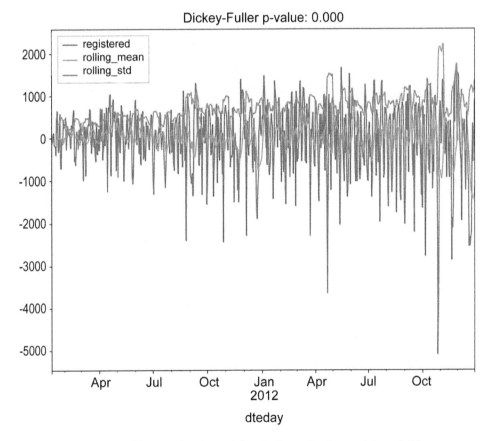

Figure 1.30: Time series tested for stationarity for registered rides

The output for casual rides will be as follows:

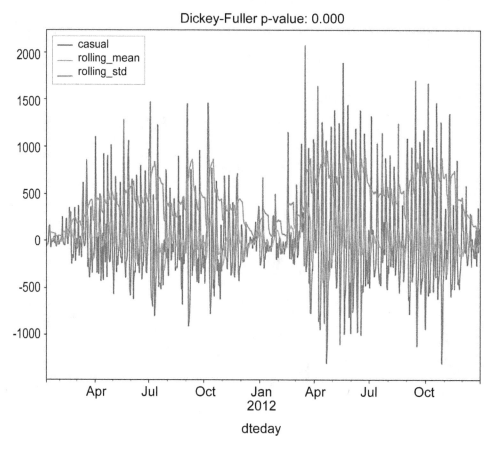

Figure 1.31: Time series tested for stationarity for casual rides

Subtracting the last value can be done in the same way:

```
# subtract last value
registered = daily_rides["registered"]
registered_diff = registered - registered.shift()
registered_diff.dropna(inplace=True)

casual = daily_rides["casual"]
casual_diff = casual - casual.shift()
casual_diff.dropna(inplace=True)

plt.figure()
test_stationarity(registered_diff, figsize=(10, 8))
```

```
plt.savefig('figs/daily_registered_diff.png', format='png')

plt.figure()
test_stationarity(casual_diff, figsize=(10, 8))
plt.savefig('figs/daily_casual_diff.png', format='png')
```

The output should be as follows:

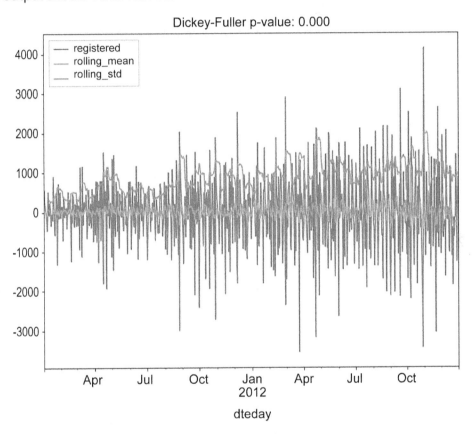

Figure 1.32: Subtracting the last values from the time series for registered rides

The output for casual rides will be as follows:

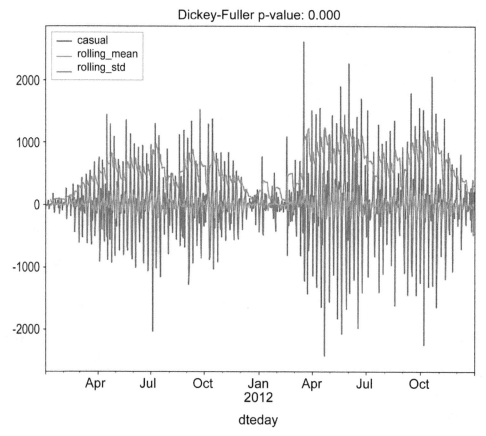

Figure 1.33: Subtracting the last values from the time series for casual rides

As you can see, both of the techniques returned a time series, which is stationary, according to the Dickey-Fuller test. Note that an interesting pattern occurs in the casual series: a rolling standard deviation exhibits a clustering effect, that is, periods in which the standard deviation is higher and periods in which it is lower. This effect is quite common in certain fields (finance, for instance) and is known as **volatility clustering**. A possible interpretation, relative to our data, is that the number of casual rides increases during summer periods and drops during the winter.

As we saw from the last analysis, removing both the rolling mean and the last value returned a stationary time series. Let's also check also the previously mentioned technique, that is, **time series decomposition**. This involves breaking the original time series into separate components:

- **Trend component**: This component represents a long-term progression of the series. A trend component is present when there is a persistent increase or decrease in the series.

- **Seasonal component**: This component represents seasonality patterns in the data. A seasonal component persists when the data is influenced by certain seasonal factors (for example, monthly, quarterly, or yearly factors).

- **Residual component**: This component represents an irregular or noisy component. This component describes random fluctuations in the data, which are not captured by the other components. In general, this is the residual of the time series, that is, once the other components have been removed.

A time series decomposition can be framed in the following way. Let's denote, with Y_t, the value of the original series at time instance t, and let T_t, S_t, and R_t represent the trend, seasonal, and residual components, respectively. We will refer to the decomposition as *additive* if the following holds:

$$Y_t = T_t + S_t + R_t$$

Figure 1.34: Decomposition as additive

And we will refer to the decomposition as multiplicative if the following holds:

$$Y_t = T_t \times S_t \times R_t$$

Figure 1.35: Decomposition as multiplicative

In the following exercise, we will illustrate how to perform time series decomposition in Python.

EXERCISE 1.06: TIME SERIES DECOMPOSITION IN TREND, SEASONALITY, AND RESIDUAL COMPONENTS

In this exercise, you will exploit seasonal decomposition in the **statsmodel** Python library in order to decompose the number of rides into three separate components, trend, seasonal, and residual components:

1. Use the **statsmodel.tsa.seasonal. seasonal_decompose()** method to decompose the **registered** and **casual** rides:

```
from statsmodels.tsa.seasonal import seasonal_decompose
registered_decomposition = seasonal_decompose(\
                        daily_rides["registered"])
casual_decomposition = seasonal_decompose(daily_rides["casual"])
```

2. To access each of these three signals, use **.trend**, **.seasonal**, and **.resid** variables. Furthermore, obtain visual results from the generated decompositions by calling the **.plot()** method:

```
# plot decompositions
registered_plot = registered_decomposition.plot()
registered_plot.set_size_inches(10, 8)

casual_plot = casual_decomposition.plot()
casual_plot.set_size_inches(10, 8)

registered_plot.savefig('figs/registered_decomposition.png', \
                        format='png')
casual_plot.savefig('figs/casual_decomposition.png', \
                    format='png')
```

The output for registered rides is as follows:

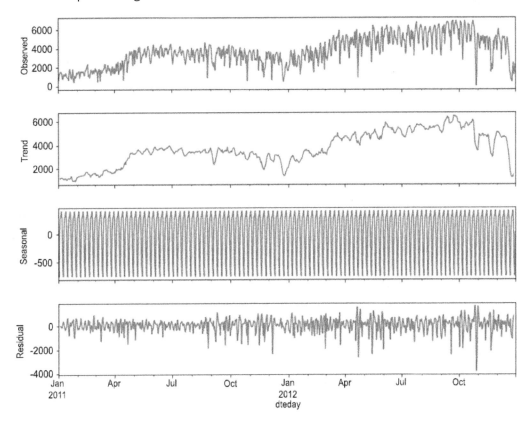

Figure 1.36: Decomposition for registered rides

The output for casual rides will be as follows:

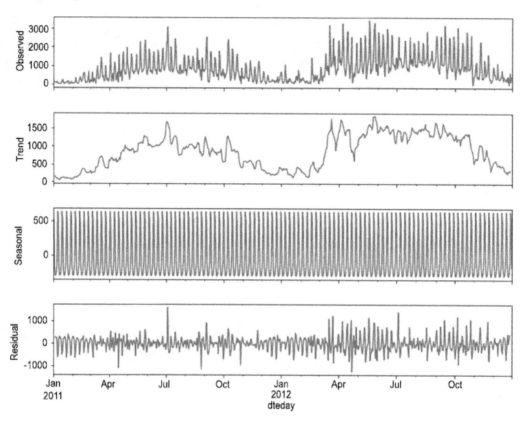

Figure 1.37: Decomposition for casual rides

3. Test the residuals obtained for stationarity:

```
# test residuals for stationarity
plt.figure()
test_stationarity(registered_decomposition.resid.dropna(), \
                  figsize=(10, 8))
plt.savefig('figs/registered_resid.png', format='png')


plt.figure()
test_stationarity(casual_decomposition.resid.dropna(), \
                  figsize=(10, 8))
plt.savefig('figs/casual_resid.png', format='png')
```

The output will be as follows:

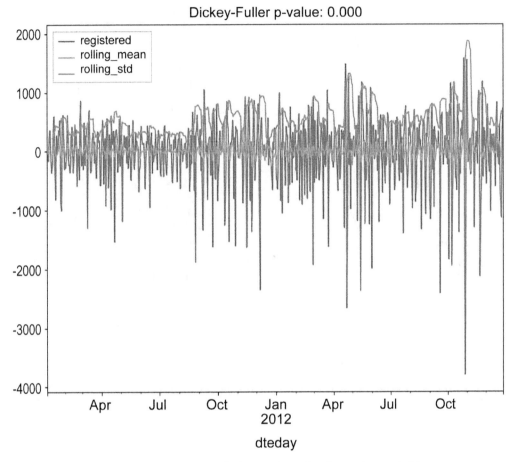

Figure 1.38: Test residuals for stationarity for registered rides

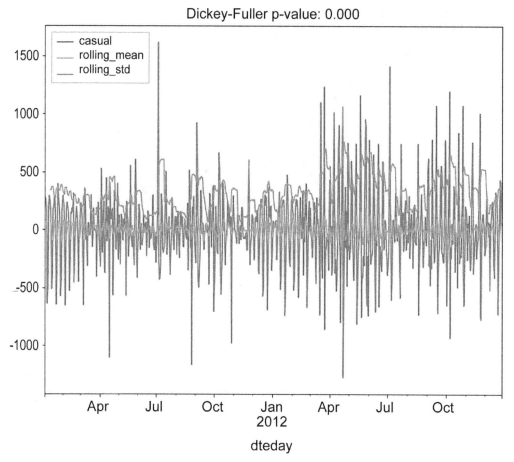

Figure 1.39: Test residuals for stationarity for casual rides

As you can see, the residuals satisfy our stationary test.

> **NOTE**
>
> To access the source code for this specific section, please refer to https://packt.live/3hB8871.
>
> You can also run this example online at https://packt.live/2BaXsLJ. You must execute the entire Notebook in order to get the desired result.

A common approach to modeling a time series is to assume that past observations somehow influence future ones. For instance, customers who are satisfied by using the bike sharing service will more likely recommend it, producing, in this way, a positive impact on the service and a higher number of customers (obviously, any negative feedback has the opposite effect, reducing the number of customers). Hence, increasing the number of customers and the quality of the service increases the number of recommendations and, therefore, the number of new customers. In this way, a positive feedback loop is created, in which the current number of rides correlates with its past values. These types of phenomena are the topic of the next section.

ARIMA MODELS

Autoregressive Integrated Moving Average (ARIMA) models are a class of statistical models that try to explain the behavior of a time series using its own past values. Being a class of models, ARIMA models are defined by a set of parameters **(p,d,q)**, each one corresponding to a different component of the ARIMA model:

- **Autoregressive of order p**: An autoregressive model of order **p (AR(p)** for short) models the current time series entry as a linear combination of its last p values. The mathematical formulation is as follows:

$$Y_t = \alpha + \beta_1 Y_{t-1} + \beta_2 Y_{t-2} + \cdots + \beta_p Y_{t-p} + \varepsilon_t$$

Figure 1.40: Expression for an autoregressive model of order p

Here, α is the intercept term, $Y_{(t-i)}$ is the lag-I term of the series with the respective coefficient β_i, while ε_t is the error term (that is, the normally distributed random variable with mean 0 and variance σ_ε^2).

- **Moving average of order q**: A moving average model of order **q** (**MA(q)** for short) attempts to model the current value of the time series as a linear combination of its past error terms. Mathematically speaking, it has the following formula:

$$Y_t = \alpha + \epsilon_t + \phi_1 \epsilon_{t-1} + \cdots + \phi_q \epsilon_{t-q}$$

Figure 1.41: Expression for the moving average model of order q

As in the autoregressive model, α represents a bias term; $\phi_1,...,\phi_q$ are parameters to be estimated in the model; and $\epsilon_t,...,\epsilon_{(t-q)}$ are the error terms at times $t,...,t-q$, respectively.

- **Integrated component of order d**: The integrated component represents a transformation in the original time series, in which the transformed series is obtained by getting the difference between Y_t and $Y_{(t-d)}$, hence the following:

$$Z_t = Y_t - Y_{t-d}$$

Figure 1.42: Expression for an integrated component of order d

The integration term is used for detrending the original time series and making it stationary. Note that we already saw this type of transformation when we subtracted the previous entry in the number of rides, that is, when we applied an integration term of order 1.

In general, when we apply an ARIMA model of order (p,d,q) to a time series, $\{Y_t\}$, we obtain the following model:

4. First, integrate the original time series of order d, and then obtain the new series:

$$Z\_t = Y\_t - Z\_{t-d}$$

Figure 1.43: Integrating the original time series

5. Then, apply a combination of the AR(p) and MA(q) models, also known as the autoregressive moving average model, or ARMA(p,q), to the transformed series, $\{Z_t\}_t$:

$$Z_t = \alpha + \beta_1 Z_{t-1} + \ldots + \beta_p Z_{t-p} + \phi_1 \epsilon_{t-1} + \ldots + \phi_q \epsilon_{t-q} + \epsilon_t$$

Figure 1.44: Expression for ARMA

Here, the coefficients $\alpha, \beta_1, \ldots, \beta_p, \phi_1, \ldots, \phi_q$ are to be estimated.

A standard method for finding the parameters (p,d,q) of an ARIMA model is to compute the autocorrelation and partial autocorrelation functions (ACF and PACF for short). The autocorrelation function measures the Pearson correlation between the lagged values in a time series as a function of the lag:

$$ACF(k) = Corr(Y_t, Y_{t-k})$$

Figure 1.45: Autocorrelation function as a function of the lag

In practice, the ACF measures the complete correlation between the current entry, Y_t, and its past entries, lagged by k. Note that when computing the ACF(k), the correlation between Y_t with all intermediate values ($Y_{(t-1)}, \ldots, Y_{(t-k+1)}$) is not removed. In order to account only for the correlation between and $Y_{(t-k)}$, we often refer to the PACF, which only measures the impact of $Y_{(t-k)}$ on Y_t.

ACF and PACF are, in general, used to determine the order of integration when modeling a time series with an ARIMA model. For each lag, the correlation coefficient and level of significance are computed. In general, we aim at an integrated series, in which only the first few lags have correlation greater than the level of significance. We will demonstrate this in the following exercise.

EXERCISE 1.07: ACF AND PACF PLOTS FOR REGISTERED RIDES

In this exercise, we will plot the autocorrelation and partial autocorrelation functions for the **registered** number of rides:

1. Access the necessary methods for plotting the ACF and PACF contained in the Python package, **statsmodels**:

```
from statsmodels.graphics.tsaplots import plot_acf, plot_pacf
```

2. Define a 3 x 3 grid and plot the ACF and PACF for the original series of registered rides, as well as for its first- and second-order integrated series:

```
fig, axes = plt.subplots(3, 3, figsize=(25, 12))

# plot original series
original = daily_rides["registered"]
axes[0,0].plot(original)
axes[0,0].set_title("Original series")
plot_acf(original, ax=axes[0,1])
plot_pacf(original, ax=axes[0,2])

# plot first order integrated series
first_order_int = original.diff().dropna()
axes[1,0].plot(first_order_int)
axes[1,0].set_title("First order integrated")
plot_acf(first_order_int, ax=axes[1,1])
plot_pacf(first_order_int, ax=axes[1,2])

# plot first order integrated series
second_order_int = first_order_int.diff().dropna()
axes[2,0].plot(first_order_int)
axes[2,0].set_title("Second order integrated")
plot_acf(second_order_int, ax=axes[2,1])
plot_pacf(second_order_int, ax=axes[2,2])
```

The output should be as follows:

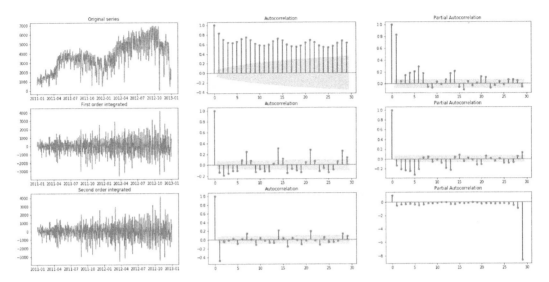

Figure 1.46: Autocorrelation and partial autocorrelation plots of registered rides

As you can see from the preceding figure, the original series exhibits several autocorrelation coefficients that are above the threshold. The first order integrated series has only a few, which makes it a good candidate for further modeling (hence, selecting an ARIMA(p,1,q) model). Finally, the second order integrated series present a large negative autocorrelation of lag 1, which, in general, is a sign of too large an order of integration.

Now focus on finding the model parameters and the coefficients for an ARIMA(p,d,q) model, based on the observed registered rides. The general approach is to try different combinations of parameters and chose the one that minimizes certain information criterion, for instance, the **Akaike Information Criterion (AIC)** or the **Bayesian Information Criterion (BIC)**:

Akaike Information Criterion:

$$AIC = 2k - 2\log(\widehat{L})$$

Figure 1.47: Expression for AIC

Bayesian Information Criterion:

$$BIC = \log(n)k - 2\log(\hat{L})$$

Figure 1.48: Expression for BIC

Here, **k** is the number of parameters in the selected model, **n** is the number of samples, and $\log(\hat{L})$ is the log likelihood. As you can see, there is no substantial difference between the two criteria and, in general, both are used. If different optimal models are selected according to the different IC, we tend to find a model in between.

3. In the following code snippet, fit an ARIMA(p,d,q) model to the **registered** column. Note that the **pmdarima** package is not a standard in Anaconda; therefore, in order to install it, you need to install it via the following:

```
conda install -c saravji pmdarima
```

And then perform the following:

```
from pmdarima import auto_arima
model = auto_arima(registered, start_p=1, start_q=1, \
                   max_p=3, max_q=3, information_criterion="aic")
print(model.summary())
```

Python's **pmdarima** package has a special function that automatically finds the best parameters for an ARIMA(p,d,q) model based on the AIC. Here is the resulting model:

```
                          Statespace Model Results
==============================================================================
Dep. Variable:                     y   No. Observations:                  731
Model:             SARIMAX(3, 1, 3)   Log Likelihood               -5854.011
Date:             Sun, 08 Dec 2019   AIC                          11724.023
Time:                     16:49:09   BIC                          11760.767
Sample:                          0   HQIC                         11738.199
                             - 731
Covariance Type:               opg
==============================================================================
                 coef    std err          z      P>|z|      [0.025      0.975]
------------------------------------------------------------------------------
intercept      0.6611      3.230      0.205      0.838      -5.670       6.992
ar.L1          1.6202      0.051     31.749      0.000       1.520       1.720
ar.L2         -1.4637      0.064    -22.954      0.000      -1.589      -1.339
ar.L3          0.3731      0.050      7.398      0.000       0.274       0.472
ma.L1         -2.1148      0.034    -61.980      0.000      -2.182      -2.048
ma.L2          2.0607      0.047     44.213      0.000       1.969       2.152
ma.L3         -0.8612      0.032    -26.886      0.000      -0.924      -0.798
sigma2      6.239e+05   2.67e+04     23.340      0.000    5.71e+05    6.76e+05
===================================================================================
Ljung-Box (Q):                      143.16   Jarque-Bera (JB):             747.95
Prob(Q):                              0.00   Prob(JB):                       0.00
Heteroskedasticity (H):               3.35   Skew:                          -1.31
Prob(H) (two-sided):                  0.00   Kurtosis:                       7.21
===================================================================================
```

Figure 1.49: The resulting model based on AIC

As you can see, the best selected model was ARIMA(3,1,3), with the **coef** column containing the coefficients for the model itself.

4. Finally, evaluate how well the number of rides is approximated by the model by using the **model.predict_in_sample()** function:

```
# plot original and predicted values
plot_data = pd.DataFrame(registered)
plot_data['predicted'] = model.predict_in_sample()
plot_data.plot(figsize=(12, 8))
plt.ylabel("number of registered rides")
plt.title("Predicted vs actual number of rides")
plt.savefig('figs/registered_arima_fit.png', format='png')
```

The output should be as follows:

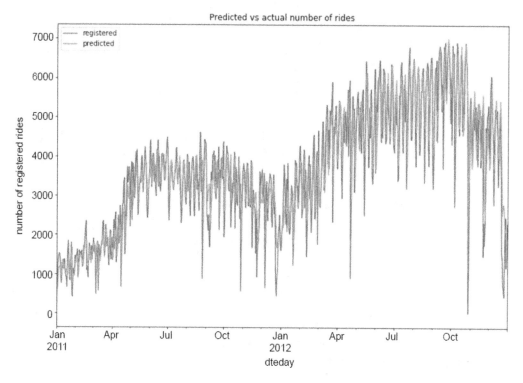

Figure 1.50: Predicted versus the actual number of registered rides

As you can see, the **predicted** column follows the original one quite well, although it is unable to correctly model a large number of rise and fall movements in the **registered** series.

> **NOTE**
>
> To access the source code for this specific section, please refer to https://packt.live/37xHHKQ.
>
> You can also run this example online at https://packt.live/30MqcFf. You must execute the entire Notebook in order to get the desired result.

In this first chapter, we presented various techniques from data analysis and statistics, which will serve as a basis for further analysis in the next chapter, in order to improve our results and to obtain a better understanding of the problems we are about to deal with.

ACTIVITY 1.01: INVESTIGATING THE IMPACT OF WEATHER CONDITIONS ON RIDES

In this activity, you will investigate the impact of weather conditions and their relationship with the other weather-related columns (**temp**, **atemp**, **hum**, and **windspeed**), as well as their impact on the number of registered and casual rides. The following steps will help you to perform the analysis:

1. Import the initial **hour** data.

2. Create a new column in which **weathersit** is mapped to the four categorical values specified in *Exercise 1.01, Preprocessing Temporal and Weather Features*. (**clear**, **cloudy**, **light_rain_snow**, and **heavy_rain_snow**).

3. Define a Python function that accepts as input the hour data, a column name, and a weather condition, and then returns a seaborn **regplot** in which regression plots are produced between the provided column name and the registered and casual rides for the specified weather condition.

4. Produce a 4 x 4 plot in which each column represents a specific weather condition (**clear**, **cloudy**, **light_rain_snow**, and **heavy_rain_snow**), and each row of the specified four columns (**temp**, **atemp**, **hum**, and **windspeed**). A useful function for producing the plot might be the **matplotlib.pyplot.subplot()** function.

> ### NOTE
>
> For more information on the **matplotlib.pyplot.subplot()** function, refer to https://pythonspot.com/matplotlib-subplot/.

5. Define a second function that accepts the hour data, a column name, and a specific weather condition as an input, and then prints the Pearson's correlation and p-value between the registered and casual rides and the provided column for the specified weather condition (once when the correlation is computed between the registered rides and the specified column and once between the casual rides and the specified column).

6. Iterating over the four columns (**temp**, **atemp**, **hum**, and **windspeed**) and four weather conditions (**clear**, **cloudy**, **light_rain_snow**, and **heavy_rain_snow**), print the correlation for each column and each weather condition by using the function defined in *Step 5*.

The output should be as follows:

```
Pearson correlation (registered, temp): corr=0.340, pval=0.000
Pearson correlation (casual, temp): corr=0.459, pval=0.000
Pearson correlation (registered, temp): corr=0.285, pval=0.000
Pearson correlation (casual, temp): corr=0.437, pval=0.000
Pearson correlation (registered, temp): corr=0.356, pval=0.000
Pearson correlation (casual, temp): corr=0.433, pval=0.000
Pearson correlation (registered, temp): corr=0.360, pval=0.766
Pearson correlation (casual, temp): corr=0.277, pval=0.821
Pearson correlation (registered, atemp): corr=0.334, pval=0.000
Pearson correlation (casual, atemp): corr=0.451, pval=0.000
Pearson correlation (registered, atemp): corr=0.285, pval=0.000
Pearson correlation (casual, atemp): corr=0.434, pval=0.000
Pearson correlation (registered, atemp): corr=0.366, pval=0.000
Pearson correlation (casual, atemp): corr=0.445, pval=0.000
Pearson correlation (registered, atemp): corr=0.810, pval=0.399
Pearson correlation (casual, atemp): corr=0.756, pval=0.454
Pearson correlation (registered, hum): corr=-0.282, pval=0.000
Pearson correlation (casual, hum): corr=-0.331, pval=0.000
Pearson correlation (registered, hum): corr=-0.156, pval=0.000
Pearson correlation (casual, hum): corr=-0.289, pval=0.000
Pearson correlation (registered, hum): corr=-0.229, pval=0.000
Pearson correlation (casual, hum): corr=-0.243, pval=0.000
Pearson correlation (registered, hum): corr=-0.423, pval=0.722
Pearson correlation (casual, hum): corr=-0.500, pval=0.667
Pearson correlation (registered, windspeed): corr=0.113, pval=0.000
Pearson correlation (casual, windspeed): corr=0.111, pval=0.000
Pearson correlation (registered, windspeed): corr=0.048, pval=0.001
Pearson correlation (casual, windspeed): corr=0.063, pval=0.000
Pearson correlation (registered, windspeed): corr=-0.005, pval=0.842
Pearson correlation (casual, windspeed): corr=0.054, pval=0.042
Pearson correlation (registered, windspeed): corr=-0.776, pval=0.435
Pearson correlation (casual, windspeed): corr=-0.828, pval=0.379
```

Figure 1.51: Correlation between weather and the registered/casual rides

NOTE

The solution to the activity can be found on page 490.

SUMMARY

In this chapter, we studied a business problem related to bike sharing services. We started by presenting some of the main visual techniques in data analysis, such as bar plots, scatter plots, and time series visualizations. We also analyzed customer behaviors based on different time frames and weather conditions. We introduced the reader to hypothesis testing and some of its main applications. Finally, we presented the basics of time series analysis, and how to identify the best time series models when dealing with nonstationary time series.

In the next chapter, we will proceed with our analysis by presenting some of the commonly used data transformation techniques, topics from probability theory, and further techniques in hypothesis testing.

2

ABSENTEEISM AT WORK

OVERVIEW

In this chapter, you will perform standard data analysis techniques, such as estimating conditional probabilities, Bayes' theorem, and Kolmogorov-Smirnov tests, for distribution comparison. You will also implement data transformation techniques, such as the Box-Cox and Yeo-Johnson transformations, and apply these techniques to a given dataset.

INTRODUCTION

In the previous chapter, we looked at some of the main techniques that are used in data analysis. We saw how hypothesis testing can be used when analyzing data, we got a brief introduction to visualizations, and finally, we explored some concepts related to time series analysis. In this chapter, we will elaborate on some of the topics we've already looked at (such as plotting and hypothesis testing) while introducing new ones coming from probability theory and data transformations.

Nowadays, work relationships are becoming more and more trust-oriented, and conservative contracts (in which working time is strictly monitored) are being replaced with more agile ones in which the employee themselves is responsible for accounting working time. This liberty may lead to unregulated absenteeism and may reflect poorly on an employee's candidature, even if absent hours can be accounted for with genuine reasons. This can significantly undermine healthy working relationships. Furthermore, unregulated absenteeism can also have a negative impact on work productivity.

In this chapter, we'll analyze absenteeism data from a Brazilian courier company, collected between July 2007 and July 2010.

> **NOTE**
>
> The original dataset can be found here: https://archive.ics.uci.edu/ml/datasets/Absenteeism+at+work.
>
> If you're interested, take a look at the following paper, which talks about the problem from a machine learning perspective: *Martiniano, A., Ferreira, R.P., Sassi, R.J., & Affonso, C. (2012). Application of neuro fuzz network on prediction of absenteeism at work. In Information Systems and Technologies (CISTI), 7th Iberian Conference on (pp. 1-4). IEEE.*
>
> This dataset can also be found on our GitHub repository here: https://packt.live/3e4rorX.

Our goal is to discover hidden patterns in the data, which might be useful for distinguishing genuine work absences from fraudulent ones. During this chapter, the following topics will be addressed:

- Introduction to probability, conditional probability, and Bayes' theorem
- Kolmogorov-Smirnov tests for equality of probability distributions
- Box-Cox and Yeo-Johnson transformations

We will apply these techniques to our analysis as we try to identify the main drivers for absenteeism.

INITIAL DATA ANALYSIS

As a rule of thumb, when starting the analysis of a new dataset, it is good practice to check the dimensionality of the data, type of columns, possible missing values, and some generic statistics on the numerical columns. We can also get the first 5 to 10 entries in order to acquire a feeling for the data itself. We'll perform these steps in the following code snippets:

```
import pandas as pd
import seaborn as sns
import matplotlib.pyplot as plt

%matplotlib inline

# import data from the GitHub page of the book
data = pd.read_csv('https://raw.githubusercontent.com'\
                   '/PacktWorkshops/The-Data-Analysis-Workshop'\
                   '/master/Chapter02/data/'\
                   'Absenteeism_at_work.csv', sep=";")
```

Note that we are providing the separator parameter when reading the data because, although the original data file is in the CSV format, the ";" symbol has been used to separate the various fields.

In order to print the dimensionality of the data, column types, and the number of missing values, we can use the following code:

```
"""
print dimensionality of the data, columns, types and missing values
"""
print(f"Data dimension: {data.shape}")
for col in data.columns:
    print(f"Column: {col:35} | type: {str(data[col].dtype):7} \
| missing values: {data[col].isna().sum():3d}")
```

This returns the following output:

```
Data dimension: (740, 21)
Column: ID                              | type: int64   | missing values:   0
Column: Reason for absence              | type: int64   | missing values:   0
Column: Month of absence                | type: int64   | missing values:   0
Column: Day of the week                 | type: int64   | missing values:   0
Column: Seasons                         | type: int64   | missing values:   0
Column: Transportation expense          | type: int64   | missing values:   0
Column: Distance from Residence to Work | type: int64   | missing values:   0
Column: Service time                    | type: int64   | missing values:   0
Column: Age                             | type: int64   | missing values:   0
Column: Work load Average/day           | type: float64 | missing values:   0
Column: Hit target                      | type: int64   | missing values:   0
Column: Disciplinary failure            | type: int64   | missing values:   0
Column: Education                       | type: int64   | missing values:   0
Column: Son                             | type: int64   | missing values:   0
Column: Social drinker                  | type: int64   | missing values:   0
Column: Social smoker                   | type: int64   | missing values:   0
Column: Pet                             | type: int64   | missing values:   0
Column: Weight                          | type: int64   | missing values:   0
Column: Height                          | type: int64   | missing values:   0
Column: Body mass index                 | type: int64   | missing values:   0
Column: Absenteeism time in hours       | type: int64   | missing values:   0
```

Figure 2.1: Dimensions of the Absenteeism_at_work dataset

As we can see from these 21 columns, only one (**Work Load Average/day**) does not contain integer values. Since no missing values are present in the data, we can consider it quite clean. We can also derive some basic statistics by using the **describe** method:

```
# compute statistics on numerical features
data.describe().T
```

The output will be as follows:

	count	mean	std	min	25%	50%	75%	max
ID	740.0	18.017568	11.021247	1.000	9.000	18.000	28.000	36.000
Reason for absence	740.0	19.216216	8.433406	0.000	13.000	23.000	26.000	28.000
Month of absence	740.0	6.324324	3.436287	0.000	3.000	6.000	9.000	12.000
Day of the week	740.0	3.914865	1.421675	2.000	3.000	4.000	5.000	6.000
Seasons	740.0	2.544595	1.111831	1.000	2.000	3.000	4.000	4.000
Transportation expense	740.0	221.329730	66.952223	118.000	179.000	225.000	260.000	388.000
Distance from Residence to Work	740.0	29.631081	14.836788	5.000	16.000	26.000	50.000	52.000
Service time	740.0	12.554054	4.384873	1.000	9.000	13.000	16.000	29.000
Age	740.0	36.450000	6.478772	27.000	31.000	37.000	40.000	58.000
Work load Average/day	740.0	271.490235	39.058116	205.917	244.387	264.249	294.217	378.884
Hit target	740.0	94.587838	3.779313	81.000	93.000	95.000	97.000	100.000
Disciplinary failure	740.0	0.054054	0.226277	0.000	0.000	0.000	0.000	1.000
Education	740.0	1.291892	0.673238	1.000	1.000	1.000	1.000	4.000
Son	740.0	1.018919	1.098489	0.000	0.000	1.000	2.000	4.000
Social drinker	740.0	0.567568	0.495749	0.000	0.000	1.000	1.000	1.000
Social smoker	740.0	0.072973	0.260268	0.000	0.000	0.000	0.000	1.000
Pet	740.0	0.745946	1.318258	0.000	0.000	0.000	1.000	8.000
Weight	740.0	79.035135	12.883211	56.000	69.000	83.000	89.000	108.000
Height	740.0	172.114865	6.034995	163.000	169.000	170.000	172.000	196.000
Body mass index	740.0	26.677027	4.285452	19.000	24.000	25.000	31.000	38.000
Absenteeism time in hours	740.0	6.924324	13.330998	0.000	2.000	3.000	8.000	120.000

Figure 2.2: Output of the describe() method

Note that some of the columns, such as **Month of absence**, **Day of the week**, **Seasons**, **Education**, **Disciplinary failure**, **Social drinker**, and **Social smoker**, are encoding categorical values. So, we can back-transform the numerical values to their original categories so that we have better plotting features. We will perform the transformation by defining a Python **dict** object containing the mapping and then applying the **apply()** function to each feature, which applies the provided function to each of the values in the column. First, let's define the encoding **dict** objects:

```
# define encoding dictionaries
month_encoding = {1: "January", 2: "February", 3: "March", \
                  4: "April", 5: "May", 6: "June", 7: "July", \
                  8: "August", 9: "September", 10: "October", \
```

```
                    11: "November", 12: "December", 0: "Unknown"}

dow_encoding = {2: "Monday", 3: "Tuesday", 4: "Wednesday", \
                5: "Thursday", 6: "Friday"}

season_encoding = {1: "Spring", 2: "Summer", 3: "Fall", 4: "Winter"}
education_encoding = {1: "high_school", 2: "graduate", \
                      3: "postgraduate", 4: "master_phd"}
yes_no_encoding = {0: "No", 1: "Yes"}
```

Afterward, we apply the encoding dictionaries to the relevant features:

```
# backtransform numerical variables to categorical
preprocessed_data = data.copy()
preprocessed_data["Month of absence"] = preprocessed_data\
                                        ["Month of absence"]\
                                        .apply(lambda x: \
                                            month_encoding[x])


preprocessed_data["Day of the week"] = preprocessed_data\
                                       ["Day of the week"]\
                                       .apply(lambda x: \
                                           dow_encoding[x])


preprocessed_data["Seasons"] = preprocessed_data["Seasons"]\
                               .apply(lambda x: season_encoding[x])
preprocessed_data["Education"] = preprocessed_data["Education"]\
                                 .apply(lambda x: \
                                     education_encoding[x])
preprocessed_data["Disciplinary failure"] = \
preprocessed_data["Disciplinary failure"].apply(lambda x: \
                                            yes_no_encoding[x])


preprocessed_data["Social drinker"] = \
preprocessed_data["Social drinker"].apply(lambda x: \
                                     yes_no_encoding[x])


preprocessed_data["Social smoker"] = \
```

```
preprocessed_data["Social smoker"].apply(lambda x: \
                                 yes_no_encoding[x])
# transform columns
preprocessed_data.head().T
```

The output will be as follows:

	0	1	2	3	4
ID	11	36	3	7	11
Reason for absence	26	0	23	7	23
Month of absence	July	July	July	July	July
Day of the week	Tuesday	Tuesday	Wednesday	Thursday	Thursday
Seasons	Spring	Spring	Spring	Spring	Spring
Transportation expense	289	118	179	279	289
Distance from Residence to Work	36	13	51	5	36
Service time	13	18	18	14	13
Age	33	50	38	39	33
Work load Average/day	239.554	239.554	239.554	239.554	239.554
Hit target	97	97	97	97	97
Disciplinary failure	No	Yes	No	No	No
Education	high_school	high_school	high_school	high_school	high_school
Son	2	1	0	2	2
Social drinker	Yes	Yes	Yes	Yes	Yes
Social smoker	No	No	No	Yes	No
Pet	1	0	0	0	1
Weight	90	98	89	68	90
Height	172	178	170	168	172
Body mass index	30	31	31	24	30
Absenteeism time in hours	4	0	2	4	2

Figure 2.3: Transformation of columns

In the previous code snippet, we created a clean copy of the original dataset by calling the `.copy()` method on the **data** object. In this way, a new copy of the original data is created. This is a convenient way to create new pandas DataFrames, without taking the risk of modifying the original raw data (as it might serve us later). Afterward, we created a set of dictionaries where the numerical values are keys and the categorical values are values. Finally, we used the `.apply()` method on each column we wanted to encode by mapping each value in the original column to its corresponding value in the encoding dictionary, which contains the target values. Note that in the **Month of absence** column, a 0 value is present, which is encoded as **Unknown** as no month corresponds to 0.

Based on the description of the data, the **Reason for absence** column contains information about the absence, which is encoded based on the **International Code of Diseases** (**ICD**). The following table represents the various encodings:

Code	Description
1	Certain infectious and parasitic diseases
2	Neoplasms
3	Diseases of the blood and blood-forming organs and certain disorders involving the immune system
4	Endocrine, nutritional, and metabolic diseases
5	Mental and behavioral disorders
6	Diseases of the nervous system
7	Diseases of the eye and adnexa
8	Diseases of the ear and mastoid process
9	Diseases of the circulatory system
10	Diseases of the respiratory system
11	Diseases of the digestive system
12	Diseases of the skin and subcutaneous tissue
13	Diseases of the musculoskeletal system and connective tissue
14	Diseases of the genitourinary system
15	Pregnancy, childbirth, and the puerperium
16	Certain conditions originating in the perinatal period
17	Congenital malformations, deformations, and chromosomal abnormalities
18	Symptoms, signs, and abnormal clinical and laboratory findings not elsewhere classified
19	Injury, poisoning, and certain other consequences of external causes
20	External causes of morbidity and mortality
21	Factors influencing health status and contact with health services
22	Patient follow-up
23	Medical consultation
24	Blood donation
25	Laboratory examination
26	Unjustified absence
27	Physiotherapy
28	Dental consultation
0	Unknown

Figure 2.4: Reason for absence encoding

Note that only values 1 to 21 represent ICD encoding; values 22 to 28 are separate reasons, which do not represent a disease, while value 0 is not defined—hence the encoded reason **Unknown**. As all values contained in the ICD represent some type of disease, it makes sense to create a new binary variable that indicates whether the current reason for absence is related to some sort of disease or not. We will do this in the following exercise.

EXERCISE 2.01: IDENTIFYING REASONS FOR ABSENCE

In this exercise, you will create a new variable, called **Disease**, which indicates whether a specific reason for absence is present in the ICD table or not. Please complete the initial data analysis before you begin this exercise. Now, follow these steps:

1. First, define a function that returns **Yes** if a provided encoded value is contained in the ICD (values 1 to 21); otherwise, **No**:

```
"""
define function, which checks if the provided integer value
is contained in the ICD or not
"""
def in_icd(val):
    return "Yes" if val >= 1 and val <= 21 else "No"
```

2. Combine the `.apply()` method with the previously defined `in_icd()` function in order to create the new **Disease** column in the preprocessed dataset:

```
# add Disease column
preprocessed_data["Disease"] = \
preprocessed_data["Reason for absence"].apply(in_icd)
```

3. Use bar plots in order to compare the absences due to disease reasons:

```
plt.figure(figsize=(10, 8))
sns.countplot(data=preprocessed_data, x='Disease')
plt.savefig('figs/disease_plot.png', format='png', dpi=300)
```

The output will be as follows:

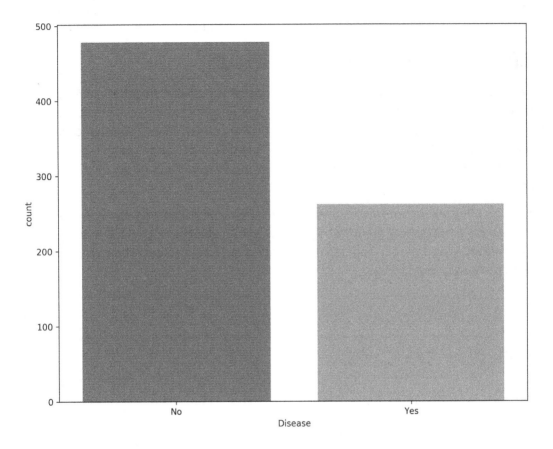

Figure 2.5: Comparing absence count to disease

Here, we are using the seaborn `.countplot()` function, which is quite handy when creating this type of bar plot, in which we want to know the total number of entries for each specific class. As we can see, the number of reasons for absence that are not listed in the ICD table is almost twice the number of listed ones.

> **NOTE**
>
> To access the source code for this specific section, please refer to https://packt.live/2B9AqVJ.
>
> You can also run this example online at https://packt.live/2UPwlr1. You must execute the entire Notebook in order to get the desired result.

In this section, we performed some simple data exploration and transformations on the initial absenteeism dataset. In the next section, we will go deeper into our data exploration and analyze some of the possible reasons for absence.

INITIAL ANALYSIS OF THE REASON FOR ABSENCE

Let's start with a simple analysis of the **Reason for absence** column. We will try to address questions such as, what is the most common reason for absence? Does being a drinker or smoker have some effect on the causes? Does the distance to work have some effect on the reasons? And so on. Starting with these types of questions is often important when performing data analysis, as this is a good way to obtain confidence and understanding of the data.

The first thing we are interested in is the overall distribution of the absence reasons in the data—that is, how many entries we have for a specific reason for absence in our dataset. We can easily address this question by using the **countplot()** function from the **seaborn** package:

```
# get the number of entries for each reason for absence
plt.figure(figsize=(10, 5))
ax = sns.countplot(data=preprocessed_data, x="Reason for absence")
ax.set_ylabel("Number of entries per reason of absence")
plt.savefig('figs/absence_reasons_distribution.png', \
            format='png', dpi=300)
```

The output will be as follows:

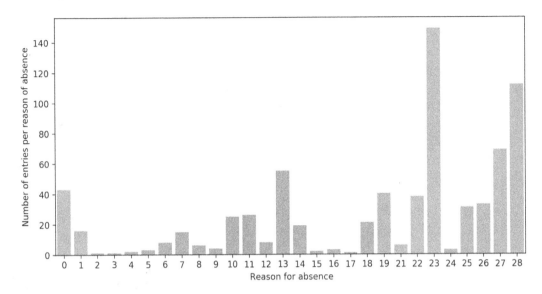

Figure 2.6: Number of entries for all reasons for absence

Note that we also used the **Disease** column as the **hue** parameter. This helps us to distinguish between disease-related reasons (listed in the ICD encoding) and those that aren't. Following *Figure 2.3*, we can assert that the most frequent reasons for absence are related to medical consultations (23), dental consultations (28), and physiotherapy (27). On the other hand, the most frequent reasons for absence encoded in the ICD encoding are related to diseases of the musculoskeletal system and connective tissue (13) and injury, poisoning, and certain other consequences of external causes (19).

In order to perform a more accurate and in-depth analysis of the data, we will investigate the impact of the various features on the **Reason for absence** and **Absenteeism in hours** columns in the following sections. First, we will analyze the data on social drinkers and smokers in the next section.

ANALYSIS OF SOCIAL DRINKERS AND SMOKERS

Let's begin with an analysis of the impact of being a drinker or smoker on employee absenteeism. As smoking and frequent drinking have a negative impact on health conditions, we would expect that certain diseases are more frequent in smokers and drinkers than others. Note that in the absenteeism dataset, 56% of the registered employees are drinkers, while only 7% are smokers. We can produce a figure, similar to *Figure 2.6* for the social drinkers and smokers with the following code:

```
# plot reasons for absence against being a social drinker/smoker
plt.figure(figsize=(8, 6))
sns.countplot(data=preprocessed_data, x="Reason for absence", \
            hue="Social drinker", hue_order=["Yes", "No"])
plt.savefig('figs/absence_reasons_drinkers.png', \
            format='png', dpi=300)
plt.figure(figsize=(8, 6))
sns.countplot(data=preprocessed_data, x="Reason for absence", \
            hue="Social smoker", hue_order=["Yes", "No"])
plt.savefig('figs/absence_reasons_smokers.png', \
            format='png', dpi=300)
```

The following is the output of the preceding code:

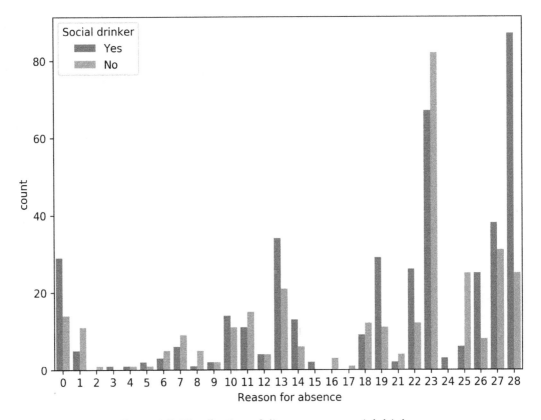

Figure 2.7: Distribution of diseases over social drinkers

Similarly, the distribution of diseases for social smokers can be visualized as follows:

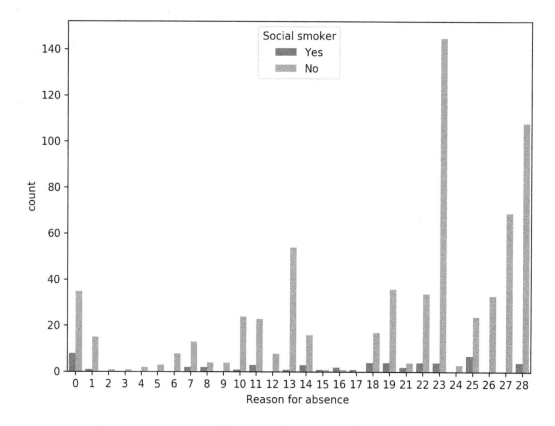

Figure 2.8: Distribution of diseases over social smokers

Next, calculate the actual count for social drinkers and smokers from the preprocessed data:

```
print(preprocessed_data["Social drinker"]\
    .value_counts(normalize=True))
print(preprocessed_data["Social smoker"]\
    .value_counts(normalize=True))
```

The output will be as follows:

```
Yes     0.567568
No      0.432432
Name: Social drinker, dtype: float64
No      0.927027
Yes     0.072973
Name: Social smoker, dtype: float64
```

As we can see from the resulting plots, a significant difference between drinkers and non-drinkers can be observed in absences related to Dental consultations (28). Furthermore, as the number of social smokers is quite small (only 7% of the entries), it is very hard to say whether there is actually a relationship between the absence reasons and smoking. A more rigorous approach in this direction would be to analyze the conditional probabilities of the different absence reasons, which are based on being a social drinker or smoker.

Conditional probability is a measure that tells us the probability of an event's occurrence, assuming that another event has occurred. From a mathematical perspective, given a set of events **Ω** and a probability measure **P** on **Ω** and given two events **A** and **B** in **Ω** with the unconditional probability of **B** being greater than zero (that is, **P(B) > 0)**, we can define the conditional probability of **A** given **B** as follows:

$$P(A \mid B) = \frac{P(A \cap B)}{P(B)}$$

Figure 2.9: Formula for conditional probability

In other words, the probability of **A** given **B** is equal to the probability of **A** and **B** both happening, divided by the probability of **B** happening. Let's consider a simple example that will help us understand the usage of conditional probability. This is a classic probability problem. Suppose that your friend has two children, and you know that one of them is male. We want to know what the probability is that your friend has two sons. First, we have to identify all the possible events in our event space **Ω**. If we denote with **B** the event of having a boy, and with **G** the event of having a girl, then the event space contains four possible events:

$$\Omega = \{BB, BG, GB, GG\}$$

Figure 2.10: Event space Ω

They each have a probability of 0.25. Following the notations from the definition, we can define the first event like so:

$$A = \{having\ two\ boys\} = \{BB\}$$

Figure 2.11: Event A

We can define the latter event like so:

$$B = \{one\ of\ the\ children\ is\ a\ boy\} = \{BG, GB, BB\}$$

Figure 2.12: Event B

Now, our initial problem translates into computing **P (A|B)**. With this, we get the following equation:

$$P(A \mid B) = \frac{A(A \cap B)}{P(B)} = \frac{P(\{BB\})}{P(\{BG, GB, BB\})} = \frac{1/4}{3/4} = 1/3$$

Figure 2.13: Probability of event A conditioned to B

We can also perform this example computationally:

```
# computation of conditional probability
sample_space = set(["BB", "BG", "GB", "GG"])
event_a = set(["BB"])
event_b = set(["BB", "BG", "GB"])

cond_prob = (0.25*len(event_a.intersection(event_b))) \
            / (0.25*len(event_b))
print(round(cond_prob, 4))
```

The output will be as follows:

```
0.3333
```

Note that by using the definition of conditional probability, we could address questions such as, "What is the probability of a reason for absence being related to laboratory examinations, assuming that an employee is a social drinker?" In other words, if we denote the "employee is absent for laboratory examinations" event with A, and the "employee is a social drinker" event with B, the probability of the "employee is absent due to laboratory examination reasons, given that employee is a social drinker" event can be computed by the previous formula.

The following exercise illustrates how the conditional probability formula can identify reasons for absence with higher probability among smokers and drinkers.

EXERCISE 2.02: IDENTIFYING REASONS OF ABSENCE WITH HIGHER PROBABILITY AMONG DRINKERS AND SMOKERS

In this exercise, you will compute the conditional probabilities of the different reasons for absence, assuming that the employee is a social drinker or smoker. Please execute the code mentioned in the previous section and *Exercise 2.01, Identifying Disease Reasons for Absence* before attempting this exercise. Now, follow these steps:

1. To identify the conditional probabilities, first compute the unconditional probabilities of being a social drinker or smoker. Verify that both the probabilities are greater than zero, as they appear in the denominator of the conditional probabilities. Do this by counting the number of social drinkers and smokers and dividing these values by the total number of entries, like so:

$$P\,(social\ drinker) = \frac{number\ of\ social\ drinkers}{total\ number\ of\ entries}$$

Figure 2.14: Probability of being a social drinker

$$P\,(social\ smoker) = \frac{number\ of\ social\ smokers}{total\ number\ of\ entries}$$

Figure 2.15: Probability of being a social smoker

The following code snippet does this for you:

```
# compute probabilities of being a drinker and smoker
drinker_prob = preprocessed_data["Social drinker"]\
            .value_counts(normalize=True)["Yes"]
smoker_prob = preprocessed_data["Social smoker"]\
            .value_counts(normalize=True)["Yes"]
print(f"P(social drinker) = {drinker_prob:.3f} \
| P(social smoker) = {smoker_prob:.3f}")
```

The output will be as follows:

```
P(social drinker) = 0.568 | P(social smoker) = 0.073
```

As you can see, the probability of being a drinker is almost 57%, while the probability of being a smoker is quite low (only 7.3%).

2. Next, compute the probabilities of being a social drinker/smoker and being absent for each reason of absence. For a specific reason of absence (say R$_i$), these probabilities are defined as follows:

$$P(social\ drinker\ and\ absent\ for\ reason\ R_1) = \frac{number\ of\ social\ drinkers\ absent\ for\ reason\ R_i}{total\ number\ of\ entries}$$

Figure 2.16: Probability of being a drinker and absent

$$P(social\ smoker\ and\ absent\ for\ reason\ R_1) = \frac{number\ of\ social\ smokers\ absent\ for\ reason\ R_i}{total\ number\ of\ entries}$$

Figure 2.17: Probability of being a smoker and absent

3. In order to carry the required computations, define masks in the data, which only account for entries where employees are drinkers or smokers:

```
#create mask for social drinkers/smokers
drinker_mask = preprocessed_data["Social drinker"] == "Yes"
smoker_mask = preprocessed_data["Social smoker"] == "Yes"
```

4. Compute the total number of entries and the number of absence reasons, masked by drinkers/smokers:

```
total_entries = preprocessed_data.shape[0]
absence_drinker_prob = preprocessed_data["Reason for absence"]\
                    [drinker_mask].value_counts()/total_entries

absence_smoker_prob = preprocessed_data["Reason for absence"]\
                    [smoker_mask].value_counts()/total_entries
```

5. Compute the conditional probabilities by dividing the computed probabilities for each reason of absence in *Step 2* by the unconditional probabilities obtained in *Step 1*:

```
# compute conditional probabilities
cond_prob = pd.DataFrame(index=range(0,29))
cond_prob["P(Absence | social drinker)"] = absence_drinker_prob\
                                /drinker_prob
cond_prob["P(Absence | social smoker)"] = absence_smoker_prob\
                                /smoker_prob
```

6. Create bar plots for the conditional probabilities:

```
# plot probabilities
plt.figure()
ax = cond_prob.plot.bar(figsize=(10,6))
ax.set_ylabel("Conditional probability")
plt.savefig('figs/conditional_probabilities.png', \
            format='png', dpi=300)
```

The output will be as follows:

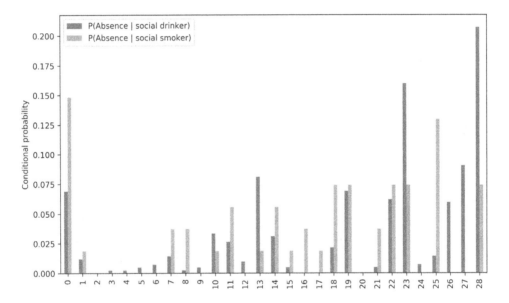

Figure 2.18: Bar plots for conditional probabilities

As we can observe from the previous plot, the highest reason for absence for drinkers is dental consultations (28), followed by medical consultations (23). Smokers' absences, however, are mostly due to unknown reasons (0) and laboratory examinations (25).

> **NOTE**
>
> To access the source code for this specific section, please refer to https://packt.live/2Y7KQhv.
>
> You can also run this example online at https://packt.live/3d7pFk3. You must execute the entire Notebook in order to get the desired result.

In the previous exercise, we saw how to compute the conditional probabilities of the reason for absence, conditioned on the employee being a social smoker or drinker. Furthermore, we saw that in order to perform the computation, we had to compute the probability of being absent and being a social smoker/drinker. Due to the nature of the problem, computing this value might be difficult, or we may only have one conditional probability (say, **P (A|B)**) where we actually need **P (B|A)** . In these cases, the Bayesian theorem can be used:

Let **Ω** denote a set of events with probability measure **P** on **Ω**. Given two events A and B in **Ω** , with **(P (B) > 0)** the Bayesian theorem states the following:

$$P(A \mid B) = \frac{P(B \mid A)P(A)}{P(B)}$$

Figure 2.19: Bayesian theorem

Before proceeding further, we will provide a practical example of applying the Bayesian theorem in practice. Suppose that we have two bags. The first one contains four blue and three red balls, while the second one contains two blue and five red balls. Let's assume that a ball is drawn at random from one of the two bags, and its color is blue. We want to know what the probability is that the ball has been drawn from the first bag. Let's use B_1 to denote the "ball is drawn from the first bag" event and B_2 to denote the "ball is drawn from the second bag" event. Since the number of balls is equal in both bags, the probability of the two events is equal to 0.5, as follows:

$$P(B_1) = P(B_2) = \frac{1}{2}$$

Figure 2.20: Probability of both events

If we use **A** to denote the "a blue ball has been drawn" event, then we have the following:

$$P(A \mid B_1) = \frac{4}{7} \quad and \quad P(A \mid B_2) = \frac{2}{7}$$

Figure 2.21: Probability of event A, where a blue ball is drawn

This is because we have four balls in the first bag and only two in the second one. Furthermore, based on the defined events, the probability we need to compute translates into **P(B₁ | A)**. By applying Bayes' theorem, we get the following:

$$P(B_1 \mid A) = \frac{P(A \mid B_1)P(B_1)}{P(A)} = \frac{P(A \mid B_1)P(B_1)}{P(A \mid B_1)P(B_1) + P(A \mid B_2)P(B_2)} = \frac{\frac{4}{7} \cdot \frac{1}{2}}{\frac{4}{7} \cdot \frac{1}{2} + \frac{2}{7} \cdot \frac{1}{2}} = \frac{\frac{2}{7}}{\frac{3}{7}} = \frac{2}{3}$$

Figure 2.22: Probability of the event that a blue ball is drawn

Now, let's apply Bayes' theorem to our dataset in the following exercise. In addition to applying Bayes' theorem, we will also be using the **Kolmogorov-Smirnov** test. The Kolmogorov-Smirnov test is used to determine whether two samples are statistically different from each other, i.e. whether or not they follow the same distribution. We can implement the Kolmogorov-Smirnov test directly from SciPy, as we will see in the exercise.

EXERCISE 2.03: IDENTIFYING THE PROBABILITY OF BEING A DRINKER/SMOKER, CONDITIONED TO ABSENCE REASON

In this exercise, you will compute the conditional probability of being a social drinker or smoker, conditioned on the reason for absence. In other words (where R_i is the reason for which an employee is absent), we want to compute the probabilities of an employee being a social drinker **P(social drinker |Ri)**, or smoker **P(social smoker |Ri)**, as follows:

$$P(social\ drinker \mid R_i) = \frac{P(R_i \mid social\ drinker)\,P(social\ drinker)}{P(R_i)}$$

Figure 2.23: Conditional probability of being a drinker, conditioned to an absence reason R_i

$$P(social\ smoker \mid R_i) = \frac{P(R_i \mid social\ smoker)\,P(social\ smoker)}{P(R_i)}$$

Figure 2.24: Conditional probability of being a smoker, conditioned to an absence reason R_i

Execute the code mentioned in the previous section, as well as the previous exercises, before attempting this exercise. Now, follow these steps:

1. Since you already computed **P(Ri | social drinker)**, **P(Ri | social smoker)**, **P(social drinker)**, and **P(social smoker)**, in the previous exercise, you only need to compute **P(R$_i$)** for each reason of absence **R_i**:

```
# compute reason for absence probabilities
absence_prob = preprocessed_data["Reason for absence"]\
              .value_counts(normalize=True)
```

2. Now that you have all the necessary values, compute the conditional probabilities according to the equations in *Step 1*:

```
# compute conditional probabilities for drinker/smoker
cond_prob_drinker_smoker = pd.DataFrame(index=range(0,29))
cond_prob_drinker_smoker["P(social drinker | Absence)"] = \
cond_prob["P(Absence | social drinker)"]*drinker_prob/absence_prob

cond_prob_drinker_smoker["P(social smoker | Absence)"] = \
cond_prob["P(Absence | social smoker)"]*smoker_prob/absence_prob

plt.figure()
ax = cond_prob_drinker_smoker.plot.bar(figsize=(10,6))
ax.set_ylabel("Conditional probability")
plt.savefig('figs/conditional_probabilities_drinker_smoker.png', \
            format='png', dpi=300)
```

The following is the output of the preceding code:

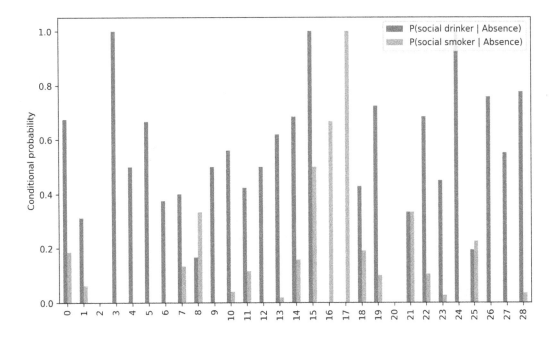

Figure 2.25: Conditional probabilities of being a drinker/smoker, conditioned to being absent

As you can see from the resulting plot, the conditional probabilities of being a social drinker/smoker are quite high, once an absence with a certain reason occurs. This is due to the fact that the number of entries is very small; as such, if all the registered employees who were absent for a certain reason are smokers, the probability of being a smoker, once that reason has been registered, will be equal to one (based on the available data).

3. To complete your analysis on the social drinkers and smokers, analyze the distribution of the hours of absenteeism based on the two classes (being a social drinker/smoker versus not being). A useful type of plot for this type of comparison is the violin plot, which can be produced using the **seaborn violinplot()** function:

```
# create violin plots of the absenteeism time in hours
plt.figure(figsize=(8,6))
sns.violinplot(x="Social drinker", y="Absenteeism time in hours", \
            data=preprocessed_data, order=["No", "Yes"])
plt.savefig('figs/drinkers_hour_distribution.png', \
            format='png', dpi=300)
plt.figure(figsize=(8,6))
```

```
sns.violinplot(x="Social smoker", y="Absenteeism time in hours", \
               data=preprocessed_data, order=["No", "Yes"])
plt.savefig('figs/smokers_hour_distribution.png', \
            format='png', dpi=300)
```

The following is the output of the preceding code:

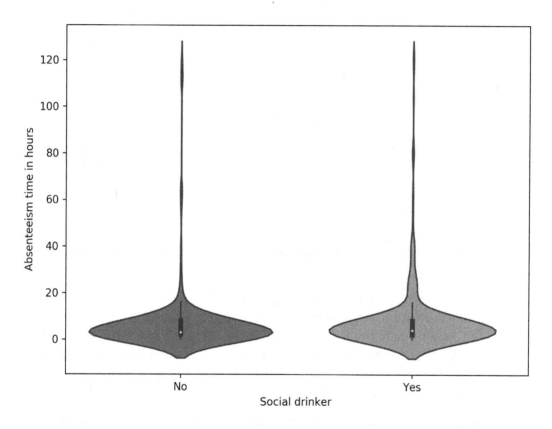

Figure 2.26: Violin plots of the absenteeism time in hours for social drinkers

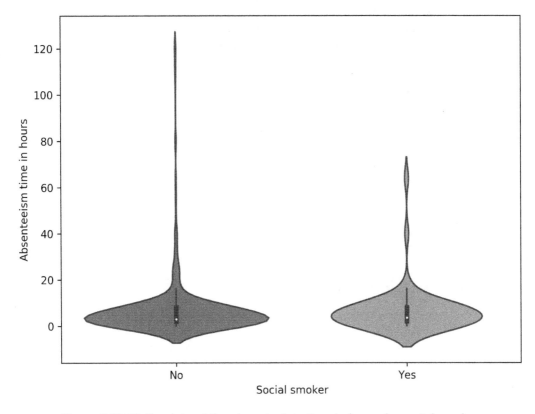

Figure 2.27: Violin plots of the absenteeism time in hours for social smokers

As you can observe from *Figure 2.27*, despite some differences in the outliers between smokers and non-smokers, there is no substantial difference in the distribution of absenteeism hours in drinkers and smokers.

4. To assess this statement in a rigorous statistical way, perform hypothesis testing on the absenteeism hours (with a null hypothesis stating that the average absenteeism time in hours is the same for drinkers and non-drinkers):

```
from scipy.stats import ttest_ind
hours_col = "Absenteeism time in hours"


# test mean absenteeism time for drinkers
drinkers_mask = preprocessed_data["Social drinker"] == "Yes"
hours_drinkers = preprocessed_data.loc[drinker_mask, hours_col]
hours_non_drinkers = preprocessed_data\
                    .loc[~drinker_mask, hours_col]
drinkers_test = ttest_ind(hours_drinkers, hours_non_drinkers)
print(f"Statistic value: {drinkers_test[0]}, \
p-value: {drinkers_test[1]}")
```

The output will be as follows:

```
Statistic value: 1.7713833295243993, p-value: 0.07690961828294651
```

5. Perform the same test on the social smokers:

```
# test mean absenteeism time for smokers
smokers_mask = preprocessed_data["Social smoker"] == "Yes"
hours_smokers = preprocessed_data.loc[smokers_mask, hours_col]
hours_non_smokers = preprocessed_data\
                    .loc[~smokers_mask, hours_col]
smokers_test = ttest_ind(hours_smokers, hours_non_smokers)
print(f"Statistic value: {smokers_test[0]}, \
p-value: {smokers_test[1]}")
```

The output will be as follows:

```
Statistic value: -0.24277795417700243, p-value: 0.8082448720154971
```

As you can see, the p-value of both tests is above the critical value of 0.05, which means that you cannot reject the null hypothesis. In other words, you cannot say that there is a statistically significant difference in the absenteeism hours between drinkers (and smokers) and non-drinkers (and non-smokers).

Note that in the previous paragraph, you performed hypothesis tests, with a null hypothesis for the average absenteeism hours being equal for drinkers (and smokers) and non-drinkers (and non-smokers). Nevertheless, the average hours may still be equal, but their distributions may be different.

6. Perform a **Kolmogorov-Smirnov** test to assess the difference in the distributions of two samples:

```
# perform Kolmogorov-Smirnov test for comparing the distributions
from scipy.stats import ks_2samp

ks_drinkers = ks_2samp(hours_drinkers, hours_non_drinkers)
ks_smokers = ks_2samp(hours_smokers, hours_non_smokers)

print(f"Drinkers comparison: statistics={ks_drinkers[0]:.3f}, \
pvalue={ks_drinkers[1]:.3f}")
print(f"Smokers comparison:  statistics={ks_smokers[0]:.3f}, \
pvalue={ks_smokers[1]:.3f}")
```

The output will be as follows:

```
Drinkers comparison: statistics=0.135, pvalue=0.002
Smokers comparison:  statistics=0.104, pvalue=0.607
```

The p-value for the drinkers dataset is lower than the critical 0.05, which is strong evidence against the null hypothesis of the two distributions being equal. On the other hand, as the p-value for the smokers dataset is higher than 0.05, you cannot reject the null hypothesis.

> **NOTE**
>
> To access the source code for this specific section, please refer to https://packt.live/3hxt3l6.
>
> You can also run this example online at https://packt.live/2BeAweq. You must execute the entire Notebook in order to get the desired result.

In this section, we investigated the relationship between the different reasons for absence, as well as social information about the employees (such as being smokers or drinkers). In the next section, we will analyze the impact of the employees' body mass index on their absenteeism.

BODY MASS INDEX

The **Body Mass Index** (**BMI**) is defined as a person's weight in kilograms, divided by the square of their height in meters:

$$BMI = \frac{weight\ [kg]}{height\ [m]}$$

Figure 2.28: Expression for BMI

BMI is a universal way to classify people as **underweight**, **healthy weight**, **overweight**, and **obese**, based on tissue mass (muscle, fat, and bone) and height. The following plot indicates the relationship between weight and height for the various categories:

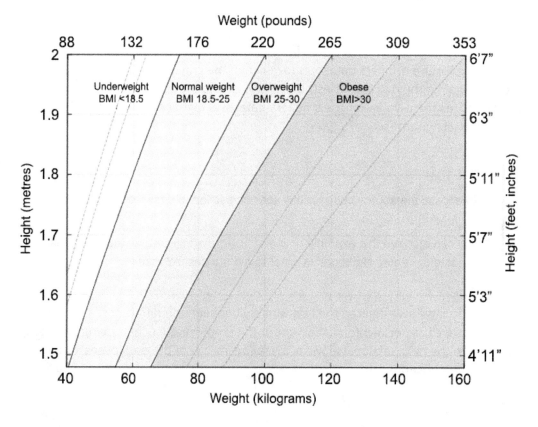

Figure 2.29: Body Mass Index categories
(**source:** https://en.wikipedia.org/wiki/Body_mass_index)

According to the preceding plot, we can build the four categories (**underweight**, **healthy weight**, **overweight**, and **obese**) based on the BMI values:

```
"""
define function for computing the BMI category, based on BMI value
"""
def get_bmi_category(bmi):
    if bmi < 18.5:
        category = "underweight"
    elif bmi >= 18.5 and bmi < 25:
        category = "healthy weight"
    elif bmi >= 25 and bmi < 30:
        category = "overweight"
    else:
        category = "obese"
    return category
# compute BMI category
preprocessed_data["BMI category"] = preprocessed_data\
                                    ["Body mass index"]\
                                    .apply(get_bmi_category)
```

We can plot the number of entries for each category:

```
# plot number of entries for each category
plt.figure(figsize=(10, 6))
sns.countplot(data=preprocessed_data, x='BMI category', \
            order=["underweight", "healthy weight", \
                "overweight", "obese"], \
            palette="Set2")
plt.savefig('figs/bmi_categories.png', format='png', dpi=300)
```

The following is the output of the preceding code:

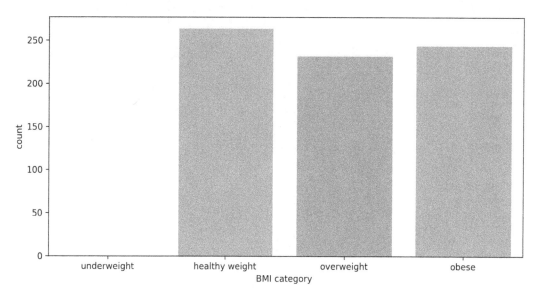

Figure 2.30: BMI categories

We can see that no entries for the **underweight** category are present, with the data being almost uniformly distributed among the remaining three categories. Of course, this is an alarming indicator, as more than 60% of the employees are either overweight or obese.

Now, let's check how the different BMI categories are related to the reason for absence. More precisely, we would like to see how many employees there are based on their body mass index and their reason for absence. This can be done with the following code:

```
# plot BMI categories vs Reason for absence
plt.figure(figsize=(10, 16))
ax = sns.countplot(data=preprocessed_data, \
                y="Reason for absence", hue="BMI category", \
                hue_order=["underweight", "healthy weight", \
                        "overweight", "obese"], \
                palette="Set2")
ax.set_xlabel("Number of employees")
plt.savefig('figs/reasons_bmi.png', format='png', dpi=300)
```

The output will be as follows:

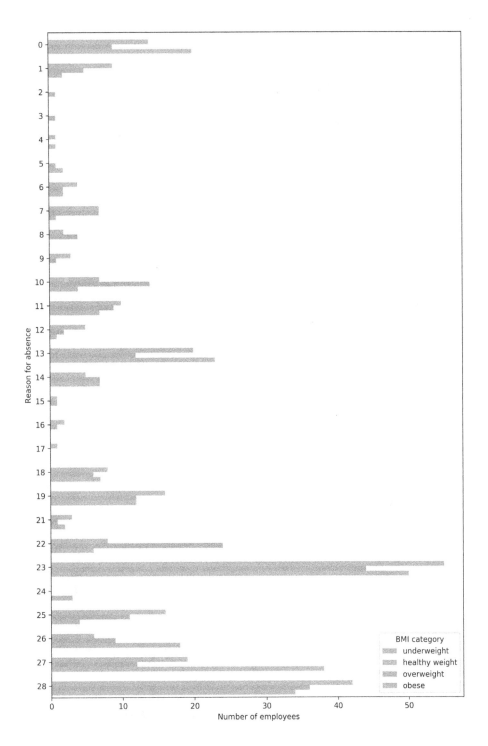

Figure 2.31: Absence reasons, based on BMI category

Unfortunately, no clear pattern arises from the preceding plot. In other words, for each reason for absence, an (almost) equal number of employees with different body mass indexes are present.

We can also investigate the distribution of absence hours for the different BMI categories:

```
# plot distribution of absence time, based on BMI category
plt.figure(figsize=(8,6))
sns.violinplot(x="BMI category", \
               y="Absenteeism time in hours", \
               data=preprocessed_data, \
               order=["healthy weight", "overweight", "obese"])
plt.savefig('figs/bmi_hour_distribution.png', format='png')
```

The output will be as follows:

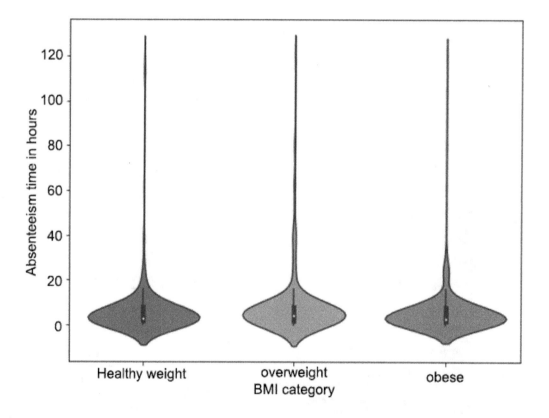

Figure 2.32: Absence time in hours, based on the BMI category

As we can observe from *Figure 2.31* and *Figure 2.32*, no evidence states that BMI and obesity levels influence the employees' absenteeism.

AGE AND EDUCATION FACTORS

Age and education may also influence employees' absenteeism. For instance, older employees might need more frequent medical treatment, while employees with higher education degrees, covering positions of higher responsibility, might be less prone to being absent.

First, let's investigate the correlation between age and absence hours. We will create a regression plot, in which we'll plot the **Age** column on the *x* axis and **Absenteeism time in hours** on the *y* axis. We'll also include the Pearson's correlation coefficient and its p-value, where the null hypothesis is that the correlation coefficient between the two features is equal to zero:

```
from scipy.stats import pearsonr
# compute Pearson's correlation coefficient and p-value
pearson_test = pearsonr(preprocessed_data["Age"], \
            preprocessed_data["Absenteeism time in hours"])
"""
create regression plot and add correlation coefficient in the title
"""
plt.figure(figsize=(10, 6))
ax = sns.regplot(x="Age", y="Absenteeism time in hours", \
            data=preprocessed_data, scatter_kws={"alpha":0.1})
ax.set_title(f"Correlation={pearson_test[0]:.03f} \
| p-value={pearson_test[1]:.03f}")
plt.savefig('figs/correlation_age_hours.png', \
        format='png', dpi=300)
```

The output will be as follows:

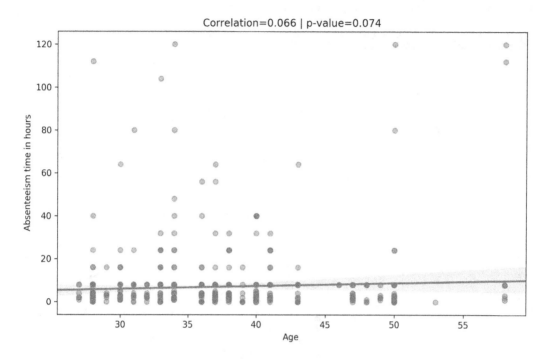

Figure 2.33: Correlation plot for absenteeism time and age

As we can observe from the resulting plot, no significant pattern occurs. Furthermore, the correlation coefficient is extremely small (0.066), and its p-value is above the threshold of 0.05, which is an additional indicator that no relationship is present between the **Age** and **Absenteeism time in hours** features.

We can also check whether age has some impact on the reason for absence. We'll perform this analysis in the next exercise.

EXERCISE 2.04: INVESTIGATING THE IMPACT OF AGE ON REASON FOR ABSENCE

In this exercise, we'll investigate the relationship between the **Age** feature and the various reasons for absence. Please execute the code mentioned in the previous section and exercises before attempting this exercise. Now, follow these steps:

1. First, create a violin plot between the **Age** and **Disease** features. This will give you your first insight into the relationship between the two columns:

```
# create violin plot between the Age and Disease columns
plt.figure(figsize=(8,6))
sns.violinplot(x="Disease", y="Age", data=preprocessed_data)
```

```
plt.savefig('figs/exercise_204_age_disease.png', \
            format='png', dpi=300)
```

The output will be as follows:

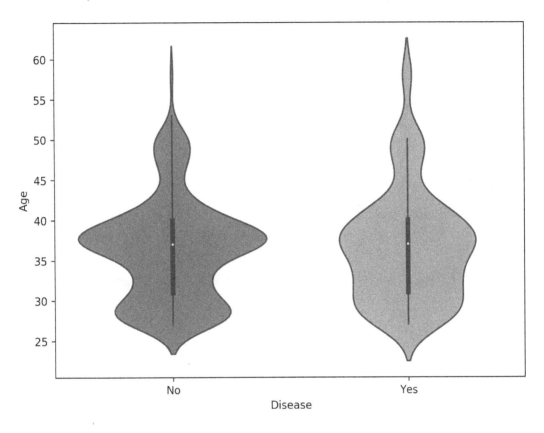

Figure 2.34: Violin plot for disease versus age

2. From *Step 1*, you can see some differences between the two distributions of age. In fact, for samples with ICD encoded reasons for absence (labeled **Yes** in the **Disease** column), you can observe that slightly more samples are present for older employees. To confirm this difference in distributions, perform hypothesis tests on the means and distributions of the two groups:

```
"""
get Age entries for employees with Disease == Yes and Disease == No
"""
disease_mask = preprocessed_data["Disease"] == "Yes"
disease_ages = preprocessed_data["Age"][disease_mask]
no_disease_ages = preprocessed_data["Age"][~disease_mask]
```

```
# perform hypothesis test for equality of means
test_res = ttest_ind(disease_ages, no_disease_ages)
print(f"Test for equality of means: \
statistic={test_res[0]:0.3f}, pvalue={test_res[1]:0.3f}")

# test equality of distributions via Kolmogorov-Smirnov test
ks_res = ks_2samp(disease_ages, no_disease_ages)
print(f"KS test for equality of distributions: \
statistic={ks_res[0]:0.3f}, pvalue={ks_res[1]:0.3f}")
```

The output will be as follows:

```
Test for equality of means: statistic=0.630, pvalue=0.529
KS test for equality of distributions: statistic=0.057,
pvalue=0.619
```

From the results of the two tests, you can conclude that there is no statistically significant difference between the two distributions. Thus, age is neither an indicator for the length of an absence nor for its type.

3. Now investigate the relationship between age and reason for absence:

```
# violin plot of reason for absence vs age
plt.figure(figsize=(20,8))
sns.violinplot(x="Reason for absence", y="Age", \
               data=preprocessed_data)
plt.savefig('figs/exercise_204_age_reason.png', format='png')
```

The output will be as follows:

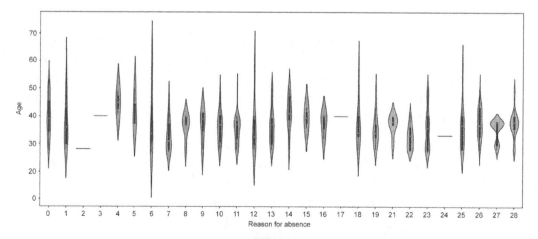

Figure 2.35: Violin plot for age and reason for absence

In light of the previously performed analysis, you can conclude that age has no impact on the employees' absenteeism.

> **NOTE**
>
> To access the source code for this specific section, please refer to https://packt.live/2Y7jEj6.
>
> You can also run this example online at https://packt.live/3d7q5qD. You must execute the entire Notebook in order to get the desired result.

Now, let's analyze the impact of education level on absenteeism.

EXERCISE 2.05: INVESTIGATING THE IMPACT OF EDUCATION ON REASON FOR ABSENCE

In this exercise, you will analyze the existing relationship between the **Reason for absence** and **Education** columns. You will start by looking at the percentage of employees with a certain educational degree, and then relate those numbers to the various reasons for absence. Please execute the code mentioned in the previous section and exercises before attempting this exercise. Now, follow these steps:

1. Before starting the analysis, check the percentage of employees in the data that hold a certain degree:

```
# compute percentage of employees per education level
education_types = ["high_school", "graduate", \
                   "postgraduate", "master_phd"]
counts = preprocessed_data["Education"].value_counts()
percentages = preprocessed_data["Education"]\
              .value_counts(normalize=True)
for educ_type in education_types:
    print(f"Education type: {educ_type:12s} \
| Counts : {counts[educ_type]:6.0f} \
| Percentage: {100*percentages[educ_type]:4.1f}")
```

The output will be as follows:

```
Education type: high_school   | Counts :    611 | Percentage: 82.6
Education type: graduate      | Counts :     46 | Percentage:  6.2
Education type: postgraduate  | Counts :     79 | Percentage: 10.7
Education type: master_phd    | Counts :      4 | Percentage:  0.5
```

You can see that most of the employees in the data have a high school degree (82.6%), which means that the data is highly biased toward these employees.

2. Create a distribution plot of the number of hours of absence, based on the level of education of the employees:

```
# distribution of absence hours, based on education level
plt.figure(figsize=(8,6))
sns.violinplot(x="Education", y="Absenteeism time in hours",\
            data=preprocessed_data, \
            order=["high_school", "graduate", \
                "postgraduate", "master_phd"])
plt.savefig('figs/exercise_205_education_hours.png', format='png')
```

The output will be as follows:

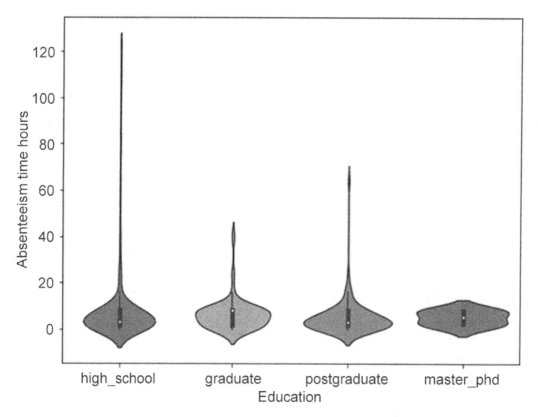

Figure 2.36: Violin plot for number of hours of absence for each level of education

3. It seems most of the extreme cases of absence are among employees with lower education levels. Compute the mean and standard deviation of the absence duration for the different levels of education:

```
# compute mean and standard deviation of absence hours
education_types = ["high_school", "graduate", \
                   "postgraduate", "master_phd"]
for educ_type in education_types:
    mask = preprocessed_data["Education"] == educ_type
    hours = preprocessed_data["Absenteeism time in hours"][mask]
    mean = hours.mean()
    stddev = hours.std()
    print(f"Education type: {educ_type:12s} | Mean : {mean:.03f} \
| Stddev: {stddev:.03f}")
```

The output will be as follows:

```
Education type: high_school  | Mean : 7.190 | Stddev: 14.259
Education type: graduate     | Mean : 6.391 | Stddev: 6.754
Education type: postgraduate | Mean : 5.266 | Stddev: 7.963
Education type: master_phd   | Mean : 5.250 | Stddev: 3.202
```

You can see that both the mean and standard deviation of the hours of absence are decreasing, meaning that highly educated employees tend to have shorter absences. Of course, a higher degree of education is not a cause for such a phenomenon and is more of an indication of it.

4. Now, check the reasons for absence based on the education level:

```
# plot reason for absence, based on education level
plt.figure(figsize=(10, 16))
sns.countplot(data=preprocessed_data, y="Reason for absence",\
              hue="Education", \
              hue_order=["high_school", "graduate", \
                         "postgraduate", "master_phd"])
plt.savefig('figs/exercise_205_education_reason.png', format='png')
```

The output will be as follows:

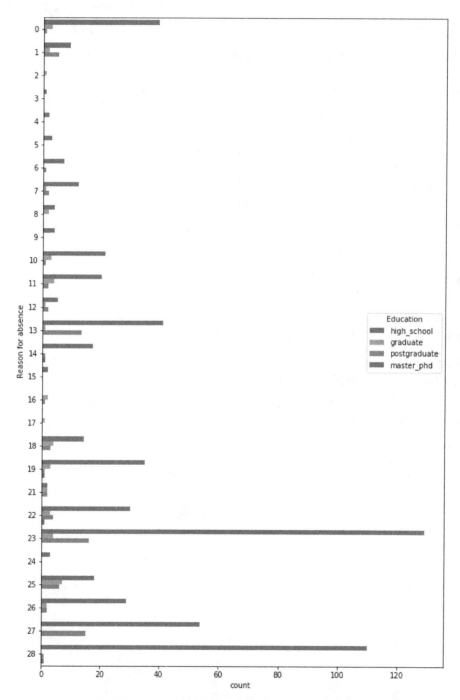

Figure 2.37: Reasons for absence for each level of education

From the preceding plot, you can observe that most of the absences relate to employees with a **high_school** level of education. This is, of course, due to the fact that most of the employees only have a high school degree (as observed in *Step 1*). Furthermore, from our analysis in *Step 2*, we saw that most of the absences that consisted of a greater number of hours were among employees with a **high_school** education level.

One question that comes to mind is whether the probability of being absent for more than one working week (40 hours) is greater for employees with a high school degree compared to graduates. In order to address this question, use the definition of conditional probability:

$$P\left(\text{extreme absence} \mid \text{degree} = \text{high\_school}\right) = \frac{P\left(\text{extreme absence}, \text{degree} = \text{high\_school}\right)}{P\left(\text{extreme absence}\right)}$$

Figure 2.38: Conditional probability for extreme absences by employees with a high school degree

$$P\left(\text{extreme absence} \mid \text{degree} \neq \text{high\_school}\right) = \frac{P\left(\text{extreme absence}, \text{degree} \neq \text{high\_school}\right)}{P\left(\text{extreme absence}\right)}$$

Figure 2.39: Conditional probability for extreme absences by employees without a high school degree

The following code snippet computes the conditional probabilities:

```
"""
define threshold for extreme hours of absenteeism and get total number
of entries
"""
threshold = 40
total_entries = len(preprocessed_data)


# find entries with Education == high_school
high_school_mask = preprocessed_data["Education"] == "high_school"


# find entries with absenteeism time in hours more than threshold
extreme_mask = preprocessed_data\
                ["Absenteeism time in hours"] > threshold


# compute probability of having high school degree
prob_high_school = len(preprocessed_data[high_school_mask])\
```

```
                          /total_entries

# compute probability of having more than high school degree
prob_graduate = len(preprocessed_data[~high_school_mask])\
               /total_entries

"""
compute probability of having high school and being absent for more
than "threshold" hours
"""

prob_extreme_high_school = len(preprocessed_data\
                              [high_school_mask & extreme_mask])\
                              /total_entries

"""
compute probability of having more than high school and being absent
for more than "threshold" hours
"""

prob_extreme_graduate = len(preprocessed_data\
                           [~high_school_mask & extreme_mask])\
                           /total_entries

# compute and print conditional probabilities
cond_prob_extreme_high_school = prob_extreme_high_school\
                               /prob_high_school
cond_prob_extreme_graduate = prob_extreme_graduate/prob_graduate
print(f"P(extreme absence | degree = high_school) = \
{100*cond_prob_extreme_high_school:3.2f}")
print(f"P(extreme absence | degree != high_school) = \
{100*cond_prob_extreme_graduate:3.2f}")
preprocessed_data.head().T
```

The output will be as follows:

```
P(extreme absence | degree = high_school) = 2.29
P(extreme absence | degree != high_school) = 0.78
```

The preprocessed data now looks as follows:

	0	1	2	3	4
ID	11	36	3	7	11
Reason for absence	26	0	23	7	23
Month of absence	July	July	July	July	July
Day of the week	Tuesday	Tuesday	Wednesday	Thursday	Thursday
Seasons	Spring	Spring	Spring	Spring	Spring
Transportation expense	289	118	179	279	289
Distance from Residence to Work	36	13	51	5	36
Service time	13	18	18	14	13
Age	33	50	38	39	33
Work load Average/day	239.554	239.554	239.554	239.554	239.554
Hit target	97	97	97	97	97
Disciplinary failure	No	Yes	No	No	No
Education	high_school	high_school	high_school	high_school	high_school
Son	2	1	0	2	2
Social drinker	Yes	Yes	Yes	Yes	Yes
Social smoker	No	No	No	Yes	No
Pet	1	0	0	0	1
Weight	90	98	89	68	90
Height	172	178	170	168	172
Body mass index	30	31	31	24	30
Absenteeism time in hours	4	0	2	4	2
Disease	No	No	No	Yes	No
BMI category	obese	obese	obese	healthy weight	obese

Figure 2.40: Analysis of data

NOTE

To access the source code for this specific section, please refer to https://packt.live/3fxhorg.

You can also run this example online at https://packt.live/2YDVBr0. You must execute the entire Notebook in order to get the desired result.

From the preceding computations, we can see that the probability of having an absence of more than 40 hours for employees with a high school education degree is 2.29%, which is approximately three times greater than the same probability for employees with a university degree (0.78%).

TRANSPORTATION COSTS AND DISTANCE TO WORK FACTORS

Two possible indicators for absenteeism may also be the distance between home and work (the **Distance from Residence to Work** column) and transportation costs (the **Transportation expense** column). Employees who have to travel longer, or whose costs for commuting to work are high, might be more prone to absenteeism.

In this section, we will investigate the relationship between these variables and the absence time in hours. Since we do not believe the aforementioned factors might be indicative of disease problems, we will not consider a possible relationship with the **Reason for absence** column.

First, let's start our analysis by plotting the previously mentioned columns (**Distance from Residence to Work** and **Transportation expense**) against the **Absenteeism time in hours** column:

```
# plot transportation costs and distance to work against hours
plt.figure(figsize=(10, 6))
sns.jointplot(x="Distance from Residence to Work", \
              y="Absenteeism time in hours", \
              data=preprocessed_data, kind="reg")
plt.savefig('figs/distance_vs_hours.png', format='png')


plt.figure(figsize=(10, 6))
sns.jointplot(x="Transportation expense", \
              y="Absenteeism time in hours", \
              data=preprocessed_data, kind="reg")
plt.savefig('figs/costs_vs_hours.png', format='png')
```

Note that, here, we used the **seaborn jointplot()** function, which not only produces the regression plot between the two variables but also estimates their distribution. The output will be as follows:

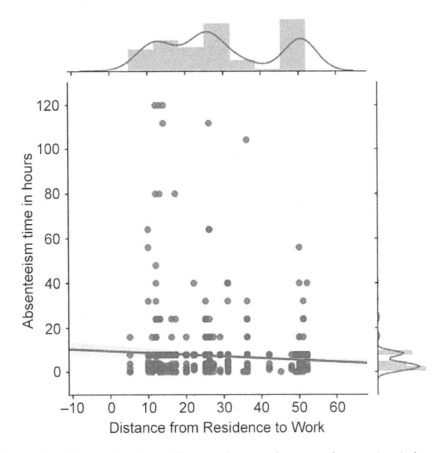

Figure 2.41: Regression plot of distance from work versus absenteeism in hours

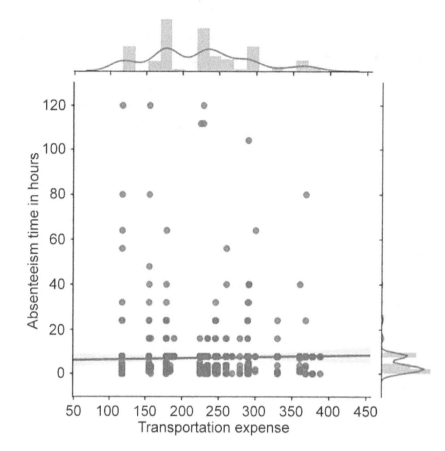

Figure 2.42: Regression plot of transportation costs versus absenteeism in hours (on the right)

As we can see, the distributions of `Distance from Residence to Work` and `Transportation expense` look close to normal distributions, while the absenteeism time in hours is heavily right-skewed. This makes the comparison between the variables difficult to interpret. One solution to this problem is to transform the data into something close to a normal distribution. A handy way to perform this transformation is to use the **Box-Cox** or **Yeo-Johnson** transformations. Both are defined as a family of functions, depending on a parameter λ, under which the transformed data is as close to normal as possible.

The Box-Cox transformation is defined as follows:

$$f_\lambda(x) = \frac{x^\lambda - 1}{\lambda} \quad if \ \lambda \neq 0$$

Figure 2.43: Expression for Box-Cox transformation if λ is not equal to 0

$$f_\lambda(x) = log(x) \quad if \ \lambda = 0$$

Figure 2.44: Expression for Box-Cox transformation if λ is equal to 0

The optimal value of the parameter **λ** is the one that results in the best approximation of a normal distribution. Note that the Box-Cox transformation fails if the data assumes negative values or zero. If this is the case, the **Yeo-Johnson** transformation can be used:

$$f_\lambda(x) = \frac{((x+1)^\lambda - 1)}{\lambda} \quad if \ \lambda \neq 0, \ x \geq 0$$

$$f_\lambda(x) = log(x+1) \quad if \ \lambda = 0, \ x \geq 0$$

$$f_\lambda(x) = \frac{\left[(-x+1)^{(2-\lambda)} - 1\right]}{2-\lambda} \quad if \ \lambda \neq 2, \ x < 0$$

$$f_\lambda(x) = -log(-\lambda + 1) \quad if \ \lambda = 2, \ x < 0$$

Figure 2.45: Expression for Yeo-Johnson transformation

In Python, both transformations can be found in the **scipy.stats** module (in the **boxcox()** and **yeojohnson()** functions, respectively).

Since the **Absenteeism time in hours** column contains zeros, we will apply the Yeo-Johnson transformation in order to reproduce the plots from *Figure 2.42*:

```
# run Yeo-Johnson transformation and recreate previous plots
from scipy.stats import yeojohnson

hours = yeojohnson(preprocessed_data\
                   ["Absenteeism time in hours"].apply(float))
distances = preprocessed_data["Distance from Residence to Work"]
expenses = preprocessed_data["Transportation expense"]

plt.figure(figsize=(10, 6))
ax = sns.jointplot(x=distances, y=hours[0], kind="reg")
ax.set_axis_labels("Distance from Residence to Work",\
                   "Transformed absenteeism time in hours")
plt.savefig('figs/distance_vs_hours_transformed.png', format='png')

plt.figure(figsize=(10, 6))
ax = sns.jointplot(x=expenses, y=hours[0], kind="reg")
ax.set_axis_labels("Transportation expense", \
                   "Transformed absenteeism time in hours")
plt.savefig('figs/costs_vs_hours_transformed.png', format='png')
```

The output will be as follows:

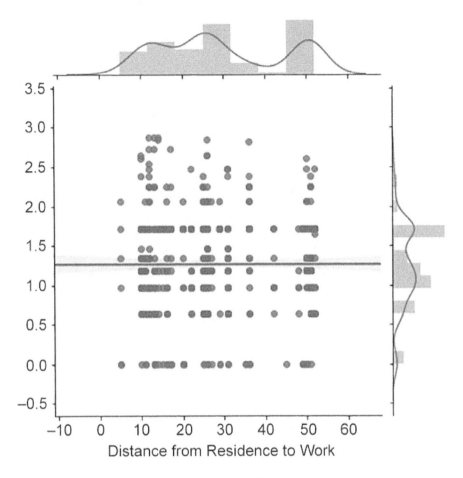

Figure 2.46: Regression plot of distance from work versus transformed
absenteeism in hours

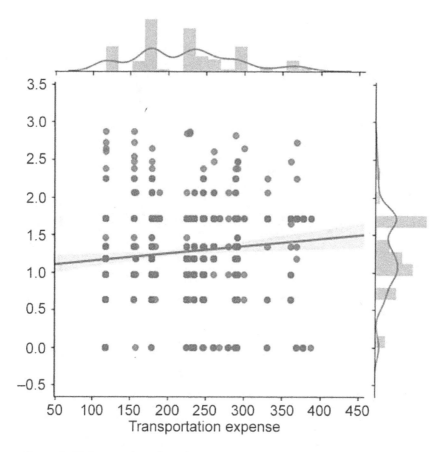

Figure 2.47: Regression plot of transportation costs versus transformed absenteeism in hours

We can also produce kernel density estimation plots (that is, plots that help us visualize the probability density functions of continuous variables) by just changing the type of the **jointplot()** function to **kde**.

```
# produce KDE plots
plt.figure(figsize=(10, 6))
ax = sns.jointplot(x=distances, y=hours[0], kind="kde")
ax.set_axis_labels("Distance from Residence to Work",\
                   "Transformed absenteeism time in hours")
plt.savefig('figs/distance_vs_hours_transformed_kde.png', \
            format='png')


plt.figure(figsize=(10, 6))
ax = sns.jointplot(x=expenses, y=hours[0], kind="kde")
ax.set_axis_labels("Transportation expense", \
                   "Transformed absenteeism time in hours")
plt.savefig('figs/costs_vs_hours_transformed_kde.png', \
            format='png')
```

The KDE plot for distance from residence to work versus absent hours will be as follows:

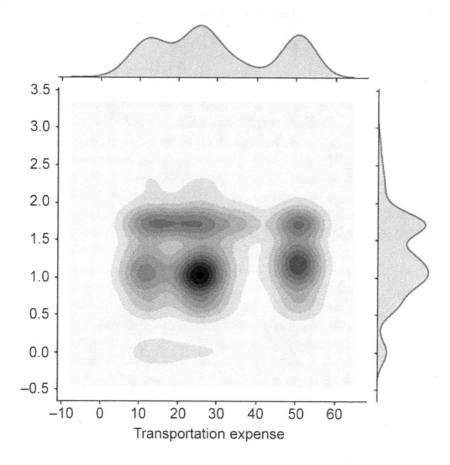

Figure 2.48: KDE plot for distance from residence to work versus absent hours

The KDE plot for transport expense versus absent hours will be as follows:

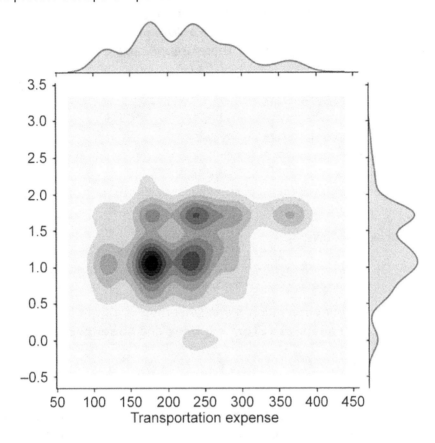

Figure 2.49: KDE plot for transport expense versus absent hours

From *Figure 2.46*, we can also see that the regression line between the variables is almost flat for the **Distance from Residence to Work** column (which is a clear indicator of zero correlation) but has a slight upward slope for the **Transportation Expense** column. Therefore, we can expect a small positive correlation:

```
# investigate correlation between the columns
distance_corr = pearsonr(hours[0], distances)
expenses_corr = pearsonr(hours[0], expenses)
print(f"Distances correlation: corr={distance_corr[0]:.3f}, \
pvalue={distance_corr[1]:.3f}")
print(f"Expenses comparison:  corr={expenses_corr[0]:.3f}, \
pvalue={expenses_corr[1]:.3f}")
```

The output will be as follows:

```
Distances correlation: corr=-0.000, pvalue=0.999
Expenses comparison: corr=0.113, pvalue=0.002
```

These results confirm our observation, stating that there is a slight positive correlation between **Transportation expense** and **Absenteeism time in hours**.

TEMPORAL FACTORS

Factors such as day of the week and month may also be indicators for absenteeism. For instance, employees might prefer to have their medical examinations on Friday when the workload is lower, and it is closer to the weekend. In this section, we will analyze the impact of the **Day of the week** and **Month of absence** columns, and their impact on the employees' absenteeism.

Let's begin with an analysis of the number of entries for each day of the week and each month:

```python
# count entries per day of the week and month
plt.figure(figsize=(12, 5))
ax = sns.countplot(data=preprocessed_data, \
                x='Day of the week', \
                order=["Monday", "Tuesday", \
                    "Wednesday", "Thursday", "Friday"])
ax.set_title("Number of absences per day of the week")
plt.savefig('figs/dow_counts.png', format='png', dpi=300)
plt.figure(figsize=(12, 5))
ax = sns.countplot(data=preprocessed_data, \
                x='Month of absence', \
                order=["January", "February", "March", \
                    "April", "May", "June", "July", \
                    "August", "September", "October", \
                    "November", "December", "Unknown"])
ax.set_title("Number of absences per month")
plt.savefig('figs/month_counts.png', format='png', dpi=300)
```

The output will be as follows:

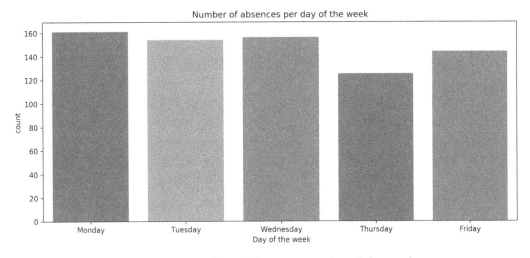

Figure 2.50: Number of absences per day of the week

The number of absences per month can be visualized as follows:

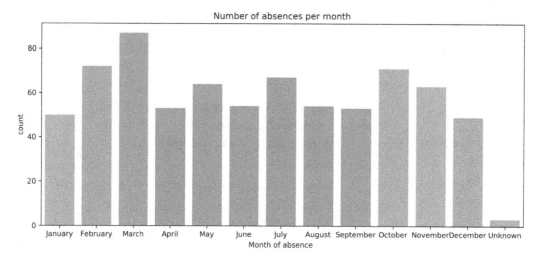

Figure 2.51: Number of absences per month

From the preceding plots, we can't really see a substantial difference between the different days of the week or months. It seems that fewer absences occur on Thursday, while the month with the most absences is March, but it is hard to say that the difference is significant.

Now, let's focus on the distribution of absence hours among the days of the week and the months of the year. This analysis will be performed in the following exercise.

EXERCISE 2.06: INVESTIGATING ABSENCE HOURS, BASED ON THE DAY OF THE WEEK AND THE MONTH OF THE YEAR

In this exercise, you will be looking at the hours during which the employees were absent for days of the week and months of the year. Execute the code mentioned in the previous section and exercises before attempting this exercise. Now, follow these steps:

1. Consider the distribution of absence hours among the days of the week and months of the year:

```
# analyze average distribution of absence hours
plt.figure(figsize=(12,5))
sns.violinplot(x="Day of the week", \
               y="Absenteeism time in hours",\
               data=preprocessed_data, \
               order=["Monday", "Tuesday", \
                    "Wednesday", "Thursday", "Friday"])
plt.savefig('figs/exercise_206_dow_hours.png', \
            format='png', dpi=300)
plt.figure(figsize=(12,5))
sns.violinplot(x="Month of absence", \
               y="Absenteeism time in hours",\
               data=preprocessed_data, \
               order=["January", "February", \
                    "March", "April", "May", "June", "July",\
                    "August", "September", "October", \
                    "November", "December", "Unknown"])
plt.savefig('figs/exercise_206_month_hours.png', \
            format='png', dpi=300)
```

The output will be as follows:

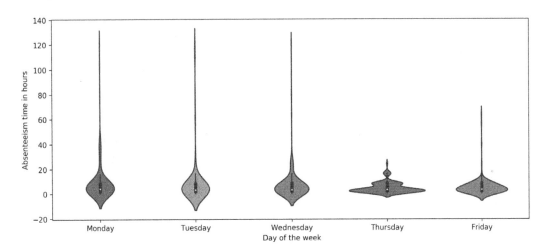

Figure 2.52: Average absent hours during the week

The violin plot for the average absent hours over the year can be visualized as follows:

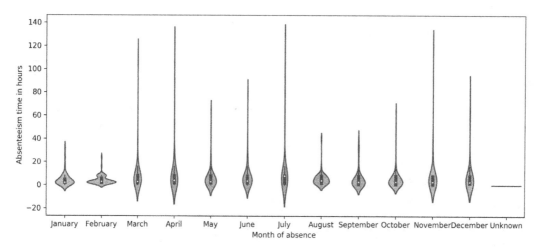

Figure 2.53: Average absent hours over the year

2. Compute the mean and standard deviation of the absences based on the day of the week:

```
"""
compute mean and standard deviation of absence hours per day of the
week
"""
dows = ["Monday", "Tuesday", "Wednesday", \
        "Thursday", "Friday"]
for dow in dows:
    mask = preprocessed_data["Day of the week"] == dow
    hours = preprocessed_data["Absenteeism time in hours"][mask]
    mean = hours.mean()
    stddev = hours.std()
    print(f"Day of the week: {dow:10s} | Mean : {mean:.03f} \
| Stddev: {stddev:.03f}")
```

The output will be as follows:

```
Day of the week: Monday    | Mean : 9.248 | Stddev: 15.973
Day of the week: Tuesday   | Mean : 7.981 | Stddev: 18.027
Day of the week: Wednesday | Mean : 7.147 | Stddev: 13.268
Day of the week: Thursday  | Mean : 4.424 | Stddev: 4.266
Day of the week: Friday    | Mean : 5.125 | Stddev: 7.911
```

Figure 2.54: Mean and standard deviation of absent hours per day of the week

3. Similarly, compute the mean and standard deviation based on the month, as follows:

```
"""
compute mean and standard deviation of absence hours per day of the
month
"""
months = ["January", "February", "March", "April", "May", \
          "June", "July", "August", "September", "October", \
          "November", "December"]
for month in months:
    mask = preprocessed_data["Month of absence"] == month
    hours = preprocessed_data["Absenteeism time in hours"][mask]
    mean = hours.mean()
    stddev = hours.std()
    print(f"Month: {month:10s} | Mean : {mean:8.03f} \
| Stddev: {stddev:8.03f}")
```

The output will be as follows:

```
Month: January   | Mean :    4.440 | Stddev:    5.786
Month: February  | Mean :    4.083 | Stddev:    3.710
Month: March     | Mean :    8.793 | Stddev:   16.893
Month: April     | Mean :    9.094 | Stddev:   18.024
Month: May       | Mean :    6.250 | Stddev:   10.314
Month: June      | Mean :    7.611 | Stddev:   12.359
Month: July      | Mean :   10.955 | Stddev:   21.547
Month: August    | Mean :    5.333 | Stddev:    5.749
Month: September | Mean :    5.509 | Stddev:    8.407
Month: October   | Mean :    4.915 | Stddev:    8.055
Month: November  | Mean :    7.508 | Stddev:   16.121
Month: December  | Mean :    8.449 | Stddev:   16.049
```

Figure 2.55: Mean and standard deviation of absent hours per month

4. Observe that the average duration of the absences is slightly shorter on Thursday (4.424 hours), while absences during July have the longest average duration (10.955 hours). To determine whether these values are statistically significant—that is, whether there is a statistically significant difference regarding the rest of the days/months—use the following code snippet:

```
# perform statistical test for avg duration difference
thursday_mask = preprocessed_data\
            ["Day of the week"] == "Thursday"


july_mask = preprocessed_data\
            ["Month of absence"] == "July"
thursday_data = preprocessed_data\
            ["Absenteeism time in hours"][thursday_mask]
```

```
no_thursday_data = preprocessed_data\
                    ["Absenteeism time in hours"][~thursday_mask]
july_data = preprocessed_data\
            ["Absenteeism time in hours"][july_mask]
no_july_data = preprocessed_data\
                    ["Absenteeism time in hours"][~july_mask]

thursday_res = ttest_ind(thursday_data, no_thursday_data)
july_res = ttest_ind(july_data, no_july_data)

print(f"Thursday test result: statistic={thursday_res[0]:.3f}, \
pvalue={thursday_res[1]:.3f}")
print(f"July test result: statistic={july_res[0]:.3f}, \
pvalue={july_res[1]:.3f}")
```

The output will be as follows:

```
Thursday test result: statistic=-2.307, pvalue=0.021
July test result: statistic=2.605, pvalue=0.009
```

5. Summarize and visualize the data as follows:

```
preprocessed_data.head().T
preprocessed_data["Service time"].hist()
```

The output will be as follows:

	0	1	2	3	4
ID	11	36	3	7	11
Reason for absence	26	0	23	7	23
Month of absence	July	July	July	July	July
Day of the week	Tuesday	Tuesday	Wednesday	Thursday	Thursday
Seasons	Spring	Spring	Spring	Spring	Spring
Transportation expense	289	118	179	279	289
Distance from Residence to Work	36	13	51	5	36
Service time	13	18	18	14	13
Age	33	50	38	39	33
Work load Average/day	239.554	239.554	239.554	239.554	239.554
Hit target	97	97	97	97	97
Disciplinary failure	No	Yes	No	No	No
Education	high_school	high_school	high_school	high_school	high_school
Son	2	1	0	2	2
Social drinker	Yes	Yes	Yes	Yes	Yes
Social smoker	No	No	No	Yes	No
Pet	1	0	0	0	1
Weight	90	98	89	68	90
Height	172	178	170	168	172
Body mass index	30	31	31	24	30
Absenteeism time in hours	4	0	2	4	2
Disease	No	No	No	Yes	No
BMI category	obese	obese	obese	healthy weight	obese

Figure 2.56: Statistics of data

6. Visualize the plot as follows:

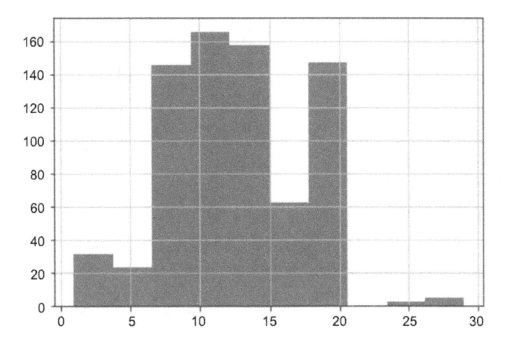

Figure 2.57: Histogram for preprocessed data

NOTE

To access the source code for this specific section, please refer to https://packt.live/2AIFO1X.

You can also run this example online at https://packt.live/37y5omt. You must execute the entire Notebook in order to get the desired result.

Since the p-values from both the statistical tests are below the critical value of 0.05, we can conclude the following:

- There is a statistically significant difference between Thursdays and other days of the week. Absences on Thursday have a shorter duration, on average.

- Absences during July are the longest over the year. Also, in this case, we can reject the null hypothesis of having no difference.

From the analysis we've performed in this exercise, we can conclude that our initial observations about the difference in absenteeism during the month of July and on Thursdays are correct. Of course, we cannot claim that this is the cause, but only state that certain trends exist in the data.

ACTIVITY 2.01: ANALYZING THE SERVICE TIME AND SON COLUMNS

In this activity, you will extend the analysis of the absenteeism dataset by exploring the impact of two additional columns: `Service time` and `Son`.

This activity is based on the techniques that have been presented in this chapter—that is, distribution analysis, hypothesis testing, and conditional probability estimation.

The following steps will help you complete this activity:

1. Import the data and the necessary libraries:

```
import pandas as pd
import seaborn as sns
import matplotlib.pyplot as plt
%matplotlib inline
```

2. Analyze the distribution of the **Service time** column by creating a kernel density estimation plot (use the **seaborn.kdeplot()** function). Perform a hypothesis test for normality (that is, a Kolmogorov-Smirnov test with the **scipy.stats.kstest()** function). The KDE plot will be as follows:

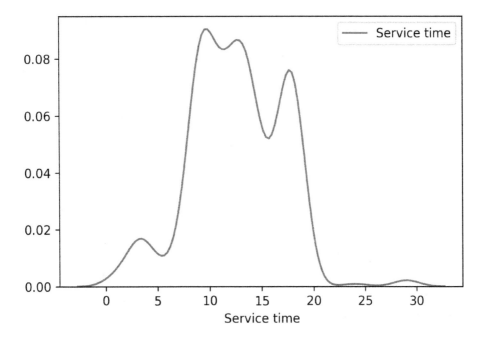

Figure 2.58: KDE plot for service time

3. Create a violin plot of the **Service time** column and the **Reason for absence** column. Draw a conclusion about the observed relationship.

    The output will be as follows:

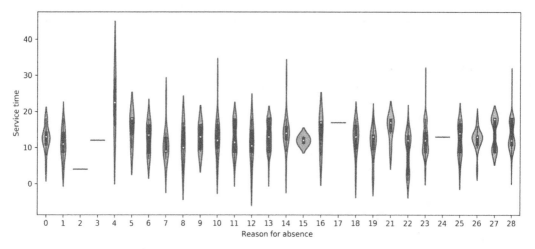

Figure 2.59: Violin plot for the Service time column

4. Create a correlation plot between the **Service time** and **Absenteeism time in hours** columns, similar to the one in *Figure 2.47*. The output will be as follows:

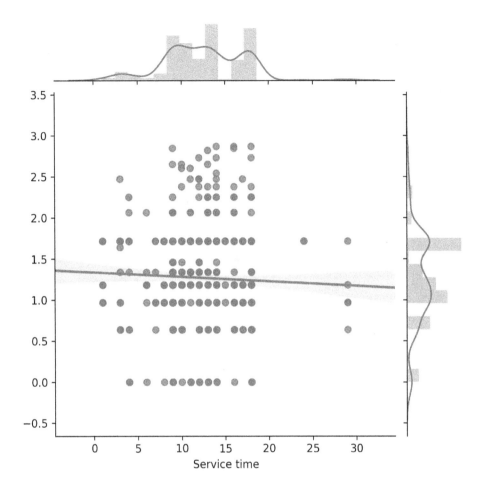

Figure 2.60: Correlation plot for service time

5. Analyze the distributions of **Absenteeism time in hours** for employees with a different number of children (the **Son** column).

The output will be as follows:

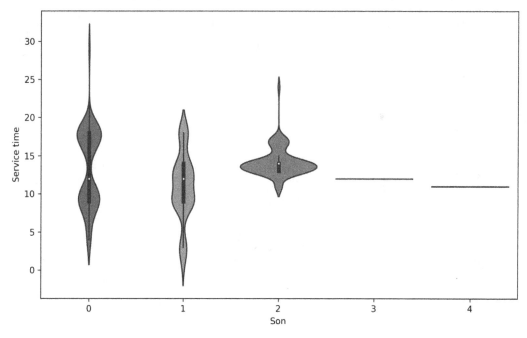

Figure 2.61: Distribution of absent time for employees with a different number of children

> **NOTE**
>
> The solution to the activity can be found on page 494.

From this analysis, we can infer that the number of absence hours for employees with a greater number of children lies in the range of 10-15 hours. Employees with less than three children appear to be absent in a varying range of 1-20 hours. To be specific, employees with no children still have a varying number of absent hours within the range of 10-15 hours, owing to other reasons, which now opens up a new area of analysis. On the contrary, employees with one child are absent only for an average of 5 hours. Employees with two children have an average of 15-25 absent hours, which could be analyzed further.

Thus, we have successfully drawn measurable conclusions to help us understand employee behavior in an organization to tackle unregulated absenteeism and take necessary measures to ensure the optimal utilization of human resources.

SUMMARY

In this chapter, we analyzed a dataset containing employees' absences and their relationship to additional health and socially related factors. We introduced various data analysis techniques, such as distribution plots, conditional probabilities, Bayes' theorem, data transformation techniques (such as Box-Cox and Yeo-Johnson), and the Kolmogorov-Smirnov test, and applied these to the dataset.

In the next chapter, we will be analyzing the marketing campaign dataset of a Portuguese bank and the impact it had on acquiring new customers.

3

ANALYZING BANK MARKETING CAMPAIGN DATA

OVERVIEW

In this chapter, we will analyze marketing campaign data related to new financial products. We will pay particular attention to modeling the relationships between the different features in the data and their impact on the final outcome of the campaign. We will also introduce fundamental topics in data analysis, such as linear and logistic regression models, and see how they can be used when analyzing the outcome of a marketing campaign.

INTRODUCTION

In the previous chapter, we looked at various techniques to do with probability theory and hypothesis testing, which are often applied in data analysis. In this chapter, we will extend our knowledge by introducing mathematical models that are suitable for both data analysis and predictions. In this way, we will obtain the fundamental tools for deriving explanatory models and provide a generic framework for identifying causalities and effects when performing data analysis.

Direct marketing campaigns are a classical approach to increasing business revenue, informing potential customers about new products, and merchandising them. Having targeted marketing campaigns can significantly increase success rates and revenue since the audience is based on precise criteria and the analysis of past marketing campaigns. Thus, extracting information about successful campaigns and customers can significantly reduce marketing costs and increase sales.

In this chapter, we will analyze data from the direct marketing campaign of a Portuguese banking institution based on phone calls that were performed between May 2008 and November 2010. We will not only use the techniques presented in the previous chapters but will introduce new concepts, such as linear and logistic regression, that are widely used in data analysis and predictive modeling (predictive modeling being the process of using data patterns to predict future outcomes). These types of models have several advantages, but two of the most important ones are their simplicity and interpretability.

> **NOTE**
>
> The original dataset can be found here: https://archive.ics.uci.edu/ml/datasets/Bank+Marketing.
>
> You can also find it in our GitHub repository at: https://packt.live/2UOmlyp.
>
> For further reading on this topic, refer to the following article: [Moro et al., 2014] S. Moro, P. Cortez and P. Rita. *A Data-Driven Approach to Predict the Success of Bank Telemarketing*. Decision Support Systems, Elsevier, 62:22-31, June 2014.

The scope of the marketing campaign is selling long-term deposits. For each call, information about the client and the outcome of the call is registered. For instance, client information contains family and education status and the client's current financial situation (the data is anonymized). Information about the last call from the previous marketing campaign is also registered. In this way, we have a clear picture of the type of client that has been contacted, as well as information about the historical outcome from previous marketing campaigns.

INITIAL DATA ANALYSIS

We'll start our analysis by loading the data into Python and performing some simple analysis, which will give us a feeling about the type of data and the different features of the dataset (this is presented in detail in *Figure 3.2*):

```python
import pandas as pd
import numpy as np
import seaborn as sns
import matplotlib.pyplot as plt

%matplotlib inline

# pull data from github
bank_data = pd.read_csv("https://raw.githubusercontent.com/"\
                        "PacktWorkshops/"\
                        "The-Data-Analysis-Workshop/"\
                        "master/Chapter03/data/bank-additional/"\
                        "bank-additional-full.csv", sep=";")

# visualize the head of the dataset
bank_data.head().T
```

In the following screenshot, we can see the values that were returned by the previous command:

	0	1	2	3	4
age	56	57	37	40	56
job	housemaid	services	services	admin.	services
marital	married	married	married	married	married
education	basic.4y	high.school	high.school	basic.6y	high.school
default	no	unknown	no	no	no
housing	no	no	yes	no	no
loan	no	no	no	no	yes
contact	telephone	telephone	telephone	telephone	telephone
month	may	may	may	may	may
day_of_week	mon	mon	mon	mon	mon
duration	261	149	226	151	307
campaign	1	1	1	1	1
pdays	999	999	999	999	999
previous	0	0	0	0	0
poutcome	nonexistent	nonexistent	nonexistent	nonexistent	nonexistent
emp.var.rate	1.1	1.1	1.1	1.1	1.1
cons.price.idx	93.994	93.994	93.994	93.994	93.994
cons.conf.idx	-36.4	-36.4	-36.4	-36.4	-36.4
euribor3m	4.857	4.857	4.857	4.857	4.857
nr.employed	5191	5191	5191	5191	5191
y	no	no	no	no	no

Figure 3.1: Snapshot of the banking data, returned by the head().T function (first five entries)

Note that in this chapter, we are using the data provided in the **bank-additional-full.csv** file as a dataset. It contains slightly more features than the bank data itself (that is, **bank-full.csv**) as we believe that we will be able to perform more extensive analysis on the dataset by taking advantage of the additional information available.

A list of the available features of the dataset and their values can be found in the following table:

Column name	Description	Values
Age	Age of the contacted client	Numerical
Job	Type of job	admin., blue- collar, entrepreneur, housemaid, management, retired, self-employed, services, student, technician, unemployed, unknown
Marital	Marital status (note: "divorced" means divorced or widowed)	divorced, married, single, unknown
Education	Education level of the contacted client	basic.4y, basic.6y, basic.9y, high.school, illiterate, professional.course, university. degree, unknown
Default	Does the client have credit in default?	yes, no, unknown
Housing	Does the client have a housing loan?	yes, no, unknown
Loan	Does the client have a personal loan?	yes, no, unknown
Contact	Type of communication with the client	cellular, telephone
Month	Last contact, month of the year	jan, feb, …, nov, dec
day_of_week	Last contact, day of the week	mon, tue, wed, thu, fri
Duration	Last contact duration (in seconds)	Numeric
Campaign	Number of contacts performed during this campaign for this client	Numeric
Pdays	Number of days passed by after the client was contacted from a previous campaign	numeric (999 means the client was notcontacted)
Previous	Number of contacts performed before this campaign and for this client	Numeric
Poutcome	Outcome of the previous marketing campaign	failure, nonexistent, success
emp.var.rate	Employment variation rate (quarterly indicator)	Numeric
cons.price.idx	Consumer price index (monthly indicator)	Numeric
cons.conf.idx	Consumer confidence index (monthly indicator)	Numeric
euribor3m	Euribor 3-month rate	Numeric
nr.employed	Number of employees (quarterly indicator)	Numeric
Y	Has the client subscribed to a term deposit (outcome of the marketing campaign)?	yes, no

Figure 3.2: List of columns and their values, provided in the bank-additional-full.csv file

As shown in the preceding table, we have two types of columns in the dataset: numerical and categorical. A good practice in data analysis is to start by looking at the different features, their distributions, and possible outliers. We will do this in the following exercises.

EXERCISE 3.01: ANALYZING DISTRIBUTIONS OF NUMERICAL FEATURES IN THE BANKING DATASET

In this exercise, you will perform a simple analysis of the numerical features in the banking dataset. It is important to always start data analysis on a new dataset by deriving basic statistics. In this way, you will obtain general knowledge and a "feel" for the data. A typical example could be computing the minimum and maximum values in the **age** column. If those values are not aligned with your expectations (for example, a minimum age of 18, and a maximum in the range 70-90), you should investigate further to determine the reason for the disparity.

You will start by selecting the relevant numerical features in a programmatic way, computing some basic statistics (such as mean, standard deviation, and minimum and maximum values) on them, and plotting their distributions. This will give you an idea of the numerical features in the dataset. Follow these steps to complete this exercise:

1. First, select the relevant numerical features. A straightforward approach would be to just list them, but as in certain cases, the dimension of the data might be quite large (with tens or even hundreds of features), so you need a scalable approach that is independent of the size of the data. For this reason, use the **np.issubdtype()** function, which checks whether the type of the first argument is equal or a subtype of the second one:

```
# define numerical features
numerical_features = [col for col in bank_data.columns \
                      if np.issubdtype(bank_data[col]\
                      .dtype, np.number)]
print(numerical_features)
```

The following is the output of the preceding code:

```
['age', 'duration', 'campaign', 'pdays', 'previous',
 'emp.var.rate', 'cons.price.idx', 'cons.conf.idx',
 'euribor3m', 'nr.employed']
```

The detected numerical features are in line with those defined in *Figure 3.2*.

2. Next, compute some basic statistics on the identified numerical features (such as mean, standard deviation, minimum and maximum values, and quartiles):

```
# print statistics about the different numerical columns
bank_data[numerical_features].describe().T
```

The output will be as follows:

	count	mean	std	min	25%	50%	75%	max
age	41188.0	40.024060	10.421250	17.000	32.000	38.000	47.000	98.000
duration	41188.0	258.285010	259.279249	0.000	102.000	180.000	319.000	4918.000
campaign	41188.0	2.567593	2.770014	1.000	1.000	2.000	3.000	56.000
pdays	41188.0	962.475454	186.910907	0.000	999.000	999.000	999.000	999.000
previous	41188.0	0.172963	0.494901	0.000	0.000	0.000	0.000	7.000
emp.var.rate	41188.0	0.081886	1.570960	-3.400	-1.800	1.100	1.400	1.400
cons.price.idx	41188.0	93.575664	0.578840	92.201	93.075	93.749	93.994	94.767
cons.conf.idx	41188.0	-40.502600	4.628198	-50.800	-42.700	-41.800	-36.400	-26.900
euribor3m	41188.0	3.621291	1.734447	0.634	1.344	4.857	4.961	5.045
nr.employed	41188.0	5167.035911	72.251528	4963.600	5099.100	5191.000	5228.100	5228.100

Figure 3.3: Description of numerical features

3. Finally, plot the distributions of the single numerical columns:

```
# plot distributions of numerical features
plt.figure(figsize=(10,18))
for index, col in enumerate(numerical_features):
    plt.subplot(5, 2, index+1)
    sns.distplot(bank_data[col])
plt.savefig("figs/exercise_3_01_distributions.png", \
            format="png", dpi=500)
```

The following is the output of the preceding code:

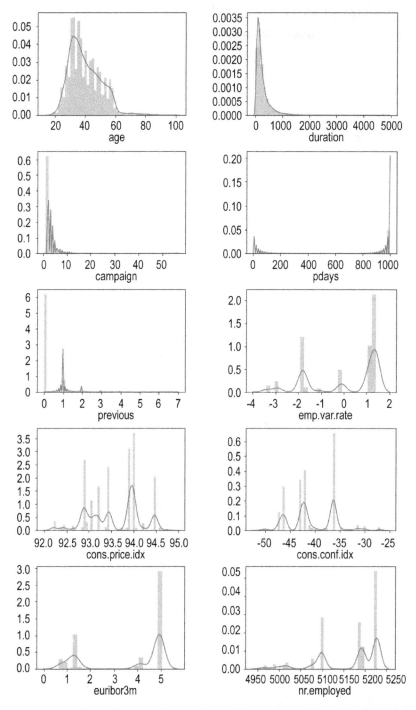

Figure 3.4: Distributions of the numerical features in the banking dataset

> **NOTE**
>
> The above code can sometimes result in an error, depending on the version of statsmodels that is used. If you do encounter an error, you can achieve a similar output by replacing `sns.distplot(bank_data[col])` with `sns.distplot(bank_data[col], kde_kws={'bw': 0.1})`. This manually passes in a small bandwidth value and avoids the plotting error. There will be small variations between your output and the one above if you use this method.

From the preceding plot, we can see that, besides the **age** and **duration** columns, the rest of the numerical features do not seem to have a regular distribution of values since their distributions seem scattered and only a few values are present.

> **NOTE**
>
> To access the source code for this specific section, please refer to https://packt.live/30MuxlH.
>
> You can also run this example online at https://packt.live/2Y63lgL. You must execute the entire Notebook in order to get the desired result.

In the following exercise, we will focus on the analysis of the categorical features.

EXERCISE 3.02: ANALYZING DISTRIBUTIONS OF CATEGORICAL FEATURES IN THE BANKING DATASET

In this exercise, you will perform a simple analysis of the categorical features. This will give you an idea of their distributions and the most frequent value in each categorical feature, and, in general, it will serve as a reference for later analysis. You will start by programmatically selecting them, and then create bar plots for the number of entries in each class for each feature. This will give you a general overview of their distributions. Finally, you will explicitly check the number of entries in the **y** column, which contains information about whether the marketing campaign was successful or not. Follow these steps to complete this exercise:

1. Select the categorical features in the banking dataset. Note that in **pandas**, categorical features are of the **object** type and are encoded as strings:

```
# define categorical features
categorical_features = [col for col in bank_data.columns \
                        if pd.api.types\
                        .is_string_dtype(bank_data[col])]
print(categorical_features)
```

The following is the output of the preceding code:

```
['job', 'marital', 'education', 'default', 'housing', 'loan',
 'contact', 'month', 'day_of_week', 'poutcome', 'y']
```

You will now plot the distributions of entries among the different features.

2. Use the **matplotlib.pyplot.subplot()** function to create multiple plots in the same figure:

```
# plot distributions of numerical features
plt.figure(figsize=(25,35))
for index, col in enumerate(categorical_features):
    plt.subplot(6, 2, index+1)
    ax = sns.countplot(y=col, data=bank_data)
    ax.set_xlabel("count", fontsize=20)
    ax.set_ylabel(col, fontsize=20)
    ax.tick_params(labelsize=20)

plt.savefig("figs/exercise_3_02_counts.png", \
            format="png", dpi=500)
```

The resulting plot is shown in the following output:

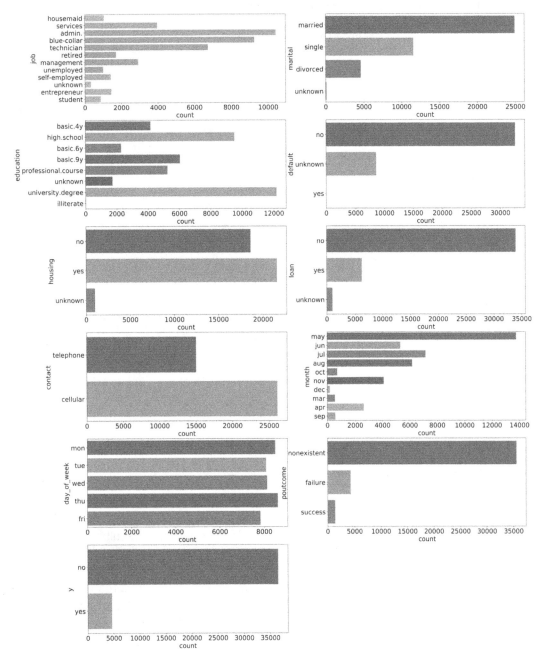

Figure 3.5: Bar plots of the categorical features

3. Finally, explicitly compute the number of entries in the **y** column since it contains information about the outcome of the marketing campaign:

```
# compute number of entries in y column
print("Total number of entries:")
print(bank_data["y"].value_counts(ascending=True))
print()
print("Percentages:")
print(bank_data["y"].value_counts(normalize=True, \
                            ascending=True)*100)
```

The following is the output of the preceding code:

```
Total number of entries:
yes      4640
no       36548
Name: y, dtype: int64

Percentages:
yes      11.265417
no       88.734583
Name: y, dtype: float64
```

From the preceding output, we can derive that only 11% of the contacted customers decided to accept the offer from the bank.

> **NOTE**
>
> To access the source code for this specific section, please refer to https://packt.live/2B9ieLM.
>
> You can also run this example online at https://packt.live/30HWlbM. You must execute the entire Notebook in order to get the desired result.

In this section, we acquired some basic understanding of the various features (numerical and categorical). This is always important as understanding the basic statistics and distributions of the features serves as a basis for further and more detailed analysis. In the next section, we will analyze the relationships between the feature columns and the outcome of each call (that is, the **y** column).

IMPACT OF NUMERICAL FEATURES ON THE OUTCOME

In this section, we will analyze the relationship between the numerical features (already identified in *Exercise 3.01, Analyzing Distributions of Numerical Features in the Banking Dataset*) and the outcome of a marketing campaign, which is identified in the **y** column in the banking dataset.

We will start our analysis by addressing the following question: Is there a statistically significant difference in numerical features for successful and non-successful marketing campaigns? For this reason, we will create violin plots (as shown in the previous chapters) that compare the distribution of the numerical features for the two types of outcomes ("yes" for a successful marketing campaign, "no" for an unsuccessful one):

```
"""
create violin plots for successful and non-successful marketing campaigns
"""
plt.figure(figsize=(10,18))
for index, col in enumerate(numerical_features):
    plt.subplot(5, 2, index+1)
    sns.violinplot(x=col, y="y", data=bank_data, \
                   order=["yes", "no"])
plt.savefig("figs/violin_plots_numerical_features.png", \
            format="png", dpi=500)
```

The following is the output of the preceding code:

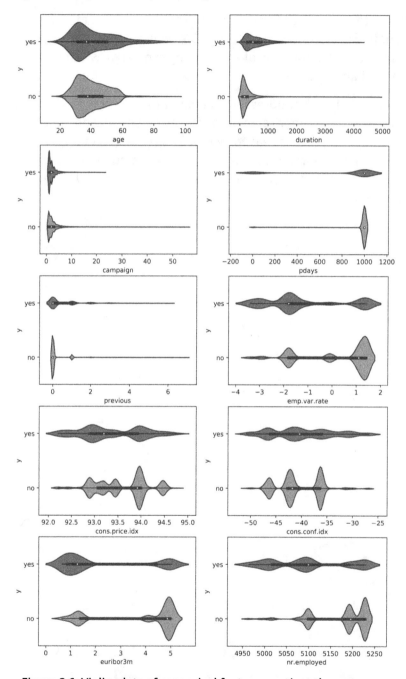

Figure 3.6: Violin plots of numerical features against the outcome
of the marketing campaign

The preceding figure shows that the distributions of most of the numerical features vary between successful marketing campaigns (those whose **y** column value is equal to "yes") and unsuccessful ones (those whose **y** column value is equal to "no"). We can assess this difference from a statistical perspective by running a hypothesis test on each of the numerical features, in which we will test whether the average value of the respective numerical feature is different for "yes" entries for the **y** column against "no" entries for each numerical feature.

First, let's define a function that returns the average values of the column in the "yes" and "no" groups for the provided column, as well as the **test statistic** and **p-value** from the equality of means test:

```python
from scipy.stats import ttest_ind
"""
define function for computing mean of column for yes and no cases,
as well as the test statistics and pvalue for equality of means test
"""
def test_means(data, col):
    yes_mask = data["y"] == "yes"
    values_yes = data[col][yes_mask]
    values_no = data[col][~yes_mask]
    mean_yes = values_yes.mean()
    mean_no = values_no.mean()

    ttest_res = ttest_ind(values_yes, values_no)

    return [col, mean_yes, mean_no, \
            round(ttest_res[0], 4), round(ttest_res[1],4)]
```

Then, we define a **pandas** DataFrame that will contain the values that were returned by the **test_means** function:

```
# define pandas dataframe, in which values should be filled
test_df = pd.DataFrame(columns=["column", "mean yes", \
                                "mean no", "ttest stat", \
                                "ttest pval"])
"""
for each column in the numerical_features, compute means and test
statistics and fill the values in the dataframe
"""
for index, col in enumerate(numerical_features):
    test_df.loc[index] = test_means(bank_data, col)

test_df
```

The results of the preceding code snippet can be seen in the following output:

	column	mean yes	mean no	ttest stat	ttest pval
0	age	40.913147	39.911185	6.1721	0.0
1	duration	553.191164	220.844807	89.9672	0.0
2	campaign	2.051724	2.633085	-13.4965	0.0
3	pdays	792.035560	984.113878	-69.7221	0.0
4	previous	0.492672	0.132374	48.0027	0.0
5	emp.var.rate	-1.233448	0.248875	-63.4337	0.0
6	cons.price.idx	93.354386	93.603757	-27.9032	0.0
7	cons.conf.idx	-39.789784	-40.593097	11.1539	0.0
8	euribor3m	2.123135	3.811491	-65.6466	0.0
9	nr.employed	5095.115991	5176.166600	-76.9845	0.0

Figure 3.7: Difference in mean and results of the equality of means test for numerical columns

As we can see from the previous plot, there is a statistically significant difference in the mean values for each of the numerical columns (the results from the p-value in the **ttest pval** column). This means that for each of the numerical features, the average value for successful marketing campaigns is significantly different than the average value for unsuccessful marketing campaigns.

We can not only analyze the difference in means but also the distribution difference for each numerical column. We will do this in the following exercise.

EXERCISE 3.03: HYPOTHESIS TEST OF THE DIFFERENCE OF DISTRIBUTIONS IN NUMERICAL FEATURES

In this exercise, you will programmatically test the difference between the distributions of successful and unsuccessful marketing calls for each numerical feature. This is a good way to structure algorithmic-based reasoning and perform hypothesis testing on a variety of features. More precisely, you will perform a Kolmogorov-Smirnov test for the equality of distributions for each of the numerical features for successful versus unsuccessful marketing campaigns. Follow these steps to complete this exercise:

1. First, define a function that, for a provided column, computes the Kolmogorov-Smirnov test and returns the values in an array:

```
from scipy.stats import ks_2samp

"""
define function which performs Kolmogorov-Smirnov test,
for provided column
"""
def test_ks(data, col):
    yes_mask = data["y"] == "yes"
    values_yes = data[col][yes_mask]
    values_no = data[col][~yes_mask]

    kstest_res = ks_2samp(values_yes, values_no)
    return [col, round(kstest_res[0], 4), \
            round(kstest_res[1],4)]
```

2. Next, define a **pandas** DataFrame that contains the results from the function defined in *Step 1* by applying it to each numerical feature:

```
# define pandas dataframe, in which values should be filled
test_df = pd.DataFrame(columns=["column", "ks stat", "ks pval"])


"""
for each column in the numerical_features,
compute test statistics and fill the values in the dataframe
"""
for index, col in enumerate(numerical_features):
    test_df.loc[index] = test_ks(bank_data, col)


test_df
```

The following is the output of the preceding code:

	column	ks stat	ks pval
0	age	0.0861	0.0
1	duration	0.4641	0.0
2	campaign	0.0808	0.0
3	pdays	0.1934	0.0
4	previous	0.2102	0.0
5	emp.var.rate	0.4324	0.0
6	cons.price.idx	0.2281	0.0
7	cons.conf.idx	0.1998	0.0
8	euribor3m	0.4326	0.0
9	nr.employed	0.4324	0.0

Figure 3.8: Results from the Kolmogorov-Smirnov test for equality of distributions

From the preceding figure, we can also observe that the distributions of the various numerical features present a significant difference between successful and unsuccessful marketing campaigns.

NOTE

To access the source code for this specific section, please refer to https://packt.live/2CdYyqH.

You can also run this example online at https://packt.live/3e7FU1v. You must execute the entire Notebook in order to get the desired result.

In order to further deepen our analysis, also create pairplots between the numerical features and divide the groups by the outcome of the marketing campaign. First, let's divide the numerical features into two groups: campaign-related features and financial features. In the first group, we will include the **age, duration, campaign**, and **previous** columns, while in the latter one, we will include the **emp.var.rate**, **cons.price.idx**, **cons.conf.idx**, and **euribor3m** columns:

```
# create arrays containing campaign and financial columns
campaign_columns = ["age", "duration", "campaign", "previous"]
financial_columns = ["emp.var.rate", "cons.price.idx", \
                     "cons.conf.idx", "euribor3m"]
```

The following code snippet plots the campaign columns:

```
# create pairplot between campaign columns
plot_data = bank_data[campaign_columns + ["y"]]
plt.figure(figsize=(10,10))
sns.pairplot(plot_data, hue="y", palette="bright")
plt.savefig("figs/pairplot_campaign.png", \
            format="png", dpi=300)
```

The following is the output of the preceding code:

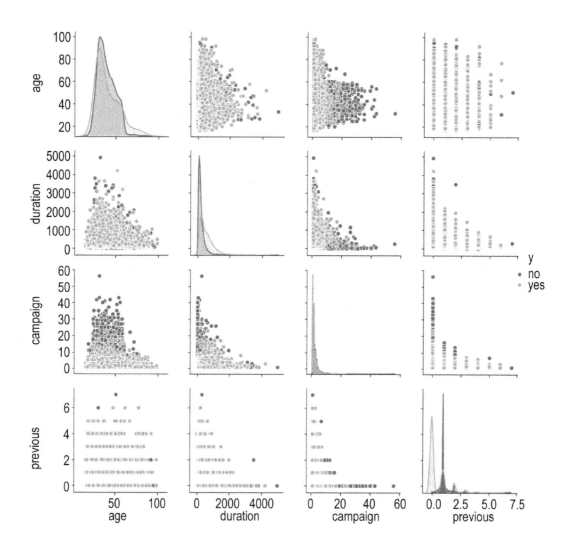

Figure 3.9: Pairplot of the campaign features, grouped by marketing outcome

> **NOTE**
>
> As in the earlier exercise, if you get an error due to a known issue with the packages used, you can get a similar output by using **sns. pairplot(plot_data, hue="y", palette="bright", diag_kws={'bw': 0.1})**. This will give a slightly different output due to the manual bandwidth setting, but the plot shapes should be a similar shape to those shown above.

From the preceding figure, we can immediately see that, in the **previous** column, most of the successful marketing campaigns were with newly contacted customers, while a substantial peak is present for customers who were contacted the second time, but without success.

Now, consider the financial columns:

```
# create pairplot between financial features
plot_data = bank_data[financial_columns + ["y"]]
plt.figure(figsize=(10,10))
sns.pairplot(plot_data, hue="y", palette="bright")
plt.savefig("figs/pairplot_financial.png", \
            format="png", dpi=300)
```

The following is the output of the preceding code:

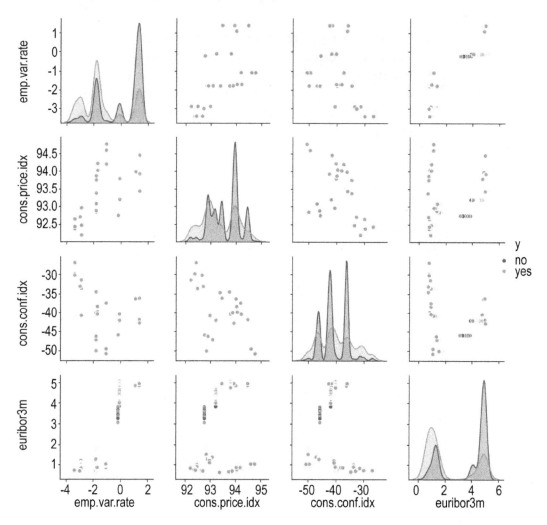

Figure 3.10: Pairplot of the financial features, grouped by marketing outcome

Interestingly, for lower values for the 3-month interest rates (the **euribor3m** column), the number of successful marketing calls is larger than the number of unsuccessful ones. The inverse situation happens when interest rates are higher. A possible explanation for this phenomenon is customer optimism when interest rates are lower. You will investigate the market indicators and their impact on the outcome of the marketing calls later in this section.

Analyze the correlations between the different numerical features. This is important so that we have a clear picture of how the different features behave with respect to each other. We will do this by distinguishing between the two cases, that is, successful and unsuccessful customer calls:

```
# create mask for successful calls
successful_calls = bank_data.y == "yes"

# plot correlation matrix for successful calls
plot_data = bank_data[campaign_columns + financial_columns]\
                [successful_calls]
successful_corr = plot_data.corr()
successful_corr.style.background_gradient(cmap='coolwarm')\
.set_precision(2)
```

The following is the output of the preceding code:

	age	duration	campaign	previous	emp.var.rate	cons.price.idx	cons.conf.idx	euribor3m
age	1	-0.059	-0.0079	0.075	-0.082	-0.025	0.14	-0.085
duration	-0.059	1	0.16	-0.23	0.5	0.24	-0.14	0.5
campaign	-0.0079	0.16	1	-0.1	0.22	0.12	-0.043	0.21
previous	0.075	-0.23	-0.1	1	-0.28	0.091	0.13	-0.39
emp.var.rate	-0.082	0.5	0.22	-0.28	1	0.66	-0.27	0.93
cons.price.idx	-0.025	0.24	0.12	0.091	0.66	1	-0.33	0.41
cons.conf.idx	0.14	-0.14	-0.043	0.13	-0.27	-0.33	1	-0.12
euribor3m	-0.085	0.5	0.21	-0.39	0.93	0.41	-0.12	1

Figure 3.11: Correlation matrix of numerical features for successful customer calls

In the preceding figure, we can see the correlation matrix of the numerical features, filtered only for successful customer calls. Do the same for unsuccessful calls:

```
# plot correlation matrix for unsuccessful calls
plot_data = bank_data[campaign_columns + financial_columns]\
                     [~successful_calls]
unsuccessful_corr = plot_data.corr()
unsuccessful_corr.style.background_gradient(cmap='coolwarm')\
.set_precision(2)
```

The following is the output of the preceding code:

	age	duration	campaign	previous	emp.var.rate	cons.price.idx	cons.conf.idx	euribor3m
age	1	0.0008	0.0084	-0.003	0.027	0.011	0.12	0.041
duration	0.0008	1	-0.083	-0.0043	0.0035	0.018	0.0042	0.0065
campaign	0.0084	-0.083	1	-0.068	0.13	0.12	-0.0071	0.12
previous	-0.003	-0.0043	-0.068	1	-0.42	-0.27	-0.14	-0.44
emp.var.rate	0.027	0.0035	0.13	-0.42	1	0.8	0.32	0.98
cons.price.idx	0.011	0.018	0.12	-0.27	0.8	1	0.15	0.73
cons.conf.idx	0.12	0.0042	-0.0071	-0.14	0.32	0.15	1	0.39
euribor3m	0.041	0.0065	0.12	-0.44	0.98	0.73	0.39	1

Figure 3.12: Correlation matrix of numerical features for unsuccessful customer calls

As we can observe from the preceding two figures, the correlation between **euribor3m** and **emp.var.rate** is very high (approximately 0.93 for successful and 0.98 for unsuccessful calls). That is quite an interesting phenomenon as the first one relates to the average interest rate at which European banks lend money to other banks with a maturity of 3 months, while the second one relates to the employment variation, that is, the rate at which people are hired or fired in an economy.

A positive correlation between those values means that in an expanding economy, in which more people are hired than fired (hence, the positive values in **emp.var. rate**), interest rates tend to be higher. Another column that is also highly correlated with the previous two is the **Consumer Price Index** (**CPI**) column: **cons.price.idx**.

By definition (https://www.investopedia.com/terms/c/consumerpriceindex.asp), the CPI is a measure that observes the change of prices of a basket of consumers' goods and services (food, transportation, households, and medical care). The basket itself is a collection of goods and services from eight major areas: medical care, food and beverages, housing, apparel, transportation, education, recreation, and other goods and services. The formula for the CPI is as follows:

$$CPI = \frac{Cost\ of\ Market\ Basket\ in\ Given\ Year}{Cost\ of\ Market\ Basket\ in\ Base\ Year} \times 100$$

Figure 3.13: Formula for the CPI

In the preceding equation, the cost of the market basket is compared between two different years. Changes in the CPI are related to changes in the cost of living and are therefore a clear indicator of inflation or deflation.

A high positive correlation of the **cons.price.idx** column with the **emp.var.rate** and **euribor3m** columns is a clear indicator of an expanding economy, in which growing employment means more people with money—hence more spending and higher inflation. In such situations, central banks tend to increase interest rates (in order to keep inflation under control), which is totally in line with our observation of increasing the **euribor3m** column.

Finally, returning to our marketing campaign problem, consider the difference between the correlation matrices for successful and unsuccessful calls:

```
"""
plot difference of successful - unsuccessful correlation matrices
"""
diff_corr = successful_corr - unsuccessful_corr
diff_corr.style.background_gradient(cmap='coolwarm')\
.set_precision(2)
```

The following is the output of the preceding code:

	age	duration	campaign	previous	emp.var.rate	cons.price.idx	cons.conf.idx	euribor3m
age	0	-0.06	-0.016	0.078	-0.11	-0.036	0.016	-0.13
duration	-0.06	0	0.24	-0.23	0.5	0.22	-0.15	0.49
campaign	-0.016	0.24	0	-0.036	0.089	-0.0068	-0.036	0.097
previous	0.078	-0.23	-0.036	0	0.14	0.36	0.27	0.05
emp.var.rate	-0.11	0.5	0.089	0.14	0	-0.14	-0.59	-0.05
cons.price.idx	-0.036	0.22	-0.0068	0.36	-0.14	0	-0.48	-0.32
cons.conf.idx	0.016	-0.15	-0.036	0.27	-0.59	-0.48	0	-0.51
euribor3m	-0.13	0.49	0.097	0.05	-0.05	-0.32	-0.51	0

Figure 3.14: Difference between correlation matrices for successful and unsuccessful calls

In the preceding figure, you can see the difference between the correlation matrices, one for successful calls and one for unsuccessful calls. The values indicated in the matrix can provide us with information about strong differences in correlations between successful and unsuccessful calls. You can immediately see that there is a significant difference in the correlations between the **duration** and **emp.var. rate** columns for successful (correlation: **0.5**) and unsuccessful (correlation: **0.0035**) calls.

This might look like a significant indicator at first, but note that the **duration** column represents the duration of the call. Therefore, we can expect successful calls to have a longer duration (as information about the product has to be presented and the customer's data has to be gathered). On the other hand, the **emp.var.rate** column represents the employment variation rate, a macroeconomic factor that is definitely not influenced by the length of certain phone calls. It is always important to remember that correlation does not imply causation. Another interesting relationship is the one between the **cons.conf.idx** column and the **emp.var.rate, cons. price.idx**, and **euribor3m** columns.

The **cons.conf.idx** column represents the Consumer Confidence Index, an economic indicator that defines the degree of optimism in an economy. The correlations between the **cons.conf.idx** and **emp.var.rate** columns and the **cons.price.idx** and **euribor3m** columns for successful and unsuccessful calls are given in the following table:

Columns	Successful Calls	Unsuccessful Calls
cons.conf.idx – emp.var.rate	-0.27	0.32
cons.conf.idx – cons.price.idx	-0.33	0.15
cons.conf.idx – euribor3m	-0.12	0.39

Figure 3.15: Correlations between the columns

This is quite an interesting phenomenon as the **emp.var.rate, cons.price. idx**, and **euribor3m** columns are strongly correlated. We already mentioned that during periods of expanding economy, the employment rate increases, leading to higher consumer price index and higher interest rates (the situation is the inverse in contracting economy and periods of depression).

From the preceding table, an interesting fact arises: the consumer confidence index is negatively correlated with the three mentioned columns for successful customer calls, and positively correlated for unsuccessful ones. This means that when the overall economic sentiment is pessimistic, people are willing to accept the new banking products and vice versa.

MODELING THE RELATIONSHIP VIA LOGISTIC REGRESSION

We will dedicate the rest of this chapter to one of the fundamental techniques in data analysis and machine learning: linear and logistic regression.

Suppose that we are estimating the relationship between m different features.

In both linear and logistic regression, a set of features, $\mathbf{X}_1, \ldots, \mathbf{X}_m$, and a target variable, $\mathbf{Y}$, are provided to model the target variable, $\mathbf{Y}$, as a function of the features, $\mathbf{X}_1, \ldots, \mathbf{X}_m$, as in the following equation:

$$Y \approx f(X_1, \ldots, X_m)$$

Figure 3.16: General form of linear/logistic regression

LINEAR REGRESSION

In linear regression, the target variable, Y, is a continuous variable, meaning that it assumes all possible values in a bounded or unbounded interval, (a,b) $\subseteq$ R, where R is the set of real numbers. In this way, the preceding equation assumes the following concrete form:

$$Y \approx \alpha_0 + \sum_{j=1}^{m} \alpha_j X_j$$

Figure 3.17: Linear regression equation

Let's denote the right-hand side of the preceding equation with $\hat{\mathbf{Y}}$, as follows:

$$\widehat{Y} = \alpha_0 + \sum_{j=1}^{m} \alpha_i X_j$$

Figure 3.18: Linear regression equation

Then, if we have n samples in our data (where for each $i \in \{1,..., n\}$, we denote the entries for the m features with $x_{i,1},....x_{i,m}$ and the target variable with y_i), we can rewrite the previous equation in a more specific form, as follows:

$$y_i \approx \hat{y}_i = \alpha_0 + \sum_{j=1}^{m} \alpha_j X_{i,j}$$

Figure 3.19: Linear regression equation in a specific form

Note that in *Figure 3.17* and *Figure 3.19*, we assume that the dependency of Y from the feature vectors $X_1,...,X_m$ is either linear or can be approximated with a linear equation. With this assumption, estimating the relationship between Y and the features $X_1,...,X_m$ means finding the parameters $\alpha_0, ..., \alpha_m$ so that the "distance" between Y and $\hat{Y}$ is minimized. One of the most common methods that's used to minimize the distance between the two vectors Y and $\hat{Y}$ is the *least squares* method, which aims to find the coefficients $\alpha = (\alpha_0, ..., \alpha_m)$ so that the residual sum of squares is minimized:

$$RSS(\alpha) = \sum_{i=1}^{n} (y_i - \hat{y}_i)^2 = \sum_{i=1}^{n} \left(y_i - \alpha_0 - \sum_{j=1}^{m} \alpha_j X_{i,j} \right)^2$$

Figure 3.20: Residual sum of squares for linear regression

In order to solve the preceding equation, we need to introduce the matrix notations of the target variable, Y, the feature matrix, X, and the parameter vector, α, which are defined as follows:

$$Y = \begin{bmatrix} y_1 \\ \cdot \\ y_n \end{bmatrix} \quad X = \begin{bmatrix} 1 x_{11} & \cdots & x_{1m} \\ \cdots & & \\ 1 x_{n1} & \cdots & x_{nm} \end{bmatrix} \quad \alpha = \begin{bmatrix} \alpha_1 \\ \cdot \\ \alpha_m \end{bmatrix}$$

Figure 3.21: Definitions of the matrix notation of Y, X, and α

With these notations, *Figure 3.20* becomes the following, where X^T denotes the transpose of the matrix, X:

$$RSS(a) = \left(Y - X_\alpha \right)^T \left(Y - X_\alpha \right)$$

Figure 3.22: Expression for RSS(α)

In order to compute the values of the vector, **α**, that minimize the equation in *Figure 3.19*, we need to impose the conditions of local minima for the function RSS(.) with respect to **α** —that is, that the gradient of RSS is equal to zero and its Hessian matrix (meaning the second derivative of the function RSS with respect to the vector, **α**) is positive definite. In other words, the following conditions have to be imposed on **α**, in order to minimize the equation in *Figure 3.20*:

$$\frac{\partial RSS}{\partial \alpha}(\alpha) = -2X^T(y - X\alpha) = 0$$

Figure 3.23: Condition of the gradient of RSS to be equal to zero

$$\frac{\partial^2 RSS}{\partial \alpha^2}(\alpha) = 2X^T X \text{ positive definite}$$

Figure 3.24: Condition of the hessian matrix of RSS to be positive definite

Note that from the second conditions (*Figure 3.24*), it follows that the matrix X^TX is invertible with the inverse matrix $(X^TX)^{-1}$. We can rewrite the equation in *Figure 3.23* as follows:

$$\hat{\alpha} = (X^TX)^{-1}X^Ty$$

Figure 3.25: Analytical solution of equation in Figure 3.20

This is the value of **α**, which minimizes the function in the right-hand side of the equation in *Figure 3.20*.

From a data analysis perspective, the computation of the preceding matrices is performed automatically in various Python packages, leaving the analyst the more interesting task of analyzing the data and drawing important business conclusions, rather than implementing the matrix multiplications personally. Let's see how we can apply linear regression to our banking data in order to create a linear model that's able to identify the relationship between the various numerical features.

In this section, we will be applying linear regression in order to predict the consumer confidence index (the **cons.conf.idx** column) based on the employment variation rate, the CPI, and the **euribor** 3-month interest rate (the **emp.var.rate**, **cons.price.idx**, and **euribor3m** columns, respectively). In Python, we can easily fit a linear regression model by using the **OLS()** function from the **statsmodels.api** package:

```
import statsmodels.api as sm

# create feature matrix and target variable
X = bank_data[["emp.var.rate", "cons.price.idx", "euribor3m"]]
# add constant value for the intercept term
X = sm.add_constant(X)
y = bank_data["cons.conf.idx"]

# define and fit model
lineare_regression_model = sm.OLS(y, X)
result = lineare_regression_model.fit()
print(result.summary())
```

The summary of the result is shown in the following figure:

```
                            OLS Regression Results
==============================================================================
Dep. Variable:          cons.conf.idx   R-squared:                     0.177
Model:                            OLS   Adj. R-squared:                0.177
Method:                 Least Squares   F-statistic:                   2960.
Date:                Mon, 10 Feb 2020   Prob (F-statistic):             0.00
Time:                        23:28:51   Log-Likelihood:           -1.1753e+05
No. Observations:               41188   AIC:                       2.351e+05
Df Residuals:                   41184   BIC:                       2.351e+05
Df Model:                           3
Covariance Type:            nonrobust
==============================================================================
                 coef    std err          t      P>|t|      [0.025      0.975]
------------------------------------------------------------------------------
const         -82.4025      5.999    -13.736      0.000     -94.161     -70.644
emp.var.rate   -4.1814      0.072    -57.960      0.000      -4.323      -4.040
cons.price.idx  0.2828      0.063      4.478      0.000       0.159       0.407
euribor3m       4.3582      0.057     76.618      0.000       4.247       4.470
==============================================================================
Omnibus:                     3246.559   Durbin-Watson:                 0.001
Prob(Omnibus):                  0.000   Jarque-Bera (JB):           4034.493
Skew:                           0.761   Prob(JB):                       0.00
Kurtosis:                       2.811   Cond. No.                   2.72e+04
==============================================================================
```

Figure 3.26: Results from the OLS model

Several statistics are provided in the result from the **summary()** function. Some of the most important ones are the **R-squared** and **Adj. R-squared** metrics and the **coef** and **P>| t |** columns. Let's investigate those values in more detail.

The **R-squared** metric, also known as **coefficient of determination**, is the proportion of variance in the dependent variable (**cons.conf.idx**, in our case) that is predicted by our model. From a mathematical perspective, it can be computed by the following formula:

$$R^2 = 1 - \frac{\sum_{i=1}^{n}(y_i - \hat{y}_i)^2}{\sum_{i=1}^{n}(y_i - \bar{y})^2}$$

Figure 3.27: Definition of R^2

Here, $\hat{y}_i$ is the predicted value by the model and can be expressed as follows:

$$\hat{y}_i = \alpha_0 + \sum_{j=1}^{m} \alpha_j X_{i,j}$$

Figure 3.28: Definition of $\hat{y}_i$

That $\bar{y}$ is the average value of y and can be expressed as follows:

$$\bar{y} = \frac{1}{n} \sum_{i=1}^{n} y_i$$

Figure 3.29: Definition of $\bar{y}$

In general, the R-squared metric is limited in the interval [0, 1], where R-squared values close to 0 mean predicting the average value of the target variable (thus, almost no predictive power), while values close to 1 indicate a very accurate prediction model. One interesting property of the R-squared metric is that it tends to increase by increasing the complexity of the model (that is, adding more features). This doesn't always mean that our model is becoming more accurate as sometimes, those features are completely irrelevant. For this reason, we often tend to consider the **Adjuster R-squared** metric, which not only takes into account the accuracy of the model but also its complexity:

$$\overline{R^2} = 1 - (1 - R^2) \frac{n-1}{n-m-1}$$

Figure 3.30: Definition of $\overline{R^2}$

Now, let's consider the **coef** column in *Figure 3.25*. It provides the coefficients of the linear regression formula in *Figure 3.17*. More precisely, our model assumes the following form:

$$cons.conf.idx = -82.4025 - 4.1814 \; .emp.var.rate + 0.2828 \; .cons.price.idx + 4.3582.euribor3m$$

Figure 3.31: Linear regression model of cons.conf.idx as a function of emp.var.rate, cons. price.idx, and euribor3m

The single values of the coefficients are quite important. They tell us how much **cons.conf.idx** will increase if we increase one of the variables by 1 while keeping the other constant. For instance, the **cons.conf.idx** value will increase by 4.3582, if the value of the **euribor3m** is increased by 1, while it will decrease by 4.1814 at any increase of **emp.var.rate**. This means that **cons.conf.idx** is positively correlated with the **cons.price.idx** and **euribor3m** columns, and negatively correlated with **emp.var.rate**.

Finally, the **P>| t |** column in *Figure 3.26* returns the p-value of a hypothesis test, in which the null hypothesis is that the relative coefficient is equal to zero. In *Figure 3.26*, we can see that all those p-values are 0, meaning that each of the coefficients is statistically significant in our equation. Sometimes, these p-values become large, which means that the feature associated with that value is not relevant for our linear regression model and can be removed from the equation, without deteriorating the accuracy of the model.

LOGISTIC REGRESSION

Logistic regression is very similar to the linear regression technique we introduced in the previous section, with the only difference that the target variable, **Y**, assumes only values in a discrete set; say, for simplicity {0, 1}. If we were to approach such a problem as a logistic regression problem, the output of the right-hand side of the equation in *Figure 3.17* could easily go way beyond the values 0 and 1. Furthermore, even by limiting the output, it will still be able to assume all the values in the interval [0, 1]. For this reason, the idea behind logistic regression is to model the *probability* of the target variable Y, to assume one of the values (say 1). In this case, all the values between 0 and 1 will be reasonable.

With **p**, let's denote the probability of the target variable, **Y**, being equal to 1 when it's given a specific feature **x**:

$$p = Pr(\,Y = y \big| X = x)$$

Figure 3.32: Definition of p

Let's also define the **logit** function:

$$logit(\,p) = \log\!\left(\frac{p}{1-p}\right)$$

Figure 3.33: Definition of the logit function

Note that the **logit** function maps the interval (0, 1) into $(-\infty, +\infty)$, as shown in *Figure 3.32*, as generated by the following code snippet:

```
# plot logit function
x = np.arange(0, 1, 0.01)
logit = np.log(x/(1-x))

plt.figure(figsize=(6,6))
plt.plot(x,logit)
plt.xlabel("p")
plt.ylabel("$\log(\\frac{p}{1-p})$")
plt.grid()
plt.savefig("figs/logit_function.png", \
            format="png", dpi=300)
```

The output will be as follows:

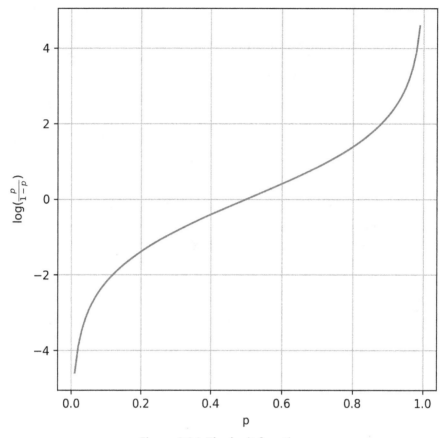

Figure 3.34: The logit function

With the help of the **logit** function, we can transform the output from the linear model in the equation in *Figure 3.17* into a probability:

$$\text{logit}(p) = \log\left(\frac{p}{1-p}\right) = \alpha_0 + \sum_{j=1}^{m} \alpha_j X_j$$

Figure 3.35: Transforming output into probability

By solving the last equation with respect to p, we can obtain the estimation of the probability of the target variable, Y, being equal to 1, given the feature vector **X = x**, as follows:

$$Pr(Y=1|X=x) = \frac{exp(\alpha_0 + \sum_{j=1}^{m} \alpha_j X_j)}{1 + exp(\alpha_0 + \sum_{j=1}^{m} \alpha_j X_j)}$$

Figure 3.36: Probability estimation via logistic regression (Y = 1)

$$Pr(Y=0|X=x) = \frac{1}{1 + exp(\alpha_0 + \sum_{j=1}^{m} \alpha_j X_j)}$$

Figure 3.37: Probability estimation via logistic regression (Y = 0)

As is the case of linear regression, Python's **statsmodels.api** package already contains a function that implements the logistic regression model. Let's look at how we can use this in order to create a logistic regression model that has the **age**, **duration**, **campaign**, and **previous** columns as feature vectors and the **y** column as the target variable:

```
# create feature matrix and target variable
X = bank_data[["age", "duration", "campaign", "previous"]]
# add constant value for the intercept term
X = sm.add_constant(X)
# target has to be numeric
y = np.where(bank_data["y"] == "yes", 1, 0)

# define and fit model
logistic_regression_model = sm.Logit(y, X)
result = logistic_regression_model.fit()
print(result.summary())
```

The result of the **summary()** function can be seen in the following figure:

```
                        Logit Regression Results
==================================================================================
Dep. Variable:                        y   No. Observations:               41188
Model:                            Logit   Df Residuals:                   41183
Method:                             MLE   Df Model:                           4
Date:                 Tue, 11 Feb 2020   Pseudo R-squ.:                 0.2331
Time:                          17:19:35   Log-Likelihood:               -11119.
converged:                         True   LL-Null:                      -14499.
Covariance Type:              nonrobust   LLR p-value:                    0.000
==================================================================================
                 coef    std err          z      P>|z|      [0.025      0.975]
----------------------------------------------------------------------------------
const         -3.7793      0.076    -49.435      0.000      -3.929      -3.629
age            0.0091      0.002      5.665      0.000       0.006       0.012
duration       0.0039   6.16e-05     62.973      0.000       0.004       0.004
campaign      -0.1163      0.011    -10.706      0.000      -0.138      -0.095
previous       1.0579      0.027     39.232      0.000       1.005       1.111
==================================================================================
```

Figure 3.38: Results from the logistic regression model

As in the case of linear regression, the model returns the parameters from the logistic regression equation. Hence, we can easily construct the estimation of the probabilities of the **y** variable being equal to "yes" or "no" as follows:

$$Pr(y = yes) = \frac{exp(-3.7793 + 0.0091.\,age + 0.0039.duration - 0.1163.\,campaign + 1.0579.\,previous)}{1 + exp(-3.7793 + 0.0091.\,age + 0.0039.duration - 0.1163.\,campaign + 1.0579.\,previous)}$$

Figure 3.39: Probability of the y column being equal to "yes," according to the logistic regression model

$$Pr(y = yes) = \frac{1}{1 + exp(-3.7793 + 0.0091.\,age + 0.0039.duration - 0.1163.\,campaign + 1.0579.\,previous)}$$

Figure 3.40: Probability of the y column being equal to "no," according to the logistic regression model

Furthermore, from the **P>|z|** column in *Figure 3.38*, we can see that all the parameters are statistically significant for our probability estimation.

One important aspect of both the linear and logistic regression models is that both the feature and target vectors must be numeric variables. We already saw how to transform the target variable from categorical into numerical values using the **numpy.where()** function:

```
# target has to be numeric
y = np.where(bank_data["y"] == "yes", 1, 0)
```

We can also use the **apply()** function on a **pandas.Series** object if we need more sophisticated mappings. None of these methods scale well when we have lots of features with categorical values. In order to solve this problem, we can use the **pandas.get_dummies()** function, which automatically creates dummy variables for all non-numeric columns. With this technique (also known as **one-hot encoding**), we convert each categorical column into a set of new columns, each one indicating that the original one contains a specific value. Let's provide a simple example. Consider the **education** column in the bank marketing campaign. Originally, it contains 8 distinct classes, as shown in the following code:

```
print(bank_data["education"].unique())
```

The output will be as follows:

```
['basic.4y' 'high.school' 'basic.6y' 'basic.9y'
 'professional.course' 'unknown' 'university.degree' 'illiterate']
```

By applying the **pandas.get_dummies()** function to the **education** column, we get 8 new columns with 0 or 1 as the only possible values, depending on the value in the original **education** column. Here is the output of the **pandas.get_dummies()** function when applied to the **education** column (we also attach the original column for better understanding):

```
hot_encoded = pd.get_dummies(bank_data["education"])
hot_encoded["education"] = bank_data["education"]
hot_encoded.head(10)
```

The following is the output of the preceding code:

	basic.4y	basic.6y	basic.9y	high.school	illiterate	professional.course	university.degree	unknown	education
0	1	0	0	0	0	0	0	0	basic.4y
1	0	0	0	1	0	0	0	0	high.school
2	0	0	0	1	0	0	0	0	high.school
3	0	1	0	0	0	0	0	0	basic.6y
4	0	0	0	1	0	0	0	0	high.school
5	0	0	1	0	0	0	0	0	basic.9y
6	0	0	0	0	0	1	0	0	professional.course
7	0	0	0	0	0	0	0	1	unknown
8	0	0	0	0	0	1	0	0	professional.course
9	0	0	0	1	0	0	0	0	high.school

Figure 3.41: Result of the get_dummies() function being applied to the education column

As shown in the preceding figure, eight new columns have been created, all of which have values equal to 0, except the column corresponding to the original value in the **education** column, which has a value of 1.

In the following exercise, we will apply the techniques we've presented so far to our bank marketing campaign data.

EXERCISE 3.04: LOGISTIC REGRESSION ON THE FULL MARKETING CAMPAIGN DATA

In this exercise, you will create a logistic regression model based on the full marketing campaign data. By doing this, you will be able to create a mathematical model that explains the relationship between the different features in the data and the final outcome of the marketing campaign. This could serve as a basis for marketing campaign optimization (for instance, contacting only customers with certain characteristics). In this way, not only could the outcome be improved, but also marketing campaign costs could be reduced.

Although creating and fitting the model is straightforward, you will need to transform all the features into numerical ones by using the **pandas.get_dummies()** function. Follow these steps to complete this exercise:

1. First, preprocess the feature matrix so that it contains only numerical values. This is not a problem for columns such as **age** or **duration** as they already contain numerical values, but columns such as **job** or **month** should be preprocessed. For this reason, apply the **pandas.get_dummies()** function:

```
"""
transform all features into numerical ones, by using
the get_dummies() function
"""
X = bank_data.drop("y", axis=1)
X = pd.get_dummies(X)
X = sm.add_constant(X)
print(X.columns)
```

The output will be as follows:

```
Index(['const', 'age', 'duration', 'campaign', 'pdays', 'previous',
       'emp.var.rate', 'cons.price.idx', 'cons.conf.idx', 'euribor3m',
       'nr.employed', 'job_admin.', 'job_blue-collar', 'job_entrepreneur',
       'job_housemaid', 'job_management', 'job_retired', 'job_self-employed',
       'job_services', 'job_student', 'job_technician', 'job_unemployed',
       'job_unknown', 'marital_divorced', 'marital_married', 'marital_single',
       'marital_unknown', 'education_basic.4y', 'education_basic.6y',
       'education_basic.9y', 'education_high.school', 'education_illiterate',
       'education_professional.course', 'education_university.degree',
       'education_unknown', 'default_no', 'default_unknown', 'default_yes',
       'housing_no', 'housing_unknown', 'housing_yes', 'loan_no',
       'loan_unknown', 'loan_yes', 'contact_cellular', 'contact_telephone',
       'month_apr', 'month_aug', 'month_dec', 'month_jul', 'month_jun',
       'month_mar', 'month_may', 'month_nov', 'month_oct', 'month_sep',
       'day_of_week_fri', 'day_of_week_mon', 'day_of_week_thu',
       'day_of_week_tue', 'day_of_week_wed', 'poutcome_failure',
       'poutcome_nonexistent', 'poutcome_success'],
      dtype='object')
```

Figure 3.42: Resulting features, which will be used in the logistic regression model

2. Transform the target variable:

```
# extract and transform target variable
y = np.where(bank_data["y"] == "yes", 1 ,0)
```

3. Finally, create a logistic regression model based on the full set of features:

```
# define and fit model
full_logistic_regression_model = sm.Logit(y, X)
result = full_logistic_regression_model.fit(maxiter=500)
print(result.summary())
```

The result of the model is shown in the following figure:

```
                          Logit Regression Results
==============================================================================
Dep. Variable:                    y   No. Observations:                41188
Model:                        Logit   Df Residuals:                    41135
Method:                         MLE   Df Model:                           52
Date:              Wed, 12 Feb 2020   Pseudo R-squ.:                  0.4111
Time:                      17:31:02   Log-Likelihood:                -8538.9
converged:                    False   LL-Null:                       -14499.
Covariance Type:            nonrobust   LLR p-value:                    0.000
==============================================================================
                                 coef     std err          z      P>|z|       [0.025      0.975]
------------------------------------------------------------------------------
const                        -68.6994         nan        nan        nan          nan         nan
age                            0.0002       0.002      0.081      0.936       -0.005       0.005
duration                       0.0047    7.46e-05     63.108      0.000        0.005       0.005
campaign                      -0.0401       0.012     -3.473      0.001       -0.063      -0.017
pdays                         -0.0009       0.000     -4.326      0.000       -0.001      -0.001
previous                      -0.0628       0.059     -1.062      0.288       -0.179       0.053
emp.var.rate                  -1.7576       0.142    -12.380      0.000       -2.036      -1.479
cons.price.idx                 2.1905       0.252      8.679      0.000        1.696       2.685
cons.conf.idx                  0.0207       0.008      2.664      0.008        0.005       0.036
euribor3m                      0.3316       0.130      2.551      0.011        0.077       0.586
nr.employed                    0.0054       0.003      1.738      0.082       -0.001       0.012
job_admin.                    -5.5134    2.11e+06  -2.62e-06      1.000    -4.13e+06    4.13e+06
job_blue-collar               -5.7481    1.82e+06  -3.16e-06      1.000    -3.56e+06    3.56e+06
job_entrepreneur              -5.6914    1.77e+06  -3.22e-06      1.000    -3.46e+06    3.46e+06
job_housemaid                 -5.5377         nan        nan        nan          nan         nan
job_management                -5.5695     1.9e+06  -2.92e-06      1.000    -3.73e+06    3.73e+06
job_retired                   -5.2276    1.37e+06   -3.8e-06      1.000    -2.69e+06    2.69e+06
job_self-employed             -5.6712    1.69e+06  -3.36e-06      1.000     -3.3e+06     3.3e+06
job_services                  -5.6532    2.42e+06  -2.34e-06      1.000    -4.74e+06    4.74e+06
job_student                   -5.3100    1.93e+06  -2.76e-06      1.000    -3.77e+06    3.77e+06
job_technician                -5.5274     1.9e+06   -2.9e-06      1.000    -3.73e+06    3.73e+06
job_unemployed                -5.4922    1.38e+06  -3.97e-06      1.000    -2.71e+06    2.71e+06
job_unknown                   -5.5838    2.55e+06  -2.19e-06      1.000    -5.01e+06    5.01e+06
marital_divorced             -16.6541    9.63e+05  -1.73e-05      1.000    -1.89e+06    1.89e+06
marital_married              -16.6569    3.31e+05  -5.04e-05      1.000    -6.48e+05    6.48e+05
marital_single               -16.5982     3.1e+05  -5.36e-05      1.000    -6.07e+05    6.07e+05
marital_unknown              -16.6247     7.8e+05  -2.13e-05      1.000    -1.53e+06    1.53e+06
education_basic.4y            -8.5265    1.47e+06  -5.79e-06      1.000    -2.89e+06    2.89e+06
education_basic.6y            -8.4039    1.46e+06  -5.77e-06      1.000    -2.86e+06    2.86e+06
education_basic.9y            -8.5275    1.44e+06  -5.92e-06      1.000    -2.82e+06    2.82e+06
education_high.school        -8.4779    1.46e+06  -5.83e-06      1.000    -2.85e+06    2.85e+06
education_illiterate         -7.4598    1.45e+06  -5.14e-06      1.000    -2.84e+06    2.84e+06
education_professional.course -8.4115   1.47e+06  -5.72e-06      1.000    -2.88e+06    2.88e+06
education_university.degree   -8.3306    1.44e+06  -5.77e-06      1.000    -2.83e+06    2.83e+06
education_unknown            -8.3768    1.44e+06  -5.83e-06      1.000    -2.82e+06    2.82e+06
default_no                   -16.6776         nan        nan        nan          nan         nan
default_unknown              -16.9779         nan        nan        nan          nan         nan
default_yes                  -32.8750         nan        nan        nan          nan         nan
housing_no                   -22.1674         nan        nan        nan          nan         nan
housing_unknown              -22.2021         nan        nan        nan          nan         nan
housing_yes                  -22.1721         nan        nan        nan          nan         nan
loan_no                      -22.1438    3.57e+05   -6.2e-05      1.000       -7e+05       7e+05
loan_unknown                 -22.2024         nan        nan        nan          nan         nan
loan_yes                     -22.1954    3.73e+05  -5.95e-05      1.000    -7.32e+05    7.32e+05
contact_cellular             -32.9450         nan        nan        nan          nan         nan
contact_telephone            -33.5910         nan        nan        nan          nan         nan
month_apr                     -6.9063    1.54e+06   -4.5e-06      1.000    -3.01e+06    3.01e+06
month_aug                     -6.0410    1.53e+06  -3.94e-06      1.000       -3e+06       3e+06
month_dec                     -6.5871    1.53e+06  -4.32e-06      1.000    -2.99e+06    2.99e+06
month_jul                     -6.7717     1.5e+06  -4.51e-06      1.000    -2.94e+06    2.94e+06
month_jun                     -7.4306    1.41e+06  -5.26e-06      1.000    -2.77e+06    2.77e+06
month_mar                     -4.8922    1.52e+06  -3.22e-06      1.000    -2.98e+06    2.98e+06
month_may                     -7.3502     1.5e+06   -4.9e-06      1.000    -2.94e+06    2.94e+06
month_nov                     -7.3243    1.48e+06  -4.95e-06      1.000     -2.9e+06     2.9e+06
month_oct                     -6.7123    1.46e+06  -4.59e-06      1.000    -2.86e+06    2.86e+06
month_sep                     -6.5323    1.47e+06  -4.44e-06      1.000    -2.88e+06    2.88e+06
day_of_week_fri              -13.4901         nan        nan        nan          nan         nan
day_of_week_mon              -13.6069         nan        nan        nan          nan         nan
day_of_week_thu              -13.4341         nan        nan        nan          nan         nan
day_of_week_tue              -13.3929         nan        nan        nan          nan         nan
day_of_week_wed              -13.3148         nan        nan        nan          nan         nan
poutcome_failure             -22.8763         nan        nan        nan          nan         nan
poutcome_nonexistent         -22.4505         nan        nan        nan          nan         nan
poutcome_success             -21.9166         nan        nan        nan          nan         nan
==============================================================================
```

Figure 3.43: Result of the logistic regression model when run on the full set of features

As shown in the preceding figure, the model we obtained is quite large. In fact, we have 64 different features (after encoding the categorical variables as dummy ones). It would be quite optimistic to expect that all the obtained features have a significant impact on our model. Also, a model with so many parameters would be difficult to interpret.

> **NOTE**
>
> To access the source code for this specific section, please refer to https://packt.live/3hwyUgU.
>
> You can also run this example online at https://packt.live/2AwGGH9. You must execute the entire Notebook in order to get the desired result.

In fact, observing the **P>|z|** column in the preceding figure shows us that for most of the features, the p-value is equal to one, which means that we cannot reject the null hypothesis, stating that the coefficient for the respective column should be equal to zero. In other words, we have lots of redundant columns in our model.

Furthermore, for some of the coefficients, we cannot even compute the p-values (in fact, there is a lot of NaN present in the result, indicating that the optimization model running on the back of the **Logit.fit()** function is not able to converge, which is another reason to reduce the number of features).

We will deal with this issue in the next activity. For now, it is important to remember that even if we might be able to achieve a higher accuracy model with more features, it is not always the best choice, especially if we are trying to explain the impact the different features have on our target variable.

Let's perform an activity to create a more detailed logistic regression model.

ACTIVITY 3.01: CREATING A LEANER LOGISTIC REGRESSION MODEL

The aim of this activity is to create a leaner logistic regression model by accurately selecting the important features and, in this way, improve the result of the model from *Exercise 3.04, Logistic Regression on the Full Marketing Campaign Data.* In this way, you will obtain an explainable logistic regression model with far fewer features to be combined.

It is always important to use as few features as possible when training linear models as one of their greatest advantages is their interpretability. By the end of this activity, you should be confident in building logistic regression models, improving their results, and interpreting the values of the different parameters from a business perspective.

The following steps should help you complete this activity:

1. Import the necessary Python packages.

```
import pandas as pd
import numpy as np
import statsmodels.api as sm
```

2. Upload the **bank-additional-full.csv** dataset from the data folder on GitHub.

3. Create a feature matrix using a selection of the variables with a p-value smaller than 0.05 (see Figure 3.43 for the appropriate p-values). See the table below for a list of variables to include:

The output will be as follows:

	const	duration	campaign	pdays	cons.price.idx	cons.conf.idx	euribor3m
0	1.0	261	1	999	93.994	-36.4	4.857
1	1.0	149	1	999	93.994	-36.4	4.857
2	1.0	226	1	999	93.994	-36.4	4.857
3	1.0	151	1	999	93.994	-36.4	4.857
4	1.0	307	1	999	93.994	-36.4	4.857

Figure 3.44: Feature matrix to be used in the logistic regression model

4. Transform the target variable into an array containing **0** and **1** (where 0 corresponds to "no" entries in the **y** column).

5. Fit the logistic regression model on the selected features.

The output will be as follows:

```
Optimization terminated successfully.
         Current function value: 0.222140
         Iterations 8
                      Logit Regression Results
================================================================================
Dep. Variable:                      y   No. Observations:              41188
Model:                          Logit   Df Residuals:                  41181
Method:                           MLE   Df Model:                          6
Date:                Wed, 12 Feb 2020   Pseudo R-squ.:                0.3690
Time:                        19:53:11   Log-Likelihood:              -9149.5
converged:                       True   LL-Null:                     -14499.
Covariance Type:            nonrobust   LLR p-value:                   0.000
================================================================================
                   coef    std err          z      P>|z|      [0.025      0.975]
--------------------------------------------------------------------------------
const          -43.1379      3.524    -12.240      0.000     -50.046     -36.230
duration         0.0045   7.11e-05     63.505      0.000       0.004       0.005
campaign        -0.0495      0.011     -4.331      0.000      -0.072      -0.027
pdays           -0.0016   6.81e-05    -22.928      0.000      -0.002      -0.001
cons.price.idx   0.4921      0.038     12.877      0.000       0.417       0.567
cons.conf.idx    0.0699      0.003     20.137      0.000       0.063       0.077
euribor3m       -0.7200      0.015    -47.462      0.000      -0.750      -0.690
================================================================================
```

Figure 3.45: Results from the logistic regression model

6. Derive the equations for the probabilities **Pr (y=yes)** and **Pr (y=no)** in explicit form (see *Figure 3.36* and *Figure 3.37* for reference).

7. Finally, compare the pseudo R-squared value from the obtained model with the ones from *Figure 3.38* and *Figure 3.43*. What can we deduce?

> **NOTE**
>
> The solution to the activity can be found on page 499.

With this analysis, we can see that it is easy to derive explainable mathematical models that are capable of catching the relationships and dependencies within the data. Furthermore, these techniques can be used to further optimize results and reduce costs.

SUMMARY

In this chapter, we analyzed campaign marketing data in which new financial services were offered to customers. We paid particular attention to linear models and investigated how the probability of a successful outcome can be modeled as a function of different macroeconomics factors. From a technical perspective, we introduced linear models (such as linear and logistic regression) and paid particular attention to their interpretation.

In the next chapter, we will be analyzing a Polish company's bankruptcy data to try and understand the main reasons behind bankruptcy and see whether it is possible to identify early warning signs.

TACKLING COMPANY BANKRUPTCY

OVERVIEW

In this chapter, we will be looking at a Polish company's bankruptcy data to try and understand the main reasons behind bankruptcy and whether it could be possible to identify early warning signs. By the end of this chapter, you will be able to perform exploratory data analysis using pandas profiling. You will also be able to apply missing value treatments with two different types of imputers and successfully handle imbalances in the data.

INTRODUCTION

In the previous chapter, we analyzed the data derived from the direct marketing campaign of a Portuguese bank using techniques such as hypothesis testing and clustering to be able to identify the impact it had on acquiring new customers for the bank.

In this chapter, we will be using exploratory data analysis to identify early warning signs of fatigue in the financial data. The dataset is about the bankruptcy prediction of Polish companies. The data was collected from the Emerging Markets Information Service. The bankrupt companies were analyzed for the period of 2000-2012, while the still-operating companies were evaluated from 2007 to 2013.

> **NOTE**
>
> The dataset that's being used for this chapter can be found in the UCI repository:
>
> https://archive.ics.uci.edu/ml/datasets/Polish+companies+bankruptcy+data
>
> Additionally, the dataset is also available on our GitHub repository:
>
> https://packt.live/2JMSiqj.
>
> For further information on this topic, you can refer to the following article: Zieba, M., Tomczak, S. K., & Tomczak, J. M. (2016). *Ensemble Boosted Trees with Synthetic Features Generation in Application to Bankruptcy Prediction. Expert Systems with Applications*

Bankruptcy is a legal process that is initiated by a debtor (the entity that owes debt to other entities) who cannot repay some or all of their debts they owe to the creditors (the bank or institution to whom money is owed). In most countries, bankruptcy is imposed by a court order. Bankruptcy happens when a company is unable to repay its debts or meet its obligations. This bankruptcy status can last from a few months to several years. In some cases, bankruptcy can be permanent.

Bankruptcy not only happens due to poor money management but also due to external market factors such as economic slowdown or natural calamities. Bankruptcy prediction comes in handy for predicting whether a company might enter financial distress in the near future. This can be achieved with the help of a predictive model that classifies the company as financially sound or financially unsound (where the probability of bankruptcy is high).

The importance of bankruptcy prediction has been a very important topic in the world of finance for more than a century. One of the major reasons for this is that the creditors can put a robust risk management system in place that can mitigate losses to a greater extent. As the saying goes, "Prevention is better than a cure".

In this chapter, we will be studying the important factors that lead to bankruptcy through the example debtor of a Polish company. The data that we will be using in this chapter consists of various financial ratios from the company. With the help of regularization techniques, we will be able to narrow down the important financial ratios that lead to bankruptcy. By knowing the factors that lead to bankruptcy, creditors can put a system in place that monitors these financial ratios and can take action when the threshold is breached—in the form of additional collateral or an increase in the interest rate, for example.

In this chapter, we will be taking the following approach:

Figure 4.1: Analyzing bankruptcy data

EXPLANATION OF SOME OF THE IMPORTANT FEATURES

Some of the most important terms in the dataset are as follows:

- **Net profits**: The amount that is left after all operating expenses, interest, and taxes are subtracted from the total revenue.

- **Total liabilities**: The aggregate sum that is owed as debt and other financial obligations owed by an entity.

- **Total assets**: This is the total amount of assets owned by an entity.

- **Current assets**: This is cash and other assets that can be converted to cash within a year.

- **Gross profit**: This is the profit the company makes after deducting the associated cost of manufacturing or services provided.

- **Inventory**: This is the complete list of finished goods or goods used in production by a company.

- **Working capital**: This is the capital of the company used for its day-to-day operations.

- **EBIT**: This refers to earnings before interest and tax.

IMPORTING THE DATA

There is a total of five ARFF data files with the names **1year**, **2year**, **3year**, **4year**, and **5year**, respectively.

We need to load the files and convert them into a pandas DataFrame. The columns are given a new header, as follows:

- `dataframe[0]` corresponds to **1year**.

- `dataframe[1]` corresponds to **2year**.

- `dataframe[2]` corresponds to **3year**.

- `dataframe[3]` corresponds to **4year**.

- `dataframe[4]` corresponds to **5year**.

An **Attribute-Relation File Format** (**ARFF**) file is an ASCII text file. It essentially provides a list of instances that commonly share an attribute set.

We will now begin importing our data into a DataFrame by completing the following exercise.

EXERCISE 4.01: IMPORTING DATA INTO DATAFRAMES

In this exercise, you will load the data files and import the data into the DataFrames.

Before you begin, ensure you have downloaded the ARFF data files with the names **1year**, **2year**, **3year**, **4year**, and **5year** and saved them into your working directory (i.e. the same directory as your Jupyter Notebook file).

Once you have saved the files to the correct location, you can follow these steps to complete this exercise:

1. Import the **warnings** package to suppress the warnings. We are suppressing the warnings to make the code more legible and readable:

```
# To suppress warnings
import warnings
warnings.filterwarnings("ignore")
warnings.filterwarnings("ignore", category=DeprecationWarning)
```

2. Import the basic libraries, **numpy**, **pandas**, **matplotlib inline**, and **arff**, which are required for data organization, statistical operations, and plotting:

```
import numpy as np
import pandas as pd
%matplotlib inline
# For loading .arff files
from scipy.io import arff
```

3. Load the five files into a list:

```
# Load the 5 raw .arff files into a list
def load_arff_raw_data():
    N=5
    return [arff.loadarff(str(i+1) \
            + 'year.arff') for i in range(N)]
```

4. Load the five **.arff** files into the pandas DataFrames:

```
# Loads the 5 raw .arff files into pandas dataframes
def load_dataframes():
    return [pd.DataFrame(data_i_year[0]) for data_i_year in \
            load_arff_raw_data()]
```

5. Set the column headers and labels for the DataFrames:

```
"""
Set the column headers from X1 ... X64 and the class label as Y, for
all the 5 dataframes.
"""

def set_new_headers(dataframes):
    cols = ['X' + str(i+1) for i in range\
            (len(dataframes[0].columns)-1)]
    cols.append('Y')
    for df in dataframes:
        df.columns = cols
```

6. Call the **load_dataframes** function to load the **.arff** files into a list:

```
"""
dataframes is the list of pandas dataframes for the 5 year datafiles.
We now call the function load_dataframes
"""

dataframes = load_dataframes()
```

7. Set new headers for the DataFrames. The new headers will have the renamed set of features (**X1** to **X64**):

```
# Set the new headers for the DataFrames.
set_new_headers(dataframes)
```

The DataFrames have been successfully created.

8. Print the first five rows of **year1**:

```
# print the first 5 rows of a dataset 'year1'
dataframes[0].head()
```

The output will be as follows:

	X1	X2	X3	X4	X5	X6
0	0.200550	0.37951	0.39641	2.0472	32.3510	0.38825
1	0.209120	0.49988	0.47225	1.9447	14.7860	0.00000
2	0.248660	0.69592	0.26713	1.5548	-1.1523	0.00000
3	0.081483	0.30734	0.45879	2.4928	51.9520	0.14988
4	0.187320	0.61323	0.22960	1.4063	-7.3128	0.18732

5 rows × 65 columns

Figure 4.2: Top five rows of the DataFrame

NOTE

The output has been truncated for presentation purposes. You can find the complete output at https://packt.live/2JLG6pF.

9. Now run the following code to find the shape of the **year1** DataFrame:

```
dataframes[0].shape
```

The output is as follows:

```
(7027, 65)
```

10. Once the DataFrame has been created, convert the datatype of the columns for further analysis. The numeric data (other than the class label columns) shown in the preceding DataFrame is the Python object, so we need to convert the numeric features for all the DataFrames into a **float**:

```
"""
Convert the dtypes of all the columns (other than the class label
columns) to float.
"""

def convert_columns_type_float(dfs):
    for i in range(5):
        index = 1
        while(index<=63):
            colname = dfs[i].columns[index]
            col = getattr(dfs[i], colname)
            dfs[i][colname] = col.astype(float)
            index+=1
            convert_columns_type_float(dataframes)
```

11. Convert the class label types into an **int**. If we look at the class label **'Y'**, the values are shown either as **b'0'** or **b'1'**. They actually correspond to bankruptcy being false and true. It is always advisable to convert them into binary integers 0 and 1:

```
"""
The class labels for all the dataframes are originally in object
type.
Convert them to int types
"""

def convert_class_label_type_int(dfs):
    for i in range(len(dfs)):
        col = getattr(dfs[i], 'Y')
        dfs[i]['Y'] = col.astype(int)
convert_class_label_type_int(dataframes)
```

> **NOTE**
>
> To access the source code for this specific section, please refer to https://packt.live/2JLG6pF.
>
> You can also run this example online at https://packt.live/2UQFwNg. You must execute the entire Notebook in order to get the desired result.

Thus, we have successfully converted the ARFF data files into DataFrames for further analysis.

PANDAS PROFILING

The next step in data analysis, after importing the data and installing the required packages, is pandas profiling.

In this section, we will be focusing on pandas profiling—a simple and fast approach toward exploratory data analysis. It is essentially a package that promises a more efficient method of data analysis.

In order to use pandas profiling, the following packages have to be installed in an anaconda prompt:

```
pip install pandas-profiling
```

The output will be as follows:

```
Collecting pandas-profiling
  Downloading pandas-profiling-2.5.0.tar.gz (192 kB)
     |████████████████████████████████| 192 kB 5.1 MB/s eta 0:00:01
Requirement already satisfied: numpy>=1.16.0 in /srv/conda/envs/notebook/lib/py
thon3.6/site-packages (from pandas-profiling) (1.18.1)
Requirement already satisfied: scipy>=1.4.1 in /srv/conda/envs/notebook/lib/pyt
hon3.6/site-packages (from pandas-profiling) (1.4.1)
Collecting pandas==0.25.3
  Downloading pandas-0.25.3-cp36-cp36m-manylinux1_x86_64.whl (10.4 MB)
     |████████████████████████████████| 10.4 MB 9.5 MB/s eta 0:00:01
Requirement already satisfied: matplotlib>=3.0.3 in /srv/conda/envs/notebook/li
b/python3.6/site-packages (from pandas-profiling) (3.2.1)
Collecting confuse==1.0.0
  Downloading confuse-1.0.0.tar.gz (32 kB)
Collecting jinja2==2.11.1
```

Figure 4.3: Pandas profiling installation

RUNNING PANDAS PROFILING

Now, we need to initiate a loop to perform pandas profiling for the five DataFrames. The major advantage of using pandas profiling is that it provides you with an interactive HTML report of the various statistical parameters of the columns in a DataFrame. Some of the parameters are missing values, skewness, kurtosis, most frequent values, histograms, and correlations.

We will run the following code to apply pandas profiling to all the five DataFrames that we imported in the previous step. We will be using a for loop to perform this:

```python
import pandas_profiling
for i in range(0,5):
    profile = dataframes[i]\
                .profile_report(title='Pandas Profiling Report', \
                                plot={'histogram': {'bins': 8}})
    profile.to_file(output_file=str(i)+"output.html")
```

The output of pandas profiling is in HTML. Each of the five DataFrames has a pandas profiling report.

We will be primarily focusing on the following aspects of the DataFrame:

- **Number of variables**: This feature refers to the number of features present in a DataFrame.

- **Number of observations**: This feature refers to the number of records present in the DataFrame.

- **Missing values**: This feature represents the number of records that are missing in a column of a DataFrame.

- **Duplicate rows**: This feature represents the number of records that are not unique in a column of a DataFrame.

- **Types of variables**: This refers to the number of numerical, categorical, Boolean, Date values, and URLs present in a DataFrame.

- **Skewness**: This is the amount of asymmetry or distortion in the probability distribution of a real-valued random variable around its mean:

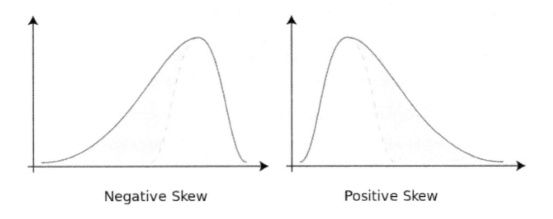

Figure 4.4: Skewness

The relationship between the mean, median, and mode of different skewness distributions is represented in the following plots:

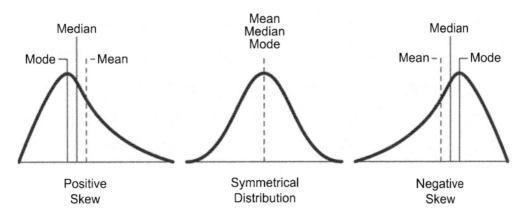

Figure 4.5: Relationship between the mean, median, and mode
of the different types of skewness

The skewness value can be positive, negative, or undefined.

- **Correlation**: Correlation talks about the relationship between two variables and the strength of the relationship. If two features in a DataFrame are highly correlated, one of the features can be rejected. Pandas profiling provides you with a list of features that are correlated and can be rejected.

- **Descriptive statistics of the variables**: Descriptive statistics of the variables represents the various parameters for that particular feature, such as mean, median, variance, coefficient of variation, kurtosis, and sum.

PANDAS PROFILING REPORT FOR DATAFRAME 1

The output of pandas profiling is an HTML file. We will be discussing the various aspects of the findings shown in the following screenshot.

> **NOTE**
>
> You can find the relevant HTML files at https://packt.live/2Vbq1z1.

The HTML file looks as follows:

Overview

Dataset info

Number of variables	65
Number of observations	7027
Missing cells	5835 (1.3%)
Duplicate rows	82 (1.2%)
Total size in memory	3.5 MiB
Average record size in memory	520.0 B

Variables types

Numeric	32
Categorical	0
Boolean	1
Date	0
URL	0
Text (Unique)	0
Rejected	32
Unsupported	0

Figure 4.6: View of the HTML file

From the preceding screenshot, we can easily derive that the dataset has 65 features with 7,027 observations. The total number of missing values is 5,835.

Now, let's look at the features and find out whether the feature is skewed or not. Apart from the skewness, we will also be looking at correlation. If two variables are correlated, we can reject one variable and go with the other.

The following screenshot is a continuation of the report for pandas profiling:

Figure 4.7: Skewness report for pandas profiling

X40 is highly correlated with X4 (ρ = 0.9701274201)   `Rejected`

X41 is highly skewed (γ1 = 47.35382405)   `Skewed`

X41 has 84 (1.2%) missing values   `Missing`

X42 is highly correlated with X39 (ρ = 0.9998701166)   `Rejected`

X43 is highly correlated with X42 (ρ = 0.9406389015)   `Rejected`

X44 is highly correlated with X43 (ρ = 0.9999561902)   `Rejected`

X45 is highly skewed (γ1 = -82.81126254)   `Skewed`

X45 has 134 (1.9%) missing values   `Missing`

X46 is highly correlated with X40 (ρ = 0.9894204681)   `Rejected`

X47 is highly skewed (γ1 = 42.88570765)   `Skewed`

X47 has 134 (1.9%) zeros   `Zeros`

X48 is highly correlated with X22 (ρ = 0.9712548784)   `Rejected`

X49 is highly skewed (γ1 = -83.0700054)   `Skewed`

X49 has 93 (1.3%) zeros   `Zeros`

X5 is highly skewed (γ1 = -52.54575303)   `Skewed`

X50 is highly skewed (γ1 = 27.74571026)   `Skewed`

X51 is highly correlated with X2 (ρ = 0.986503155)   `Rejected`

X52 is highly correlated with X32 (ρ = 0.9350348729)   `Rejected`

X53 is highly skewed (γ1 = 48.42455391)   `Skewed`

X54 is highly correlated with X53 (ρ = 0.9999168608)   `Rejected`

X55 is highly skewed (γ1 = 36.49483815)   `Skewed`

X56 is highly correlated with X49 (ρ = 0.996863638)   `Rejected`

X57 is highly skewed (γ1 = -50.90330617)   `Skewed`

X57 has 85 (1.2%) zeros   `Zeros`

X58 is highly correlated with X44 (ρ = 0.9992375305)   `Rejected`

X59 is highly skewed (γ1 = -27.1389892)   `Skewed`

X59 has 2743 (39.0%) zeros   `Zeros`

X6 is highly skewed (γ1 = -22.48347901)   `Skewed`

X6 has 2675 (38.1%) zeros   `Zeros`

X60 is highly skewed (γ1 = 79.8472124)   `Skewed`

X60 has 135 (1.9%) missing values   `Missing`

X61 is highly correlated with X54 (ρ = 0.9756267533)   `Rejected`

X62 is highly correlated with X58 (ρ = 0.9603598692)   `Rejected`

X63 is highly correlated with X34 (ρ = 0.9181490041)   `Rejected`

X64 is highly correlated with X61 (ρ = 0.9547454624)   `Rejected`

X7 is highly correlated with X24 (ρ = 0.972130258)   `Rejected`

X8 is highly correlated with X26 (ρ = 0.9410821494)   `Rejected`

X9 is highly correlated with X38 (ρ = 0.9121392064)   `Rejected`

Figure 4.8: Skewness report for pandas profiling (continued)

From the preceding report, we can see that 32 features have a high correlation.

In supervised learning, features with high correlation are removed due to the following reasons:

- Correlated features, due to duplication of information, hurt a predictive model.

- According to Occam's Razor rule, when in a dilemma, always go with a model that is simple—that is, it has a smaller number of features.

- The curse of dimensionality will kick in if we don't remove the correlated features, and it makes the machine learning model slower.

The list of features that we can reject during the model-building phase are as follows:

Rejected features = **X14, X17, X18, X20, X22, X23, X24, X26, X30, X31, X36, X38, X39, X40**

X42, X43, X44, X46, X48, X51, X52, X54, X56, X58, X61, X62, X63, X64, X7, X8, X9

As we can see from the preceding report, we have several features that are skewed, and some of the features have missing values as well. In the upcoming sections, we will be treating the missing values using different imputation methods.

PANDAS PROFILING REPORT FOR DATAFRAME 2

Now, let's have a look at the findings of the pandas profiling report for DataFrame 2. The following screenshot shows the HTML report for DataFrame 2:

Overview

Dataset info

Number of variables	65
Number of observations	10173
Missing cells	12157 (1.8%)
Duplicate rows	90 (0.9%)
Total size in memory	5.0 MiB
Average record size in memory	520.0 B

Variables types

Numeric	31
Categorical	0
Boolean	1
Date	0
URL	0
Text (Unique)	0
Rejected	33
Unsupported	0

Figure 4.9: HTML report for DataFrame 2

As shown in the preceding screenshot, the dataset has 65 features with 10,173 observations. The total number of missing values is 12,157.

Let's have a look at the skewness in the following screenshot:

Dataset has 90 (0.9%) duplicate rows   `Warning`
x_1 is highly skewed ($\gamma 1$ = -54.87572795)   `Skewed`
x_{10} is highly skewed ($\gamma 1$ = -65.96113425)   `Skewed`
x_{11} is highly skewed ($\gamma 1$ = 98.17201689)   `Skewed`
x_{12} is highly skewed ($\gamma 1$ = 59.72452287)   `Skewed`
x_{13} is highly skewed ($\gamma 1$ = 81.53270203)   `Skewed`
x_{14} is highly correlated with x_{11} (ρ = 0.9945728728)   `Rejected`
x_{16} is highly correlated with x_{12} (ρ = 0.9829626236)   `Rejected`
x_{17} is highly skewed ($\gamma 1$ = 56.77942088)   `Skewed`
x_{18} is highly correlated with x_{14} (ρ = 0.9956605702)   `Rejected`
x_{19} is highly correlated with x_{13} (ρ = 0.9999391131)   `Rejected`
x_2 is highly skewed ($\gamma 1$ = 67.33198497)   `Skewed`
x_{20} is highly skewed ($\gamma 1$ = 57.49019325)   `Skewed`
x_{20} has 494 (4.9%) zeros   `Zeros`
x_{21} is highly skewed ($\gamma 1$ = 71.12634035)   `Skewed`
x_{21} has 3164 (31.1%) missing values   `Missing`
x_{22} is highly correlated with x_{18} (ρ = 0.9907848864)   `Rejected`
x_{23} is highly correlated with x_{19} (ρ = 0.9998548525)   `Rejected`
x_{24} is highly correlated with x_{22} (ρ = 0.9897842345)   `Rejected`
x_{25} is highly correlated with x_{10} (ρ = 0.9891914684)   `Rejected`
x_{26} is highly skewed ($\gamma 1$ = 66.64906612)   `Skewed`
x_{27} is highly skewed ($\gamma 1$ = 82.51367014)   `Skewed`
x_{27} has 694 (6.8%) zeros   `Zeros`
x_{27} has 706 (6.9%) missing values   `Missing`
x_{28} is highly skewed ($\gamma 1$ = 50.34323013)   `Skewed`
x_{28} has 212 (2.1%) missing values   `Missing`
x_3 is highly correlated with x_{25} (ρ = 0.9861867189)   `Rejected`
x_{30} is highly skewed ($\gamma 1$ = 93.68093872)   `Skewed`

Figure 4.10: Skewness report for DataFrame 2

The skewness for DataFrame 2(continued) is as follows:

Figure 4.11: Skewness report for DataFrame 2 (continued)

The skewness for DataFrame 2(continued) is as follows:

X53 has 212 (2.1%) missing values	Missing
X54 is highly correlated with X53 (ρ = 0.9979360336)	Rejected
X55 is highly skewed (γ1 = 26.72438574)	Skewed
X56 is highly skewed (γ1 = -95.46610006)	Skewed
X57 is highly skewed (γ1 = -61.43873646)	Skewed
X57 has 102 (1.0%) zeros	Zeros
X58 is highly skewed (γ1 = 84.85409887)	Skewed
X59 is highly skewed (γ1 = 98.86067649)	Skewed
X59 has 4518 (44.4%) zeros	Zeros
X6 is highly correlated with X38 (ρ = 0.9805575145)	Rejected
X60 is highly skewed (γ1 = 45.98396136)	Skewed
X60 has 543 (5.3%) missing values	Missing
X61 is highly skewed (γ1 = 80.73350979)	Skewed
X62 is highly correlated with X44 (ρ = 0.9541577267)	Rejected
X63 is highly correlated with X48 (ρ = 0.9871164205)	Rejected
X64 is highly skewed (γ1 = 69.20225913)	Skewed
X64 has 212 (2.1%) missing values	Missing
X7 is highly correlated with X63 (ρ = 0.9833365706)	Rejected
X8 is highly correlated with X17 (ρ = 0.9999978802)	Rejected
X9 is highly correlated with X7 (ρ = 0.9822032554)	Rejected

Figure 4.12: Skewness report for DataFrame 2 (continued)

From the preceding report, we can see that 33 features have a high correlation.

The list of features that we can reject during the model-building phase are as follows:

Rejected variables= X14, X16, X18, X19, X22, X23, X24, X25, X3, X31, X33, X34, X35, X36, X38, X40, X42, X43, X44, X46, X47, X48, X49, X50, X51, X52, X54, X6, X62, X63, X7, X8,X9

> **NOTE**
>
> It is advised to perform analysis on the results generated from pandas profiling for the three remaining HTML files: `2output.html`, `3output.html`, and `4output.html`.

MISSING VALUE ANALYSIS

One of the major steps in data analysis is missing value analysis. The primary reason we need to perform missing value analysis is to know how much data is missing in a column and how we are going to handle it.

In general, missing values can be handled in two ways. The first way is to drop the rows with missing values, unless the percentage of missing values is high (for example, 40% missing values in a column) as this will lead to loss of information.

The second method is imputing missing values, which is where we fill in the missing values based on the imputation method employed. For example, in mean imputation, we use the mean value of the particular column to fill in the missing values.

The next step is missing value analysis.

In order to find out how many missing values are present in the DataFrame, we are going to introduce you to a package called **missingno**, which will help you visualize the count of missing values in the DataFrames.

EXERCISE 4.02: PERFORMING MISSING VALUE ANALYSIS FOR THE DATAFRAMES

In this section, we will be implementing a missing value analysis on the first DataFrame to find the missing values. This exercise is a continuation of *Exercise 4.01, Importing Data into DataFrames*. Follow these steps to complete this exercise:

1. Import the **missingno** package:

```
# To analyze the missing data
!pip install missingno
import missingno as msno
```

2. Find the missing values in the first DataFrame and visualize the missing values in a plot:

```
# Missing Values in the first DataFrame
msno.bar(dataframes[0],color='red',labels=True,\
        sort="ascending")
```

The output will be as follows:

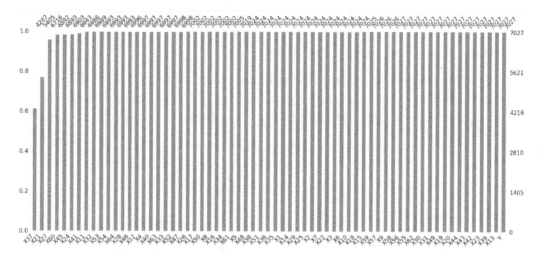

Figure 4.13: Bar plot for missing values in the first DataFrame

In the preceding plot, the *x* axis represents the features of a DataFrame, while the *y* axis represents the percentage of values present; for example, for feature **X37**, the value of the *y* axis is .6, which signifies that 60% of the data is present and the rest (40%) is missing.

> **NOTE**
>
> For the first DataFrame, we have a high number of missing values in the **X37**, **X21**, **X27**, and **X60** columns, with other columns exhibiting a lower percentage.

3. Perform the same analysis for the second DataFrame and visualize it in a bar plot, as we did previously:

```
# Missing Values in the second DataFrame
msno.bar(dataframes[1],color='blue',labels=True,\
        sort="ascending")
```

The output will be as follows:

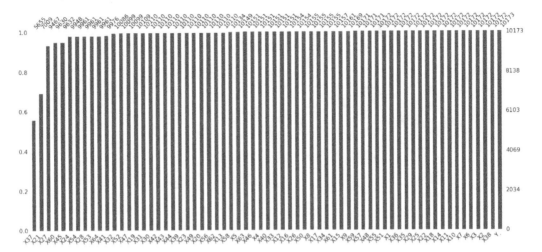

Figure 4.14: Bar plot for missing values in the second DataFrame

In the preceding plot, the *x* axis represents the features of a DataFrame, while the *y* axis represents the percentage of values present.

> **NOTE**
>
> For the second DataFrame, we have a high number of missing values in the **X37**, **X21**, **X27**, and **X60** columns, with the other columns exhibiting a lower number of missing values.

4. Perform the same analysis for the third DataFrame as well and visualize it in a bar plot, as we did previously:

```
# Missing Values in the third DataFrame
msno.bar(dataframes[2],labels=True,sort="ascending")
```

The output will be as follows:

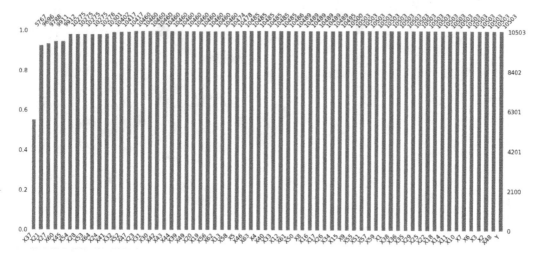

Figure 4.15: Bar plot for missing values in the third DataFrame

In the preceding plot, the *x* axis represents the features of a DataFrame, while the *y* axis represents the percentage of values present.

Similar to the previous DataFrames, this one exhibits almost the same level of missing values in the columns.

> **NOTE**
>
> It is advisable to perform this analysis on the rest of the DataFrames as well.

From this analysis, we are able to observe that dropping the missing values or eliminating the features might not be a good option due to data loss. In order to overcome this hurdle, we need to go with imputation.

> **NOTE**
>
> To access the source code for this specific section, please refer to https://packt.live/30Vju01.
>
> You can also run this example online at https://packt.live/3dauOHM. You must execute the entire Notebook in order to get the desired result.

Now, let's look at the imputation of missing values. In the next section, we will be focusing on two different types of imputations.

IMPUTATION OF MISSING VALUES

In this section, we will be looking at two different methods that we can use to handle the missing values:

- Mean imputation

- Iterative imputation

Let's look at each of these methods in detail.

MEAN IMPUTATION

In mean imputation, the missing values are filled with the mean of each column where the missing values are located. We will be performing mean imputation on the DataFrames in the next exercise.

EXERCISE 4.03: PERFORMING MEAN IMPUTATION ON THE DATAFRAMES

In this exercise, you will perform mean imputation on the first DataFrame. This exercise is a continuation of *Exercise 4.02, Performing Missing Value Analysis for the DataFrames*. Follow these steps to complete this exercise:

1. Import **Imputer** from **sklearn.preprocessing** to perform mean imputation to fill in the missing values:

```
from sklearn.impute import SimpleImputer
imputer = SimpleImputer(missing_values=np.nan, \
                        strategy='mean')
```

2. Fit the imputer on the first DataFrame, which will perform mean imputation on the columns with missing values:

```
mean_imputed_df1 = pd.DataFrame(imputer.fit_transform\
                                (dataframes[0]),\
                                columns=dataframes[0].columns)
```

3. Once the imputation has been performed, check for the missing values in the DataFrame with the following code snippet:

```
msno.bar(mean_imputed_df1,color='red',labels=True,\
        sort="ascending")
```

The output will be as follows:

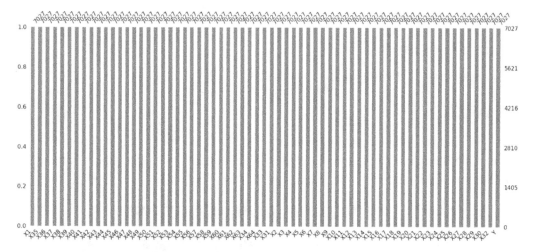

Figure 4.16: Bar plot for missing values in the dataframe[0]

In the preceding plot, the *x* axis represents the features of a DataFrame, while the *y* axis represents the percentage of values present.

From the preceding plot, we can see that the missing values have been filled.

4. Similarly, perform mean imputation on the second DataFrame:

```
# Imputation for the second DataFrame

mean_imputed_df2 = pd.DataFrame(imputer.fit_transform\
                                (dataframes[1]),\
                                columns=dataframes[1].columns)

#check for missing values
msno.bar(mean_imputed_df2,color='red',labels=True, \
        sort="ascending")
```

The output will be as follows:

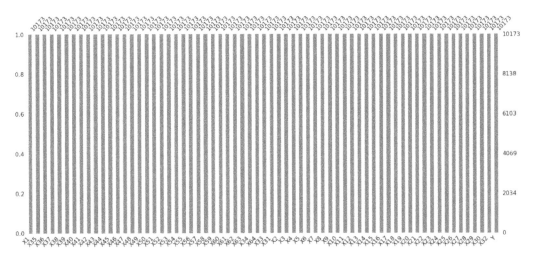

Figure 4.17: Bar plot for missing values in the dataframe[1]

In the preceding plot, the *x* axis represents the features of a DataFrame, while the *y* axis represents the percentage of values present.

From the preceding plot, we can see that the missing values have been filled.

5. Similarly, perform mean imputation on the third DataFrame:

```
# Imputation for the third  DataFrame

mean_imputed_df3 = pd.DataFrame(imputer.fit_transform\
                                (dataframes[2]),\
                                columns=dataframes[2].columns)


#checking missing values
msno.bar(mean_imputed_df3,color='red',labels=True, \
        sort="ascending")
```

The output will be as follows:

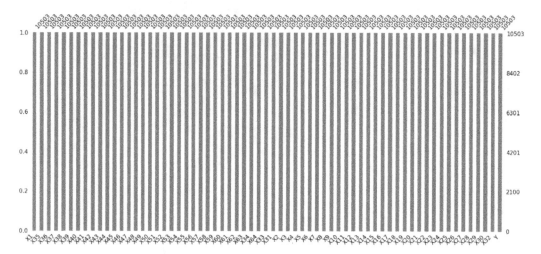

Figure 4.18: Bar plot for missing values in the dataframe[2]

In the preceding plot, the *x* axis represents the features of a DataFrame, while the *y* axis represents the percentage of values present.

Thus, we can conclude that the missing values in the DataFrames have been filled. Imputing the missing values in a DataFrame is a prerequisite to performing lasso regularization, with which we can identify the important features that are responsible for bankruptcy. (Lasso regularization will be covered in more detail later in this chapter.)

> **NOTE**
>
> To access the source code for this specific section, please refer to https://packt.live/3hAMMXy.
>
> You can also run this example online at https://packt.live/30N9HJ4. You must execute the entire Notebook in order to get the desired result.

It is advised to perform imputation on **dataframe[3]** and **dataframe[4]** before moving on:

```
#Imputation for the fourth Dataframe
mean_imputed_df4=pd.DataFrame(imputer.fit_transform\
                            (dataframes[3]), \
                            columns=dataframes[0].columns)
# Imputation for the fifth Dataframe
mean_imputed_df5=pd.DataFrame(imputer.fit_transform\
                            (dataframes[4]), \
                            columns=dataframes[1].columns)
```

ITERATIVE IMPUTATION

An iterative imputer models every feature with a missing value as a function of the other features and uses that estimate to impute the missing values. This is done in a round-robin function where the feature with missing values is defined as a target variable and the other features are considered as being independent. A regressor is then fit on *(X, y)* for a known value of *y* and is used to predict the missing values of *y*.

Let's perform iterative imputation on our DataFrames in the following exercise.

EXERCISE 4.04: PERFORMING ITERATIVE IMPUTATION ON THE DATAFRAME

In this exercise, you will implement iterative imputation on the DataFrames to fill in the missing values. This exercise is a continuation of *Exercise 4.03, Performing Mean Imputation on the DataFrames*. Follow these steps to complete this exercise:

1. Import **IterativeImputer** from **sklearn.impute** and **sklearn. experimental** from **enable_iterative_imputer** to fill in the missing values:

    ```
    from sklearn.experimental import enable_iterative_imputer
    from sklearn.impute import IterativeImputer
    ```

2. Initialize the iterative imputer:

    ```
    imputer = IterativeImputer()
    ```

3. Create a DataFrame called **`iterative_imputed_df1`** for **`dataframe[0]`** where the missing values are filled in with the help of the iterative imputer:

```
iterative_imputed_df1 = pd.DataFrame(imputer.fit_transform\
                                    (dataframes[0]), \
                                    columns=dataframes[0].columns)
```

4. Once the imputation has been performed, check for missing values in the DataFrame:

```
msno.bar(iterative_imputed_df1,color='red',labels=True, \
        sort="ascending")
```

The output will be as follows:

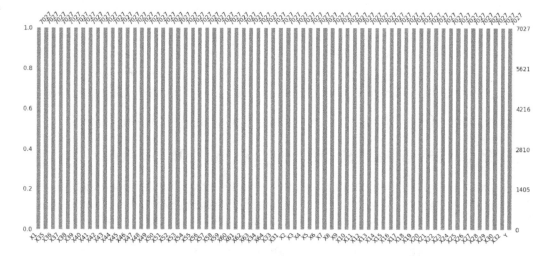

Figure 4.19: Bar plot for missing values in the dataframe[0]

In the preceding plot, the *x* axis represents the features of a DataFrame, while the *y* axis represents the percentage of values present. From this, you can see that the missing values have been filled.

5. Perform iterative imputation for the second DataFrame, **dataframe[1]**:

```
"""
Creating a dataframe iterative_imputed_df2 for dataframe[1] where
missing values are filled with the help of iterative imputer
"""

iterative_imputed_df2 = pd.DataFrame(imputer.fit_transform\
                                     (dataframes[1]), \
                                     columns=dataframes[1].columns)
#check for the missing values in the dataframe.
msno.bar(iterative_imputed_df2,color='red',labels=True, \
         sort="ascending")
```

The output will be as follows:

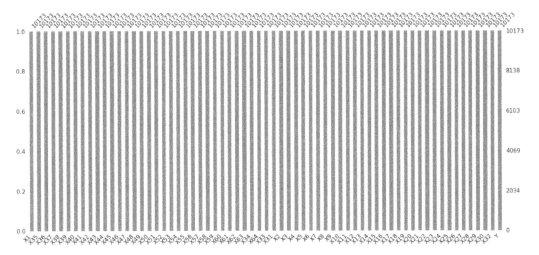

Figure 4.20: Bar plot for missing values in dataframe[1]

In the preceding plot, the x axis represents the features of a DataFrame, while the y axis represents the percentage of values present. From this, we can see that the missing values have been filled.

6. Similarly, perform iterative imputation for the third DataFrame,
    dataframe[2]:

```
"""
Creating a dataframe iterative_imputed_df3 for dataframe[2] where
missing values are filled with the help of iterative imputer
"""

iterative_imputed_df3 = pd.DataFrame(imputer.fit_transform\
                                    (dataframes[2]), \
                        columns=dataframes[2].columns)
#check for the missing values in the dataframe.
msno.bar(iterative_imputed_df3,color='red',labels=True, \
        sort="ascending")
```

The output will be as follows:

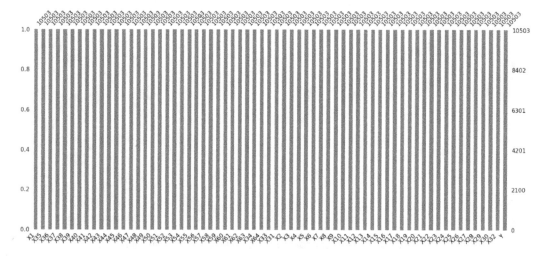

Figure 4.21: Bar plot for missing values in dataframe[2]

In the preceding plot, the *x* axis represents the features of a DataFrame, while the *y* axis represents the percentage of values present.

Finally, perform imputation on **dataframe[3]** and **dataframe[4]** before moving on:

```
iterative_imputed_df4 = pd.DataFrame(imputer.fit_transform\
                                    (dataframes[3]), \
                                    columns=dataframes[0].columns)
iterative_imputed_df5 = pd.DataFrame(imputer.fit_transform\
                                    (dataframes[4]), \
                                    columns=dataframes[1].columns)
```

> **NOTE**
>
> To access the source code for this specific section, please refer to https://packt.live/2N8mu0A.
>
> You can also run this example online at https://packt.live/3fuHN8N. You must execute the entire Notebook in order to get the desired result.

We have now performed imputation on the DataFrames and can conclude that the missing values have been filled as shown in the preceding bar plots.

SPLITTING THE FEATURES

In the previous section, we saw how the missing values are filled with different types of imputation.

In this section, we will be splitting the dependent variables in the DataFrame into *y* and the independent variables into *X*. The dependent variables are an outcome of a process. In our case, this process is whether a company is bankrupt or not. Independent variables (also called features) are the input to our process, which in this case is the rest of the variables.

Splitting the features acts as a precursor to our next step, where we select the most important *X* variables that determine the dependent variable.

We will need to split the features for mean-imputed DataFrames, as shown in the following code:

```
#First DataFrame
X0=mean_imputed_df1.drop('Y',axis=1)
y0=mean_imputed_df1.Y

#Second DataFrame
X1=mean_imputed_df2.drop('Y',axis=1)
y1=mean_imputed_df2.Y

#Third DataFrame
X2=mean_imputed_df3.drop('Y',axis=1)
y2=mean_imputed_df3.Y

X6=mean_imputed_df4.drop('Y',axis=1)
y6=mean_imputed_df4.Y
X7=mean_imputed_df5.drop('Y',axis=1)
y7=mean_imputed_df5.Y
```

Split the features for the fourth and fifth mean-imputed DataFrames as well, as shown in the preceding code.

Next, we need to split the features for iterative-imputed DataFrames, as shown in the following code snippet:

```
#First DataFrame
X3=iterative_imputed_df1.drop('Y',axis=1)
y3=iterative_imputed_df1.Y

#Second DataFrame
X4=iterative_imputed_df2.drop('Y',axis=1)
y4=iterative_imputed_df2.Y

#Third DataFrame
X5=iterative_imputed_df3.drop('Y',axis=1)
y5=iterative_imputed_df3.Y
```

```
X8=iterative_imputed_df4.drop('Y',axis=1)
y8=iterative_imputed_df4.Y

X9=iterative_imputed_df5.drop('Y',axis=1)
y9=iterative_imputed_df5.Y
```

Split the features for the fourth and fifth iterative-imputed DataFrames as well.

Now that we have split the features for both mean and iterative-imputed DataFrames, we will move on to feature selection.

FEATURE SELECTION WITH LASSO

Feature selection is one of the most important steps to be performed before building any kind of machine learning model. In a dataset, not all the columns are going to have an impact on the dependent variable. If we include all the irrelevant features for model building, we'll end up building a model with bad performance. This gives rise to the need to perform feature selection. In this section, we will be performing feature selection using the **lasso** method.

Lasso regularization is a method of feature selection where the coefficients of irrelevant features are set to zero. By doing so, we remove the features that are insignificant and only the remaining significant features are included for further analysis.

Let's perform lasso regularization for our mean- and iterative-imputed DataFrames.

LASSO REGULARIZATION FOR MEAN-IMPUTED DATAFRAMES

Let's perform lasso regularization for the mean-imputed DataFrame 1.

As the first step, import **Lasso** from **sklearn.linear_model** and **SelectFromModel** from **sklearn.feature_selection**:

```
from sklearn.linear_model import Lasso
from sklearn.feature_selection import SelectFromModel
```

We will be storing the independent feature names in a list called **features_names**:

```
features_names=X0.columns.tolist()
```

Let's initialize the **lasso** method:

```
lasso = Lasso(alpha=0.01 ,positive=True)
```

Fit **Lasso** for **X0** and **y0**:

```
lasso.fit(X0,y0)
```

Get the feature names after fitting **lasso**:

```
coef_list=sorted(zip(map(lambda x: round(x,4), \
                    lasso.coef_.reshape(-1)), \
                    features_names),reverse=True)
coef_list [0:5]
```

The output will be as follows:

```
[(0.0016, 'X2'), (0.0003, 'X34'), (0.0001, 'X51'),
 (0.0, 'X9'), (0.0, 'X8')]
```

By performing lasso regularization, we end up with only 3 significant features out of 64. The columns that are significant are as follows:

- **X2**: Total liabilities/total assets

- **X34**: Operating expenses/total liabilities

- **X51**: Short-term liabilities/total assets

> **NOTE**
>
> Columns **X9** and **X8** have zero significance.

Similarly, we will perform lasso regularization for our mean-imputed DataFrame 2:

```
"""
We are storing the independent feature names to a list called
Features_names
"""
features_names=X1.columns.tolist()
#We are initializing lasso
```

```
lasso = Lasso(alpha=0.01 ,positive=True)
#We are fitting Lasso for X1 and y1

lasso.fit(X1,y1)
#We are getting the feature names after fitting Lasso

coef_list=sorted(zip(map(lambda x: round(x,4), \
                 lasso.coef_.reshape(-1)), \
                 features_names),reverse=True)
coef_list [0:5]
```

The output will be as follows:

```
[(0.0009, 'X2'), (0.0002, 'X49'), (0.0, 'X9'),
 (0.0, 'X8'), (0.0, 'X7')]
```

By performing lasso regularization, we end up with only 2 significant features out of 64. The columns that are significant are as follows:

- **X2**: Total liabilities/total assets

- **X49**: EBITDA (profit on operating activities – depreciation)/sales

> **NOTE**
>
> Columns **X9**, **X8**, and **X7** have zero significance.

Similarly, we will perform lasso regularization for mean-imputed DataFrame 3:

```
"""
We are storing the independent feature names to a list called
Features_names
"""
features_names=X2.columns.tolist()
#We are initializing lasso

lasso = Lasso(alpha=0.01 ,positive=True)
#We are fitting Lasso for X2 and y2
```

```
lasso.fit(X2,y2)
#We are getting the feature names after fitting Lasso

coef_list=sorted(zip(map(lambda x: round(x,4), \
                    lasso.coef_.reshape(-1)), \
                    features_names),reverse=True)
coef_list [0:5]
```

The output will be as follows:

```
[(0.0009, 'X2'), (0.0001, 'X33'), (0.0, 'X9'),
 (0.0, 'X8'), (0.0, 'X7')]
```

By performing lasso regularization, we end up with only 2 significant features out of 64. The columns that are significant are as follows:

- **X2**: Total liabilities/total assets

- **X33**: Operating expenses/short-term liabilities

> **NOTE**
>
> Columns **X9**, **X8**, and **X7** have zero significance.

LASSO REGULARIZATION FOR ITERATIVE-IMPUTED DATAFRAMES

We will now perform lasso regularization for iterative-imputed DataFrame 1.

First, store the independent feature names in a list called **features_names**:

```
features_names=X3.columns.tolist()
```

Next, initialize the **lasso** method:

```
lasso = Lasso(alpha=0.01 ,positive=True)
```

Fit the lasso for **X3** and **y3**:

```
lasso.fit(X3,y3)
```

Get the feature names after fitting **lasso**:

```
coef_list=sorted(zip(map(lambda x: round(x,4), \
                    lasso.coef_.reshape(-1)), \
                    features_names),reverse=True)
coef_list [0:5]
```

The output will be as follows:

```
[(0.0018, 'X2'),
 (0.0002, 'X50'),
 (0.0002, 'X34'),
 (0.0001, 'X40'),
 (0.0, 'X9')]
```

By performing lasso regularization, we end up with only 4 significant features out of 64. The columns that are significant are as follows:

- **X2**: Total liabilities/total assets

- **X50**: Current assets/total liabilities

- **X34**: Operating expenses/total liabilities

- **X40**: (current assets – inventory – receivables)/short-term liabilities

> **NOTE**
>
> Column **X9** has zero significance.

Similarly, perform lasso regularization for iterative-imputed DataFrame 2:

```
"""
We are storing the independent feature names to a list called
Features_names
"""

features_names=X4.columns.tolist()
#We are initializing lasso
```

```
lasso = Lasso(alpha=0.01 ,positive=True)
#We are fitting Lasso for X4 and y4


lasso.fit(X4,y4)
#We are getting the feature names after fitting Lasso


coef_list=sorted(zip(map(lambda x: round(x,4), \
                    lasso.coef_.reshape(-1)), \
                    features_names),reverse=True)
coef_list [0:5]
```

The output will be as follows:

```
[(0.0011, 'X2'), (0.0002, 'X49'), (0.0, 'X9'),
 (0.0, 'X8'), (0.0, 'X7')]
```

By performing lasso regularization, we end up with only 2 significant features out of 64. The columns that are significant are as follows:

- **X2**: Total liabilities/total assets

- **X49**: EBITDA (profit on operating activities – depreciation)/sales

> **NOTE**
>
> Columns X9, X8, and X7 have zero significance.

Perform lasso regularization for iterative-imputed DataFrame 3 as well:

```
"""
We are storing the independent feature names to a list called
Features_names
"""
features_names=X5.columns.tolist()
#We are initializing lasso


lasso = Lasso(alpha=0.01 ,positive=True)
#We are fitting Lasso for X5 and y5
```

```
lasso.fit(X5,y5)
#We are getting the feature names after fitting Lasso

coef_list=sorted(zip(map(lambda x: round(x,4), \
                    lasso.coef_.reshape(-1)), \
                    features_names),reverse=True)
coef_list [0:5]
```

The output will be as follows:

```
[(0.0008, 'X2'), (0.0001, 'X33'), (0.0, 'X9'),
 (0.0, 'X8'), (0.0, 'X7')]
```

By performing lasso regularization, we end up with only 2 significant features out of 64. The columns that are significant are as follows:

- **X2**: Total liabilities/total assets

- **X33**: Operating expenses/short-term liabilities

> **NOTE**
>
> Columns **X9**, **X8**, and **X7** have zero significance.

ACTIVITY 4.01: FEATURE SELECTION WITH LASSO

In this activity, you will select the features of importance by using the lasso regularization method for the mean-imputed DataFrame **df4**, mean-imputed DataFrame **df5**, iterative-imputed DataFrame **df4**, and iterative-imputed DataFrame **df5**.

Perform the following steps to complete this activity:

1. Import **Lasso** from the **sklearn.linear_model** package.

2. Fit the independent and dependent variables with lasso regularization for the **mean_imputed_df4** DataFrame.

3. Print the coefficients of lasso regularization.

    The output will be as follows:

    ```
    [(0.0009, 'X21'), (0.0002, 'X2'), (0.0001, 'X42'),
     (0.0, 'X9'), (0.0, 'X8')]
    ```

4. Get the significant features and write down the variable's description from the data dictionary.

5. Perform the preceding steps for the **mean_imputed_df5** DataFrame as well.

    The output will be as follows:

    ```
    [(0.0216, 'X51'),
     (0.0015, 'X2'),
     (0.001, 'X9'),
     (0.001, 'X36'),
     (0.0003, 'X59'),
     (0.0003, 'X52'),
     (0.0001, 'X61'),
     (0.0001, 'X31'),
     (0.0001, 'X30'),
     (0.0001, 'X20')]
    ```

6. Perform the same steps for **iterative_imputed_df4**.

    The output will be as follows:

    ```
    [(0.0009, 'X21'), (0.0002, 'X2'), (0.0001, 'X42'),
     (0.0, 'X9'), (0.0, 'X8')]
    ```

7. Similarly, perform the same steps for **iterative_imputed_df5**.

The output will be as follows:

```
[(0.0213, 'X51'),
 (0.0015, 'X2'),
 (0.0012, 'X9'),
 (0.0009, 'X36'),
 (0.0003, 'X59'),
 (0.0003, 'X52'),
 (0.0001, 'X61'),
 (0.0001, 'X31'),
 (0.0001, 'X30'),
 (0.0001, 'X20')]
```

From this analysis, we can conclude that the columns that are significant are as follows:

X51: Short-term liabilities/total assets

X2: Total liabilities/total assets

X9: Sales/total assets

X36: Total sales/total assets

X59: Long-term liabilities/equity

X52: (short-term liabilities * 365)/cost of products sold)

X61: Sales/receivables

X31: (gross profit + interest)/sales

X30: (total liabilities - cash)/sales

X20: (inventory * 365)/sales

> **NOTE**
>
> The solution to the activity can be found on page 503.

Owing to these factors, we can now determine the actual reasons for bankruptcy, and the necessary action plan can be now be formulated.

SUMMARY

In this chapter, we learned how to import an ARFF file into a pandas DataFrame. Pandas profiling was performed on the DataFrame to get the correlated features. We detected the missing values using the **missingno** package and performed imputation using the mean and iterative imputation methods.

In order to find the important features that contribute to bankruptcy, we performed lasso regularization. With lasso regularization, we found which features are responsible for bankruptcy. Even though we get the different important features across all five DataFrames, one of the features occurs across all five DataFrames, which is nothing but the ratio of total liabilities to total assets. This particular ratio has a very high significance in leading to bankruptcy.

However, our analysis is not fully complete since we only found the factors that affect bankruptcy, but not the direction (whether bankruptcy may occur when a particular ratio increases or decreases).

To get a complete view of these factors, we need to build a classification model to expand our analysis. This more advanced process, however, is beyond the scope of this book.

In the next chapter, we will discuss various factors that affect a purchaser's decisions while shopping in an online store using clustering techniques.

5

ANALYZING THE ONLINE SHOPPER'S PURCHASING INTENTION

OVERVIEW

By the end of this chapter, you will be able to perform univariate and bivariate analysis on a given dataset. You will also be able to implement clustering and make recommendations based on the predictions. These recommendations will help you gain actionable insights and make effective decisions.

INTRODUCTION

In the previous chapter, we practiced tackling company bankruptcy using various techniques such as pandas profiling for exploratory data analytics and lasso regularization to find feature importance. In this chapter, we will analyze online shoppers' purchasing intentions.

Consumer shopping on the internet is growing year by year. However, the conversion rates have remained more or less the same. For example, most of us browse through e-commerce websites such as Amazon, perhaps adding items to a wish list or even an online shopping cart, only to end up buying nothing.

From this common truth comes the need for tools and solutions that can customize promotions and advertisements for online shoppers and improve this conversion. In this chapter, we will be analyzing various factors that affect a purchaser's decision.

NOTE

This chapter will be using data from the Online Shoppers Purchasing Intention Dataset, which can be obtained from the UCI repository. You can find the original dataset here: https://archive.ics.uci.edu/ml/datasets/Online+Shoppers+Purchasing+Intention+Dataset.

You can also find it stored in our GitHub at: https://packt.live/3hzHWcW.

For further reading on this topic, you can refer to the following article: Sakar, C.O., Polat, S.O., Katircioglu, M. et al. *Neural Comput & Applic* (2018).

DATA DICTIONARY

The following table shows and describes the various numerical features of the dataset we are going to use:

Feature Name	Description
Administrative	Pages related to account management, such as a profile page.
Administrative Duration	The amount of time spent on an administrative page in seconds.
Informational	Pages related to information about the website, such as their address or contact information.
Informational Duration	The amount of time spent on an information page in seconds.
Product Related	Pages related to products on a website.
Product Related Duration	The amount of time spent on a product-related page in seconds.
Bounce Rate	Refers to the percentage of visitors who access the site from a page and then leave the page without creating any requests for the server during the session.
Exit Rate	This is a metric that presents the number of exits made from that particular page to leave the site.
Page Value	Refers to the average value for a web page that a user visited before completing an e-commerce transaction.
Special Day	Refers to the closeness of the site visiting time to a specific day (for example, Childrens' Day).

Figure 5.1: Description of the numerical features

NOTE

The information presented in the preceding table has been picked from the UCI data description.

The following table shows and describes the various categorical features of the dataset we are going to use:

Feature Name	Description
Operating Systems	Type of operating system used, such as Windows or Mac OS.
Browser	Type of browser used, such as Chrome, Internet Explorer, or Safari.
Region	Geographic region of the visitor.
Traffic Type	Source of the traffic, such as direct or through a different website.
Visitor Type	Type of visitor – New visitor, Returning visitor, or Other.
Weekend	Whether or not the day is a weekend – a Boolean value.
Month	Month of the visit.
Revenue	Whether the session culminated in a purchase.

Figure 5.2: Description of the categorical features

IMPORTING THE DATA

To begin with the actual data analysis, we need to import a few necessary packages. As one of these packages requires installation, the first step is to run the following in Anaconda Prompt:

```
conda install -c conda-forge imbalanced-learn
```

You can then proceed with the imports in your Jupyter Notebook:

```
import pandas as pd
import numpy as np
import seaborn as sns
import matplotlib.pyplot as plt
from sklearn.cluster import KMeans
from sklearn import preprocessing
from sklearn.preprocessing import RobustScaler
from sklearn.preprocessing import StandardScaler
from sklearn.preprocessing import Normalizer
from imblearn.over_sampling import SMOTE
from sklearn.model_selection import train_test_split
import warnings
warnings.filterwarnings("ignore")
```

Next, import the dataset into the work environment:

```
df= pd.read_csv("https://raw.githubusercontent.com/"\
               "PacktWorkshops/"\
               "The-Data-Analysis-Workshop/master/"\
               "Chapter05/Datasets/online_shoppers_intention.csv")
df.head()
```

Part of the output is shown below:

	Administrative	Administrative_Duration	Informational	Informational_Duration	ProductRelated	ProductRelated_Duration
0	0	0.0	0	0.0	1	0.000000
1	0	0.0	0	0.0	2	64.000000
2	0	0.0	0	0.0	1	0.000000
3	0	0.0	0	0.0	2	2.666667
4	0	0.0	0	0.0	10	627.500000

Figure 5.3: Top five rows of the DataFrame

Now, we'll check the metadata of the DataFrame:

```
# Getting Meta Data Information about the DataFrame
df.info()
```

The output will be similar to the image shown below:

```
<class 'pandas.core.frame.DataFrame'>
RangeIndex: 12330 entries, 0 to 12329
Data columns (total 18 columns):
Administrative           12330 non-null int64
Administrative_Duration  12330 non-null float64
Informational            12330 non-null int64
Informational_Duration   12330 non-null float64
ProductRelated           12330 non-null int64
ProductRelated_Duration  12330 non-null float64
BounceRates              12330 non-null float64
ExitRates                12330 non-null float64
PageValues               12330 non-null float64
SpecialDay               12330 non-null float64
Month                    12330 non-null object
OperatingSystems         12330 non-null int64
Browser                  12330 non-null int64
Region                   12330 non-null int64
TrafficType              12330 non-null int64
VisitorType              12330 non-null object
Weekend                  12330 non-null bool
Revenue                  12330 non-null bool
dtypes: bool(2), float64(7), int64(7), object(2)
memory usage: 1.5+ MB
```

Figure 5.4: Metadata of the DataFrame

Next, we'll check for null values:

```
# Checking for Null Values
df.isnull().sum()
```

The output will be as follows:

```
Administrative              0
Administrative_Duration     0
Informational               0
Informational_Duration      0
ProductRelated              0
ProductRelated_Duration     0
BounceRates                 0
ExitRates                   0
PageValues                  0
SpecialDay                  0
Month                       0
OperatingSystems            0
Browser                     0
Region                      0
TrafficType                 0
VisitorType                 0
Weekend                     0
Revenue                     0
dtype: int64
```

Figure 5.5: Checking null values

There is no null value in the DataFrame, so we don't have to do any kind of imputation to fill in the null values.

Next, we will look at exploratory data analysis.

EXPLORATORY DATA ANALYSIS

In your typical data science project, the majority of your time will be spent investigating the data to find hidden patterns and outliers, often by plotting them in a visualization. This process is called **Exploratory Data Analysis (EDA)** and, through summary statistics, allows you to uncover underlying data structures and test your hypotheses.

We can split exploratory data analytics into three parts:

- Univariate analysis

- Bivariate analysis

- Linear relationships

Let's look at each of these analysis techniques in detail.

UNIVARIATE ANALYSIS

Univariate analysis is the simplest form of analysis and is where we analyze each feature (column of a DataFrame) and try to uncover the pattern or distribution of the data. In this section, we will be looking at the following features:

- Revenue column

- Visitor type

- Traffic type

- Region

- Weekend-wise distribution

- Browser and operating system

- Administrative page

- Information page

- Special day

Now, let's analyze each of these features in detail.

BASELINE CONVERSION RATE FROM THE REVENUE COLUMN

This feature simply refers to how many of the online shopping sessions ended in a purchase.

Let's look at the countplot of the Revenue column. We will be using the seaborn package to visualize the countplot:

```
sns.countplot(df['Revenue'])
plt.title('Baseline Revenue conversion', fontsize = 20)
plt.show()
```

The output will be as follows:

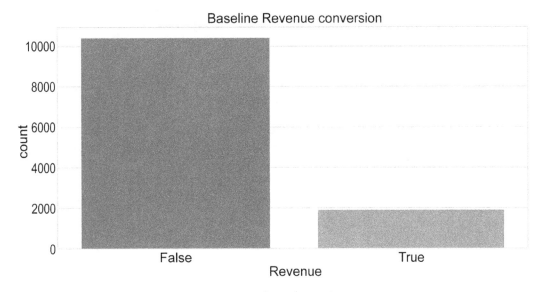

Figure 5.6: Baseline conversion rate

From the preceding graph, we can see that **False** has a higher number count than **True**. In order to get the exact value, consider the value counts of each subcategory:

```
print(df['Revenue'].value_counts())
print()
print(df['Revenue'].value_counts(normalize=True))
```

The output will be as follows:

```
False     10422
True       1908
Name: Revenue, dtype: int64

False     0.845255
True      0.154745
Name: Revenue, dtype: float64
```

Figure 5.7: Value count of the Revenue column

As you can see from the preceding data, a total of 1,908 customers ended up making a purchase, while 10,422 customers did not.

The baseline conversion rate of online visitors versus overall visitors is a ratio between the total number of online sessions that led to a purchase divided by the total number of sessions. This is calculated as follows:

```
1908/12330 * 100 = 15.47%
```

The overall number of visitors is 12,330, as shown by *Figure 5.4*. Thus, the conversion rate is 15.47%.

VISITOR-WISE DISTRIBUTION

Now, let's look at the distribution of visitors to the website. We want to determine which visitor type is most frequent—whether this is new visitors, returning visitors, or any other category.

First, we draw a countplot using seaborn (imported as **sns**):

```
sns.countplot(df['VisitorType'])
plt.title('Visitor Type wise Distribution', fontsize = 20)
plt.show()
```

The output will be as follows:

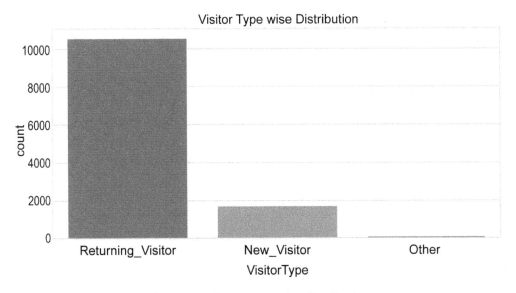

Figure 5.8: Visitor type-wise distribution

Next, we calculate the exact number of visitors belonging to each type:

```
#calculation exact number of each visitor type
print(df['VisitorType'].value_counts())
print()
print(df['VisitorType'].value_counts(normalize=True))
```

The output will be as follows:

```
Returning_Visitor      10551
New_Visitor             1694
Other                     85
Name: VisitorType, dtype: int64

Returning_Visitor      0.855718
New_Visitor            0.137388
Other                  0.006894
Name: VisitorType, dtype: float64
```

Figure 5.9: Visitor type count

From the preceding information, we can see that the number of returning customers is higher than that of new visitors. This is good news as it means we have been successful in attracting customers back to our website.

Now, let's proceed with further analysis.

TRAFFIC-WISE DISTRIBUTION

Now, let's consider the distribution of traffic. We want to find out how the visitors visit our page to determine what amount of site traffic is accounted for by direct visitors (meaning they enter the URL into the browser) and how much is generated through other mediums, such as blogs or advertisements.

Let's plot a countplot for the traffic type:

```
sns.countplot(df['TrafficType'])
plt.title('Traffic Type wise Distribution', fontsize = 20)
plt.show()
```

The output will be as follows:

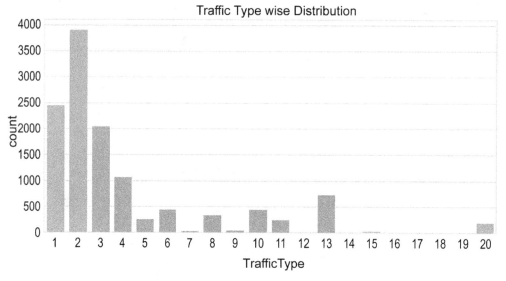

Figure 5.10: Traffic type-wise distribution

From the preceding graph, we can see that traffic type **2** has the highest count. To get the exact value, normalize the count to get the percentage value for each source:

```
print(df['TrafficType'].value_counts(normalize=True))
```

The output will be as follows:

```
2     0.317356
1     0.198783
3     0.166423
4     0.086699
13    0.059854
10    0.036496
6     0.036010
8     0.027818
5     0.021087
11    0.020032
20    0.016058
9     0.003406
7     0.003244
15    0.003082
19    0.001379
14    0.001054
18    0.000811
16    0.000243
12    0.000081
17    0.000081
Name: TrafficType, dtype: float64
```

Figure 5.11: Traffic type-wise count

From the preceding information, we can see that sources 2, 1, 3, and 4 account for the majority of our web traffic.

In the following section, we will check the weekend distribution of the customer.

NOTE

All the exercises/activities in this chapter are to be performed one after the other in a single Jupyter notebook.

EXERCISE 5.01: ANALYZING THE DISTRIBUTION OF CUSTOMERS SESSION ON THE WEBSITE

In this exercise, you will consider the distribution of customers over days of the week to determine whether customers are more active on weekends or weekdays.

The following steps will help you to complete this exercise:

1. Plot a countplot using seaborn for the **weekend** column of the DataFrame:

```
sns.countplot(df['Weekend'])
plt.title('Weekend Session Distribution', fontsize = 20)
plt.show()
```

The output will be as follows:

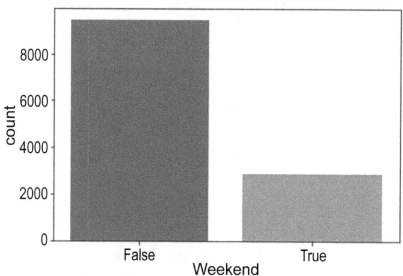

Figure 5.12: Weekend session distribution

2. Now, look at the count of each subcategory in the **weekend** column:

```
print(df['Weekend'].value_counts())
print()
print(df['Weekend'].value_counts(normalize=True))
```

The output should tell you which subcategory has the highest count, as shown in the following screenshot:

```
False    9462
True     2868
Name: Weekend, dtype: int64


False    0.767397
True     0.232603
Name: Weekend, dtype: float64
```

> **NOTE**
>
> To access the source code for this specific section, please refer to https://packt.live/2zBF3XY.
>
> You can also run this example online at https://packt.live/3e4uuvA. You must execute the entire Notebook in order to get the desired result.

From the count of the **False** subcategory, we can see that more visitors visit during weekdays than weekend days.

REGION-WISE DISTRIBUTION

In this section, we look at the region-wise distribution of the sessions. The main motive behind this analysis is to find out which region has the highest number of visitors visiting our website.

Let's plot the countplot for the **Region** column:

```
sns.countplot(df['Region'])
plt.title('Region wise Distribution', fontsize = 20)
plt.show()
```

The output will be as follows:

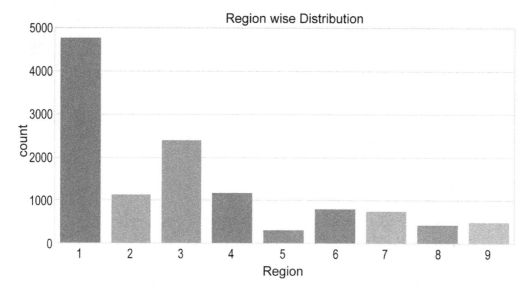

Figure 5.13: Region-wise distribution of customers

From the preceding graph, the numbers 1, 2, and so on represent the different regions that the data is sourced from. We can see that **Region 1** has the highest number of visitors visiting our website. Let's print the value count of each region and normalize the value to find the percentage contribution of each:

```
print(df['Region'].value_counts())
print()
print(df['Region'].value_counts(normalize=True))
```

The output will be as follows:

```
1       4780
3       2403
4       1182
2       1136
6        805
7        761
9        511
8        434
5        318
Name: Region, dtype: int64

1       0.387672
3       0.194891
4       0.095864
2       0.092133
6       0.065288
7       0.061719
9       0.041444
8       0.035199
5       0.025791
Name: Region, dtype: float64
```

Figure 5.14: Count of customers, region-wise

From the preceding data, we can see that regions **1** and **3** account for 50% of online sessions; thus, we can infer that regions **1** and **3** are where most potential consumers reside. With this information, we can target our marketing campaigns better.

In the following exercise, we will plot the distribution of browsers and operating systems preferred by the users.

EXERCISE 5.02: ANALYZING THE BROWSER AND OS DISTRIBUTION OF CUSTOMERS

In this exercise, we will be checking the distribution of browsers and operating systems used by customers to determine which type of browser and OS is used by our visitors. This information will allow us to configure our website so that we can make it more responsive and user-friendly.

Perform the following steps to complete this exercise:

1. Draw a countplot using the Browser column of the DataFrame:

```
sns.countplot(df['Browser'])
plt.title('Browser wise session Distribution', fontsize = 20)
plt.show()
```

2. Use the resulting plot to determine which browser type is the most popular among visitors:

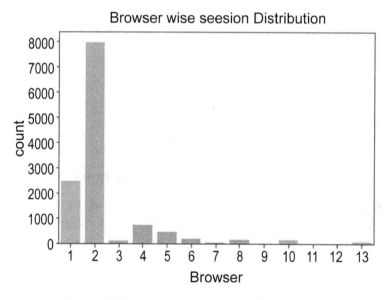

Figure 5.15: Browser-wise session distribution

From the preceding graph, we can see that browser type **2** contributes the most to the website traffic.

3. Determine the count of each subcategory with the help of the `.value_counts()` function:

```
print(df['Browser'].value_counts())
print()
print(df['Browser'].value_counts(normalize=True))
```

The output of the preceding function is as follows:

```
2      7961
1      2462
4       736
5       467
6       174
10      163
8       135
3       105
13       61
7        49
12       10
11        6
9         1
Name: Browser, dtype: int64

2      0.645661
1      0.199676
4      0.059692
5      0.037875
6      0.014112
10     0.013220
8      0.010949
3      0.008516
13     0.004947
7      0.003974
12     0.000811
11     0.000487
9      0.000081
Name: Browser, dtype: float64
```

Figure 5.16: Count of each subcategory in the browser

4. Draw a countplot with the **OperatingSystems** column of the DataFrame:

```
sns.countplot(df['OperatingSystems'])
plt.title('OS wise session Distribution', fontsize = 20)
plt.show()
```

5. Once the plot has been drawn, determine which OS type contributes the most to website traffic:

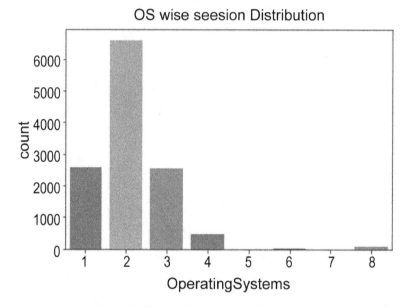

Figure 5.17: OS-wise session distribution

From the preceding graph, we can see that OS type 2 contributes the most to the website traffic.

6. Determine the count of each subcategory with the help of the **.value_counts()** function:

```
print(df['OperatingSystems'].value_counts())
print()
print(df['OperatingSystems'].value_counts(normalize=True))
```

The output of the preceding function is as follows:

```
2      6601
1      2585
3      2555
4       478
8        79
6        19
7         7
5         6
Name: OperatingSystems, dtype: int64

2      0.535361
1      0.209651
3      0.207218
4      0.038767
8      0.006407
6      0.001541
7      0.000568
5      0.000487
Name: OperatingSystems, dtype: float64
```

Figure 5.18: Count of each subcategory of the OS type

NOTE

To access the source code for this specific section, please refer to https://packt.live/3hC3CFy.

You can also run this example online at https://packt.live/3hyL9tt. You must execute the entire Notebook in order to get the desired result.

As you know, the visual method of representation is easier to understand as visual data is certainly more appealing and easier to interpret. If we know which OS type is the most predominant, we can ask the tech team to configure the website for that particular OS and take the necessary actions, such as explicitly defining CSS for that particular OS and defining valid doctypes.

ADMINISTRATIVE PAGEVIEW DISTRIBUTION

Administrative pages on a website can be pages where the content is being added to the site or the pages where the site is managed. For example, for a WordPress site, ../wp-admin will be the admin page, which, in turn, will have multiple pages within itself.

Now, let's plot the countplot for the **Administrative** page:

```
sns.countplot(df['Administrative'])
plt.title('Administrative Pageview Distribution', fontsize = 16)
plt.show()
```

The output will be as follows:

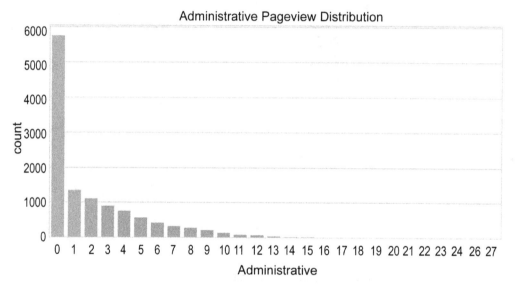

Figure 5.19: Administrative page-wise distribution

We can see from the preceding plot that users tend to visit page **0** the most often.

INFORMATION PAGEVIEW DISTRIBUTION

The information pages of a site are the pages where the direct information is presented. The simple web pages that do not generate leads or that are not connected to lead-generating pages can be classified as information pages. For example, contact pages that simply display contact information could be considered as information pages.

Now, let's plot the count of visitors visiting the information page.

Plot the countplot for the **Informational** page:

```
sns.countplot(df['Informational'])
plt.title('Information Pageview Distribution', fontsize = 16)
plt.show()
```

The output will be as follows:

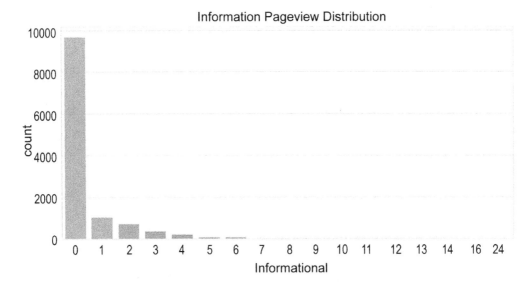

Figure 5.20: Information pageview distribution

From the preceding graph, we can see that Information page **0** has the highest number of visitors. In order to get the exact count of customers visiting each information page, we will use the **.value_count()** function:

```
print(df['Informational'].value_counts(normalize=True))
```

To get the percentage count for each information page, we use the **normalize=True** parameter.

The output will be as follows:

```
0       0.786618
1       0.084428
2       0.059043
3       0.030819
4       0.018005
5       0.008029
6       0.006326
7       0.002920
9       0.001217
8       0.001135
10      0.000568
12      0.000406
14      0.000162
11      0.000081
13      0.000081
24      0.000081
16      0.000081
Name: Informational, dtype: float64
```

Figure 5.21: Percentage distribution of views on the information page

79% of users are visiting pages **0** and **1**.

SPECIAL DAY SESSION DISTRIBUTION

In this section, we will be looking at the number of visitors during a special day. We would like to know whether special days (such as Valentine's Day) impact the number of users visiting our website.

Let's plot the countplot for special days:

```
sns.countplot(df['SpecialDay'])
plt.title('Special Day session Distribution', fontsize = 16)
plt.show()
```

The output will be as follows:

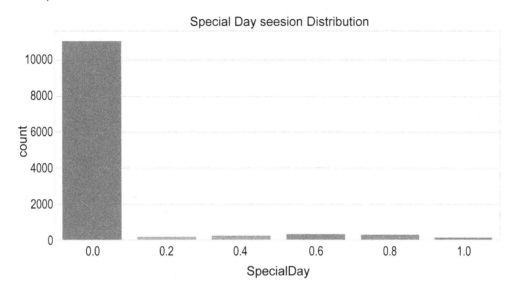

Figure 5.22: Special day session distribution

From the preceding plot, we can see that special days have no impact on the number of visitors to our website.

Now, let's look at the percentage distribution for special days:

```
print(df['SpecialDay'].value_counts(normalize=True))
```

The output will be as follows:

```
0.0     0.898540
0.6     0.028467
0.8     0.026358
0.4     0.019708
0.2     0.014436
1.0     0.012490
Name: SpecialDay, dtype: float64
```

From the preceding screenshot, we can see that 89.8% of visitors visited during a non-special day (special day subcategory **0**), showing that there is no affinity of web traffic toward special days.

This section covered the analysis of distribution plots for factors such as region, month, and type of browser. With this, we have come to the end of univariate analysis. In the next section, we will practice implementing bivariate analysis.

BIVARIATE ANALYSIS

In this section, we will be focusing on bivariate analysis. Bivariate analysis is performed between two variables to look at their relationship—for example, to determine which type of browser leads to a successful transaction, or which region has the highest number of customers who ended up making a transaction.

We will be performing bivariate analysis between the revenue column and the following categories:

- Visitor type
- Traffic type
- Region
- Browser type
- Operating system
- Month
- Special day

Now, let's analyze each feature through its relationship to the revenue.

REVENUE VERSUS VISITOR TYPE

First, consider the relationship between revenue and visitor type.

We will be plotting a categorical plot between **Revenue** and **VisitorType**. The categorical plot gives you the number of users in each subcategory, and whether each culminated in a purchase. The plot will define those users who did make a purchase as **True**, and those who did not as **False**:

```
g = sns.catplot("Revenue", col="VisitorType", col_wrap=3,\
                data=df,kind="count", height=5, aspect=1)
plt.show()
```

The output will be as follows:

Figure 5.23: Revenue versus visitor type

As you can see, more revenue conversions happen for returning customers than new customers. This clearly implies that we need to find ways to incentivize new customers to make a transaction with us.

REVENUE VERSUS TRAFFIC TYPE

Next, consider the relationship between **Revenue** and **TrafficType**.

We will be plotting a countplot between revenue and traffic type. The countplot gives you the number of users in each traffic type, and whether or not they made a purchase (shown as **True** or **False** in the plot):

```
sns.countplot(x="TrafficType", hue="Revenue", data=df)
plt.legend(loc='right')
plt.show()
```

The output will be as follows:

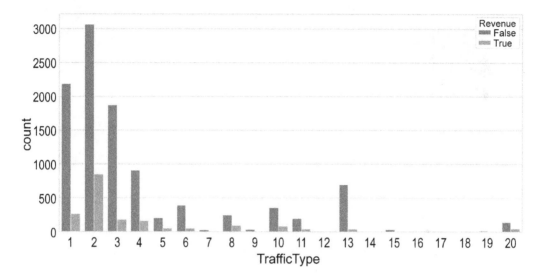

Figure 5.24: Revenue versus traffic type

From the preceding plot, we can see that more revenue conversion happens for web traffic generated from source 2. Even though source 13 generated a considerable amount of web traffic, conversion is very low compared to others.

EXERCISE 5.03: ANALYZING THE RELATIONSHIP BETWEEN REVENUE AND OTHER VARIABLES

In this exercise, you will evaluate the relationship between revenue and other variables, such as region, browser, operating system, and month of the year, to determine how these variables contribute to sales. This information will allow us to plan our marketing campaigns and logistics better.

Perform the following steps to complete this exercise:

1. Plot a countplot for each region by keeping **Revenue** as the **hue** parameter.

2. Find the number of customers who end up with a purchase region-wise:

```
sns.countplot(x="Region", hue="Revenue", data=df)
plt.show()
```

The output will be as follows:

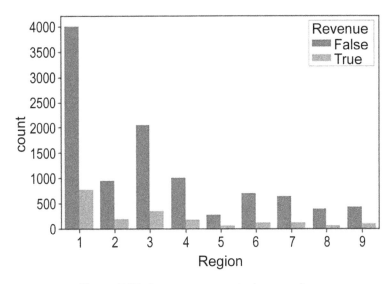

Figure 5.25: Revenue generated per region

From the preceding plot, we can see that region 1 accounts for most sales, and region 3 the second most. With this information, we can plan our marketing and supply chain activities in a better way. For example, we might propose building a warehouse specifically catering to the needs of region 1 to increase delivery rates and ensure that products in the highest demand are always well stocked.

Now, we will consider the relationship between **Revenue** and the **Browser** type.

3. Create a countplot between revenue and browser type that shows the number of users per browser type and whether or not they made a purchase (**True** or **False**):

```
sns.countplot(x="Browser", hue="Revenue", data=df)
plt.show()
```

The output will be as follows:

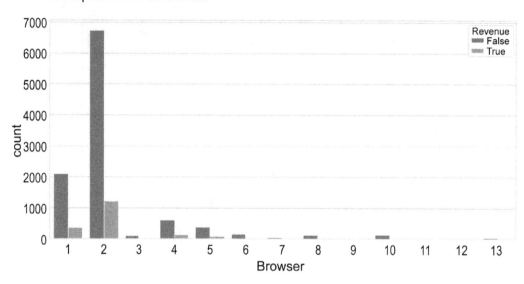

Figure 5.26: Revenue versus browser type

As you can see, more revenue-generating transactions have been performed from Browser 2. Even though Browser 1 creates a considerable number of sessions, the conversion rate is low. This is something we need to investigate further.

Now, consider the relationship between **Revenue** and the **OperatingSystems** type.

4. Create a countplot between **Revenue** and the **OperatingSysytems** type that shows the number of users per OS type and whether or not they made a purchase (**True** or **False**):

```
sns.countplot(x="OperatingSystems", hue="Revenue", data=df)
plt.show()
```

The output will be as follows:

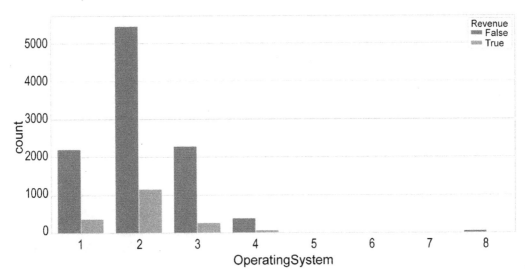

Figure 5.27: Revenue generated by the OS type

As you can see, more revenue-generating transactions happened with OS **2** than the other types.

Now consider the relationship between **Revenue** (did the session end with a purchase?) and **Months**.

5. Plot a countplot between revenue and month. The countplot gives you the number of users in any given month ending with a purchase or not (**True** or **False**):

```
sns.countplot(x="Month", hue="Revenue",\
              data=df,order=['Feb','Mar','May','June',\
                             'Jul','Aug','Sep','Oct',\
                             'Nov','Dec'])
plt.show()
```

The output will be as follows:

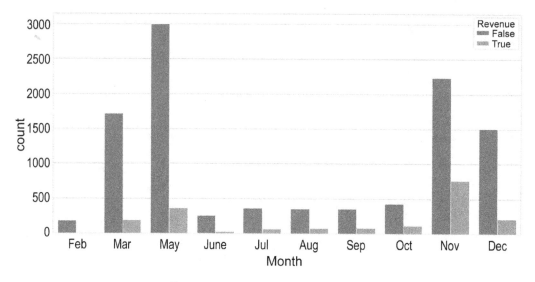

Figure 5.28: Revenue versus month

> **NOTE**
>
> To access the source code for this specific section, please refer to https://packt.live/2Y9r1qg.
>
> You can also run this example online at https://packt.live/3darQTU. You must execute the entire Notebook in order to get the desired result.

Website visitors may be high in May, but we can observe from the preceding bar plot that a greater number of purchases were made in the month of November.

LINEAR RELATIONSHIPS

The main purpose behind this section is to determine whether any two columns are linearly related. The variables are said to have a linear relationship if, and only if, they satisfy one of the following conditions:

- The value of one variable increases, while the other variable's value increases
- The value of one variable increases, while the other variable's value decreases

In this section, we will be studying the linear relationship between the following variables:

- Bounce rate versus exit rate

- Page value versus bounce rate

- Page value versus exit rate

- Impact of administration page views and administrative pageview duration on revenue

- Impact of information page views and information pageview duration on revenue

Let's start exploring the linear relationships between these variables.

BOUNCE RATE VERSUS EXIT RATE

The linear relationship between bounce rate versus exit rate can be studied by plotting an LM plot from seaborn.

We are setting the x axis as **BounceRates**, and the y axis as **ExitRates**. The data is taken from the **df** DataFrame:

```
sns.set(style="whitegrid")
ax = sns.lmplot(x="BounceRates", y="ExitRates", data=df)
```

The output will be as follows:

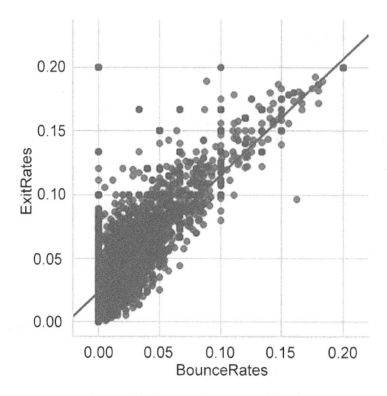

Figure 5.29: Bounce rate versus exit rate

As you can see, there is a positive correlation between the bounce rate and the exit rate. With the increase in bounce rate, the exit rate of the page increases.

PAGE VALUE VERSUS BOUNCE RATE

The linear relationship between the page value and the bounce rate can be studied by plotting an LM plot with seaborn. Set the x axis as **PageValue** and the y axis as **BounceRates**. The data is taken from the **df** DataFrame:

```
sns.set(style="whitegrid")
ax = sns.lmplot(x="PageValues", y="BounceRates" , data=df)
```

The output will be as follows:

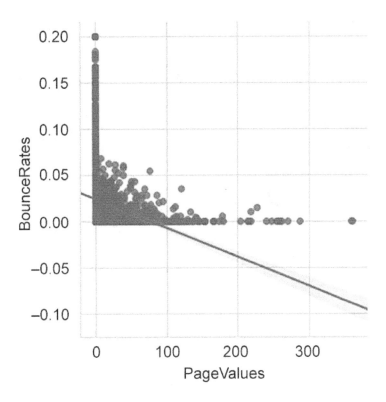

Figure 5.30: Page value versus bounce rate

As we can see in the preceding plot, there is a negative correlation between page value and bounce rate. As the page value increases, the bounce rate decreases. To increase the probability of a customer purchasing with us, we need to improve the page value—perhaps by making the content more engaging or by using images to convey the information.

PAGE VALUE VERSUS EXIT RATE

The linear relationship between **PageValues** and **ExitRates** can be studied by plotting an LM plot with seaborn.

Set the x axis as **PageValues** and the y axis as **ExitRates**. The data is taken from the **df** DataFrame:

```
sns.set(style="whitegrid")
ax = sns.lmplot(x="PageValues", y="ExitRates" , data=df)
```

The output will be as follows:

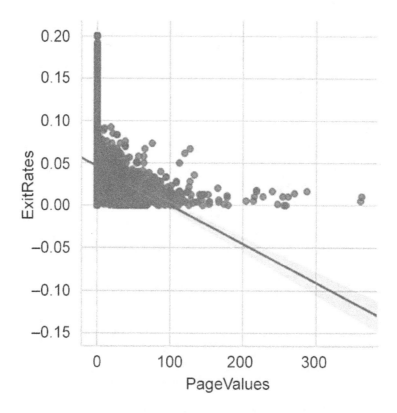

Figure 5.31: Page value versus exit rate

As we can see in the preceding plot, there is a negative correlation between page value and exit rate. Web pages with a better page value have a lower exit rate.

IMPACT OF ADMINISTRATION PAGE VIEWS AND ADMINISTRATIVE PAGEVIEW DURATION ON REVENUE

In this section, we want to look at the relationship between administrative pageviews and the amount of time spent on it. Does this relationship have an impact on revenue? If so, how?

To study the relationship, draw the LM plot with the x axis as **Administrative** and the y axis as **Administrative_Duration**, and with the **hue** parameter as **Revenue**:

```
sns.set(style="whitegrid")
ax = sns.lmplot(x="Administrative", y="Administrative_Duration",\
                hue='Revenue', data=df)
```

The output will be as follows:

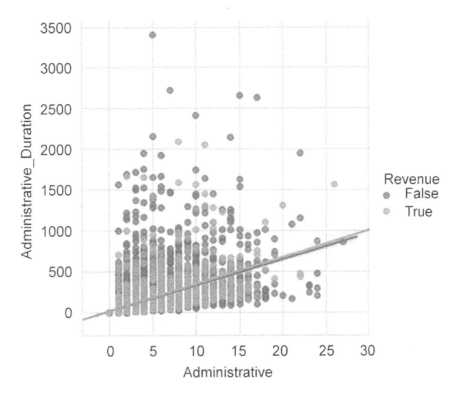

Figure 5.32: Administrative page views versus duration

From the preceding plot, we can infer that administrative-related pageviews and the administrative-related pageview duration are positively correlated. When there is an increase in the number of administrative pageviews, the administrative pageview duration also increases.

IMPACT OF INFORMATION PAGE VIEWS AND INFORMATION PAGEVIEW DURATION ON REVENUE

In this section, we want to look at the relationship between the number of views of the information pages and the amount of time spent on them. Does this relationship have an impact on revenue? If so, how?

To study the relationship, draw the LM plot with the x axis as **Informational** and the y axis as **Informational_Duration**, and with the **hue** parameter as **Revenue**:

```
sns.set(style="whitegrid")
ax = sns.lmplot(x="Informational", y="Informational_Duration",\
                hue='Revenue', data=df)
```

The output will be as follows:

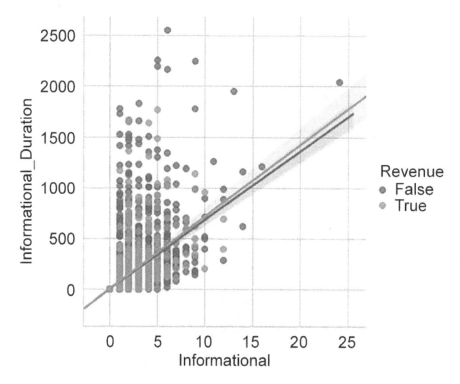

Figure 5.33: Informational page views versus duration

From the preceding plot, we can conclude the following:

- Information page views and information pageview duration are positively correlated. With an increase in the number of information pageviews, the information pageview duration also increases.

- Customers who have made online purchases visited fewer numbers of informational pages. This implies that informational pageviews don't have much effect on revenue generation.

CLUSTERING

Clustering is an unsupervised learning technique in which you group categorically similar data points into batches, called **clusters**. Here, we will be focusing on the k-means clustering method.

K-means clustering is a clustering algorithm based on iterations where similar data points are grouped into a cluster based on their closeness to the cluster centroid. This means that the model runs iteratively to find the cluster centroid.

The optimum number of clusters for a dataset is found by using the elbow method.

METHOD TO FIND THE OPTIMUM NUMBER OF CLUSTERS

The logic behind k-means clustering is to define a cluster in such a way that, within the cluster, the **sum of square (WSS)** is minimized. The smaller the value of WSS, the better the compactness of the cluster. The clusters that are compact have data points that are similar to one another. We will be using the elbow method to find the optimum number of clusters.

The elbow method gets its name from the arm-like shape of its line plot. The point at which the curve inflects is called the **elbow** and is an indication that the model fits best at that particular value of k, where "k" is the number of clusters. As shown in the following diagram, the curve bends at the value 2:

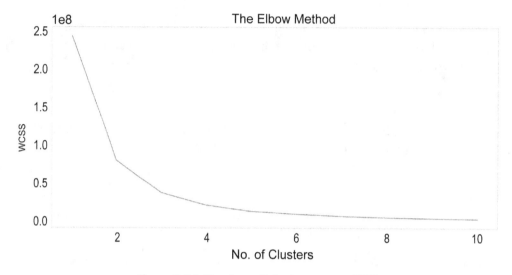

Figure 5.34: Number of clusters versus WSS

You need to complete the following steps to find the optimum cluster value through the elbow method:

1. Compute k-means clustering for different values of k.

2. Vary the value of K from 1-10 in increments of 1.

3. For each k, calculate the total cluster sum of square WSS.

4. Plot the curve for WSS.

The location of a bend in the plot is considered the optimum number of clusters. In the preceding graph, *K=2* is the optimum value.

The following exercise will guide you through how to use this clustering method on our example dataset.

EXERCISE 5.04: PERFORMING K-MEANS CLUSTERING FOR INFORMATIONAL DURATION VERSUS BOUNCE RATE

In this exercise, you will perform clustering between the information pageview duration and bounce rate columns of our dataset. Perform the following steps to complete this exercise:

1. Select the columns and assign them to a variable called **x**:

```
x = df.iloc[:, [3, 6]].values
```

2. Run the k-means algorithm for different values of **k**. **km** is the k-means clustering algorithm:

```
wcss = []
for i in range(1, 11):
    km = KMeans(n_clusters = i, init = 'k-means++', \
                max_iter = 300, n_init = 10, \
                random_state = 0, algorithm = 'elkan', tol = 0.001)
```

3. Fit the k-means algorithm to the **x** variable we defined in the preceding steps:

```
    km.fit(x)
    labels = km.labels_
```

4. Append the inertia value calculated using **Kmeans** to **wcss**:

```
    wcss.append(km.inertia_)
```

5. Plot the value of **wcss** with the value of **k**:

```
plt.rcParams['figure.figsize'] = (15, 7)
plt.plot(range(1, 11), wcss)
plt.grid()
plt.tight_layout()
plt.title('The Elbow Method', fontsize = 20)
plt.xlabel('No. of Clusters')
plt.ylabel('wcss')
plt.show()
```

The elbow graph will be displayed as follows:

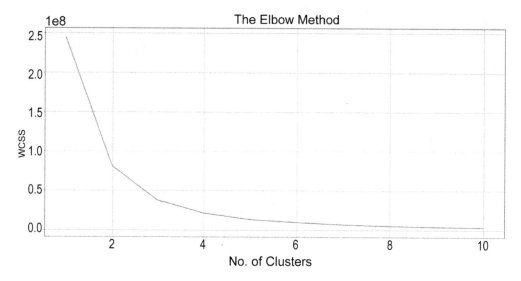

Figure 5.35: Elbow graph for informational duration versus bounce rate

From the preceding elbow graph, we can infer that **k=2** is the optimum value for clustering.

6. Now, run k-means clustering with **k=2**:

```
km = KMeans(n_clusters = 2, init = 'k-means++', \
            max_iter = 300, n_init = 10, random_state = 0)
y_means = km.fit_predict(x)
```

7. Plot the scatter plot between **Bounce Rates** and **Informational Duration**.

To make the graph more readable, assign the color **pink** for uninterested customers (in which **Revenue** is **False**), **yellow** for target customers (in which **Revenue** is **True**), and **blue** for the centroid of the cluster:

```
plt.scatter(x[y_means == 0, 0], x[y_means == 0, 1], s = 100, \
            c = 'pink', label = 'Un-interested Customers')
plt.scatter(x[y_means == 1, 0], x[y_means == 1, 1], s = 100, \
            c = 'yellow', label = 'Target Customers')
plt.scatter(km.cluster_centers_[:,0], km.cluster_centers_[:, 1], \
            s = 50, c = 'blue' , label = 'centeroid')
```

```
plt.title('Informational Duration vs Bounce Rates', fontsize = 20)
plt.grid()
plt.xlabel('Informational Duration')
plt.ylabel('Bounce Rates')
plt.legend()
plt.show()
```

The output will be as follows:

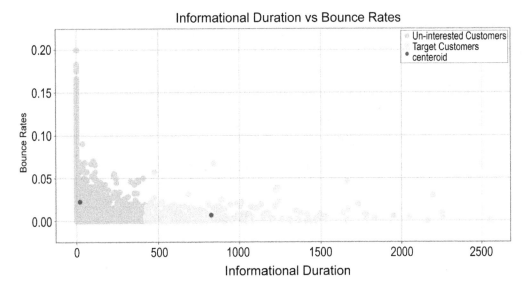

Figure 5.36: Scatterplot for informational duration versus bounce rate

NOTE

To access the source code for this specific section, please refer
to https://packt.live/30LJn29.

You can also run this example online at https://packt.live/2N2FwWb. You
must execute the entire Notebook in order to get the desired result.

From the preceding graph, we can see that our target customers spend around
850-900 seconds on average on the Information page.

PERFORMING K-MEANS CLUSTERING FOR INFORMATIONAL DURATION VERSUS EXIT RATE

We are now going to perform clustering between the information pageview duration and exit rate columns. Select the columns and assign them to a variable called **x**:

```
x = df.iloc[:, [4, 7]].values
wcss = []


for i in range(1, 11):
```

Km is the k-means clustering algorithm. Run the k-means algorithm for different values of **k (1–10)**:

```
km = KMeans(n_clusters = i, init = 'k-means++', \
            max_iter = 300, n_init = 10, \
            random_state = 0, algorithm = 'elkan', \
            tol = 0.001)
```

Now, fit the k-means algorithm to the **x** variable we defined previously:

```
km.fit(x)
labels = km.labels_
```

Now, append the inertia value we calculated using **Kmeans** to **wcss**:

```
wcss.append(km.inertia_)
```

Now, plot the value of **wcss** with the value of **k**:

```
plt.rcParams['figure.figsize'] = (15, 7)
plt.plot(range(1, 11), wcss)
plt.grid()
plt.tight_layout()
plt.title('The Elbow Method', fontsize = 20)
plt.xlabel('No. of Clusters')
plt.ylabel('wcss')
plt.show()
```

The elbow graph for this clustering can be realized as follows:

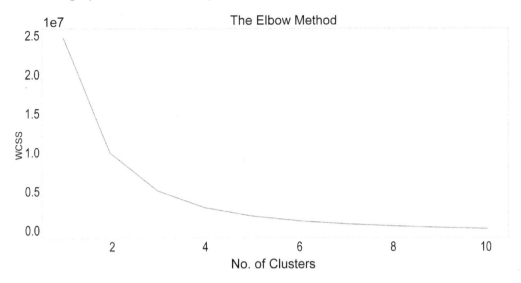

Figure 5.37: Elbow graph for informational duration versus exit rate

From the preceding elbow graph, we can see that **k=2** is the optimum value for clustering. Now, let's run k-means clustering with **k=2**:

```
km = KMeans(n_clusters = 2, init = 'k-means++', max_iter = 300, \
            n_init = 10, random_state = 0)
y_means = km.fit_predict(x)
plt.scatter(x[y_means == 0, 0], x[y_means == 0, 1], s = 100, \
            c = 'pink', label = 'Un-interested Customers')
```

We plot the scatter plot between the exit rate and information pageview duration. To make the graph more readable, we'll assign the color **pink** for uninterested customers (where **Revenue** is **False**), **yellow** for target customers (where **Revenue** is **True**), and **blue** for the centroid of the cluster:

```
plt.scatter(x[y_means == 1, 0], x[y_means == 1, 1], s = 100, \
            c = 'yellow', label = 'Target Customers')
plt.scatter(km.cluster_centers_[:,0], km.cluster_centers_[:, 1], \
            s = 50, c = 'blue' , label = 'centeroid')
plt.title('Informational Duration vs Exit Rates', fontsize = 20)
plt.grid()
plt.xlabel('Informational Duration')
plt.ylabel('Exit Rates')
plt.legend()
plt.show()
```

The scatterplot for **Informational Duration** versus **Exit Rate** can be realized as follows:

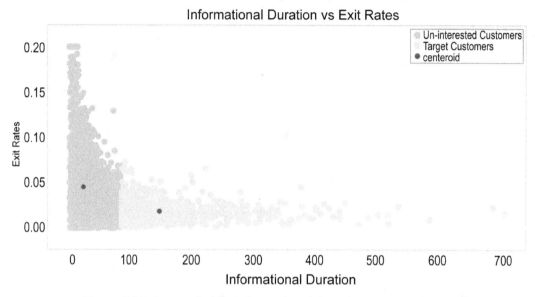

Figure 5.38: Scatterplot for informational duration versus exit rate

From the preceding cluster, we can infer that our target customers spend around 150 seconds more on average than the other customers before exiting.

We are now ready to complete an activity regarding the performance of clustering for administrative duration versus bounce rate.

ACTIVITY 5.01: PERFORMING K-MEANS CLUSTERING FOR ADMINISTRATIVE DURATION VERSUS BOUNCE RATE AND ADMINISTRATIVE DURATION VERSUS EXIT RATE

In this activity, you will perform K-means clustering for administrative pageview duration versus bounce rate. You need to perform the initial data analysis and check the null values before solving this activity.

> **NOTE**
>
> The clusters that were formed for informational duration versus bounce rate can be taken as a sample to perform this exercise.

The following steps will help you to complete this activity:

1. Select the **Administrative Pageview Duration** and **Bounce Rate** columns. Assign the column to a variable called **x**.

2. Initialize the k-means algorithm.

3. For the different values of **K**, compute the k-means inertia and store it as a variable called **wcss**.

4. Plot a graph between **wcss** and the corresponding **k** value.

   The output will be as follows:

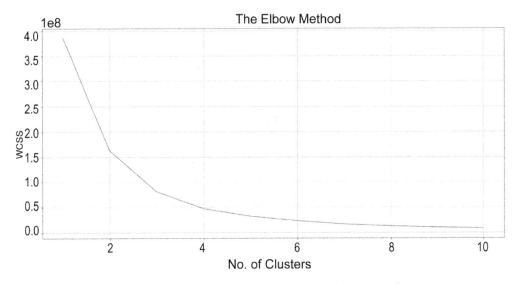

Figure 5.39: Elbow graph for administrative duration versus bounce rate

5. Perform k-means clustering between administrative duration versus bounce rate with **k=2**. By performing k-means clustering, we get the centroids of both clusters.

6. Assign the color **pink** for uninterested customers and the color **cyan** for our target customer.

7. Use the color **blue** to denote the centroid of the cluster, which can be obtained from the cluster.

8. Plot a scatter plot between **Administrative Duration vs Bounce Rate**.

The output will be as follows:

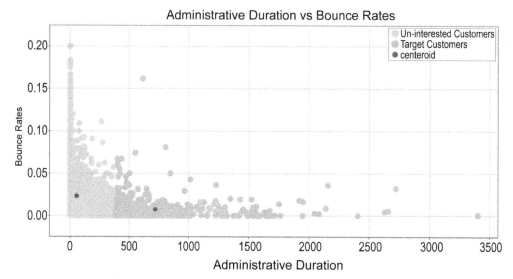

Figure 5.40: Scatterplot for administrative duration versus bounce rate

9. Select the **Administrative Duration** and **Exit Rate** columns. Assign the column to a variable called **x**.

10. Initialize the k-means algorithm.

11. For the different values of K, compute the **Kmeans** inertia and store it in a variable called **wcss**.

12. Plot a graph between **wcss** and the corresponding **k** value.

The output is as follows:

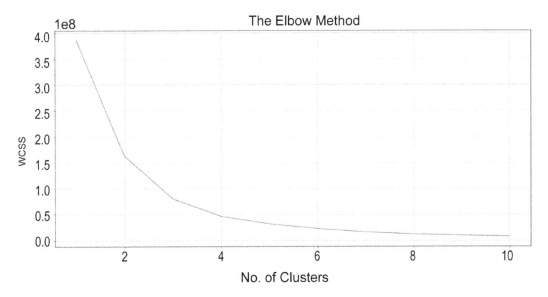

Figure 5.41: Elbow method for administrative duration versus exit rate

13. Perform k-means clustering between **Administrative Duration** versus **Exit Rate** with **k=2** to get the centroids of both clusters.

14. Assign the color **pink** for uninterested customers and the color **yellow** for our target customer.

15. Use the color **blue** to denote the centroid of the cluster, which can be obtained from the cluster.

16. Plot a scatter plot between **Administrative Duration vs Bounce Rate**.

The output will be as follows:

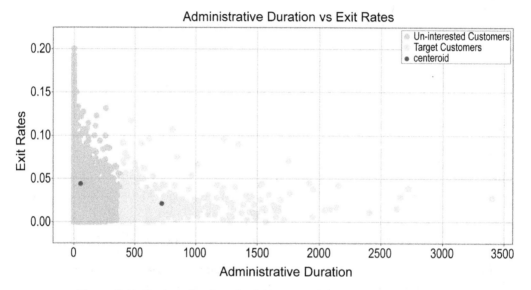

Figure 5.42: Scatterplot for administrative duration versus exit rate

> **NOTE**
>
> The solution to the activity can be found on page 507.

From the preceding graph, we can see that the uninterested customer spends less time in administrative pages compared with the target customers, who spend around 750 seconds on the administrative page before exiting.

From all the analysis we've performed in this chapter, we can conclude the following:

- The conversion rates of new visitors are high compared to those of returning customers.

- While the number of returning customers to the website is high, the conversion rate is low compared to that of new customers.

- Pages with a high page value have a lower bounce rate. We should be talking with our tech team to find ways to improve the page value of the web pages.

These factors will largely influence the next plan of action and open new avenues for more research and new business strategies and plans.

SUMMARY

In this chapter, we focused on the online shopping dataset, wherein we are trying to draw insights from a customer's behavior on the site. We analyzed a number of factors, such as conversion rate and total revenue generated.

We also performed univariate and bivariate analysis while taking various dataset features into consideration, such as pageview duration, types of visitors, types of traffic, and browsers used. Then, we implemented the K-means algorithm and elbow method to find the optimum value of clusters, and visualized scatterplots based on this value. These plots, in turn, provided us with useful information so that we can plan our next course of action.

In the next chapter, we will be looking at credit card defaults of Taiwanese customers and how data analytics can be used to prevent them.

6

ANALYSIS OF CREDIT CARD DEFAULTERS

OVERVIEW

In this chapter, you will analyze the characteristics of the customers who are most likely to default on their credit card payments using univariate and bivariate analysis techniques. Using the `crosstab` function, you will investigate the relationship between different features of the dataset. And, by the end of this chapter, you will be able to build a profile of a customer who is the most statistically likely to default on their credit card payments.

INTRODUCTION

In the previous chapter, we analyzed online shoppers' purchasing intent and derived various useful insights from our findings. We explored and utilized the K-means clustering technique, along with univariate and bivariate analysis, and also studied the linear relationships between each feature of the dataset to build a proper evaluation of the dataset. The results derived from the analysis would help a business to identify the pain points and develop new business strategies to tackle them.

In this chapter, we will analyze credit card payments of customers and use their transactional data to study the characteristics of the customers who are most likely to default, eventually building a profile of these customers.

Credit card default has been a field of interest and extensive analysis for more than a decade. There are two types of loan – secured and unsecured. A secured loan is one where some collateral is mandatory, so whenever a default happens, the banking institutions can take control of the underlying assets. This asset can vary from real estate to automobiles. In general, a secured loan is considered to be low risk.

Unlike a secured loan, an unsecured loan does not require any underlying collateral.

Lines of credit are unsecured by their very nature, so whenever a default on the payments happens, it is the credit card company or the bank that has to take the loss.

This concern has prompted banks and companies to invest heavily in the analysis and prediction of credit card defaults.

In this chapter, we will be building a profile of the customers most likely to default using techniques such as univariate and bivariate analysis. With this analysis, we will be able to understand the factors or characteristics of a customer who is likely to default. This profile will act as a criterion for the bank or lending facility to detect potential defaulters and take appropriate actions in a timely manner.

> **NOTE**
>
> The data is obtained from the UCI repository. You can find the original dataset at https://archive.ics.uci.edu/ml/datasets/default+of+credit+card+clients. You can also find it in our GitHub at: https://packt.live/3hzJ2W6.
>
> Citation:
>
> Yeh, I. C., & Lien, C. H. (2009), *The comparisons of data mining techniques for the predictive accuracy of probability of default of credit card clients. Expert Systems with Applications*, 36(2), 2473-2480.

The dataset's features can be explained by the data dictionary as follows:

Column	Description
ID	Identification number of the record
LIMIT_BAL	Amount of credit extended
SEX	Gender of the customer
EDUCATION	Highest level of education of the customer
MARRIAGE	Marital status of the customer
AGE	Age of the customer
PAY_0	The repayment status in September 2005
PAY_2	The repayment status in August 2005
PAY_3	The repayment status in July 2005
PAY_4	The repayment status in June 2005
PAY_5	The repayment status in May 2005
PAY_6	The repayment status in April 2005
BILL_AMT1	Amount on the bill statement in September 2005
BILL_AMT2	Amount on the bill statement in August 2005
BILL_AMT3	Amount on the bill statement in July 2005
BILL_AMT4	Amount on the bill statement in June 2005
BILL_AMT5	Amount on the bill statement in May 2005
BILL_AMT6	Amount on the bill statement in April 2005
PAY_AMT1	Amount paid in September 2005
PAY_AMT2	Amount paid in August 2005
PAY_AMT3	Amount paid in July 2005
PAY_AMT4	Amount paid in June 2005
PAY_AMT5	Amount paid in May 2005
PAY_AMT6	Amount paid in April 2005
default payment next month	Default of the loan

Figure 6.1: Data dictionary

We will first import the dataset into the Jupyter notebook.

IMPORTING THE DATA

Before we begin with the actual analysis, we will need to import the required packages as follows:

```
# Import basic libraries
import numpy as np
import pandas as pd

# import visualization libraries
import seaborn as sns
import matplotlib.pyplot as plt
%matplotlib inline
```

Next, read/import the dataset into the work environment:

```
df = pd.read_excel('default_credit.xls')
df.head(5)
```

The output will be as follows:

	ID	LIMIT_BAL	SEX	EDUCATION	MARRIAGE	AGE	PAY_0	PAY_2	PAY_3	PAY_4	...
0	1	20000	2	2	1	24	2	2	-1	-1	...
1	2	120000	2	2	2	26	-1	2	0	0	...
2	3	90000	2	2	2	34	0	0	0	0	...
3	4	50000	2	2	1	37	0	0	0	0	...
4	5	50000	1	2	1	57	-1	0	-1	0	...

5 rows × 25 columns

Figure 6.2: Top five rows of the DataFrame

Check the metadata of the DataFrame:

```
# Getting Meta Data Information about the dataset
df.info()
```

The output will be similar to the image shown below:

```
<class 'pandas.core.frame.DataFrame'>
RangeIndex: 30000 entries, 0 to 29999
Data columns (total 25 columns):
ID                          30000 non-null int64
LIMIT_BAL                   30000 non-null int64
SEX                         30000 non-null int64
EDUCATION                   30000 non-null int64
MARRIAGE                    30000 non-null int64
AGE                         30000 non-null int64
PAY_0                       30000 non-null int64
PAY_2                       30000 non-null int64
PAY_3                       30000 non-null int64
PAY_4                       30000 non-null int64
PAY_5                       30000 non-null int64
PAY_6                       30000 non-null int64
BILL_AMT1                   30000 non-null int64
BILL_AMT2                   30000 non-null int64
BILL_AMT3                   30000 non-null int64
BILL_AMT4                   30000 non-null int64
BILL_AMT5                   30000 non-null int64
BILL_AMT6                   30000 non-null int64
PAY_AMT1                    30000 non-null int64
PAY_AMT2                    30000 non-null int64
PAY_AMT3                    30000 non-null int64
PAY_AMT4                    30000 non-null int64
PAY_AMT5                    30000 non-null int64
PAY_AMT6                    30000 non-null int64
default payment next month  30000 non-null int64
dtypes: int64(25)
memory usage: 5.7 MB
```

Figure 6.3: Information of the DataFrame

Check the descriptive statistics for the numerical columns in the DataFrame:

```
df.describe().T
```

The output will be as follows:

	count	mean	std	min	25%	50%	75%	max
ID	30000.0	15000.500000	8660.398374	1.0	7500.75	15000.5	22500.25	30000.0
LIMIT_BAL	30000.0	167484.322667	129747.661567	10000.0	50000.00	140000.0	240000.00	1000000.0
SEX	30000.0	1.603733	0.489129	1.0	1.00	2.0	2.00	2.0
EDUCATION	30000.0	1.853133	0.790349	0.0	1.00	2.0	2.00	6.0
MARRIAGE	30000.0	1.551867	0.521970	0.0	1.00	2.0	2.00	3.0
AGE	30000.0	35.485500	9.217904	21.0	28.00	34.0	41.00	79.0
PAY_0	30000.0	-0.016700	1.123802	-2.0	-1.00	0.0	0.00	8.0
PAY_2	30000.0	-0.133767	1.197186	-2.0	-1.00	0.0	0.00	8.0
PAY_3	30000.0	-0.166200	1.196868	-2.0	-1.00	0.0	0.00	8.0
PAY_4	30000.0	-0.220667	1.169139	-2.0	-1.00	0.0	0.00	8.0
PAY_5	30000.0	-0.266200	1.133187	-2.0	-1.00	0.0	0.00	8.0
PAY_6	30000.0	-0.291100	1.149988	-2.0	-1.00	0.0	0.00	8.0
BILL_AMT1	30000.0	51223.330900	73635.860576	-165580.0	3558.75	22381.5	67091.00	964511.0
BILL_AMT2	30000.0	49179.075167	71173.768783	-69777.0	2984.75	21200.0	64006.25	983931.0
BILL_AMT3	30000.0	47013.154800	69349.387427	-157264.0	2666.25	20088.5	60164.75	1664089.0
BILL_AMT4	30000.0	43262.948967	64332.856134	-170000.0	2326.75	19052.0	54506.00	891586.0
BILL_AMT5	30000.0	40311.400967	60797.155770	-81334.0	1763.00	18104.5	50190.50	927171.0
BILL_AMT6	30000.0	38871.760400	59554.107537	-339603.0	1256.00	17071.0	49198.25	961664.0
PAY_AMT1	30000.0	5663.580500	16563.280354	0.0	1000.00	2100.0	5006.00	873552.0
PAY_AMT2	30000.0	5921.163500	23040.870402	0.0	833.00	2009.0	5000.00	1684259.0
PAY_AMT3	30000.0	5225.681500	17606.961470	0.0	390.00	1800.0	4505.00	896040.0
PAY_AMT4	30000.0	4826.076867	15666.159744	0.0	296.00	1500.0	4013.25	621000.0
PAY_AMT5	30000.0	4799.387633	15278.305679	0.0	252.50	1500.0	4031.50	426529.0
PAY_AMT6	30000.0	5215.502567	17777.465775	0.0	117.75	1500.0	4000.00	528666.0
default payment next month	30000.0	0.221200	0.415062	0.0	0.00	0.0	0.00	1.0

Figure 6.4: Descriptive statistics of the DataFrame

Next, check for null values:

```
# Checking for Null Values
df.isnull().sum()
```

The output will be as follows:

```
ID                             0
LIMIT_BAL                      0
SEX                            0
EDUCATION                      0
MARRIAGE                       0
AGE                            0
PAY_0                          0
PAY_2                          0
PAY_3                          0
PAY_4                          0
PAY_5                          0
PAY_6                          0
BILL_AMT1                      0
BILL_AMT2                      0
BILL_AMT3                      0
BILL_AMT4                      0
BILL_AMT5                      0
BILL_AMT6                      0
PAY_AMT1                       0
PAY_AMT2                       0
PAY_AMT3                       0
PAY_AMT4                       0
PAY_AMT5                       0
PAY_AMT6                       0
default payment next month     0
dtype: int64
```

Figure 6.5: Checking for null values

From the preceding output, we can see that the value corresponding to each column is zero, which implies no missing values, meaning there is no null value present in any of the columns. In previous chapters, we studied how to handle null values when present using techniques such as mean imputation and iterative imputation, wherein we simply make use of a model to replace the missing values.

The next section deals with data preprocessing before heading into exploratory data analysis. The purpose behind doing preprocessing is that the data has to be cleaned of any errors such as spellings, along with identifying the unique values in a column and making the data more meaningful by clubbing the data to form groups. In data preprocessing, we also look at data consistency, for example, a categorical column such as **SEX** (**0: Female**, **1: Male**) is displayed as an integer and so on. Without data preprocessing, visualizing the data or building a machine learning model becomes very difficult.

DATA PREPROCESSING

Before proceeding onto univariate analysis, let's look at the unique values in the columns. The motive behind looking at the unique values in a column is to identify the subcategory in each column. By knowing the subcategory in each column, we would be in a position to understand which subcategory has a higher count or vice versa. For example, let's take the **EDUCATION** column. We are interested in finding what the different subcategories in the **EDUCATION** column are and which subcategory has the higher count; that is, do our customers have their highest education as **College** or **University**?

This step acts as a precursor before we build a profile of our customers.

Let's now find unique values in the **SEX** column.

We'll print the unique values in the **SEX** column and sort them in ascending order:

```
print('SEX ' + str(sorted(df['SEX'].unique())))
```

The output will be as follows:

```
SEX [1, 2]
```

The following code prints the unique values in the **EDUCATION** column and sorts the values in ascending order:

```
print('EDUCATION ' + str(sorted(df['EDUCATION'].unique())))
```

The output will be as follows:

```
EDUCATION [0, 1, 2, 3, 4, 5, 6]
```

The following code prints the unique values in the **MARRIAGE** column and sorts the values in ascending order:

```
print('MARRIAGE ' + str(sorted(df['MARRIAGE'].unique())))
```

The output will be as follows:

```
MARRIAGE [0, 1, 2, 3]
```

The following code prints the unique values in the **PAY_0** column and sorts the values in ascending order:

```
print('PAY_0 ' + str(sorted(df['PAY_0'].unique())))
```

The output will be as follows:

```
PAY_0 [-2, -1, 0, 1, 2, 3, 4, 5, 6, 7, 8]
```

The following code prints the unique values in the **default payment next month** column and is sorted in ascending order:

```
print('default.payment.next.month ' \
      + str(sorted(df['default payment next month'].unique())))
```

The output will be as follows:

```
default.payment.next.month [0, 1]
```

The **EDUCATION** column has 7 unique values, but as per our data description, we have only 4 unique values, so we are going to club categories 0, 5, and 6 with category 4:

```
fill = (df.EDUCATION == 0) | (df.EDUCATION == 5) \
       | (df.EDUCATION == 6)
df.loc[fill, 'EDUCATION'] = 4
```

Let's look at the unique values in the **EDUCATION** column after clubbing the values:

```
print('EDUCATION ' + str(sorted(df['EDUCATION'].unique())))
```

The output will be as follows:

```
Education [1, 2, 3, 4]
```

Similarly, in the **MARRIAGE** column, according to the data description, we should have **3** unique values. But here, we have **4** values in our data. As per our data description, the **MARRIAGE** column should have three subcategories. So, we combine category **0** with category **2** (**Single**):

```
fill = (df.MARRIAGE == 0)
df.loc[fill, 'MARRIAGE'] = 2
```

Let's look at the unique values in the **MARRIAGE** column after clubbing the values:

```
print('MARRIAGE ' + str(sorted(df['MARRIAGE'].unique())))
```

The output will be as follows:

```
Marriage [1, 2, 3]
```

Rename the **PAY_0** column to **PAY_1** and the **default payment next month** column to **DEFAULT** to maintain consistency with the naming of other columns:

```
df = df.rename(columns={'default payment next month': 'DEFAULT', \
                        'PAY_0': 'PAY_1'})
df.head()
```

The output will be as follows:

	ID	LIMIT_BAL	SEX	EDUCATION	MARRIAGE	AGE	PAY_1	PAY_2	PAY_3	PAY_4	...
0	1	20000	2	2	1	24	2	2	-1	-1	...
1	2	120000	2	2	2	26	-1	2	0	0	...
2	3	90000	2	2	2	34	0	0	0	0	...
3	4	50000	2	2	1	37	0	0	0	0	...
4	5	50000	1	2	1	57	-1	0	-1	0	...

5 rows × 25 columns

Figure 6.6: Renamed columns

As you can see, we have now renamed a few of the columns for easier understanding and combined a few of the subcategories to make data analysis more efficient and easier to interpret. In the next section, we will be looking at exploratory data analysis.

EXPLORATORY DATA ANALYSIS

The majority of time in a data science project is spent on **Exploratory Data Analysis (EDA)**. In EDA, we investigate data to find hidden patterns and outliers with the help of visualization. By performing EDA, we can uncover the underlying structure of data and test our hypotheses with the help of summary statistics. We can split EDA into three parts:

- Univariate analysis
- Bivariate analysis
- Correlation

Let's look at each of the parts one by one in the following sections.

UNIVARIATE ANALYSIS

Univariate analysis is the simplest form of analysis where we analyze each feature (that is, each column of a DataFrame) and try to uncover the pattern or distribution of the data.

In univariate analysis, we will be analyzing the categorical columns (**DEFAULT**, **SEX**, **EDUCATION**, and **MARRIAGE**) to mine useful information about the data:

Let's begin with each of the variables one by one:

1. The **DEFAULT** column:

    Let's look at the count of the **DEFAULT** column by drawing the count plot from the **seaborn** library:

    ```
    sns.countplot(x="DEFAULT", data=df)
    ```

The output will be as follows:

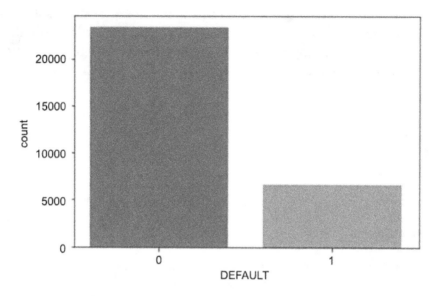

Figure 6.7: Count plot for the DEFAULT column

To analyze the distribution of the **DEFAULT** column, that is, the count of defaults versus non-defaults, use the following:

```
df['DEFAULT'].value_counts()
```

The output will be as follows:

```
0    23364
1     6636
Name: DEFAULT, dtype: int64
```

From the preceding output, we see that around **6636** customers have defaulted out of **30000** people, which is around **22%**.

2. The **SEX** column:

We will now plot a count plot for the **SEX** column to identify how many males and females there are in our data:

```
sns.countplot(x="SEX", data=df)
```

The output will be as follows:

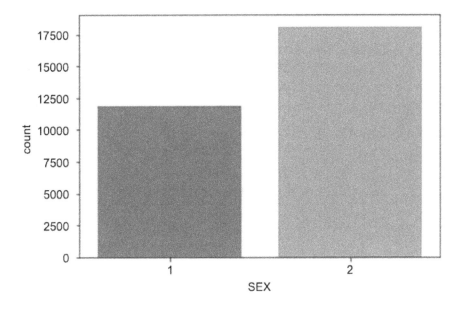

Figure 6.8: Count plot for the SEX column

In the preceding output, **1** represents male and **2** represents female.

Calculate the exact count of the values in the **SEX** column:

```
df['SEX'].value_counts()
```

The output will be as follows:

```
2 18112
1 11888
Name: SEX, dtype: int64
```

As you can see in the preceding output, there are a total of **18112** females and **11888** males in the given dataset.

3. The **EDUCATION** column:

    We'll now plot the value counts of the **EDUCATION** column. We perform this step to understand our customers with respect to their highest qualification, find out how many of them fall under each subcategory, and try to analyze whether education influences payment defaults in any way.

    The following subcategories represent the highest qualification of our customers:

Category	Qualification
1	Graduate School
2	University
3	High School
4	Others

Figure 6.9: Subcategories of education levels

Plot a count plot for the **EDUCATION** column:

```
sns.countplot(x="EDUCATION", data=df)
```

The output will be as follows:

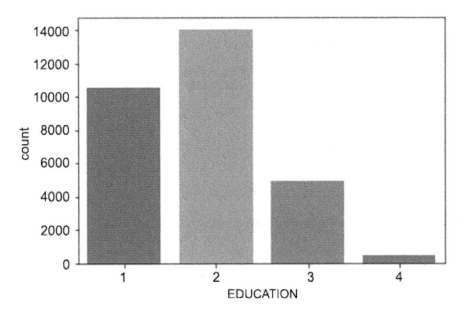

Figure 6.10: Count plot for the education column

Calculate the exact values for the **EDUCATION** column:

```
df['EDUCATION'].value_counts()
```

The output will be as follows:

```
2 14030
1 10585
3 4917
4 468
Name: EDUCATION, dtype: int64
```

From the preceding output, we can infer that most of our customers either went to graduate school or university.

4. The **MARRIAGE** column:

    Let's proceed with the value counts of the **MARRIAGE** column.

    The subcategories in the **MARRIAGE** column are as follows:

Category	Status
1	Married
2	Single
3	Divorced

    Figure 6.11: Categories of the marriage column

    Plot a count plot for the **MARRIAGE** column:

    ```
    sns.countplot(x="MARRIAGE", data=df)
    ```

    The output will be as follows:

    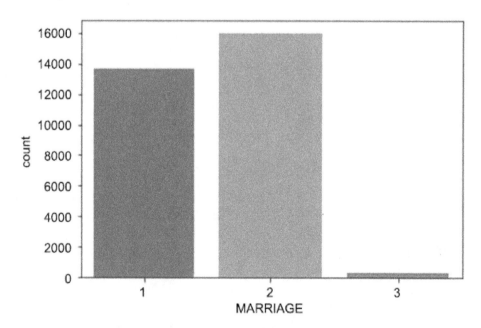

    Figure 6.12: Count plot for the marriage column

Let's calculate the number of values for the **MARRIAGE** column:

```
df['MARRIAGE'].value_counts()
```

The output will be as follows:

```
2 16018
1 13659
3 323
Name: MARRIAGE, dtype: int64
```

From the preceding output, we can infer that our dataset has a high number of people who are single (unmarried), closely followed by people who are married.

BIVARIATE ANALYSIS

Bivariate analysis is performed between two variables to look at their relationship.

In this section, you will consider the relationship between the **DEFAULT** column and other columns in the DataFrame with the help of the **crosstab** function and visualization techniques.

1. The **SEX** column versus the **DEFAULT** column:

   In this section, you will look at the relationship between the **SEX** and **DEFAULT** columns by plotting a count plot with the **hue** as **DEFAULT** to compare the number of male customers who have defaulted with the number of female customers who have defaulted:

```
sns.set(rc={'figure.figsize':(15,10)})
edu = sns.countplot(x='SEX', hue='DEFAULT', data=df)
edu.set_xticklabels(['Male','Female'])
plt.show()
```

The output will be as follows:

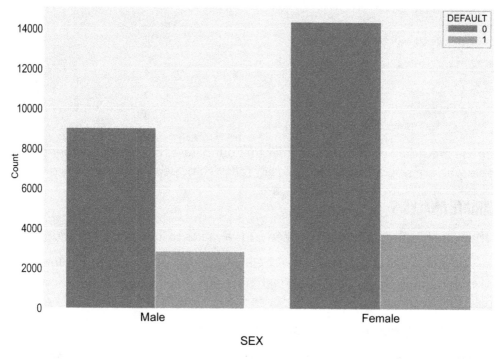

Figure 6.13: Relationship between the SEX and DEFAULT columns

From the preceding graph, you can see that females have defaulted more than males. But this graph doesn't show us the complete picture. To determine what percentage of each sex has defaulted, we will perform cross-tabulation.

Cross-tabulation is a technique used to show the relationship between two or more categorical values. For example, in this scenario, we would like to find the relationship between **DEFAULT** and **SEX**. A crosstab table will show you the count of customers for each of the following combinations:

1	Male and defaulted
2	Male and hasn't defaulted
3	Female and defaulted
4	Female and hasn't defaulted

Figure 6.14: Combinations for cross-tabulation

The output will be as follows:

DEFAULT	0	1
SEX		
1	9015	2873
2	14349	3763

Figure 6.15: Cross-tabulation table for male and female defaulters

The preceding table can be used as a sample. In this table, we can see that **SEX** subcategory **1** has **9015** people who have not defaulted (**DEFAULT** :0) and **2873** people who have defaulted, while subcategory **2** in **SEX** has **14349** people who have not defaulted and **3763** people who have defaulted.

We can also find the percentage distribution for each pair by passing in the `normalize='index'` parameter, as follows:

```
pd.crosstab(df.SEX,df.DEFAULT,normalize='index',margins=True)
```

The output will be as follows:

DEFAULT	0	1
SEX		
1	0.758328	0.241672
2	0.792237	0.207763
All	0.778800	0.221200

Figure 6.16: Cross-tabulation for the SEX and DEFAULT columns

As you can see, around 24% of male customers have defaulted and around 20% of female customers have defaulted.

In the next exercise, we will evaluate the relationship between the **EDUCATION**, **MARRIAGE** and **DEFAULT** columns.

EXERCISE 6.01: EVALUATING THE RELATIONSHIP BETWEEN THE DEFAULT COLUMN AND THE EDUCATION AND MARRIAGE COLUMNS

In this exercise, you will evaluate the relationship between the **EDUCATION** and **DEFAULT** columns using a count plot and the **crosstab** function. Our main objective is to determine which subcategory in the **EDUCATION** column has the highest default rate.

Perform the following steps to complete the exercise:

1. Plot a count plot using **seaborn** for the **EDUCATION** and **DEFAULT** columns, setting the **hue** as **DEFAULT**:

```
sns.set(rc={'figure.figsize':(15,10)})
edu = sns.countplot(x='EDUCATION', hue='DEFAULT', data=df)
edu.set_xticklabels(['Graduate School','University',\
                     'High School','Other'])
plt.show()
```

The output will be as follows:

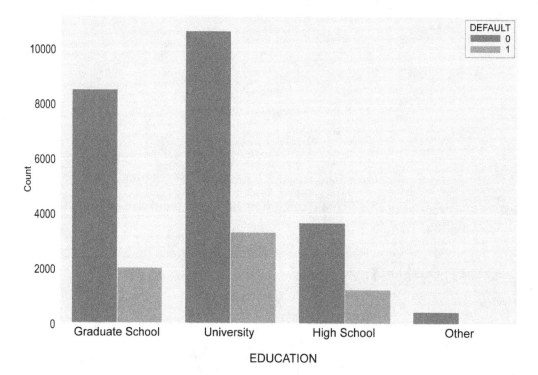

Figure 6.17: Relationship between the EDUCATION and DEFAULT columns

Observe the count plot for each subcategory. You can conclude from the plot that a greater number of defaults happen for customers whose highest qualification is **University**, but it is advisable to first perform cross-tabulation to find the exact count.

2. To determine which subcategory has a higher default percentage, perform cross-tabulation with the following code:

```
pd.crosstab(df.EDUCATION,df.DEFAULT,normalize='index')
```

The output will be as follows:

DEFAULT	0	1
EDUCATION		
1	0.807652	0.192348
2	0.762651	0.237349
3	0.748424	0.251576
4	0.929487	0.070513

Figure 6.18: Cross-tabulation of the DEFAULT and EDUCATION columns

3. To evaluate the relationship between the **MARRIAGE** and **DEFAULT** columns, plot a count plot with the **hue** as **DEFAULT** and determine how marital status corresponds to customer default rates:

```
sns.set(rc={'figure.figsize':(12,10)})
marriage = sns.countplot(x="MARRIAGE", hue='DEFAULT', data=df)
marriage.set_xticklabels(['Married','Single','Other'])
plt.show()
```

The output will be as follows:

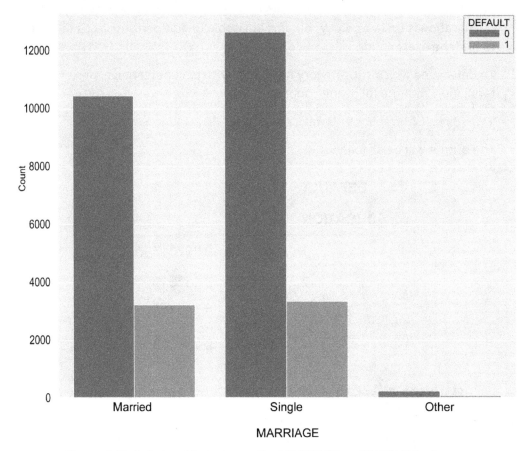

Figure 6.19: Relationship between the MARRIAGE and DEFAULT columns

From the preceding graph, we can see that married and single people have an almost equal number of defaults.

4. To determine what percentage of married/single/other people have defaulted, perform cross-tabulation:

```
pd.crosstab(df.MARRIAGE,df.DEFAULT,normalize='index',margins=True)
```

The output will be as follows:

DEFAULT	0	1
MARRIAGE		
1	0.765283	0.234717
2	0.791110	0.208890
3	0.739938	0.260062
All	0.778800	0.221200

Figure 6.20: Cross-tabulation between the DEFAULT and MARRIAGE columns

> **NOTE**
>
> To access the source code for this specific section, please refer to https://packt.live/3e4vwaW.
>
> You can also run this example online at https://packt.live/3fxjvet. You must execute the entire Notebook in order to get the desired result.

With the help of the **crosstab** function, we see that customers who belong to the **Other** subcategory have a higher percentage of defaults than the others.

Let's now look at the other possible relationships between the different variables.

PAY_1 VERSUS DEFAULT

In this section, we will be looking at the relationship between the **DEFAULT** and **PAY_1** columns (the repayment status in the month of September 2005).

The measurement scale for the repayment status is as follows:

Measurement Scale	Description
-1	Paid on time
1	Payment delay for 1 month
2	Payment delay for 2 months
3	Payment delay for 3 months
4	Payment delay for 4 months
5	Payment delay for 5 months
6	Payment delay for 6 months
7	Payment delay for 7 months
8	Payment delay for 8 months
9	Payment delay for 9 months and above

Figure 6.21: Scaling for repayment statuses

We can use the **crosstab** function to visualize the relationship between **DEFAULT** and **PAY_1**. This gives the percentage of defaults for each subcategory:

```
pd.crosstab(df.PAY_1,df.DEFAULT,margins=True)
```

The output will be as follows:

DEFAULT	0	1	All
PAY_1			
-2	2394	365	2759
-1	4732	954	5686
0	12849	1888	14737
1	2436	1252	3688
2	823	1844	2667
3	78	244	322
4	24	52	76
5	13	13	26
6	5	6	11
7	2	7	9
8	8	11	19
All	23364	6636	30000

Figure 6.22: Cross-tabulation for the PAY_1 and DEFAULT columns

From the output of the **crosstab** function, we can see that the maximum count of defaults falls under subcategory **2**—that is, a payment delay for the last 2 months. This implies that a customer who has missed payments for 2 continuous months has a high probability of default.

BALANCE VERSUS DEFAULT

In this section, we will be looking at the relationship between the **LIMIT_BAL** column and the **DEFAULT** column with the help of a categorical plot from **seaborn**. The balance is the amount given as credit. It includes both the individual consumer's credit and their family's (supplementary) credit.

We will be plotting a categorical plot between **DEFAULT** and **LIMIT_BAL**:

```
sns.catplot(x="DEFAULT", y="LIMIT_BAL", jitter=True, data=df);
```

The output will be as follows:

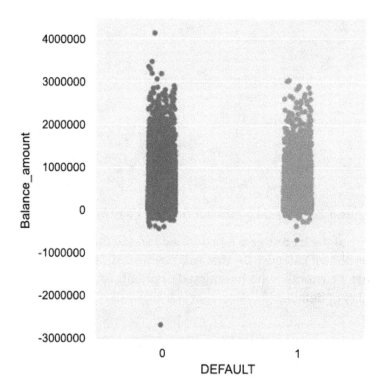

Figure 6.23: Relationship between the LIMIT_BAL and DEFAULT columns

From the preceding plot, we can infer that customers with higher balances have a lower likelihood of default than customers with lower balance amounts.

EXERCISE 6.02: EVALUATING THE RELATIONSHIP BETWEEN THE AGE AND DEFAULT COLUMNS

In this exercise, you will evaluate the relationship between the **AGE** and **DEFAULT** columns using the **crosstab** function. Our main objective is to find out which age group has the highest default rate.

Perform the following steps to complete the exercise:

1. Apply the **crosstab** function to evaluate the relationship between the **AGE** and **DEFAULT** columns:

```
pd.crosstab(df.AGE,df.DEFAULT)
```

The output will be as follows:

DEFAULT AGE	0	1
21	53	14
22	391	169
23	684	247
24	827	300
25	884	302
26	1003	253
27	1164	313
28	1123	286
29	1292	313
30	1121	274

Figure 6.24: Relationship between the AGE and DEFAULT columns

> **NOTE**
>
> The output has been truncated for presentation purposes. Please find the complete output at https://packt.live/39TIAhN.

As you can see, the age groups with the highest count of defaults are 27 and 29. In order to find the percentage-based split in each age category, we need to perform cross-tabulation, which is covered in the next step.

2. To determine which age group has the highest default percentage, perform cross-tabulation with **normalize= 'Index'**:

```
pd.crosstab(df.AGE,df.DEFAULT,normalize='index',margins=True)
```

The output will be as follows:

DEFAULT	0	1
AGE		
21	0.791045	0.208955
22	0.698214	0.301786
23	0.734694	0.265306
24	0.733807	0.266193
25	0.745363	0.254637
26	0.798567	0.201433
27	0.788084	0.211916
28	0.797019	0.202981
29	0.804984	0.195016
30	0.803584	0.196416

Figure 6.25: Cross-tabulation for the AGE and DEFAULT columns

From the preceding output, we can see that even though the ages **27** and **29** had higher counts of defaults, the percentage-wise default count paints a different picture. Those customers of the age of **22** had a higher percentage of defaulters than non-defaulters.

CORRELATION

In this section, we will cover correlation – what does correlation mean, and how do we check the correlation between the **DEFAULT** column and other columns in our dataset?

Correlation measures the degree of dependency between any two variables. Say, for example, we have two variables, A and B. If the value of B increases when the value of A is increased, we say the variables are positively correlated. On the other hand, if the value of B decreases when we increase the value of A, we say the variables are negatively correlated. There could also be a situation where an increase in the value of A doesn't affect the value of B, for which we say the variables are uncorrelated.

The value of a correlation coefficient can vary between -1 to 1, with 1 being a strong positive correlation and -1 a strong negative correlation.

By studying the correlation between the **DEFAULT** column and other columns with the help of a heatmap, we can figure out which column/variable has a high impact on the **DEFAULT** column.

In this section, we will be using Spearman's rank correlation to check the correlation between two variables. The main reason for using Spearman's rank correlation is that it does not assume that the data is normally distributed, and it can be used between ordinal variables.

A variable is said to be ordinal if it is categorical in nature and has a natural order; for example, *High*, *Medium*, and *Low* are ordinal variables. In our dataset, as we have categorical columns such as **EDUCATION**, it is a good idea to go with Spearman's rank correlation.

ACTIVITY 6.01: EVALUATING THE CORRELATION BETWEEN COLUMNS USING A HEATMAP

In this activity, you will analyze the correlation of the **DEFAULT** column with the other remaining columns of the DataFrame and visualize the analysis using a heatmap. By finding the correlation between these and the **DEFAULT** column, you can determine which features have a higher impact on the **DEFAULT** column and whether that impact is positive or negative.

Perform the following steps to complete the activity:

1. Plot the heatmap for all the columns in a DataFrame (other than the **ID** column) by using **sns.heatmap**, keeping the figure size as **30,10** for better visibility.

2. Use **Spearman** as the method parameter to compute Spearman's rank correlation coefficient.

   The output will be as follows:

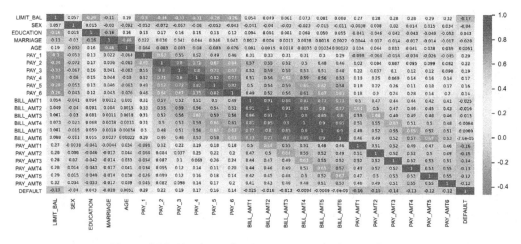

Figure 6.26: Heatmap for Spearman's rank correlation

3. Apply the `.corr()` function on each column with respect to the **DEFAULT** column to get the exact correlation coefficients.

The output will be as follows:

```
ID            -0.013952
LIMIT_BAL     -0.169586
SEX           -0.039961
EDUCATION      0.043425
MARRIAGE      -0.028174
AGE            0.005149
PAY_1          0.292213
PAY_2          0.216919
PAY_3          0.194771
PAY_4          0.173690
PAY_5          0.159043
PAY_6          0.142523
BILL_AMT1     -0.025327
BILL_AMT2     -0.015554
BILL_AMT3     -0.012670
BILL_AMT4     -0.008357
BILL_AMT5     -0.006851
BILL_AMT6     -0.000076
PAY_AMT1      -0.160493
PAY_AMT2      -0.150977
PAY_AMT3      -0.139388
PAY_AMT4      -0.127979
PAY_AMT5      -0.116587
PAY_AMT6      -0.121444
dtype: float64
```

Figure 6.27: Output for the correlation function

NOTE

The solution to the activity can be found on page 513.

From the preceding output, we can easily conclude that the **DEFAULT** column has a high positive correlation with **PAY_1** **(.29)**, which implies that if a customer has missed a payment in the first month, they have a higher chance of missing further payments in the consecutive months.

Also, the **DEFAULT** column has the highest negative correlation with **PAY_AMT1** **(-.16)**, which implies that the higher the payment for the month of September 2005, the lower the chances of default.

BUILDING A PROFILE OF A HIGH-RISK CUSTOMER

Based on the analysis performed in the previous sections, we can now build a profile of the customer who is most likely to default. With this predicted customer profile, credit card companies can take preventive steps (such as reducing credit limits or increasing the rate of interest) and can demand additional collateral from customers who are deemed to be high risk.

The customer who satisfies the majority of the following conditions can be classified as a high-risk customer. A high-risk customer is one who has a higher probability of default:

- A male customer is more likely to default than a female customer.

- People with a relationship status of *other* are more likely to default than married or single people.

- A customer whose highest educational qualification is a high-school diploma is more likely to default than a customer who has gone to graduate school or university.

- A customer who has delayed payment for 2 consecutive months has a higher probability of default.

- A customer who is 22 years of age has a higher probability of defaulting on payments than any other age group.

SUMMARY

In this chapter, we applied univariate EDA to a given dataset to plot the distribution of individual features and implemented bivariate analysis to understand the relationship between two features. We also used a correlation heatmap to determine the correlation of the features of the DataFrame. Drawing conclusions from the results of our analyses, we were able to build a statistically probable profile of a high-risk customer most likely to default on a loan.

In the next chapter, we will analyze the medical data of 303 patients and link the data features with the diagnosis of heart disease.

7

ANALYZING THE HEART DISEASE DATASET

OVERVIEW

In this chapter, we are going to analyze medical data. We will use various data analysis techniques, such as searching for missing values and outliers, and plot visualizations to observe trends and patterns that exist in the data. We will create bar charts, heatmaps, and other visualizations using seaborn and Matplotlib to understand how the features we'll be looking at affect the target column of the dataset.

INTRODUCTION

In the previous chapter, we looked at a dataset regarding credit cards, which was used to predict whether or not the customers would default. We applied different data analysis techniques, such as univariate analysis and bivariate analysis, to understand and process customers' payment histories and identify relationships between different features.

In this chapter, we are going to work with a dataset from the medical industry. This dataset is called the Heart Disease dataset and has been published in the UCI Machine Learning Repository. This dataset originally contained 75 attributes, but only 14 of those attributes have been used by published experiments, so we will also be using this subset for our data analysis. The dataset uses a lot of medical terminology that you may be unfamiliar with, but the features will be explained in the exercises so that you are aware of what you are analyzing.

We will be checking for outliers, missing values, and the trends and relationships between different features of the dataset to gain a better understanding of the available data and derive useful insights from it.

> ## NOTE
>
> The original data can be found here: https://archive.ics.uci.edu/ml/datasets/Heart+Disease.
>
> You can also find it in our GitHub: https://packt.live/3frm8hK.
>
> Principal investigators responsible for the data collection at each institution are as follows:
>
> 1. Hungarian Institute of Cardiology. Budapest: Andras Janosi, M.D.
>
> 2. University Hospital, Zurich, Switzerland: William Steinbrunn, M.D.
>
> 3. University Hospital, Basel, Switzerland: Matthias Pfisterer, M.D.
>
> 4. V.A. Medical Center, Long Beach and Cleveland Clinic Foundation:Robert Detrano, M.D., Ph.D.

The goal of this dataset is to train a model so that it predicts whether a person is likely to suffer from heart disease (whether the probability is above or below 50%); however, in this chapter, we are simply going to observe and analyze the distribution of the data, search for outliers and missing values, and assess the relationships between features.

The features are as follows:

- **Age**: Age of the patient.

- **Sex**: Sex of the patient, where **0** represents **female** and **1** represents **male**.

  Angina is a type of chest pain that occurs when the heart doesn't receive blood containing enough oxygen.

- **Cp**: Chest pain type, where the categories are as follows:

Category	Chest Pain Type
0	Typical angina
1	Atypical angina
2	Non-anginal pain
3	Asymptomatic (not exhibiting symptoms of disease)

Figure 7.1: Chest pain types

- **Trestbps**: Resting blood pressure in mm Hg on admission to the hospital.

- **Chol**: Serum cholesterol in mg/dl.

- **Fbs**: Fasting blood sugar, whether it's greater than 120 mg/dl or not, where 0 represents false and 1 presents true.

- **Restecg**: Resting ECG results, where the categories are as follows:

Category	Results
0	Normal
1	Having ST-T wave abnormality (T wave inversions and/or ST elevation or depression of > 0.05 mV)
2	Showing probable or definite left ventricular hypertrophy by Estes' criteria

Figure 7.2: ECG results

- **Thalach**: Maximum recorded heart rate achieved.

- **Exang**: Presence of exercise-induced angina, where **0** represents **no** and **1** represents **yes**.

- **Oldpeak**: ST depression induced by exercise relative to rest.

The deeper and more widespread this ST depression is, the more severe the disease. ST depression refers to a depression that's found in an electrocardiogram. This occurs when the trace of the ST segment is unusually far below the normal baseline. The ST segment refers to the ending of the S wave and the beginning of the T wave in an electrocardiogram.

- **Slope**: The slope of the peak exercise ST segment. The categories are as follows:

Category	Slope of the peak
0	Upsloping
1	Flat
2	Downsloping

Figure 7.3: Slope of peak exercise

- **Ca**: Number of major vessels colored by fluoroscopy.

- **Thal**: Thalassemia.

  Thalassemia is a hereditary blood disease wherein the body is unable to produce an adequate amount or appropriate form of hemoglobin.

- **Target**: Diagnosis of heart disease, where **0** represents where narrowing of the diameter is less than 50% and **1** represents where narrowing of the diameter is more than 50%.

> **NOTE**
>
> All the exercises and activities in this chapter are linked together, so they must be done in the same Jupyter notebook, one after the other.

EXERCISE 7.01: LOADING AND UNDERSTANDING THE DATA

In this exercise, you will read the dataset into a DataFrame, review its features, and rename them, if required, since this is a medical dataset. Follow these steps to complete this exercise:

1. Open a new Jupyter notebook and import pandas (to load and analyze the dataset), matplotlib.pyplot (for data visualization), seaborn (for data visualization), and NumPy (for linear algebra):

```
import pandas as pd
import matplotlib.pyplot as plt
import seaborn as sns
import numpy as np
```

2. Use the `.read_csv()` function to load the **heart.csv** file into a DataFrame called **df**:

```
df = pd.read_csv('https://raw.githubusercontent.com/'\
                 'PacktWorkshops/'\
                 'The-Data-Analysis-Workshop/master/'\
                 'Chapter07/Dataset/heart.csv')
```

3. Use `.describe()` to display the statistical information about **df**:

```
df.describe()
```

The output will be as follows:

	age	sex	cp	trestbps	chol	fbs	restecg
count	303.000000	303.000000	303.000000	303.000000	303.000000	303.000000	303.000000
mean	54.366337	0.683168	0.966997	131.623762	246.264026	0.148515	0.528053
std	9.082101	0.466011	1.032052	17.538143	51.830751	0.356198	0.525860
min	29.000000	0.000000	0.000000	94.000000	126.000000	0.000000	0.000000
25%	47.500000	0.000000	0.000000	120.000000	211.000000	0.000000	0.000000
50%	55.000000	1.000000	1.000000	130.000000	240.000000	0.000000	1.000000
75%	61.000000	1.000000	2.000000	140.000000	274.500000	0.000000	1.000000
max	77.000000	1.000000	3.000000	200.000000	564.000000	1.000000	2.000000

Figure 7.4: df's statistical information

This DataFrame has 14 columns, all of which are numerical. The count of instances for each column is the same (303), which means this dataset is made up of the health data of 303 patients and contains no missing values.

A lot of the column names are difficult to understand for people from a non-medical background, so let's rename some of them.

4. Use the .**rename()** function to create a dictionary of the original column name with the new column name within the **columns** parameter:

```
df.rename(index = str, \
          columns = {'cp' : 'chest_pain', \
                     'trestbps' : 'rest_bp', \
                     'fbs' : 'fast_bld_sugar', \
                     'restecg' : 'rest_ecg', \
                     'thalach' : 'max_hr', \
                     'exang' : 'ex_angina', \
                     'oldpeak' : 'st_depr', \
                     'ca' : 'colored_vessels', \
                     'thal' : 'thalassemia', }, inplace = True)
```

5. Use .**info()** to print an overview of our new DataFrame:

```
df.info()
```

The output will be as follows:

```
<class 'pandas.core.frame.DataFrame'>
Index: 303 entries, 0 to 302
Data columns (total 14 columns):
 #   Column          Non-Null Count   Dtype
---  ------          --------------   -----
 0   age             303 non-null     int64
 1   sex             303 non-null     int64
 2   chest_pain      303 non-null     int64
 3   rest_bp         303 non-null     int64
 4   chol            303 non-null     int64
 5   fast_bld_sugar  303 non-null     int64
 6   rest_ecg        303 non-null     int64
 7   max_hr          303 non-null     int64
 8   ex_angina       303 non-null     int64
 9   st_depr         303 non-null     float64
 10  slope           303 non-null     int64
 11  colored_vessels 303 non-null     int64
 12  thalassemia     303 non-null     int64
 13  target          303 non-null     int64
dtypes: float64(1), int64(13)
memory usage: 35.5+ KB
```

Figure 7.5: Information about the DataFrame

Now, the column names are easier to understand.

> **NOTE**
>
> To access the source code for this specific section, please refer to https://packt.live/2BjhPGs.
>
> You can also run this example online at https://packt.live/2Y87JRR. You must execute the entire Notebook in order to get the desired result.

In this exercise, we have successfully loaded our data into a DataFrame and observed the features. We can see that all the columns contain numerical data and none have any missing values.

Next, we are going to check to see if our dataset has any outliers. But first, let's take a look at what outliers are.

OUTLIERS

An outlier is a data point that is different from most data points. When visualized, this data point is far away from the rest—hence the name: outlier. For example, if you have a set of 12 numbers, out of which 11 are between 1 and 6 and 1 has a value of 37, that data point will be an outlier due to its significant difference from the rest of the data points. The definition of what is and what is not an outlier also depends on the context of the dataset.

For example, let's say you have a column that is measuring height in feet and you have data points ranging from 5'5" to 6'2" and then you have one data point that is 7'8". When you look at those numbers as just numbers, they're not that far off— there's only a numeric distance of 1.6 between 6'2" and 7'8". However, if you think about them as heights, then you realize how different 7'8" is. It is very unlikely for someone to be that tall, especially when your majority's maximum height is 6'2". Therefore, you can call this an outlier.

Box plots are a type of visualization that is great for visualizing outliers. They provide us with a lot of information about our data, such as the median, the first quartile, the third quartile, and the minimum and maximum values, as well as the existence of outliers, as shown in the following diagram:

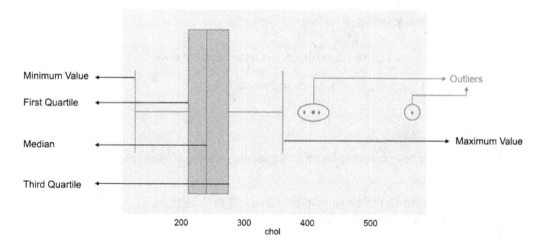

Figure 7.6: Information provided by a box plot

Let's perform an exercise to identify outliers with box plots.

EXERCISE 7.02: CHECKING FOR OUTLIERS

In the previous exercise, you displayed the statistical information of **df**, which includes the minimum and maximum values of the data in each column. Consider *Figure 7.04*. You can see there that the values seem a bit odd for a few columns, such as **chol**. The mean value is **246**, the third quartile value is **274.5**, but the maximum value is **564**. This means that there is probably at least one outlying value. The values for **st_depr**, **colored_vessels**, and **thalassemia** seem the same.

In this exercise, you will plot a box plot for **chol** to determine the existence of outliers.

First, set some basic styling for how we want our plots to look. Make sure you are using the same Jupyter notebook that you used for *Exercise 7.01, Loading and Understanding the Data*. Follow these steps to complete this exercise:

1. Use seaborn's **.set()** function to set the color palette as pastel. Within **rc**, create a dictionary wherein the figure size is (**12, 8**), the axes' title size is **18**, and the *x* and *y* axes' label sizes are **16**:

```
sns.set(palette = 'pastel', rc = {"figure.figsize": (12,8), \
                                  "axes.titlesize" : 18, \
                                  "axes.labelsize" : 16, \
                                  "xtick.labelsize" : 16, \
                                  "ytick.labelsize" : 16 })
```

2. Plot a boxplot using **sns.boxplot** for the **chol** column:

```
chol = sns.boxplot(df['chol'])
plt.show()
```

The output will be as follows:

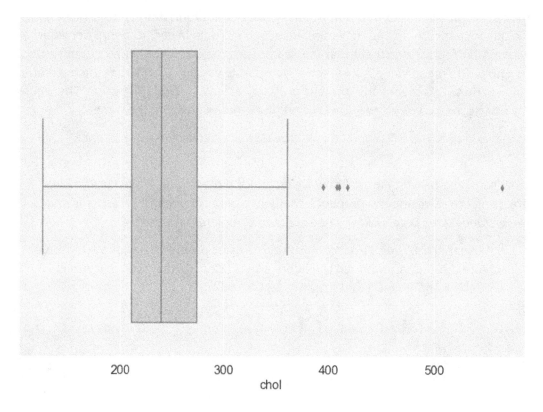

Figure 7.7: Box plot for the chol column

> **NOTE**
>
> To access the source code for this specific section, please refer to https://packt.live/2N1iYoS.
>
> You can also run this example online at https://packt.live/30QfLRm. You must execute the entire Notebook in order to get the desired result.

As hypothesized, the preceding box plot shows that there are, in fact, a few outliers (represented by the dots beyond 370). In the following activity, you will check for outliers in the other three columns we hypothesized would also have outliers.

ACTIVITY 7.01: CHECKING FOR OUTLIERS

In this activity, you will check for outliers in the **st_depr**, **colored_vessels**, and **thalassemia** columns. Follow these steps to complete this activity:

1. Plot a box plot using **sns.boxplot** for the **st_depr** column.

   The output will be as follows:

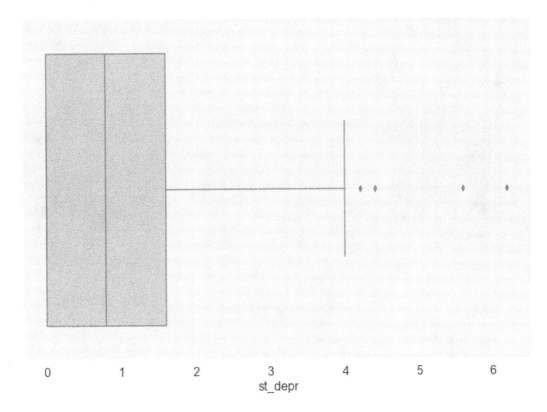

Figure 7.8: Box plot for st_depr

2. Plot a box plot using **sns.boxplot** for the **colored_vessels** column.

   The output will be as follows:

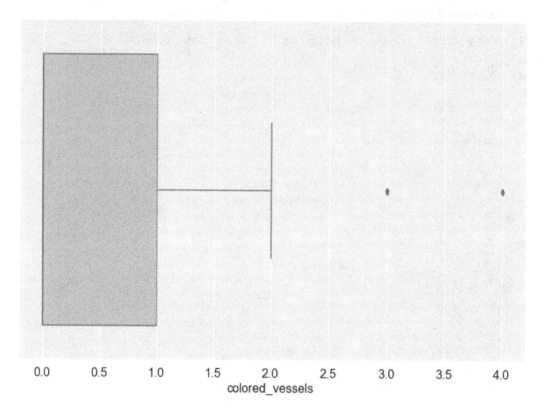

Figure 7.9: Box plot for colored_vessels

3. Plot a boxplot using **sns.boxplot** for the **thalassemia** column.

The output will be as follows:

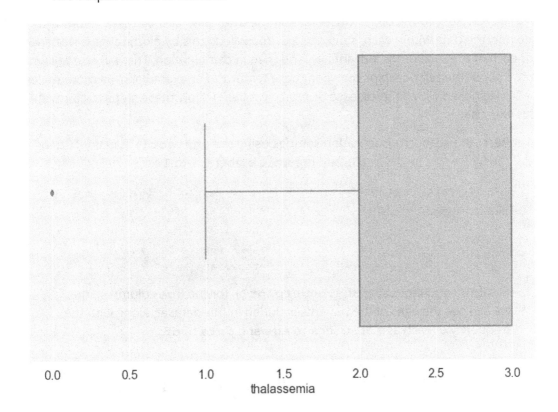

Figure 7.10: Box plot for thalassemia

> **NOTE**
>
> The solution to the activity can be found on page 515.

The preceding box plots show that each of these columns do have a few outliers. However, in this case, we are not going to delete these instances or impute them since we have so few instances to start off with. We are just observing how the data is distributed.

EXERCISE 7.03: PLOTTING THE DISTRIBUTIONS AND RELATIONSHIPS BETWEEN SPECIFIC FEATURES

In this exercise, you will take a closer look at the **age**, **sex**, and **target** columns to see how the data within each is distributed. You will do this by plotting visualizations for each of these columns individually, and then in combination. This will also tell us more about the relationships between these features. For example, have more males been diagnosed with heart disease or more females? Follow these steps to complete this exercise:

1. Reset the seaborn visualization settings using the **sns.set()** function. Change the figure size to (**16, 10**), and the **xtick** label size to **14**:

```
sns.set(palette = 'pastel', rc = {"figure.figsize": (16,10), \
                                  "axes.titlesize" : 18, \
                                  "axes.labelsize" : 16, \
                                  "xtick.labelsize" : 14, \
                                  "ytick.labelsize" : 16 })
```

2. Create a countplot using **sns.countplot()** for the **age** column so that we can see the ages of the patients included in this dataset, along with the frequency of each age. First, set **x** to **age** and **data** to **df**:

```
g = sns.countplot(x = 'age', data = df)
```

3. Use **.set_title()** to set the title of the plot to **Distribution of Age**:

```
g.set_title('Distribution of Age')
```

4. Use **plt.xlabel()** to label the x axis as **Age**:

```
plt.xlabel('Age')
```

The output will be as follows:

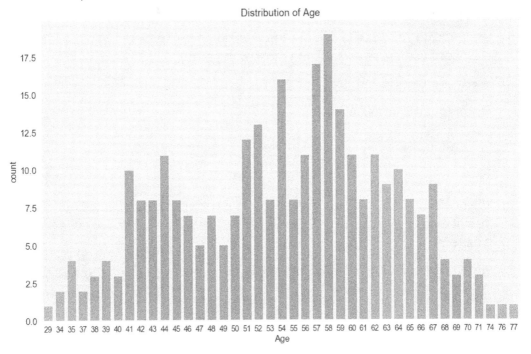

Figure 7.11: Age distribution

The preceding graph displays the number of patients of each age that have been included in this dataset. We can see that the youngest patient was 29 years old, while the oldest was 77. The majority of the patients in this experiment were in their 50s and early 60s, with the most common age being 58 years old. This gives us an idea of the data we will observe when we analyze the remaining features of this dataset. Since most of the patients are older, their health data may not be in the normal healthy ranges.

334 | Analyzing the Heart Disease Dataset

Next, look more closely at the **target** column to see how many of these patients have and have not been diagnosed with heart disease.

5. Use **.value_counts()** to print the total number of patients who have been diagnosed with heart disease and those who haven't:

```
df.target.value_counts()
```

The output will be as follows:

```
1    165
0    138
Name: target, dtype: int64
```

The preceding results tell us that our dataset is almost balanced; the number of instances in each of the two classes is similar. Let's visualize this to understand it better.

6. Plot a countplot using **sns.countplot** with **x** as **target** and **data** as **df**:

```
a = sns.countplot(x = 'target', data = df)
```

7. Use **.set_title()** to set the title to **Distribution of Presence of Heart Disease**:

```
a.set_title('Distribution of Presence of Heart Disease')
```

8. Use **.set_xticklabels()** to set the labels of the two bars to **Absent** and **Present**, respectively:

```
a.set_xticklabels(['Absent', 'Present'])
```

9. Use **plt.xlabel()** to set the label of the x axis to **Presence of Heart Disease**:

```
plt.xlabel("Presence of Heart Disease")
plt.show()
```

The output will be as follows:

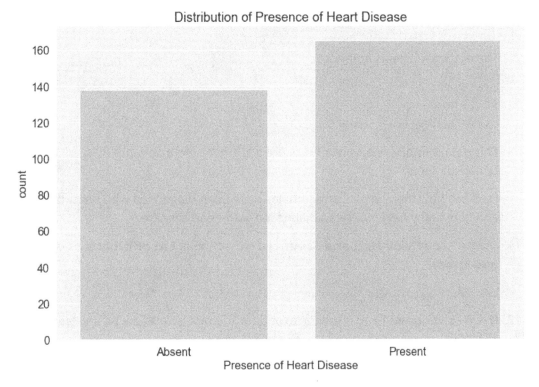

Figure 7.12: Distribution of target column

This plot confirms that the number of patients with and without heart disease are similar.

Now, we're going to add **sex** to this plot to see how many patients of each sex have and have not been diagnosed with heart disease.

10. Use `.value_counts()` to print the total number of patients who are male and female:

```
df.sex.value_counts()
```

The output will be as follows:

```
1     207
0      96
Name: sex, dtype: int64
```

This data is imbalanced since there are a lot more male patients than female patients.

Let's see how many males and females have been diagnosed with heart disease, and how many have not been diagnosed with heart disease.

11. Create a countplot using **sns.countplot** with **x** as **target**, **data** as **df**, and **hue** as **sex**:

```
b = sns.countplot(x = 'target', data = df, hue = 'sex')
```

12. Use **plt.legend()** to create a legend for the plot with **Female** and **Male** as labels:

```
plt.legend(['Female', 'Male'])
```

13. Use `.set_title()` to set **Distribution of Presence of Heart Disease by Sex** as the title of the plot:

```
b.set_title('Distribution of Presence of Heart Disease by Sex')
```

14. Use `.set_xticklabels` to set the labels of the bars as **Absent** and **Present**:

```
b.set_xticklabels(['Absent', 'Present'])
plt.show()
```

The output will be as follows:

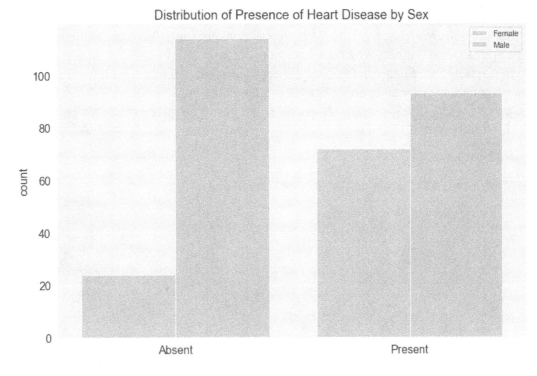

Figure 7.13: Distribution of Presence of Heart Disease by Sex

This plot tells us that, out of the 96 female patients present, around 72 of them have been diagnosed with heart disease. This case is the opposite in the male patients; a larger number of male patients have not been diagnosed with heart disease than those that have.

> **NOTE**
>
> To access the source code for this specific section, please refer to https://packt.live/2N6G4KY.
>
> You can also run this example online at https://packt.live/3e9lRjt. You must execute the entire Notebook in order to get the desired result.

In this exercise, you have successfully observed how the **age** and `target` columns are distributed, as well as how many female and male patients have been diagnosed with heart disease. In the next activity, you are going to perform a similar analysis on the other features of the dataset.

ACTIVITY 7.02: PLOTTING DISTRIBUTIONS AND RELATIONSHIPS BETWEEN COLUMNS WITH RESPECT TO THE TARGET COLUMN

In the previous exercise, you observed the relationships and distributions between age and sex, and patients who have and have not been diagnosed with heart disease. In this activity, you are going to analyze three more features in a similar fashion to see how the data is distributed and what the relationships between them and the target columns are like. These three features are chest pain type, number of colored vessels, and the slope of the ST segment.

Chest Pain

1. Print the total number of patients with each type of chest pain.

   The output will be as follows:

   ```
   0    143
   2     87
   1     50
   3     23
   Name: chest_pain, dtype: int64
   ```

2. Create a countplot with **chest_pain** as **x**, **data** as **df**, and **hue** as **target**. First, create a legend for the plot with **Absent** and **Present** as labels.

3. Set the title to **Distribution of Presence of Heart Disease by Chest Pain Type**.

4. Set the labels of the bars as the four types of chest pain, that is, **Typical Anginal**, **Atypical Anginal**, **Non-anginal Pain**, and **Asymptomatic**.

The plot will be as follows:

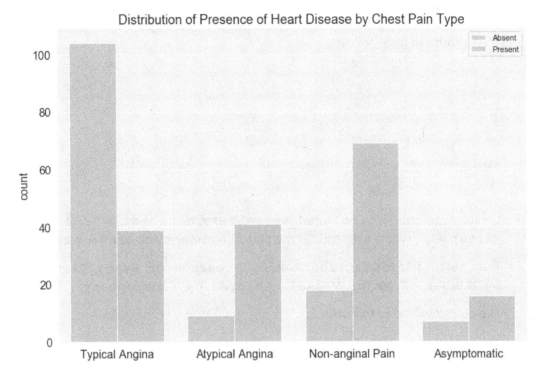

Figure 7.14: Distribution of Presence of Heart Disease by Chest Pain Type

This graph shows that most of the patients have typical angina. The next most common chest pain type is non-anginal pain, then atypical angina, and lastly, asymptomatic.

Many patients who had typical angina were not diagnosed with heart disease. The largest group of patients with a particular chest pain that had been diagnosed with heart disease had non-anginal pain.

Colored Vessels

5. Print the total number of patients with each number of colored vessels.

    The output will be as follows:

    ```
    0     175
    1      65
    2      38
    3      20
    4       5
    Name: colored_vessels, dtype: int64
    ```

6. Create a countplot with **colored_vessels** as **x**, **data** as **df**, and **hue** as **target**. First, create a legend for the plot with **Absent** and **Present** as labels.

7. Then, set the title to **Distribution of Presence of Heart Disease by Number of Major Vessels Colored by Fluoroscopy**.

    The output will be as follows:

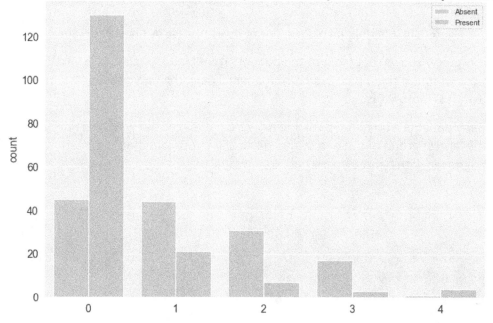

Figure 7.15: Distribution of Presence of Heart Disease by Number of Major Vessels Colored by Fluoroscopy

The preceding graph shows that most of the patients have 0 colored vessels and that most of the patients with 0 colored vessels have been diagnosed with heart disease. This implies a strong negative correlation between colored vessels and heart disease.

Slope

8. Print the total number of patients with each type of slope.

   The output will be as follows:

```
2    142
1    140
0     21
Name: slope, dtype: int64
```

9. Create a countplot with **slope** as **x**, **data** as **df**, and **hue** as **target**. First, create a legend for the plot with **Absent** and **Present** as labels.

10. Set the title to **Distribution of Presence of Heart Disease by Slope**.

11. Lastly, set the labels of the bars as the three types of slope, that is, **Upsloping**, **Flat**, and **Downsloping**.

The output will be as follows:

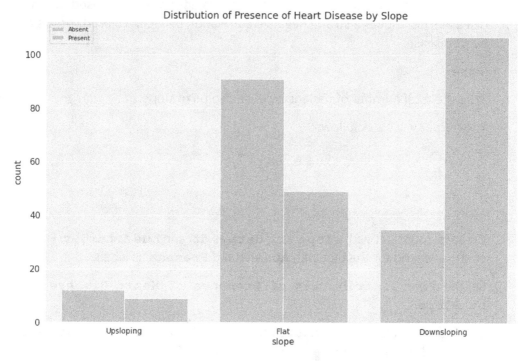

Figure 7.16: Distribution of Presence of Heart Disease by Slope

The preceding graph clearly shows that most patients with a downwards slope of the ST segment post-peak exercise have been diagnosed with heart disease, thus implying a correlation between the two. The least number of patients had an upward slope, and most of those who had a flat line have not been diagnosed with heart disease.

> **NOTE**
>
> The solution to the activity can be found on page 518.

In this activity, we have successfully observed the relationships that chest pain type, slope type, and number of colored vessels share with the diagnosis of heart disease.

Both *Exercise 7.03: Plotting the Distributions and Relationships Between Specific Features* and *Activity 7.02: Plotting Distributions and Relationships Between Columns with Respect to the Target Column* looked at the relationship between the **target** column and columns whose values represent discrete classes. In the following exercise and activity, we are going to look at the relationship between the **target** column and columns that contain continuous values.

EXERCISE 7.04: PLOTTING THE RELATIONSHIP BETWEEN THE PRESENCE OF HEART DISEASE AND MAXIMUM RECORDED HEART RATE

In this exercise, we are going to create a scatter plot to observe the effect maximum recorded heart rate and age have on the diagnosis of heart disease. Follow these steps to complete this exercise:

1. Use **sns.set** to alter the display of the plots. Set **style** as **'whitegrid'** and **palette** as **colorblind**. For **rc**, copy the same configurations we used in *Exercise 7.02, Checking for Outliers*:

```
sns.set(style = 'whitegrid', palette = 'colorblind', \
        rc = {"figure.figsize": (12,8), "axes.titlesize" : 18, \
        "axes.labelsize" : 16, "xtick.labelsize" : 16, \
        "ytick.labelsize" : 16 })
```

2. Use **sns.scatterplot** to create a scatter plot. Set **x** as **'age'**, **y** as **max_hr**, **hue** as **target**, **style** as **target**, and **data** as **df**. Use **plt.xlabel** to set the *x*-axis label to **Age**. Use **plt.ylabel** to set the *y*-axis label to **Maximum Heart Rate**:

```
f = sns.scatterplot(x = 'age', y = 'max_hr', hue = 'target', \
                    style = 'target', data = df)
f.set_title('Presence of Heart Disease based on Age and '\
            'Maximum Heart Rate')
plt.xlabel('Age')
plt.ylabel('Maximum Heart Rate')
```

The output will be as follows:

Figure 7.17: Presence of Heart Disease based on Age and Maximum Heart Rate

The preceding graph doesn't show a very distinct pattern; the points for absent and present are mixed together and there are no discrete clusters. However, it is visible that quite a few data points with a higher heart rate are a yellow cross, which means they have been diagnosed with heart disease. We can also see that, surprisingly, this is regardless of age. A lot of the patients with heart disease seem to be on the younger side but have a high heart rate.

Let's take a closer look at this age and heart disease link.

3. Create a new column in **df** called **age_category**. Create bins with intervals of 5, starting from 25 (the minimum age in the **age** column is 29) and ending at 85 (the maximum age is 77) for the **age** column, using the **.cut()** function:

```
df['age_category'] = pd.cut(df.age, \
                        bins = list(np.arange(25, 85, 5)))
```

4. Create two plots using the **age_category** column—one with patients who have heart disease and one with those who don't. Set the first subplot as (**121**):

```
plt.subplot(121)
```

5. Apply the **.groupby** function to **df** where **target == 1** (those who have heart disease) and group by the **age_category** column. Use the **.count()** function on the **age** column to count how many patients in each age category have heart disease. Apply **.plot()** to this with the **kind** parameter set as **bar** to plot a bar graph:

```
df[df.target == 1].groupby('age_category')['age']\
.count().plot(kind = 'bar')
```

6. Set **title** to **Present**, the **xlabel** to **Age Group**, and **ylabel** to **Count**:

```
plt.title('Present')
plt.xlabel('Age Group')
plt.ylabel('Count')
```

7. Set the second **subplot** as (**122**):

```
plt.subplot(122)
```

8. Apply the **.groupby** function to **df** where **target == 0** (those who don't have heart disease) and group by the **age_category** column. Use the **.count()** function on the **age** column to count how many patients in each age category don't have heart disease. Apply **.plot()** to this with the **kind** parameter set as **bar** to plot a bar graph:

```
df[df.target == 0].groupby('age_category')['age']\
.count().plot(kind = 'bar')
```

9. Set **title** to **Absent**, **xlabel** to **Age Group**, and **ylabel** to **Count**:

```
plt.title('Absent')
plt.xlabel('Age Group')
plt.ylabel('Count')
```

The output will be as follows:

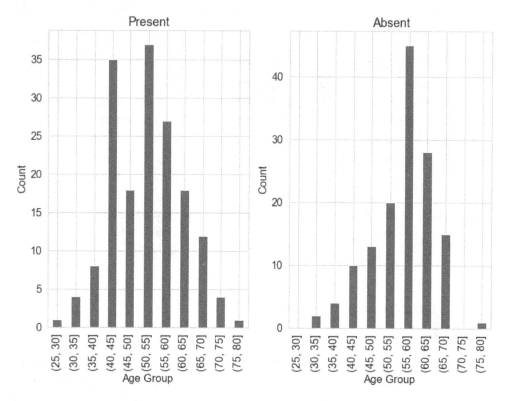

Figure 7.18: The presence of heart disease per age group

The preceding graphs confirm our earlier observation. Quite a few patients on the younger side have been diagnosed with heart disease compared to those that haven't been diagnosed with heart disease.

> **NOTE**
>
> To access the source code for this specific section, please refer to https://packt.live/2UT1Kyj.
>
> You can also run this example online at https://packt.live/3fvjtUn. You must execute the entire Notebook in order to get the desired result.

In this exercise, you successfully observed the relationship between heart rate and heart disease, as well as age and heart disease. In the following activity, you will use the same techniques on the cholesterol column.

ACTIVITY 7.03: PLOTTING THE RELATIONSHIP BETWEEN THE PRESENCE OF HEART DISEASE AND THE CHOLESTEROL COLUMN

In this activity, you are going to take a closer look at the relationship between cholesterol, age, and heart disease. Follow these steps to complete this activity:

1. Create a scatter plot with **x** as **age**, **y** as **chol**, both **hue** and **style** as **target**, and **df** as **age**.

2. Set the title to **Presence of Heart Disease based on Age and Cholesterol**.

3. Set the **x** label as **Age** and the **y** label as **Cholesterol**.

    The output will be as follows:

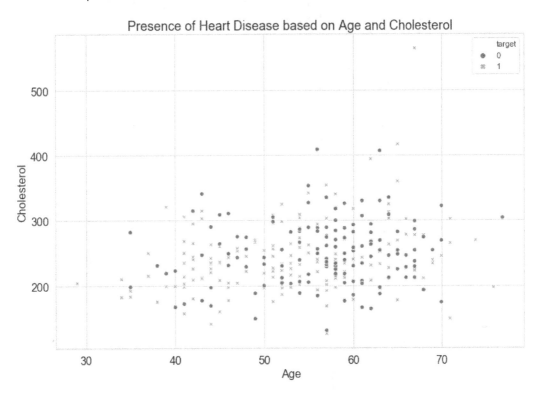

Figure 7.19: Presence of Heart Disease based on Age and Cholesterol

The preceding scatter plot doesn't show a clear correlation between age and cholesterol, or cholesterol and heart disease. However, we can observe the trend we confirmed in *Exercise 7.04, Plotting the Relationship between the Presence of Heart Disease and Maximum Recorded Heart Rate*; more younger people seem to be diagnosed with heart disease.

Now, consider the count of patients in each cholesterol group.

4. Create a new column called **chol_cat** with bins starting at **120** and ending at **380** with intervals of 20.

5. Create two subplots—one for patients with heart disease and one for patients without. Group the **target** column by the **chol_cat** column and count the number of instances in the groups. Plot a bar graph for each. Set the titles for the two as **Present** and **Absent**, respectively, with the x axis as **Cholesterol Groups** and the y axis as **Count**.

The output will be as follows:

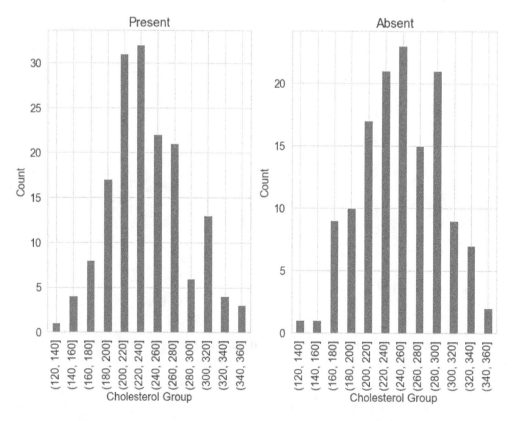

Figure 7.20: The presence of heart disease per cholesterol group

The preceding graphs don't show too much of a trend, except that, surprisingly, patients who don't have heart disease have quite high cholesterol. You would think that they would have lower cholesterol levels.

In this activity, we have seen that cholesterol doesn't have a very strong relationship with heart disease or age.

> **NOTE**
>
> The solution to the activity can be found on page 523.

EXERCISE 7.05: OBSERVING CORRELATIONS WITH A HEATMAP

While in the previous exercises and activities you observed relationships between multiple features as well as how the data within each feature has been distributed, ultimately, the main column is the **target** column. In this book, we are not going to feed any data into a machine learning model, but most datasets are prepared with that goal in mind. Therefore, it is important to determine which features actually have an impact on the **target** column. These are the features that will be fed into the model, ensuring it learns the correct patterns and trends and isn't focused on features that make no difference to the predictions.

In this exercise, you are going to observe the correlations between all the features in this dataset and the **target** column. Follow these steps to complete this exercise:

1. Set the figure size for the heatmap to **12,12** and save it in **f** and **ax**:

    ```
    f,ax = plt.subplots(figsize=(12,12))
    ```

2. Use **sns.heatmap()** to create the heatmap. The data should be the **.corr()** function applied on **df**, set annotations as **True**, the line widths as **.5**, the decimal points of the correlations as **.1f**, and **ax** as **ax**:

    ```
    sns.heatmap(df.corr(), annot = True, linewidths = .5, \
                fmt =  '.1f', ax = ax)
    ```

3. Display the plot:

    ```
    plt.show()
    ```

The output will be as follows:

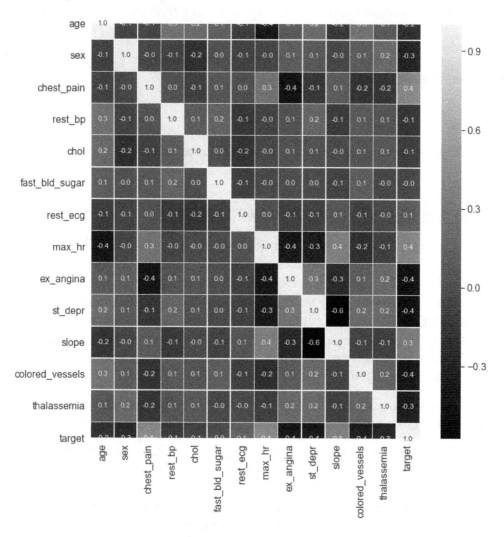

Figure 7.21: Heatmap for the features of df

The preceding heatmap tells us that only a few features (slope, maximum heart rate, and chest pain) have a noticeable positive correlation with the **target** column. You visualized all these relationships in the previous exercises and activities and did, in fact, notice trends, so our hypotheses were correct.

SUMMARY

In this chapter, we reviewed and analyzed the medical data of 303 patients and linked the features with the diagnosis of heart disease. We checked for outliers and created different visualizations depending on the type of feature we were analyzing. Additionally, we created plots with three features each to understand the relationships between all three. We also created new features from existing features to visualize trends between the presence of heart disease and age and cholesterol.

In the next chapter, we will apply similar data analysis techniques (such as searching for missing values and outliers, creating visualizations, and so on) to a dataset from the retail industry. We will also deal with missing values and outliers, rather than just leaving them be, as we did in this chapter.

8

ANALYZING ONLINE RETAIL II DATASET

OVERVIEW

In this chapter, you will search for and deal with missing values, outliers, and anomalies within a given dataset. You will learn how to create new columns from existing columns, conduct exploratory data analysis, and design visualizations. You will also practice summarizing the insights provided by your data. This chapter aims to guide you through various data analysis techniques pertaining to a specific dataset—the Online Retail II dataset—and therefore, a specific domain.

INTRODUCTION

In the previous chapter, we studied and analyzed a heart disease dataset and studied the relationships between different features of the dataset to gain a better understanding of the available data and derive useful insights from it.

This chapter follows a similar pattern as the previous chapters and guides you through data-specific analysis in a real-world domain and situation. This chapter targets the retail industry, and we're going to be analyzing data retrieved from an online retail company to observe patterns and correlations and to evaluate the business more accurately and in more depth.

> ## NOTE
>
> The dataset we are going to use has been obtained from the UCI repository of datasets and can be found at https://archive.ics.uci.edu/ml/datasets/Online+Retail+II#. To use the dataset in the exercises and activities, you can use the GitHub repo, at https://packt.live/3e7wZxs.

As you have seen in the previous chapters, transforming data into business insights consists of many steps and processes. These include the following:

1. Data cleaning

2. Data preparation and feature engineering

3. Data analysis: This comprises of asking the right questions and data visualization techniques.

Let's now begin with the cleaning of the data first.

DATA CLEANING

When doing online projects or learning from a course, the data used is often already in perfect form; there are no missing values or outliers, and all the features are accurate and useful. In reality, though, this is almost never the case. There are often rows and rows of data with inconsistencies that, if used as is, will provide us with flawed business insights, which could be disastrous if actually used to make business decisions.

For example, you're monitoring your shop's most and least active hours. This is done by tracking and storing information regarding your customers, especially what time they're coming into the shop. You have been storing the time in 24-hour clock format.

The next day, however, another employee takes over this responsibility and starts storing the time in 12-hour clock format. You suddenly have a column of data that has been stored in two different ways, and now 8:00 can mean both AM and PM. You don't notice this and begin to prepare, visualize, and analyze your data. You observe a spike at 8:00 and you think that it's AM because you've been working with the 24-hour clock, and so you might think about opening the shop even earlier or come up with deals to target your early morning customers. But in reality, that 8:00 means PM in most cases, and you've got it wrong.

"*Garbage in, garbage out*" is a famous saying in the world of data, and therefore, the first step when doing anything with data is always to clean it.

Cleaning data involves searching for missing values, outliers, and anomalies, and either deleting them or imputing new values. Let's take a closer look at these processes with the help of an exercise.

EXERCISE 8.01: LOADING AND CLEANING OUR DATA

In this exercise, you load, read, and clean one part of the Online Retail II dataset using pandas. The following steps will help you achieve this:

1. Open a new Jupyter notebook and import the required packages:

```
import pandas as pd
import numpy as np
import seaborn as sns
import matplotlib.pyplot as plt
```

2. Read the `.csv` file using pandas' **read_csv** function and store it in a DataFrame called **retail**. Print the first five rows of the DataFrame using the **.head()** function:

```
retail = pd.read_csv('https://raw.githubusercontent.com/'\
                     'PacktWorkshops/'\
                     'The-Data-Analysis-Workshop/master/'\
                     'Chapter08/Datasets/online_retail_II.csv')
retail.head()
```

The output will be as follows:

	Invoice	StockCode	Description	Quantity	InvoiceDate	Price	Customer ID	Country
0	489434	85048	15CM CHRISTMAS GLASS BALL 20 LIGHTS	12	01/12/2009 07:45	6.95	13085.0	United Kingdom
1	489434	79323P	PINK CHERRY LIGHTS	12	01/12/2009 07:45	6.75	13085.0	United Kingdom
2	489434	79323W	WHITE CHERRY LIGHTS	12	01/12/2009 07:45	6.75	13085.0	United Kingdom
3	489434	22041	RECORD FRAME 7" SINGLE SIZE	48	01/12/2009 07:45	2.10	13085.0	United Kingdom
4	489434	21232	STRAWBERRY CERAMIC TRINKET BOX	24	01/12/2009 07:45	1.25	13085.0	United Kingdom

Figure 8.1: The original retail DataFrame

3. Rename the column headings using the `.rename` function as follows: **Invoice** as **invoice**, **StockCode** as **stock_code**, **Quantity** as **quantity**, **InvoiceDate** as **date**, **Price** as **unit_price**, **Country** as **country**, **Description** as **desc**, and **Customer ID** as **cust_id**.

Set **index** as **str** and **inplace** to **True**:

```
retail.rename(index = str, \
            columns = {'Invoice' : 'invoice', \
                    'StockCode' : 'stock_code', \
                    'Quantity' : 'quantity', \
                    'InvoiceDate' : 'date', \
                    'Price' : 'unit_price', \
                    'Country' : 'country', \
                    'Description' : 'desc', \
                    'Customer ID' : 'cust_id'}, inplace = True)
retail.head()
```

The output will be as follows:

	invoice	stock_code	desc	quantity	date	unit_price	cust_id	country
0	489434	85048	15CM CHRISTMAS GLASS BALL 20 LIGHTS	12	01/12/2009 07:45	6.95	13085.0	United Kingdom
1	489434	79323P	PINK CHERRY LIGHTS	12	01/12/2009 07:45	6.75	13085.0	United Kingdom
2	489434	79323W	WHITE CHERRY LIGHTS	12	01/12/2009 07:45	6.75	13085.0	United Kingdom
3	489434	22041	RECORD FRAME 7" SINGLE SIZE	48	01/12/2009 07:45	2.10	13085.0	United Kingdom
4	489434	21232	STRAWBERRY CERAMIC TRINKET BOX	24	01/12/2009 07:45	1.25	13085.0	United Kingdom

Figure 8.2: Renamed columns

Now that we've loaded our data, let's take a closer look at it and see what needs to be cleaned up.

4. Use the `.info()` function to get a basic understanding of the **retail** DataFrame's columns and instances:

```
retail.info()
```

The output will be as follows:

```
<class 'pandas.core.frame.DataFrame'>
Index: 525461 entries, 0 to 525460
Data columns (total 8 columns):
invoice       525461 non-null object
stock_code    525461 non-null object
desc          522533 non-null object
quantity      525461 non-null int64
date          525461 non-null object
unit_price    525461 non-null float64
cust_id       417534 non-null float64
country       525461 non-null object
dtypes: float64(2), int64(1), object(5)
memory usage: 36.1+ MB
```

Figure 8.3: Using the .info() function

This information tells us that there's a total of 525,461 instances in our dataset! If we look at the total number of non-null objects in each column, we can see that **desc** and **cust_id** seem to have fewer entries.

5. Check how many missing values are present in **retail** using the **.isnull()** function. To see the total number of missing values per column, apply the **.sum()** function. Sort the columns of **retail** in descending order of their missing values using the **.sort_values()** function and set the **ascending** parameter to **False**:

```
retail.isnull().sum().sort_values(ascending = False)
```

The output will be as follows:

```
cust_id        107927
desc             2928
country             0
unit_price          0
date                0
quantity            0
stock_code          0
invoice             0
dtype:  int64
```

The information presented in the preceding screenshot tells us that only two columns in **retail** have missing values, and they are **cust_id** and **desc**. Between these two, **cust_id** has the most missing values.

6. Get some statistical information on the numerical columns of **retail** by using the **.describe()** function:

```
retail.describe()
```

The output will be as follows:

	quantity	unit_price	cust_id
count	525461.000000	525461.000000	417534.000000
mean	10.337667	4.688834	15360.645478
std	107.424110	146.126914	1680.811316
min	-9600.000000	-53594.360000	12346.000000
25%	1.000000	1.250000	13983.000000
50%	3.000000	2.100000	15311.000000
75%	10.000000	4.210000	16799.000000
max	19152.000000	25111.090000	18287.000000

Figure 8.4: Statistical information about the retail DataFrame

There are some odd values in this table. We can see once again that the **cust_id** column has fewer entries than the rest of the columns in the DataFrame, but the **unit_price** and **quantity** columns have some extreme values.

The minimum value in the **quantity** column is **-9600**, which is odd because items cannot be purchased in negative quantities. The maximum value of the **quantity** column is **19152**, which is quite large. This may or may not be an outlier or an anomaly. We'll take a look at it in a bit.

The **unit_price** column has a minimum of **-53594**, which once again is odd as items cannot cost a negative amount. Additionally, the maximum value is **25111**, which is plausible, but seems unlikely.

Let's take a closer look at the values of both these columns in the next steps.

7. Use the `.loc()` function to determine how many instances in retail have
    25111.09 as their **unit_price** value:

```
retail.loc[retail['unit_price'] == 25111.090000]
```

The output will be as follows:

	invoice	stock_code	desc	quantity	date	unit_price	cust_id	country
241824	C512770	M	Manual	-1	17/06/2010 16:52	25111.09	17399.0	United Kingdom
241827	512771	M	Manual	1	17/06/2010 16:53	25111.09	NaN	United Kingdom

Figure 8.5: The instances that have an extreme value in the unit_price column

There are only two instances that possess this value as their **unit_price**. One
of them has a quantity of **-1**. Maybe we can discard these.

8. Use the `.loc()` function again to determine how many instances in retail have
    -53594.36 as their **unit_price** value:

```
retail.loc[retail['unit_price'] == -53594.360000]
```

The output will be as follows:

	invoice	stock_code	desc	quantity	date	unit_price	cust_id	country
179403	A506401	B	Adjust bad debt	1	29/04/2010 13:36	-53594.36	NaN	United Kingdom

Figure 8.6: The instances that have an extreme negative value in the unit_price column

There is only one instance of this extreme negative value. The description
suggests that this is not related to an actual item at all. However, it is too vague
for us to conclusively determine the implications of this.

These extreme values at both ends of the spectrum are known as outlying
values, since they are very far away from the mean and median of the data
present in the respective columns. Negative values for something like **unit_
price** obviously don't make sense and therefore are also outliers. Now, we
need to decide whether to delete these instances or impute them with
different values.

Deletion is naturally a quick way of dealing with outliers, since the entire instance that contains them is dropped. However, this depends on the number of outliers present. Multiple outliers in a single column may require imputation if that column is significant. Multiple outliers can also mean that that column of data is useless and should be dropped entirely. A few outliers here and there can be dealt with by deleting just those instances. Let's take a look and see how many outliers we have.

9. Calculate the total number of instances that have negative **unit_price** values:

```
(retail['unit_price'] <= 0).sum()
```

The output will be as follows:

```
3690
```

This is only 0.7% of the total instances.

10. Calculate the total number of instances that have negative **quantity** values:

```
(retail['quantity'] <= 0).sum()
```

The output will be as follows:

```
12326
```

Though this number seems large, it is only **2.35%** of the total instances.

11. Check how many instances have negative values for both the **unit_price** and **quantity** columns, and also have missing **cust_id** values. Do this using three conditions joined together by the **&** method and wrapped by the **.sum()** function:

unit_price < 0

quantity < 0

cust_id.isnull()

```
((retail['unit_price'] <= 0) & (retail['quantity'] <= 0) \
  & (retail['cust_id'].isnull())).sum()
```

The output will be as follows:

```
2121
```

This is **0.4%** of the total instances.

From this analysis, we can see that the total percentage of instances containing these peculiar values is really small. Therefore, we can just delete these instances from **retail**. *Step 11* tells us that **2121** instances also contain missing values in the **cust_id** column, and so after deleting those only approximately **8000** instances with missing **cust_ids** will remain. Let's just delete those too.

12. Store the data with missing values in a DataFrame called **null_retail**, just in case:

```
null_retail = retail[retail.isnull().any(axis=1)]
null_retail.head()
```

The output will be as follows:

	invoice	stock_code	desc	quantity	date	unit_price	cust_id	country
263	489464	21733	85123a mixed	-96	01/12/2009 10:52	0.00	NaN	United Kingdom
283	489463	71477	short	-240	01/12/2009 10:52	0.00	NaN	United Kingdom
284	489467	85123A	21733 mixed	-192	01/12/2009 10:53	0.00	NaN	United Kingdom
470	489521	21646	NaN	-50	01/12/2009 11:44	0.00	NaN	United Kingdom
577	489525	85226C	BLUE PULL BACK RACING CAR	1	01/12/2009 11:49	0.55	NaN	United Kingdom

Figure 8.7: The DataFrame with missing values

13. Drop the rows with missing values using the **.dropna()** function. Store these in a new DataFrame called **new_retail**:

```
new_retail = retail.dropna()
```

14. Keep only those instances in **new_retail** that have positive values for both **unit_price** and **quantity**:

```
new_retail = new_retail[(new_retail['unit_price'] > 0) \
             & (new_retail['quantity'] > 0)]
```

15. Use the **.describe()** function to get an overview of our outlier-free DataFrame:

```
new_retail.describe()
```

The output will be as follows:

	quantity	unit_price	cust_id
count	407664.000000	407664.000000	407664.000000
mean	13.585585	3.294438	15368.592598
std	96.840747	34.757965	1679.762138
min	1.000000	0.001000	12346.000000
25%	2.000000	1.250000	13997.000000
50%	5.000000	1.950000	15321.000000
75%	12.000000	3.750000	16812.000000
max	19152.000000	10953.500000	18287.000000

Figure 8.8: Statistical overview of new_retail

Now there are no outliers. Take a look at the maximum values of **unit_price** and **quantity** now to see if there are any anomalies.

16. Plot a boxplot for the **unit_price** column of **new_retail**:

```
plt.subplots(figsize = (12, 6))
up = sns.boxplot(new_retail.unit_price)
```

The output will be as follows:

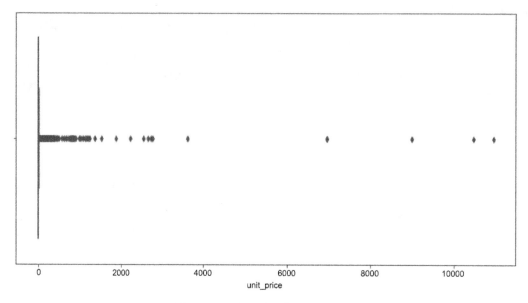

Figure 8.9: Boxplot for unit_price

Most of the data points are between **0** and **2000**, which seems fine. There are four data points beyond **6000**, though. These may be anomalies. Deleting these instances is a personal choice and you should go with your instincts. In this example, we are going to delete them.

17. Keep only those instances that have a **unit_price** lower than **6000**:

```
new_retail = new_retail[new_retail.unit_price < 6000]
new_retail.describe()
```

The output will be as follows:

	quantity	unit_price	cust_id
count	407659.000000	407659.000000	407659.000000
mean	13.585740	3.185750	15368.593562
std	96.841331	14.494341	1679.761725
min	1.000000	0.001000	12346.000000
25%	2.000000	1.250000	13997.000000
50%	5.000000	1.950000	15321.000000
75%	12.000000	3.750000	16812.000000
max	19152.000000	3610.500000	18287.000000

Figure 8.10: New retail DataFrame details

18. Plot a boxplot of the new **unit_price** column to see the changes:

```
up_new = sns.boxplot(new_retail.unit_price)
```

The output will be as follows:

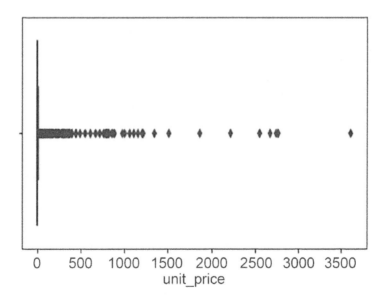

Figure 8.11: Boxplot of the updated unit_price column

Now the data looks more even.

19. Similarly, plot a boxplot of the new **quantity** column to see the changes:

```
plt.subplots(figsize = (12, 6))
q = sns.boxplot(new_retail.quantity)
```

The output will be as follows:

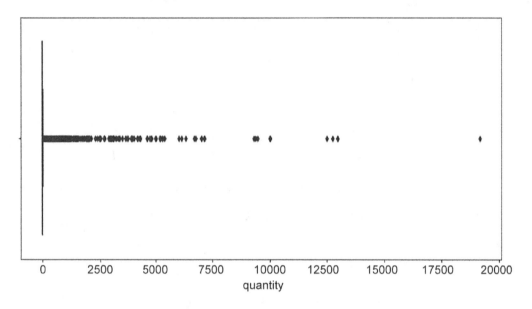

Figure 8.12: Boxplot of quantity

There seems to be one anomaly here between 17,500 and 20,000. The majority of the data points are between 1 and 7,500, with a few ranging from 7,500 to around 13,500. Let's delete the instance with the anomaly.

20. Keep only those instances whose quantity is below 15,000:

```
new_retail = new_retail[new_retail.quantity < 15000]
new_retail.describe()
```

The output will be as follows:

	quantity	unit_price	cust_id
count	407658.000000	407658.000000	407658.000000
mean	13.538792	3.185757	15368.597160
std	92.085647	14.494358	1679.762214
min	1.000000	0.001000	12346.000000
25%	2.000000	1.250000	13997.000000
50%	5.000000	1.950000	15321.000000
75%	12.000000	3.750000	16812.000000
max	12960.000000	3610.500000	18287.000000

Figure 8.13: Instances with a quantity value of less than 15,000

21. Plot a boxplot for the updated **quantity** column:

```
q_new = sns.boxplot(new_retail.quantity)
```

The output will be as follows:

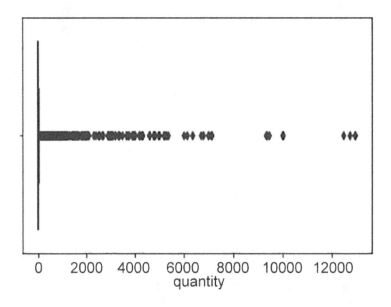

Figure 8.14: Boxplot of the updated quantity column

Now the data looks okay.

22. Use the **.info()** function to get an overview of the **new_retail** DataFrame:

```
new_retail[(new_retail.desc.isnull()) \
           & (new_retail.cust_id.isnull())]
new_retail.info()
```

The output will be as follows:

```
<class 'pandas.core.frame.DataFrame'>
Index: 407658 entries, 0 to 525460
Data columns (total 8 columns):
invoice        407658 non-null object
stock_code     407658 non-null object
desc           407658 non-null object
quantity       407658 non-null int64
date           407658 non-null object
unit_price     407658 non-null float64
cust_id        407658 non-null float64
country        407658 non-null object
dtypes: float64(2), int64(1), object(5)
memory usage: 28.0+ MB
```

Figure 8.15: Details for new_retail DataFrame

All the columns now have an equal number of instances.

23. Rename the **new_retail** DataFrame to **retail** to make it easier to use in the following exercises:

```
retail = new_retail
retail.head()
```

The output will be as follows:

	invoice	stock_code	desc	quantity	date	unit_price	cust_id	country
0	489434	85048	15CM CHRISTMAS GLASS BALL 20 LIGHTS	12	01/12/2009 07:45	6.95	13085.0	United Kingdom
1	489434	79323P	PINK CHERRY LIGHTS	12	01/12/2009 07:45	6.75	13085.0	United Kingdom
2	489434	79323W	WHITE CHERRY LIGHTS	12	01/12/2009 07:45	6.75	13085.0	United Kingdom
3	489434	22041	RECORD FRAME 7" SINGLE SIZE	48	01/12/2009 07:45	2.10	13085.0	United Kingdom
4	489434	21232	STRAWBERRY CERAMIC TRINKET BOX	24	01/12/2009 07:45	1.25	13085.0	United Kingdom

Figure 8.16: New retail DataFrame

> **NOTE**
>
> To access the source code for this specific section, please refer to https://packt.live/2YF5k0g.
>
> You can also run this example online at https://packt.live/3day32a. You must execute the entire Notebook in order to get the desired result.

We have now successfully loaded and cleaned our data and created a DataFrame from it that we are going to use in the following exercises. We have achieved this by checking for and dealing with outliers by visualizing the respective columns and deciding whether to delete the instances or impute the values with other values.

DATA PREPARATION AND FEATURE ENGINEERING

Once you have loaded and cleaned your data, you need to prepare it so that it's in a format that you can use to perform data analysis. Along with this, you need to identify features that will help you understand your data better and provide significant insights. These processes involve modifying already existing features and transforming them into new features.

For example, in the previous exercise, we saw that the dataset contains a **date** column consisting of day, month, and year. We can use this information to determine which months of the year were most popular for the online retail store. In order to do this, we need to modify the **date** column by breaking it down into columns such as day, month, year, and so on.

When preparing data for machine learning models, categorical features must be transformed into a numerical format so that the models can learn from them. However, since we are just going to be analyzing the data, we can leave the categorical features (**country**) as is.

EXERCISE 8.02: PREPARING OUR DATA

In this exercise, we are going to modify and add to the features present in the retail DataFrame that we created in *Exercise 8.01, Loading and Cleaning Our Data Using pandas*. This will help us get a more accurate view of our data and draw certain conclusions, such as which is the most popular day of the week for the online store.

1. The **description** column does not need to be converted into numerical form or be deleted, but convert all the letters in it to lowercase so that it is easier for us to process. Use the **.lower()** function to do this:

```
retail.desc = retail.desc.str.lower()
retail.head()
```

The output will be as follows:

	invoice	stock_code	desc	quantity	date	unit_price	cust_id	country
0	489434	85048	15cm christmas glass ball 20 lights	12	01/12/2009 07:45	6.95	13085.0	United Kingdom
1	489434	79323P	pink cherry lights	12	01/12/2009 07:45	6.75	13085.0	United Kingdom
2	489434	79323W	white cherry lights	12	01/12/2009 07:45	6.75	13085.0	United Kingdom
3	489434	22041	record frame 7" single size	48	01/12/2009 07:45	2.10	13085.0	United Kingdom
4	489434	21232	strawberry ceramic trinket box	24	01/12/2009 07:45	1.25	13085.0	United Kingdom

Figure 8.17: Using the lower() function

2. Convert the date column into datetime format using the **to_datetime()** function:

```
retail['date'] = pd.to_datetime(retail.date, \
                                format = '%d/%m/%Y %H:%M')
```

3. Print the first five instances of **retail** using the **.head()** function to view the changes you have made so far:

```
retail.head()
```

The output will be as follows:

	invoice	stock_code	desc	quantity	date	unit_price	cust_id	country
0	489434	85048	15cm christmas glass ball 20 lights	12	2009-12-01 07:45:00	6.95	13085.0	United Kingdom
1	489434	79323P	pink cherry lights	12	2009-12-01 07:45:00	6.75	13085.0	United Kingdom
2	489434	79323W	white cherry lights	12	2009-12-01 07:45:00	6.75	13085.0	United Kingdom
3	489434	22041	record frame 7" single size	48	2009-12-01 07:45:00	2.10	13085.0	United Kingdom
4	489434	21232	strawberry ceramic trinket box	24	2009-12-01 07:45:00	1.25	13085.0	United Kingdom

Figure 8.18: The first five rows of retail

4. Expand the **date** column to create six new features that will help us analyze the **retail** DataFrame better. To create each column, use the **.insert()** function. Add the first column at location **4**, and increment the location by 1 with each new column.

The first column is **year_month** and the values are the year and the month put together. Use **lambda** to create a function that arrives at this value:

```
retail.insert(loc = 4, column = 'year_month', \
            value = retail.date.map\
                    (lambda x: 100 * x.year + x.month))
```

The second column is **year**:

```
retail.insert(loc = 5, column = 'year', \
              value = retail.date.dt.year)
```

The third is **month**:

```
retail.insert(loc = 6, column = 'month', \
              value = retail.date.dt.month)
```

The fourth is **day**:

```
retail.insert(loc = 7, column = 'day', \
              value = retail.date.dt.day)
```

The fifth is **hour**:

```
retail.insert(loc = 8, column = 'hour', \
              value = retail.date.dt.hour)
```

The sixth is **day_of_week**:

```
retail.insert(loc = 9, column='day_of_week', \
              value=(retail.date.dt.dayofweek)+1)
```

We are adding 1 to the day of the week so that the days are numbered from 1 to 7 instead of 0 to 6.

Creating these columns is necessary because we can't perform datetime analysis on the original **date** column.

5. Print the first five rows of **retail** using the `.head()` function to view the new columns:

```
retail.head()
```

A truncated version of the output is as follows:

	invoice	stock_code	desc	quantity	year_month	year	month	day	hour	day_of_week
0	489434	85048	15cm christmas glass ball 20 lights	12	200912	2009	12	1	7	2
1	489434	79323P	pink cherry lights	12	200912	2009	12	1	7	2
2	489434	79323W	white cherry lights	12	200912	2009	12	1	7	2
3	489434	22041	record frame 7" single size	48	200912	2009	12	1	7	2
4	489434	21232	strawberry ceramic trinket box	24	200912	2009	12	1	7	2

Figure 8.19: The updated retail DataFrame

Now there are different features that help identify when an item was purchased. These columns provide a variety of insights, which you will take a look at in the next section.

The price of an item is given by **unit_price**, but that doesn't tell you the total amount spent in a particular instance. You will need to create that feature.

6. Insert a column called **spent** that multiplies the **unit_price** value by the quantity to tell us how much money was spent in each instance. Insert this column at position **11**:

```
retail.insert(loc = 11, column = 'spent', \
              value = (retail['quantity'] * retail['unit_price']))
retail.head()
```

A truncated version of the output is as follows:

	invoice	stock_code	desc	quantity	year_month	year	month	day	hour	day_of_week
0	489434	85048	15cm christmas glass ball 20 lights	12	200912	2009	12	1	7	2
1	489434	79323P	pink cherry lights	12	200912	2009	12	1	7	2
2	489434	79323W	white cherry lights	12	200912	2009	12	1	7	2
3	489434	22041	record frame 7" single size	48	200912	2009	12	1	7	2
4	489434	21232	strawberry ceramic trinket box	24	200912	2009	12	1	7	2

Figure 8.20: New retail Dataframe

7. Reposition the columns of **retail** so that they are easier to read:

```
retail = retail[['invoice', 'country', 'cust_id', 'stock_code', \
                 'desc','quantity', 'unit_price', 'date', \
                 'spent', 'year_month', 'year', 'month', 'day', \
                 'day_of_week', 'hour']]
```

8. Print the first five rows of **retail** to see the changes we have made:

```
retail.head()
```

The output will be as follows:

	invoice	country	cust_id	stock_code	desc	quantity	unit_price	date	spent
0	489434	United Kingdom	13085.0	85048	15cm christmas glass ball 20 lights	12	6.95	2009-12-01 07:45:00	83.4
1	489434	United Kingdom	13085.0	79323P	pink cherry lights	12	6.75	2009-12-01 07:45:00	81.0
2	489434	United Kingdom	13085.0	79323W	white cherry lights	12	6.75	2009-12-01 07:45:00	81.0
3	489434	United Kingdom	13085.0	22041	record frame 7" single size	48	2.10	2009-12-01 07:45:00	100.8
4	489434	United Kingdom	13085.0	21232	strawberry ceramic trinket box	24	1.25	2009-12-01 07:45:00	30.0

Figure 8.21: The final DataFrame

NOTE

To access the source code for this specific section, please refer to https://packt.live/3fAVMtJ.

You can also run this example online at https://packt.live/2UUKB7A. You must execute the entire Notebook in order to get the desired result.

We have split up the date column into multiple columns, such as **date**, **hour**, and **month**, which will help us conduct our analysis in the next section. We have also created a new column (**spent**) that consists of data calculated from two existing columns (**quantity** and **unit_price**) This is our final DataFrame. We are going to perform data analysis and visualization on this in the next section.

DATA ANALYSIS

One important thing to keep in mind while analyzing data is you need to understand what it is capable of telling you. Noting down some questions you think your data can answer helps you determine a path for your analysis.

Take a look at the **retail** DataFrame that we updated in *Exercise 8.02, Preparing Our Data*; it has 15 features. These features define who bought how much of what in which country at what time on what day in which month in which year. We can use combinations of these features to provide us with a lot of insights that would answer the following questions:

1. Which customers placed the most and fewest orders?

2. Which customers spent the most and least money?

3. Which months were the most and least popular for this online retail store?

4. Which dates of the month were the most and least popular for this online retail store?

5. Which days were the most and least popular for this online retail store?

6. Which hours of the day were most and least popular for this online retail store?

7. Which items were ordered the most and least?

8. Which countries placed the most and fewest orders?

9. Which countries spent the most and least money?

Let's now begin with the actual analysis of our data—answering these questions and gaining insights from our data.

EXERCISE 8.03: FINDING THE ANSWERS IN OUR DATA

In this exercise, you will use the DataFrame to answer each of the questions from the previous section.

Which customers placed the most and fewest orders?

1. Create a new DataFrame called **ord_cust**. Use the **.groupby()** function to group the **retail** DataFrame by **cust_id** and **country**. Use the **.count()** function to count the total number of invoices per customer. Therefore, the **ord_cust** DataFrame will have the following three columns – **cust_id**, **country**, and **invoice**:

```
ord_cust = retail.groupby(by = ['cust_id', 'country'], \
                          as_index = False)['invoice'].count()
ord_cust.head(10)
```

The output is as follows:

	cust_id	country	invoice
0	12346.0	United Kingdom	33
1	12347.0	Iceland	71
2	12348.0	Finland	20
3	12349.0	Italy	102
4	12351.0	Unspecified	21
5	12352.0	Norway	18
6	12353.0	Bahrain	20
7	12355.0	Bahrain	22
8	12356.0	Portugal	84
9	12357.0	Switzerland	165

Figure 8.22: Checking the countries with the greatest number of orders

2. Plot a bar graph for **ord_cust**, with **cust_id** as the *x* axis and **invoice** as the *y* axis. Label the **x** axis as **Customer ID**, the **y** axis as **Number of Orders**, and the graph as **Number of Orders made by Customers**. Display the plot:

```
plt.subplots(figsize = (15, 6))
oc = plt.plot(ord_cust.cust_id, ord_cust.invoice)
plt.xlabel('Customer ID')
plt.ylabel('Number of Orders')
plt.title('Number of Orders made by Customers')
plt.show()
```

The output will be as follows:

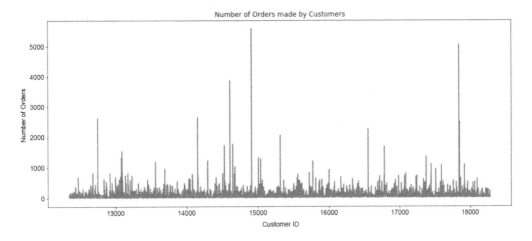

Figure 8.23: Number of orders made by customers

From this graph, you can see that the majority of customers placed less than **1000** orders. The maximum number of orders places seems to be above **5000**. Let's see who the top 5 customers were:

```
ord_cust.describe()
```

The output will be as follows:

	cust_id	invoice
count	4315.000000	4315.000000
mean	15346.442642	94.474623
std	1702.986420	201.977000
min	12346.000000	1.000000
25%	13878.500000	18.000000
50%	15346.000000	44.000000
75%	16833.500000	102.000000
max	18287.000000	5570.000000

Figure 8.24: Describing the ord_cust DataFrame

3. Sort the values in **ord_cust** by invoice in descending order and print the first five rows:

```
ord_cust.sort_values(by = 'invoice', ascending = False).head()
```

The output will be as follows:

	cust_id	country	invoice
1844	14911.0	EIRE	5570
3992	17841.0	United Kingdom	5043
1610	14606.0	United Kingdom	3866
1273	14156.0	EIRE	2648
256	12748.0	United Kingdom	2633

Figure 8.25: The five customers who ordered the most

From this table, we can conclude that the customer with customer ID 14911 from Ireland placed the most orders between December 2009 and December 2010.

4. Use the `.tail()` function to determine who placed the fewest orders:

```
ord_cust.sort_values(by = 'invoice', ascending = False).tail()
```

The output will be as follows:

	cust_id	country	invoice
1233	14095.0	United Kingdom	1
1239	14106.0	United Kingdom	1
2752	16165.0	United Kingdom	1
3655	17378.0	United Kingdom	1
1427	14366.0	United Kingdom	1

Figure 8.26: The five customers who ordered the least

These are the five customers who placed the fewest orders.

Which customers spent the most and least money on an item?

5. Group retail by **cust_id**, **country**, **quantity**, and **unit_price**. Use the `.sum()` function on the **spent** column to calculate the total amount spent by each customer. Store this in a DataFrame called **spent_cust**:

```
spent_cust = retail.groupby(by = ['cust_id', 'country', \
                                  'quantity', 'unit_price'], \
                     as_index = False)['spent'].sum()
spent_cust.head()
```

The output will be as follows:

	cust_id	country	quantity	unit_price	spent
0	12346.0	United Kingdom	1	1.00	1.00
1	12346.0	United Kingdom	1	3.25	3.25
2	12346.0	United Kingdom	1	5.95	23.80
3	12346.0	United Kingdom	1	7.49	142.31
4	12346.0	United Kingdom	5	4.50	157.50

Figure 8.27: Describing the spent_cust DataFrame

You must be wondering how the **spent** column does not actually calculate the exact amount spent. The customer with the customer ID **12346.0** has purchased an item called 'edwardian parasol' whose **unit_price** is **5.95**. They have bought this item 4 times (therefore 4 x 5.95 = 23.8). However, the invoice number for each of these four purchases is different; therefore, the **spent** column reflects the fact that the person bought 4 pieces of the same product. But, since they were separate purchases, the quantity is listed as 1.

6. Plot a bar graph for **spent_cust**:

```
plt.subplots(figsize = (15, 6))
sc = plt.plot(spent_cust.cust_id, spent_cust.spent)
plt.xlabel('Customer ID')
plt.ylabel('Total Amount Spent')
plt.title('Amount Spent by Customers')
plt.show()
```

The output will be as follows:

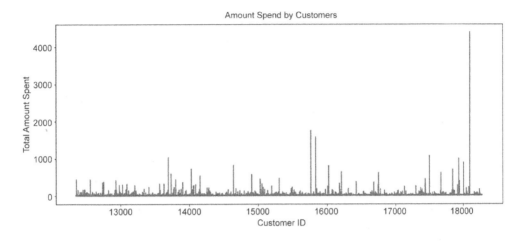

Figure 8.28: The total amount spent by customers

There are only a few customers who have spent an extreme amount during the year, with one of them having spent close to 40,000! Let's see which customer this was.

7. Sort the values in **spent_cust** by **spent** in descending order. Print the **.head()** and **.tail()** of this table to see who spent the most and least:

```
spent_cust.sort_values(by = 'spent', \
                      ascending = False).head()
```

The output will be as follows:

	cust_id	country	quantity	unit_price	spent
144871	18102.0	United Kingdom	300	4.58	43968.0
144915	18102.0	United Kingdom	600	3.00	18000.0
82744	15769.0	United Kingdom	200	1.65	17490.0
84312	15838.0	United Kingdom	9360	1.69	15818.4
144912	18102.0	United Kingdom	576	3.00	13824.0

Figure 8.29: The five customers who spent the most on a particular item

Customer **18102** spent the most on a particular product.

Use the following code to see the customers who have spent the least.

```
spent_cust.sort_values(by = 'spent', ascending = False).tail()
```

The output will be as follows:

	cust_id	country	quantity	unit_price	spent
44358	14249.0	United Kingdom	1	0.001	0.001
27696	13583.0	United Kingdom	1	0.001	0.001
48967	14459.0	United Kingdom	1	0.001	0.001
124745	17350.0	United Kingdom	1	0.001	0.001
106656	16705.0	United Kingdom	1	0.001	0.001

Figure 8.30: The customers who spent the least on a product

These are the customers who spent the least money on an item.

Which months were the most and least popular for this online retail store?

8. Group retail by **invoice** and count the number of invoices generated per month using .**unique()** and .**value_counts()**. Store this in **ord_month**:

```
ord_month = retail.groupby(['invoice'])['year_month']\
            .unique().value_counts().sort_index()
ord_month
```

The output will be as follows:

```
[200912]     1512
[201001]     1010
[201002]     1104
[201003]     1521
[201004]     1329
[201005]     1377
[201006]     1497
[201007]     1381
[201008]     1293
[201009]     1688
[201010]     2133
[201011]     2587
[201012]      776
Name: year_month, dtype: int64
```

Figure 8.31: Number of invoices generated per month

9. Plot a bar graph of **ord_month**. Set the **x** axis label as **Month**, the **y** axis label as **Number of Orders**, and the **title** as **Orders per Month**. Set the **x** tick labels as the **month** and **year**, and the **rotation** parameter as **horizontal**:

```
om = ord_month.plot(kind='bar', figsize = (15, 6))
om.set_xlabel('Month')
om.set_ylabel('Number of Orders')
om.set_title('Orders per Month')
om.set_xticklabels(('Dec 09', 'Jan 10', 'Feb 10', 'Mar 10', \
                    'Apr 10', 'May 10', 'Jun 10', 'Jul 10', \
                    'Aug 10', 'Sep 10', 'Oct 10', 'Nov 10', \
                    'Dec 10'), rotation = 'horizontal')
plt.show()
```

The output will be as follows:

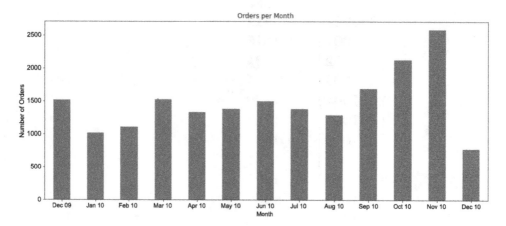

Figure 8.32: Orders per month

From this graph, you can conclude that the most popular month for this online retail store was November 2010, and the least popular month was December 2010. This seems a little odd since December is festival season, but this is what the data is telling us. Sales steadily increase from August 2010 to November 2010 and then drop drastically.

Which dates of the month were the most and least popular for this online retail store?

10. Group **retail** by **invoice** and calculate the number of invoices generated on each day by using the `.unique()` and `.value_counts()` functions on the **day** column. Store this in **ord_day**:

```
ord_day = retail.groupby('invoice')['day']\
          .unique().value_counts().sort_index()
ord_day
```

The output will be as follows:

```
[1]       708
[2]       696
[3]       610
[4]       595
[5]       661
[6]       572
[7]       812
[8]       827
[9]       689
[10]      609
[11]      655
[12]      576
[13]      512
[14]      634
[15]      732
[16]      617
[17]      600
[18]      687
[19]      601
[20]      506
[21]      649
[22]      636
[23]      573
[24]      602
[25]      667
[26]      672
[27]      517
[28]      671
[29]      614
[30]      457
[31]      251
Name: day, dtype: int64
```

Figure 8.33: Number of invoices generated on each day of the month

11. Plot a bar graph for **ord_day** with the *x* axis labeled as **Day of the Month**, the *y* axis as **Number of Orders** and the title as **Orders per Day of the Month**. Set **xticklabels** to the numbers from 1 to 31 using a list comprehension:

```
od = ord_day.plot(kind='bar', figsize = (15, 6))
od.set_xlabel('Day of the Month')
od.set_ylabel('Number of Orders')
od.set_title('Orders per Day of the Month')
od.set_xticklabels(labels = [i for i in range (1, 31)], \
                    rotation = 'horizontal')
plt.show()
```

The output will be as follows:

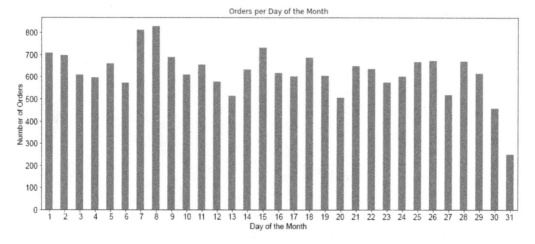

Figure 8.34: Orders per Day of the Month

From this graph, you can see that the most popular days of the month seem to be in the first and second week. The number of orders for the 31st are the lowest, but this could be a result of only 6 months out of 12 having 31 days, therefore this shouldn't be taken into consideration. Overall though, there doesn't seem to be too much of a trend other than on the 7th and 8th.

Which days of the week were the most and least popular for this online retail store?

12. Group **retail** by **invoice** and calculate the number of invoices generated on each day by using the **.unique()** and **.value_counts()** functions on the **day_of_week** column. Store this in **ord_dayofweek**:

```
ord_dayofweek = retail.groupby('invoice')['day_of_week']\
                .unique().value_counts().sort_index()
ord_dayofweek
```

The output will be as follows:

```
[1]     2985
[2]     3513
[3]     3426
[4]     3976
[5]     2612
[6]       30
[7]     2666
Name: day_of_week, dtype: int64
```

13. Plot a bar graph for **ord_dayofweek** with **Day of the Week** as the **x** axis label, **Number of Orders** as the **y** axis label, and **Orders per Day of the Week** as the title. Set **xticklabels** to the days of the week:

```
odw = ord_dayofweek.plot(kind='bar', figsize = (15, 6))
odw.set_xlabel('Day of the Week')
odw.set_ylabel('Number of Orders')
odw.set_title('Orders per Day of the Week')
odw.set_xticklabels(labels = ['Mon', 'Tues', 'Wed', 'Thurs', \
                    'Fri', 'Sat', 'Sun'], \
                rotation = 'horizontal')
plt.show()
```

The output will be as follows:

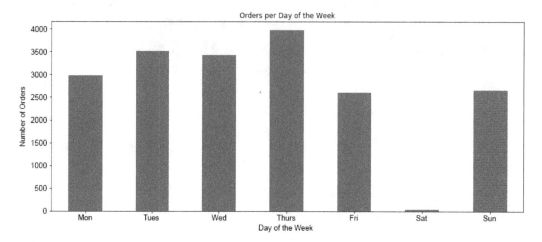

Figure 8.35: Orders per day of the week

From this graph, it is pretty evident that Saturday is the day when the fewest of orders are made, and Thursday is the day when most orders are made. The conclusion is that people tend to order more in the first four days of the week.

Which hours of the day were most and least popular for this online retail store?

14. Group **retail** by **invoice** and calculate the number of invoices generated on each hour by using the .**unique()** and .**value_counts()** functions on the **hour** column. Store this in **ord_hour**:

```
ord_hour = retail.groupby(by = ['invoice'])['hour']\
        .unique().value_counts().sort_index()
ord_hour
```

The output will be as follows:

```
[7]         49
[8]         444
[9]         1209
[10]        2232
[11]        2407
[12]        3173
[13]        2891
```

```
[14]      2365
[15]      2061
[16]      1263
[17]       637
[18]       258
[19]       185
[20]        34
Name: hour, dtype: int64
```

15. Plot a bar graph for **ord_hour** with the *x* axis labeled as **Hour of the Day**, the *y* axis as **Number of Orders**, and the title as **Orders per Hour of the Day**. Set the *x* tick labels as numbers ranging from 7 to 20 using list comprehensions:

```
oh = ord_hour.plot(kind='bar', figsize = (15, 6))
oh.set_xlabel('Hour of the Day')
oh.set_ylabel('Number of Orders')
oh.set_title('Orders per Hour of the Day')
oh.set_xticklabels(labels = [i for i in range (7, 20)], \
                   rotation = 'horizontal')
plt.show()
```

The output will be as follows:

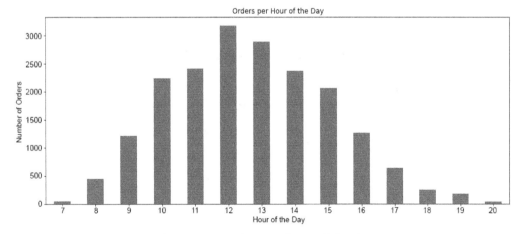

Figure 8.36: Orders per hour of the day

There is a clear trend in this graph: the number of orders increases from 7am onwards and peaks at noon, and then slowly decreases and ends at 8pm. Most people order between 11am and 2pm.

Which items were ordered the most and least?

16. Create a DataFrame called **q_item**. Group **retail** by **desc** and use the **.sum()** function to calculate the total quantity ordered of each item:

```
q_item = retail.groupby(by = ['desc'], \
                        as_index = False)['quantity'].sum()
q_item.head()
```

The output will be as follows:

	desc	quantity
0	doormat union jack guns and roses	169
1	3 stripey mice feltcraft	663
2	4 purple flock dinner candles	200
3	animal stickers	385
4	bank charges	2

Figure 8.37: Quantity of ordered items

17. Sort **q_item** by quantity in descending order. View the first five rows and last five rows to see which items were ordered the most and least:

```
q_item.sort_values(by = 'quantity', ascending = False).head()
```

The output will be as follows:

	desc	quantity
4260	white hanging heart t-light holder	56915
4366	world war 2 gliders asstd designs	54754
691	brocade ring purse	48166
2632	pack of 72 retro spot cake cases	45156
262	assorted colour bird ornament	44551

Figure 8.38: The most ordered items

The most ordered item is the **white hanging heart t-light holder**. **56915** pieces of it were sold.

18. Now look at the least ordered items from the set.

```
q_item.sort_values(by = 'quantity', ascending = False).tail()
```

The output will be as follows:

	desc	quantity
2544	opal white/silver flower necklace	1
1789	green chenille shaggy c/cover	1
2337	midnight blue crystal drop earrings	1
3728	silicon cube 25w, blue	1
1381	f.fairy s/3 sml candle, lavender	1

Figure 8.39: The least ordered items

This table shows us the items that were ordered the least.

Which countries placed the most and fewest orders?

19. Group **retail** by **country** and use the **.count()** function to calculate total number of invoices per country:

```
ord_coun = retail.groupby(['country'])['invoice']\
        .count().sort_values()
ord_coun.head()
```

The output will be as follows:

```
country
Nigeria        30
Bahrain        42
Korea          53
West Indies    54
Brazil         62
Name: invoice, dtype: int64
```

20. Plot a horizontal bar graph for **ord_coun** with the x axis labeled as **Number of Orders**, y axis as **Country**, and **title** as **Orders per Country**:

```
ocoun = ord_coun.plot(kind='barh', figsize = (15, 6))
ocoun.set_xlabel('Number of Orders')
ocoun.set_ylabel('Country')
ocoun.set_title('Orders per Country')
plt.show()
```

The output will be as follows:

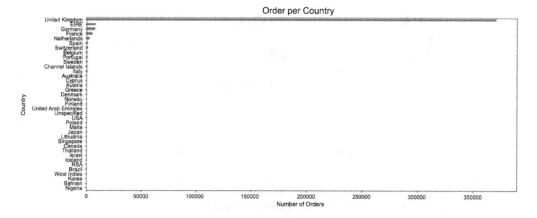

Figure 8.40: Orders per country

This store is based in the UK, so it seems obvious that customers in the UK would have placed the most orders. Remove the UK from **ord_coun** to see how the other countries are ordered.

21. Use **del** to delete **United Kingdom** from **ord_coun**:

```
del ord_coun['United Kingdom']
```

22. Now that **United Kingdom** is removed from **ord_coun**, plot a horizontal bar graph for **ord_coun** with the **x** axis labeled as **Number of Orders**, the **y** axis as **Country**, and the **title** as **Orders per Country**:

```
ocoun2 = ord_coun.plot(kind='barh', figsize = (15, 6))
ocoun2.set_xlabel('Number of Orders')
ocoun2.set_ylabel('Country')
ocoun2.set_title('Orders per Country')
plt.show()
```

The output will be as follows:

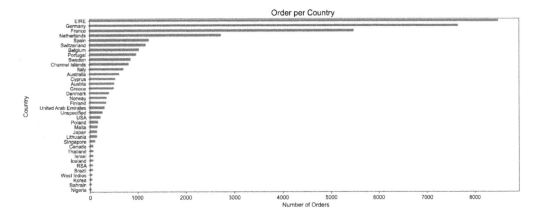

Figure 8.41: Orders per country without the UK

Now you can get a better understanding of how the countries placed orders. Customers from Ireland ordered the most and as the physical distance from the UK increases with each country, fewer orders are placed.

23. Next, group **retail** by **country** and use the **.sum()** function to calculate the amount of money spent by each country's customers. Plot a horizontal bar graph for **coun_spent** with the **x** axis labeled as **Amount Spent**, **y** axis as **Country**, and **title** as **Amount Spent per Country**:

```
coun_spent = retail.groupby('country')['spent']\
             .sum().sort_values()


cs = coun_spent.plot(kind='barh', figsize = (15, 6))
cs.set_xlabel('Amount Spent')
cs.set_ylabel('Country')
cs.set_title('Amount Spent per Country')
plt.show()
```

The output will be as follows:

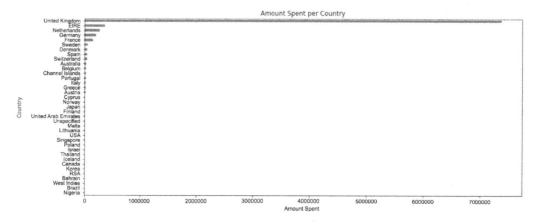

Figure 8.42: Amount spent per country

As expected, the UK spent the most money since that's where the most orders came from. Again, remove the UK and see how the other countries did.

24. Remove **United Kingdom** from **coun_spent** using **del**:

```
del coun_spent['United Kingdom']
```

25. Now that **United Kingdom** is removed from **coun_spent**, plot a horizontal bar graph for **coun_spent** with the x axis labeled as **Amount Spent**, y axis as **Country**, and title as **Amount Spent per Country**:

```
cs2 = coun_spent.plot(kind='barh', figsize = (15, 6))
cs2.set_xlabel('Amount Spent')
cs2.set_ylabel('Country')
cs2.set_title('Amount Spent per Country')
plt.show()
```

The output will be as follows:

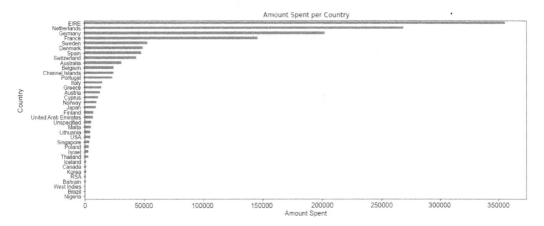

Figure 8.43: Amount spent per country without the UK

> **NOTE**
>
> To access the source code for this specific section, please refer to https://packt.live/2AL4ve9.
>
> You can also run this example online at https://packt.live/2N3KySt. You must execute the entire Notebook in order to get the desired result.

Now that our data analysis and visualization is done, we can answer the questions we asked in the previous section and see the insights our data provided.

1. Which customers placed the most orders? Which placed the fewest?

   Customer 14911 from Ireland placed the most orders (5,570). Customer 14366 from UK was one of the customers to place the fewest orders (only 1).

2. Which customers spent the most money on a particular item? Which spent the least?

   Customer 18102 from UK spent the most money on an item (43,968 on 300 pieces). Customer 16705 from UK was one of the customers who spent the least money on an item (0.001 on 1 piece).

3. Which months were the most popular for this online retail store? Which were the least?

   November 2010 was the most popular month, and December 2010 was the least popular.

4. Which dates of the month were the most popular for this online retail store? Which were the least?

   The 8th day of the month was the most popular day, and the 30th was the least (excluding 31st, as not all months have 31 days, thus we cannot consider any value for the 31st).

5. Which days were the most popular for this online retail store? Which were the least popular?

   Thursday was the most popular day, and Saturday was the least popular.

6. Which hours of the day were most popular for this online retail store? Which were the least popular?

   Noon was the most popular hour, and 8:00 PM was the least.

7. Which items were ordered the most, and which were ordered least?

   The white hanging heart t-light holder was ordered the most (56,916 pieces), and the f.fairy s/3 sml candle, lavender was the least popular item (only 1 piece).

8. Which countries placed the most and fewest orders?

    Customers from the UK placed the most orders, and after the UK, customers from Ireland placed the most orders. Customers from Nigeria placed the fewest orders.

9. Which countries spent the most and least money?

    Customers from the UK spent the most money and, after the UK, customers from the Ireland spent the most money. Customers from Nigeria spent the least money.

These insights can help you make several business decisions, such as which audience to target, when to have sales, when to increase advertising because more people are using the site, and so on.

Through this case study, we have seen how to analyze retail data and make it provide useful and significant information that can help improve the business.

ACTIVITY 8.01: PERFORMING DATA ANALYSIS ON THE ONLINE RETAIL II DATASET

In this activity, you are going to combine the Online Retail II data from 2009–2010 with that of 2010–2011, clean it, prepare it, and analyze it to come up with similar insights to the previous exercise.

1. Import the required packages:

```
import pandas as pd
import numpy as np
import seaborn as sns
import matplotlib.pyplot as plt
```

    In a Jupyter notebook, install **plotly** using the following command:

```
!pip install plotly
```

    Import **plotly.express** from the installed package:

```
import plotly.express as px
```

2. Store each of the CSV files in two different DataFrames.

3. Concatenate the two DataFrames into one called **retail** using the .**concat()** function and add the keys **09-10** and **10-11**.

4. Rename the columns as we did in *Exercise 8.01: Loading and Cleaning Our Data.*

5. Check the statistical information for **retail**.

6. Calculate how many negative values of **unit_price** and **quantity** are present in **retail**. If they are only a small percentage of the total number of instances, then remove them from **retail**.

7. Store the instances with missing values in another DataFrame.

8. Delete the instances with missing values from **retail**.

9. Plot a boxplot for **unit_price** to see if there are any outliers. If there are, remove those instances.

10. Plot a boxplot for **quantity** to see if there are any outliers. If there are, remove those instances.

11. Convert the text in the **desc** column to lowercase.

12. Convert the **date** column into datetime format.

13. Add six new columns with the following names: **Year_month**, **Year**, **Month**, **Day**, **Day_of_week**, and **Hour**.

14. Add a column called **spent**, which is the **quantity** multiplied by the **unit_price**.

15. Rearrange the columns as we did in *Exercise 8.02: Preparing Our Data.*

16. Find out which customers placed the most and fewest orders.

17. Find out which country has the customers who spent the most money on one item.

18. Find out which month had the most orders.

19. Find out which day of the month had the most orders.

20. Find out which day of the week had the most orders.

21. Find out which country has the customers who spent the most money on a product.

22. Find out which country has the customers who placed the greatest number of orders.

23. Find out which country had the customers who spent the greatest amount of money on orders.

> **NOTE**
>
> The solution to the activity can be found on page 526.

This concludes your data analysis of the Online Retail II dataset. As you can see from the visualizations, the trends seem to be similar to those we discovered in the exercises; for example, Saturday remains the least active day for this store. As expected, the customers who ordered the most spent the most, and the most popular items are different and varied over a range, as concluded from the results of the exercises.

SUMMARY

In this chapter, we performed various data cleaning, preparation, and analysis techniques on the Online Retail II dataset and observed the importance of these processes. We learned how to make the decision between keeping outlier instances and deleting them and also how to break one feature into several features to enhance the analysis. Lastly, we learned how to ask our data the right questions and manipulate it to provide the answers—the definition of successful data analysis.

In the following chapter, we will follow a similar path with a different dataset and, thus, a new domain—that of appliance energy consumption. The techniques used depend on the data we have, and so while some of the actions might be repeated, some will be new.

9

ANALYSIS OF THE ENERGY CONSUMED BY APPLIANCES

OVERVIEW

This chapter aims to display the application of general data analysis techniques to a specific use case—analyzing the energy consumed by household appliances. By the end of this chapter, you will be able to analyze individual features of the dataset to assess whether the data is skewed. You will also be equipped to perform feature engineering by creating new features from existing ones, and also to conduct **Exploratory Data Analysis** (**EDA**) and design informative visualizations.

INTRODUCTION

In the previous chapter, we took a look at the retail industry through the dataset of an online retail store based out of the UK. We applied a variety of techniques, such as breaking down the date-time column into individual columns containing the year, month, day of the week, hour, and so on, and creating line graphs to conduct a time series analysis to answer questions such as 'Which month was the most popular for the store?'

This chapter guides you through the data-specific analysis of a real-world domain and situation. This chapter focuses on a dataset containing information regarding the energy consumption of household appliances. The true goal of this dataset is to understand the relationships between the temperature and humidity of various rooms of a house (as well as outside the house) to then predict the energy consumption (usage) of appliances. However, in this chapter, we are just going to analyze the dataset to reveal patterns between the features.

This dataset has been retrieved from the UCI Machine Learning Repository. The data consists of temperature and humidity values for several rooms in a house in Belgium, monitored by wireless sensors. The data regarding the energy used by the lights and appliances was recorded by energy meters. The temperature, humidity, and pressure values for outside the house were procured from the nearest airport weather station (Cheivres Airport, Belgium). The two datasets have been merged together based on date and time.

> **NOTE**
>
> The original data can be found here: https://archive.ics.uci.edu/ml/datasets/Appliances+energy+prediction#.
>
> You can also find the dataset in our GitHub at: https://packt.live/3fxvys6.
>
> For further information on this topic, refer to the following: *Luis M. Candanedo, Veronique Feldheim, Dominique Deramaix, Data-driven prediction models of energy use of appliances in a low-energy house, Energy and Buildings, Volume 140, 1 April 2017, 81-97, ISSN 0378-7788*

To understand the dataset further, let's take a closer look.

> **NOTE**
>
> All the exercises and activities are to be done in the same Jupyter notebook, one followed by the other.

EXERCISE 9.01: TAKING A CLOSER LOOK AT THE DATASET

In this exercise, you will load the data and use different viewing methods to better understand the instances and features. You will also check for missing values, outliers, and anomalies and deal with them through imputation or deletion if required:

1. Open a new Jupyter notebook.

2. Import the required packages:

```
import pandas as pd
import numpy as np
import seaborn as sns
import matplotlib.pyplot as plt
import plotly.express as px
```

3. Read the data from the link using pandas' **read_csv** function and store it in a DataFrame called **data**:

```
data = pd.read_csv('https://raw.githubusercontent.com/'\
                   'PacktWorkshops/The-Data-Analysis-Workshop/'\
                   'master/Chapter09/Datasets/'\
                   'energydata_complete.csv')
```

4. Print the first five rows of data using the **.head()** function:

```
data.head()
```

A truncated version of the output is shown below:

	date	Appliances	lights	T1	RH_1	T2	RH_2	T3	RH_3	T4
0	2016-01-11 17:00:00	60	30	19.89	47.596667	19.2	44.790000	19.79	44.730000	19.000000
1	2016-01-11 17:10:00	60	30	19.89	46.693333	19.2	44.722500	19.79	44.790000	19.000000
2	2016-01-11 17:20:00	50	30	19.89	46.300000	19.2	44.626667	19.79	44.933333	18.926667
3	2016-01-11 17:30:00	50	40	19.89	46.066667	19.2	44.590000	19.79	45.000000	18.890000
4	2016-01-11 17:40:00	60	40	19.89	46.333333	19.2	44.530000	19.79	45.000000	18.890000

Figure 9.1: The first five rows of data

5. Check to see if there are any missing values. Use the `.isnull()` function to check for missing values in each column, and the `.sum()` function to print the total number of missing values per column:

```
data.isnull().sum()
```

The output will be as follows:

```
date              0
Appliances        0
lights            0
T1                0
RH_1              0
T2                0
RH_2              0
T3                0
RH_3              0
T4                0
RH_4              0
T5                0
RH_5              0
T6                0
RH_6              0
T7                0
RH_7              0
T8                0
RH_8              0
T9                0
RH_9              0
T_out             0
Press_mm_hg       0
RH_out            0
Windspeed         0
Visibility        0
Tdewpoint         0
rv1               0
rv2               0
dtype: int64
```

Figure 9.2: The number of missing values per column

The preceding output indicates that there are no missing values. This makes your job easier as now you don't need to figure out how to deal with them.

6. Change these column names in the current DataFrame to make them less confusing. If you click on the dataset link provided in the first **Note** box in this chapter, you'll see a section titled `Attribute Information`. This section elaborates on each column name to tell us what the values of that column actually mean. Use this information to rename the columns so that they're easier to understand. Rename these columns in a new DataFrame called **df1**:

```
df1 = data.rename(columns = {'date' : 'date_time', \
                    'Appliances' : 'a_energy', \
                    'lights' : 'l_energy', \
                    'T1' : 'kitchen_temp', \
                    'RH_1' : 'kitchen_hum', \
                    'T2' : 'liv_temp', \
                    'RH_2' : 'liv_hum', \
                    'T3' : 'laun_temp', \
                    'RH_3' : 'laun_hum', \
                    'T4' : 'off_temp', \
                    'RH_4' : 'off_hum', \
                    'T5' : 'bath_temp', \
                    'RH_5' : 'bath_hum', \
                    'T6' : 'out_b_temp', \
                    'RH_6' : 'out_b_hum', \
                    'T7' : 'iron_temp', \
                    'RH_7' : 'iron_hum', \
                    'T8' : 'teen_temp', \
                    'RH_8' : 'teen_hum', \
                    'T9' : 'par_temp', \
                    'RH_9' : 'par_hum', \
                    'T_out' : 'out_temp', \
                    'Press_mm_hg' : 'out_press', \
                    'RH_out' : 'out_hum', \
                    'Windspeed' : 'wind', \
                    'Visibility' : 'visibility', \
                    'Tdewpoint' : 'dew_point', \
                    'rv1' : 'rv1', \
                    'rv2' : 'rv2'})
```

7. Print the first five rows of **df1** using the **.head()** function:

```
df1.head()
```

A truncated version of the output is shown below:

	date_time	a_energy	l_energy	kitchen_temp	kitchen_hum	liv_temp	liv_hum	laun_temp
0	2016-01-11 17:00:00	60	30	19.89	47.596667	19.2	44.790000	19.79
1	2016-01-11 17:10:00	60	30	19.89	46.693333	19.2	44.722500	19.79
2	2016-01-11 17:20:00	50	30	19.89	46.300000	19.2	44.626667	19.79
3	2016-01-11 17:30:00	50	40	19.89	46.066667	19.2	44.590000	19.79
4	2016-01-11 17:40:00	60	40	19.89	46.333333	19.2	44.530000	19.79

Figure 9.3: The first five rows of df1

This table looks easier to understand. The **a_energy** and **l_energy** columns are the energy consumed by the appliances and lights respectively and are both in **Wh** (watt-hour). The **temperature** columns are all in **degree Celsius** and **humidity** columns are in **%**. The pressure column is in **mm Hg**, the wind speed column is in **meters per second**, visibility is in **kilometers**, and **Tdewpoint** is in **degree Celsius**.

A closer look at the **date_time** column tells us that there's a time interval of 10 minutes between each instance.

8. Print the last five rows of **df1**:

```
df1.tail()
```

The output will be as follows:

	date_time	a_energy	l_energy	kitchen_temp	kitchen_hum	liv_temp	liv_hum
19730	2016-05-27 17:20:00	100	0	25.566667	46.560000	25.890000	42.025714
19731	2016-05-27 17:30:00	90	0	25.500000	46.500000	25.754000	42.080000
19732	2016-05-27 17:40:00	270	10	25.500000	46.596667	25.628571	42.768571
19733	2016-05-27 17:50:00	420	10	25.500000	46.990000	25.414000	43.036000
19734	2016-05-27 18:00:00	430	10	25.500000	46.600000	25.264286	42.971429

Figure 9.4: The last five rows of df1

Comparing the **date_time** columns in *Figure 9.3* and *Figure 9.4* shows us that this data has been collected over approximately 4.5 months—from January 11, 2016 to May 27, 2016.

Now that we have an idea of what our data is about, let's check the values out.

9. Use the **.describe()** function to get a statistical overview of the DataFrame:

```
df1.describe()
```

The output will be as follows:

	a_energy	l_energy	kitchen_temp	kitchen_hum	liv_temp	liv_hum
count	19735.000000	19735.000000	19735.000000	19735.000000	19735.000000	19735.000000
mean	97.694958	3.801875	21.686571	40.259739	20.341219	40.420420
std	102.524891	7.935988	1.606066	3.979299	2.192974	4.069813
min	10.000000	0.000000	16.790000	27.023333	16.100000	20.463333
25%	50.000000	0.000000	20.760000	37.333333	18.790000	37.900000
50%	60.000000	0.000000	21.600000	39.656667	20.000000	40.500000
75%	100.000000	0.000000	22.600000	43.066667	21.500000	43.260000
max	1080.000000	70.000000	26.260000	63.360000	29.856667	56.026667

Figure 9.5: Overview of df1

NOTE

The output has been truncated for presentation purposes. The full output can be found here:

https://packt.live/34imyTx.

NOTE

To access the source code for this specific section, please refer to https://packt.live/34imyTx.

You can also run this example online at https://packt.live/3hAZqG0. You must execute the entire Notebook in order to get the desired result.

We can make a lot of observations based on the information present in *Figure 9.5*. These observations can help us determine whether our data requires deeper cleaning, preparation, and analysis, or whether it is fine and good to go.

For example, all the humidity and temperature columns seem fine; the minimum and maximum values seem reasonable and not extreme.

However, the two energy columns seem a bit odd. The **a_energy** column has a maximum value of 1,080, but the mean is around 97. This means that there are a few extreme values that might be outliers. The **l_energy** column has a 0 value for minimum, 25%, 50%, and 75%, and then has 70 as its maximum value. Something doesn't seem right here, so let's take a closer look.

EXERCISE 9.02: ANALYZING THE LIGHT ENERGY CONSUMPTION COLUMN

In this exercise, you will focus on the data present in one column of our DataFrame—**l_energy**, which explains the energy consumption of lights around the house:

1. Using **seaborn**, plot a boxplot for **l_energy**:

```
lights_box = sns.boxplot(df1.l_energy)
```

The output will be as follows:

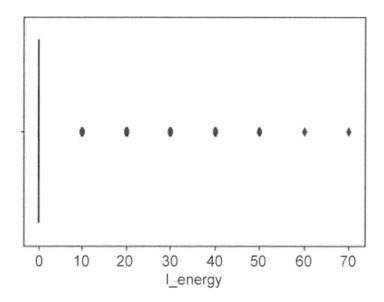

Figure 9.6: Boxplot of l_energy

This plot seems quite peculiar. It makes you wonder how many instances exist for each of these unique values.

2. Since you know that there are 8 unique **Wh** values present in the **l_energy** column, store these in a list:

```
l = [0, 10, 20, 30, 40, 50, 60, 70]
```

3. Create an empty list called **counts**, which is where we'll store the number of instances per **Wh**:

```
counts = []
```

4. Write a **for** loop that iterates over each value in **l**, calculates the total number of instances for each value in **l**, and appends that number to **counts**:

```
for i in l:
    a = (df1.l_energy == i).sum()
    counts.append(a)
```

5. Print **counts**:

```
counts
```

The output will be as follows:

```
[15252, 2212, 1624, 559, 77, 9, 1, 1]
```

The preceding results show that the majority of the values present in **l_energy** are **0**.

6. Plot a bar graph to better understand the distribution of the **l_energy** column using seaborn. Set the *x* axis as **l** (the Wh values) and the *y* axis as **counts** (the number of instances). Set the *x*-axis label as **Energy Consumed by Lights**, the *y*-axis label as **Number of Lights**, and the title as **Distribution of Energy Consumed by Lights**:

```
lights = sns.barplot(x = l, y = counts)
lights.set_xlabel('Energy Consumed by Lights')
lights.set_ylabel('Number of Lights')
lights.set_title('Distribution of Energy Consumed by Lights')
```

The output will be as follows:

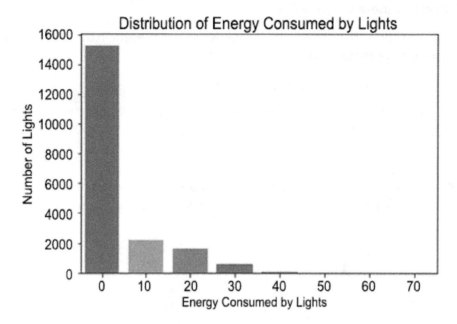

Figure 9.7: Distribution of energy consumed by lights

As you can see, most of the instances present in **df1** have 0 Wh as the energy consumed by lights.

7. Calculate the percentage of 0 values in **l_energy** by dividing the number of instances with 0 Wh by the total number of instances in **df1** and multiplying this by 100:

```
((df1.l_energy == 0).sum() / (df1.shape[0])) * 100
```

The output will be as follows:

```
77.28401317456296
```

77% of the instances have 0 Wh. This renders the **l_energy** column quite useless because we can't possibly find any links between it and the other data. So, let's get rid of this column.

8. Create a copy of **df1** called **new_data**:

```
new_data = df1
```

9. Use the **.drop()** function to drop the **l_energy** column **new_data**. Set **axis** as **1** to tell the function that we want to drop a column, not a row, and set **inplace** as **True**:

```
new_data.drop(['l_energy'], axis = 1, inplace = True)
```

10. Print the first five rows of **new_data**, using **.head()**:

```
new_data.head()
```

The output will be as follows:

	date_time	a_energy	kitchen_temp	kitchen_hum	liv_temp	liv_hum	laun_temp	laun_hum
0	2016-01-11 17:00:00	60	19.89	47.596667	19.2	44.790000	19.79	44.730000
1	2016-01-11 17:10:00	60	19.89	46.693333	19.2	44.722500	19.79	44.790000
2	2016-01-11 17:20:00	50	19.89	46.300000	19.2	44.626667	19.79	44.933333
3	2016-01-11 17:30:00	50	19.89	46.066667	19.2	44.590000	19.79	45.000000
4	2016-01-11 17:40:00	60	19.89	46.333333	19.2	44.530000	19.79	45.000000

Figure 9.8: The first five rows of new_data

Now there's no **l_energy** column.

NOTE

To access the source code for this specific section, please refer to https://packt.live/3ee7U3K.

You can also run this example online at https://packt.live/3e9tSF5. You must execute the entire Notebook in order to get the desired result.

In this exercise, we successfully analyzed the **1_energy** column to understand the data pertaining to the consumption of energy of light fittings. We observed that a majority of the instances had a **0 Wh** value for this column, which resulted in it being redundant. Therefore, we dropped the entire column from our DataFrame.

ACTIVITY 9.01: ANALYZING THE APPLIANCES ENERGY CONSUMPTION COLUMN

In this activity, you are going to analyze the **a_energy** column in a similar fashion to the **1_energy** column in *Exercise 9.02, Analyzing the Light Energy Consumption Column*. Please solve *Exercise 9.01: Taking a Closer Look at the Dataset* and *Exercise 9.02, Analyzing the Light Energy Consumption Column* before solving this activity.

1. Using seaborn, plot a boxplot for the **a_energy** column:

   The output will be as follows:

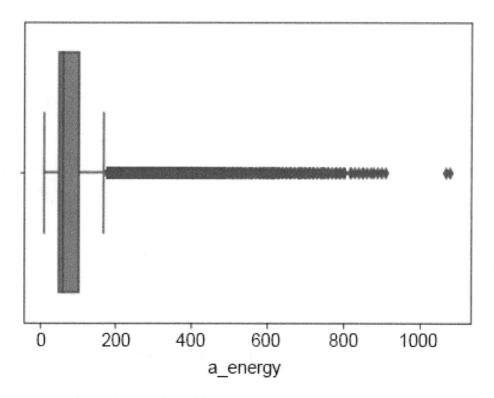

Figure 9.9: Box plot of a_energy

This box plot looks a little less weird than that of **l_energy**, but something is still off here. You can see that a majority of the values seem to lie between **50** Wh and **100** Wh. However, some values extend the upper bracket of **200** Wh and go beyond **1000** Wh. This seems odd. Check to see how many values extend above 200 Wh.

1. Use `.sum()` to determine the total number of instances wherein the value of the energy consumed by appliances is above 200 Wh.

   The output will be as follows:

   ```
   1916
   ```

2. Calculate the percentage of the number of instances wherein the value of the energy consumed by appliances is above 200 Wh.

   The output will be as follows:

   ```
   9.708639473017481
   ```

3. Use `.sum()` to check the total number of instances wherein the value of the energy consumed by appliances is above 950 Wh.

   The output will be as follows:

   ```
   2
   ```

4. Calculate the percentage of the number of instances wherein the value of the energy consumed by appliances is above 950 Wh.

   The output will be as follows:

   ```
   0.010134279199391943
   ```

   Only 0.01% of the instances have **a_energy** above 950 Wh, so deleting those 2 rows seems okay. However, close to 10% of the instances have **a_energy** above 200 Wh. The decision to remove these instances will differ from analyst to analyst, and also on the task at hand. You may decide to keep them, but in this chapter, we are going to delete them. You are encouraged to keep them in a separate set and see the impact this has on the rest of the analysis.

5. Create a new DataFrame called **energy**, that is, **new_data** without the instances where **a_energy** is above 200 Wh.

6. Print the statistical information of **energy** using `.describe()`.

The output will be as follows:

	a_energy	kitchen_temp	kitchen_hum	liv_temp	liv_hum	laun_temp
count	17819.000000	17819.000000	17819.000000	17819.000000	17819.000000	17819.000000
mean	68.728324	21.687676	40.158323	20.294921	40.470961	22.230049
std	31.378141	1.605252	3.933742	2.172435	4.062130	1.971209
min	10.000000	16.790000	27.023333	16.100000	20.463333	17.200000
25%	50.000000	20.760000	37.260000	18.790000	37.930000	20.790000
50%	60.000000	21.600000	39.560000	19.926667	40.560000	22.100000
75%	80.000000	22.600000	42.900000	21.472333	43.326667	23.290000
max	200.000000	26.200000	59.633333	29.856667	56.026667	29.200000

Figure 9.10: The first five rows of energy

Now the count of all the columns is **17819** because we dropped the instances in which **a_energy** was above 200 Wh. The maximum value in **a_energy** is now **200** Wh. There are **27** columns in the **describe** table since we dropped **l_energy**, and the **date_time** column doesn't appear here.

We have now successfully analyzed the **a_energy** column, removed the outliers, and prepared a new DataFrame that we will use for further analyses.

> **NOTE**
>
> The solution to the activity can be found on page 562.

Let's now move toward feature engineering to bring more efficacy into our analysis.

EXERCISE 9.03: PERFORMING FEATURE ENGINEERING

In this exercise, you will perform feature engineering on the **date_time** column of the **energy** DataFrame so that we can use it more efficiently to analyze the data:

1. Create a copy of the **energy** DataFrame and store it as **new_en**:

```
new_en = energy
```

2. Convert the **date_time** column of **new_en** into the DateTime format – **%Y-%m-%d %H:%M:%S** – using the **.to_datetime()** function:

```
new_en['date_time'] = pd.to_datetime(new_en.date_time, \
                                    format = '%Y-%m-%d %H:%M:%S')
```

3. Print the first five rows of **new_en**:

```
new_en.head()
```

The output will be as follows:

	date_time	a_energy	kitchen_temp	kitchen_hum	liv_temp	liv_hum	laun_temp	laun_hum
0	2016-01-11 17:00:00	60	19.89	47.596667	19.2	44.790000	19.79	44.730000
1	2016-01-11 17:10:00	60	19.89	46.693333	19.2	44.722500	19.79	44.790000
2	2016-01-11 17:20:00	50	19.89	46.300000	19.2	44.626667	19.79	44.933333
3	2016-01-11 17:30:00	50	19.89	46.066667	19.2	44.590000	19.79	45.000000
4	2016-01-11 17:40:00	60	19.89	46.333333	19.2	44.530000	19.79	45.000000

Figure 9.11: The converted date_time column

4. Insert a column at index position 1 called **month**, whose value is the month from the **date_time** column extracted using the **dt.month** function:

```
new_en.insert(loc = 1, column = 'month', \
              value = new_en.date_time.dt.month)
```

5. Insert another column at index position 2 called **day**, whose value is the day of the week extracted using the **dt.dayofweek** function. Add 1 to this value so that the numbers are between 1 and 7:

```
new_en.insert(loc = 2, column = 'day', \
              value = (new_en.date_time.dt.dayofweek)+1)
```

6. Print the first five rows of **new_en**:

```
new_en.head()
```

The output will be as follows:

	date_time	month	day	a_energy	kitchen_temp	kitchen_hum	liv_temp	liv_hum
0	2016-01-11 17:00:00	1	1	60	19.89	47.596667	19.2	44.790000
1	2016-01-11 17:10:00	1	1	60	19.89	46.693333	19.2	44.722500
2	2016-01-11 17:20:00	1	1	50	19.89	46.300000	19.2	44.626667
3	2016-01-11 17:30:00	1	1	50	19.89	46.066667	19.2	44.590000
4	2016-01-11 17:40:00	1	1	60	19.89	46.333333	19.2	44.530000

Figure 9.12: The month and day columns in new_en

> **NOTE**
>
> To access the source code for this specific section, please refer to https://packt.live/2C9Sjnz.
>
> You can also run this example online at https://packt.live/2AAaOBv. You must execute the entire Notebook in order to get the desired result.

In this exercise, we have successfully created two new features (the month and the day of the week) from one original feature (**date_time**). These new features will help us conduct a detailed time series analysis and derive greater insight from our data. This method of feature engineering can be applied to other features as well. In the previous chapter, for instance, we created a feature called **spent** whose values were the product of values from two other features.

Let's now solve an exercise to picture the dataset, which will certainly help us to have better insights into the data.

EXERCISE 9.04: VISUALIZING THE DATASET

In this exercise, you will visualize various features from the **new_en** DataFrame we created at the end of *Exercise 9.03, Performing Feature Engineering* to observe patterns and relationships. We are going to use a new Python library called **plotly** to create visualizations. **plotly** is a great library to create interactive visualizations. From **plotly**, we are going to be using the **graph_objs** module.

There are a variety of Python libraries designed for data visualization, and the decision of which one to use is most commonly based on personal preference, as in general they all possess similar methods.

1. Import **plotly.graph_objs**:

    ```
    import plotly.graph_objs as go
    ```

2. Create a scatter plot, with the **x** axis as the **date_time** column, **mode** as **lines**, and the **y** axis as the **a_energy** column:

    ```
    app_date = go.Scatter(x = new_en.date_time, \
                          mode = "lines", y = new_en.a_energy)
    ```

3. In the layout, set the title as **Appliance Energy Consumed by Date**, the **x**-axis title as **Date**, and the **y**-axis title as **Wh**:

    ```
    layout = go.Layout(title = 'Appliance Energy Consumed by Date', \
                      xaxis = dict(title='Date'), \
                      yaxis = dict(title='Wh'))
    ```

4. Plot the figure using **go.Figure**, with the data as **app_date** and the layout as **layout**:

    ```
    fig = go.Figure(data = [app_date], layout = layout)
    ```

5. Use **.show()** to display the figure:

    ```
    fig.show()
    ```

The output will be as follows:

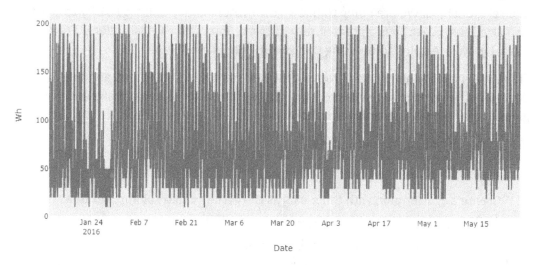

Appliance Energy Consumed by Date

Figure 9.13: The energy consumed by appliances per date

The data seems quite evenly distributed; however, there is a dip in the energy consumed toward the end of January and the beginning of April. Let's take a closer look.

6. Create a table called **app_month** that stores the total energy consumed by appliances per month. To do this, use **.groupby()** on **month** in **new_en** and **.sum()** on **a_energy**. The **groupby** function groups a DataFrame by specific columns:

```
app_mon = new_en.groupby(by = ['month'], \
                         as_index = False)['a_energy'].sum()
```

7. Print **app_mon**:

```
app_mon
```

The output will be as follows:

	month	a_energy
0	1	150060
1	2	258270
2	3	283190
3	4	274030
4	5	259120

Figure 9.14: Total energy consumed by appliances per month

8. Sort **app_mon** in descending order to find out which month the appliances consumed the most amount of energy:

```
app_mon.sort_values(by = 'a_energy', \
                ascending = False).head()
```

The output will be as follows:

	month	a_energy
2	3	283190
3	4	274030
4	5	259120
1	2	258270
0	1	150060

Figure 9.15: Sorted app_mon

As you can see, March was the month during which the appliances consumed the most energy, and it was in January that they consumed the least. The difference between the energy consumed in January and February (the month during which the second least amount of energy was consumed) is approximately 100,000 Wh itself.

9. Set the figure size as **15, 6**:

```
plt.subplots(figsize = (15, 6))
```

10. Using seaborn, create a bar plot for the **month** and **a_energy** columns in **app_mon**:

```
am = sns.barplot(app_mon.month, app_mon.a_energy)
```

11. Set the **x**-axis label as **Month**, the **y**-axis label as **Energy Consumed by Appliances**, and the title as **Total Energy Consumed by Appliances per Month**:

```
plt.xlabel('Month')
plt.ylabel('Energy Consumed by Appliances')
plt.title('Total Energy Consumed by Appliances per Month')
```

12. Display the plot using **.show()**:

```
plt.show()
```

The output will be as follows:

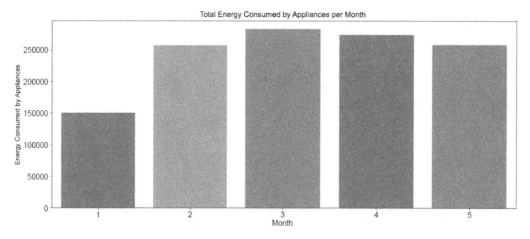

Figure 9.16: The total energy consumed by appliances per month

NOTE

To access the source code for this specific section, please refer to https://packt.live/2BbwHqy.

You can also run this example online at https://packt.live/3eat9DA. You must execute the entire Notebook in order to get the desired result.

This graph displays the observations we made in the **app_mon** table.

ACTIVITY 9.02: OBSERVING THE TREND BETWEEN A_ENERGY AND DAY

In this activity, you are going to repeat this process with the **day** column, observing the relationship between **a_energy** and **day**:

1. Create a table called **app_day** that stores the total energy consumed by appliances per day of the week. To do this, use **.groupby()** on **day** in **new_en** and **.sum()** on **a_energy**.

2. Print **app_day**.

    The output will be as follows:

	day	a_energy
0	1	161190
1	2	175930
2	3	191700
3	4	177830
4	5	161170
5	6	173640
6	7	183210

Figure 9.17: The total energy consumed by appliances per day of the week

As you can see in the preceding output, the days are numbered as 1, 2, and so on to represent Monday, Tuesday, and so on respectively.

3. Sort **app_day** in descending order to find out which day of the week the appliances consumed the most amount of energy.

   The output will be as follows:

	day	a_energy
2	3	191700
6	7	183210
3	4	177830
1	2	175930
5	6	173640
0	1	161190
4	5	161170

   Figure 9.18: The total energy consumed by appliances on different days of the week

   This table indicates that Wednesdays were the days when the appliances consumed the most energy, which is a bit odd. The following day in the table is Sunday, which makes sense since people might be at home more. The day the least energy was consumed was Friday.

4. Set the figure size as **15, 6**.

5. Using seaborn, create a bar plot for the **day** and **a_energy** columns in **app_day**.

6. Set the **x**-axis label as **Day of the Week**, the **y**-axis label as **Energy Consumed by Appliances**, and the title as **Total Energy Consumed by Appliances**.

7. Display the plot using **.show()**.

The output will be as follows:

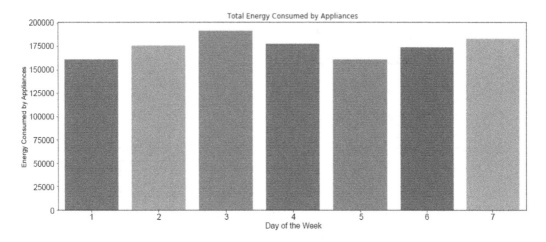

Figure 9.19: The total energy consumed by appliances each day of the week

As you can see, the greatest amount of energy is consumed on Wednesdays and the least energy is consumed on Fridays.

> **NOTE**
>
> The solution to the activity can be found on page 564.

In this activity, we successfully observed the energy consumed per day of the week. In the following exercise and activity, we are going to look into the other features more closely.

EXERCISE 9.05: PLOTTING DISTRIBUTIONS OF THE TEMPERATURE COLUMNS

In this exercise, you will plot distributions of the temperature columns to check whether any of them contain skewed data:

1. Create a list called **col_temp** containing all the column names from **new_en** that contain data regarding temperature:

```
col_temp = ['kitchen_temp', 'liv_temp', 'laun_temp', \
            'off_temp', 'bath_temp', 'out_b_temp', \
            'iron_temp', 'teen_temp', 'par_temp']
```

2. Create a DataFrame called **temp**, containing data of the columns mentioned in **col_temp**:

```
temp = new_en[col_temp]
```

3. Print the first five rows of **temp**:

```
temp.head()
```

The output will be as follows:

	kitchen_temp	liv_temp	laun_temp	off_temp	bath_temp	out_b_temp	iron_temp	teen_temp
0	19.89	19.2	19.79	19.000000	17.166667	7.026667	17.200000	18.2
1	19.89	19.2	19.79	19.000000	17.166667	6.833333	17.200000	18.2
2	19.89	19.2	19.79	18.926667	17.166667	6.560000	17.200000	18.2
3	19.89	19.2	19.79	18.890000	17.166667	6.433333	17.133333	18.1
4	19.89	19.2	19.79	18.890000	17.200000	6.366667	17.200000	18.1

Figure 9.20: The temp DataFrame

4. Plot a histogram for each of these temperature columns with **15** bins each:

```
temp.hist(bins = 15, figsize = (12, 16))
```

Since we are plotting distributions of the temperature columns, the y axis is the count and the x axis is the temperature in Celsius.

The output will be as follows:

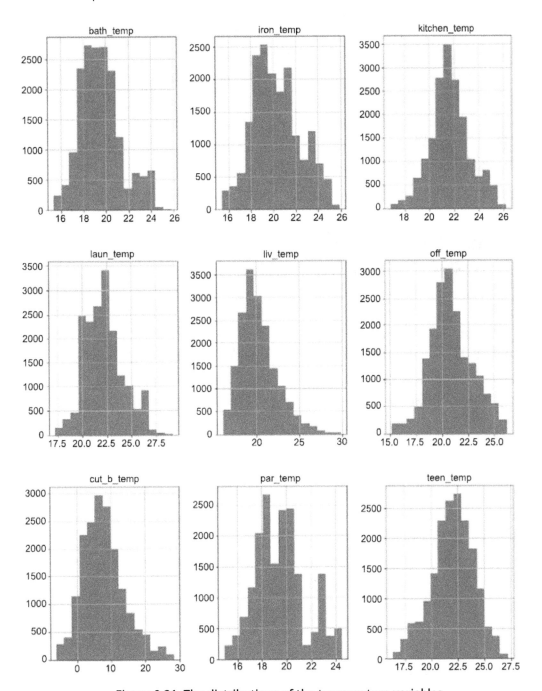

Figure 9.21: The distributions of the temperature variables

> **NOTE**
>
> To access the source code for this specific section, please refer to https://packt.live/3fA6j8P.
>
> You can also run this example online at https://packt.live/30PqdIP. You must execute the entire Notebook in order to get the desired result.

All of these distributions seem to be following the normal distribution as they are spread across the scale with a few gradual surges in between. As you can see, there are no sudden rises or falls through the distribution and so we can conclude that the temperature data is not skewed.

> **NOTE**
>
> To find out more about the normal distribution, click here:
>
> https://www.investopedia.com/terms/n/normaldistribution.asp

ACTIVITY 9.03: PLOTTING DISTRIBUTIONS OF THE HUMIDITY COLUMNS

In this activity, you will repeat the steps of *Exercise 9.05, Plotting Distributions of Temperature Columns* but for the humidity columns and the external columns:

1. Create a list called **col_hum**, consisting of the humidity columns from **new_en**.

2. Create a DataFrame called **hum**, containing data from the columns mentioned in `col_hum`.

3. Print the first five rows of **hum**.

The output will be as follows:

	kitchen_hum	liv_hum	laun_hum	off_hum	bath_hum	out_b_hum	iron_hum	teen_hum
0	47.596667	44.790000	44.730000	45.566667	55.20	84.256667	41.626667	48.900000
1	46.693333	44.722500	44.790000	45.992500	55.20	84.063333	41.560000	48.863333
2	46.300000	44.626667	44.933333	45.890000	55.09	83.156667	41.433333	48.730000
3	46.066667	44.590000	45.000000	45.723333	55.09	83.423333	41.290000	48.590000
4	46.333333	44.530000	45.000000	45.530000	55.09	84.893333	41.230000	48.590000

Figure 9.22: The hum DataFrame

4. Plot a histogram for each of these variables with 15 bins each.

Since we are plotting distributions of the humidity columns, the y axis is the count and the x axis is the humidity expressed as a percentage.

The output will be as follows:

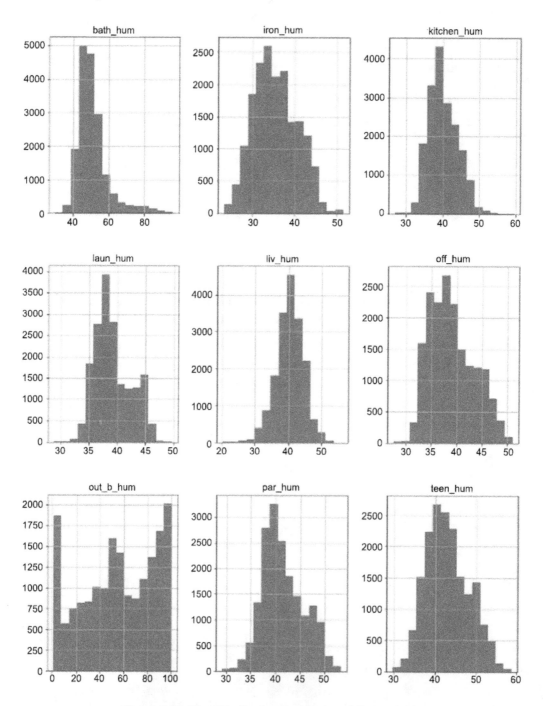

Figure 9.23: The distributions of the humidity variables

All the distributions except **out_b_hum** appear to be following the normal distribution. As you can see, the distribution of **out_b_hum** rises steeply at the extremes of the scale and the rest of the data points are spread unevenly across the x axis. Plot the distributions of the remaining variables first, and then take a closer look at **out_b_hum**.

5. Create a list called **col_weather** consisting of the remaining columns from **new_en**.

6. Create a DataFrame called **weath** containing data from the columns mentioned in **col_weather**. The first five rows of **weath** should be as follows:

	out_temp	dew_point	out_hum	out_press	wind	visibility
0	6.600000	5.3	92.0	733.5	7.000000	63.000000
1	6.483333	5.2	92.0	733.6	6.666667	59.166667
2	6.366667	5.1	92.0	733.7	6.333333	55.333333
3	6.250000	5.0	92.0	733.8	6.000000	51.500000
4	6.133333	4.9	92.0	733.9	5.666667	47.666667

Figure 9.24: The weath DataFrame

7. Plot a histogram for each of these variables with 15 bins each.

Since we are plotting distributions, the y axis is the count and the x axis is the feature we are plotting. For example, the x axis in the case of wind is windspeed.

The output should be similar to the following:

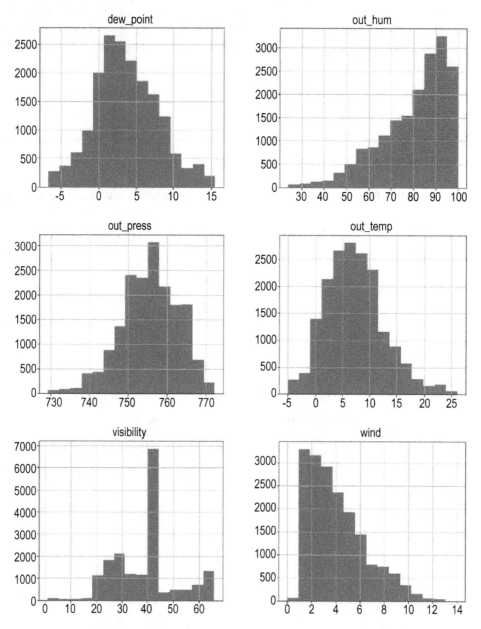

Figure 9.25: The distributions of the weather variables

NOTE

The solution to the activity can be found on page 567.

In this activity, we have successfully plotted the distributions of all the features from our data and determined which ones follow a normal distribution and which ones don't. As you can see, three of these distributions are not normal: **out_hum**, **visibility**, and **wind**, as they appear to show steep rises/falls through the plot. We need to find out the reason for this, as they will largely influence the input parameters fed to a machine learning model.

In the following exercise, we are going to take a closer look at four features that we have concluded do not seem like normal distributions. Taking a closer look at data is always beneficial since it helps us determine whether data is skewed or not, and based on that, whether those features should be used as input for machine learning models or not. Hence, this technique can be used in multiple different scenarios too, to assess the quality and distribution of your data.

EXERCISE 9.06: PLOTTING OUT_B, OUT_HUM, VISIBILITY, AND WIND

In this exercise, you will plot the distribution for the features of **out_b**, **out_hum**, **visibility**, and **wind** to determine how important these features are so that we can decide whether they can be used as inputs for machine learning models:

1. Set the axes and figure sizes:

```
f, ax = plt.subplots(2, 2, figsize = (12, 8))
```

2. Create a distribution plot using seaborn for each of the four variables:

```
obh = sns.distplot(hum["out_b_hum"], bins = 10, ax = ax[0][0])
oh = sns.distplot(weath["out_hum"], bins = 10, ax = ax[0][1])
vis = sns.distplot(weath["visibility"], bins = 10, ax = ax[1][0])
wind = sns.distplot(weath["wind"], bins = 10, ax = ax[1][1])
```

The output will be as follows:

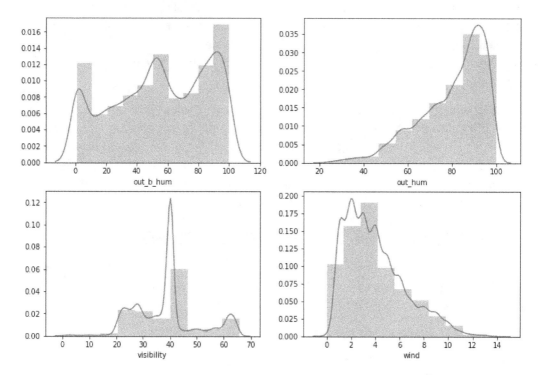

Figure 9.26: The distribution plots for the skewed columns

Let's plot a correlation plot to observe the relationship between all the variables.

3. Use `.corr()` to calculate the correlation between the variables in **new_en**. Save this in a variable called **corr**:

```
corr = new_en.corr()
```

4. Mask the repeated values:

```
mask = np.zeros_like(corr, dtype=np.bool)
mask[np.triu_indices_from(mask)] = True
```

5. Set the axes and figure sizes:

```
f, ax = plt.subplots(figsize=(16, 14))
```

6. Create a heatmap based on **corr**. Set the annotations as **True** and the number of decimal places to **two**, and mask as **mask**:

```
sns.heatmap(corr, annot = True, fmt = ".2f", mask = mask)
```

7. Set the *x*- and *y*-axis ticks as the column names:

```
plt.xticks(range(len(corr.columns)), corr.columns)
plt.yticks(range(len(corr.columns)), corr.columns)
```

8. Display the plot:

```
plt.show()
```

The output will be as follows:

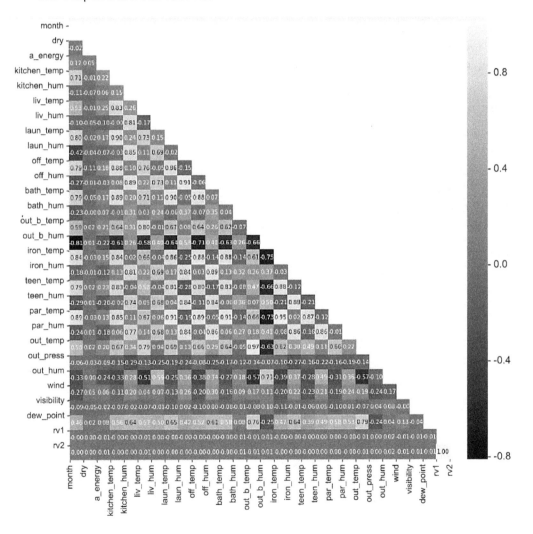

Figure 9.27: Correlation plot

> **NOTE**
>
> To access the source code for this specific section, please refer to https://packt.live/2UPoCyT.
>
> You can also run this example online at https://packt.live/30Te719. You must execute the entire Notebook in order to get the desired result.

From this heatmap, we can see that all the temperature variables have a high positive correlation with **a_energy**. The outdoor weather attributes seem to have a low correlation, as well as the humidity columns. This means that the temperature has a lot to do with how much the appliances are used.

SUMMARY

We have reached the end of this chapter and have successfully analyzed the amount of energy consumed by household appliances based on temperature, humidity, and other external weather conditions. We applied several data analysis techniques, including feature engineering and designing boxplots for specific features, to gain a better understanding of the information that the data contains. Additionally, we also plotted distributions of skewed data to observe them better.

In the next chapter, we will come to the end of our data analysis journey by applying our techniques to one last dataset. We will be analyzing and assessing the air quality of multiple localities in Beijing, China. Be ready to apply all your data analysis knowledge gained so far on this last dataset.

10

ANALYZING AIR QUALITY

OVERVIEW

In this chapter, you will search for, and handle, missing values. You will also carry out feature engineering, exploratory data analysis, design visualizations, and thereafter summarize insights provided by your data. By the end of this chapter, you will have a firm grasp of various data analysis techniques pertaining to a specific dataset—the Beijing Multi-Site Air Quality dataset.

INTRODUCTION

In the previous chapter, we performed data analysis techniques on a dataset that described the relationship between temperature, humidity, and the energy consumed by household appliances; that is, how much the appliances were used depending on the weather.

In the last chapter of this book, we will continue through the same journey of exploratory data analysis, but on a dataset describing the air quality in multiple localities of Beijing, China. We will be using several data analysis techniques (many of which you may have encountered in previous chapters) to clean the dataset and observe trends such as which time of year and which year had the highest concentration of pollutants.

ABOUT THE DATASET

The dataset we are using in this chapter has been obtained from the UCI repository of datasets. There are 12 separate CSV files consisting of approximately 35,000 entries each. Each file contains data specific to one locality. In total, across all 12 files, there are around 420,000 instances in the dataset.

The attributes include the amounts of a variety of pollutants found in the air, such as sulphur dioxide and ozone, and also the temperature and pressure. This data has been collected over 4 years—from March 1, 2013 to February 28, 2017.

Let's begin our data analysis process by taking a closer look at the data.

> **NOTE**
>
> To find out more about the dataset, click here: https://archive.ics.uci.edu/ml/datasets/Beijing+Multi-Site+Air-Quality+Data#.
>
> For further information on this topic, refer to the following: Zhang, S., Guo, B., Dong, A., He, J., Xu, Z., and Chen, S.X. (2017) *Cautionary Tales on Air Quality Improvement in Beijing*. Proceedings of the Royal Society A, Volume 473, No. 2205, pages 20170457
>
> All the exercises and activities, unless specifically mentioned, are linked together and should be conducted within the same Jupyter notebook.
>
> The datasets can be found on the following GitHub repository: https://packt.live/3e4yWei.

EXERCISE 10.01: CONCATENATING MULTIPLE DATAFRAMES AND CHECKING FOR MISSING VALUES

In this exercise, you will load the 12 CSV files into our Jupyter notebook, concatenate them into one DataFrame, and check for missing values.

Perform the following steps to complete the exercise:

1. Open a new Jupyter notebook.

2. Import the **pandas** to load, clean, and manipulate the data; **seaborn** to visualize the data; and **matplotlib.pyplot** to visualize the data:

```
import pandas as pd
import seaborn as sns
import matplotlib.pyplot as plt
```

3. Read the first CSV file for the area of 'Aotizhongxin' into its own DataFrame, called **aot**, using the **.read_csv()** function:

```
aot = pd.read_csv('https://raw.githubusercontent.com/'\
                  'PacktWorkshops/'\
                  'The-Data-Analysis-Workshop/master/'\
                  'Chapter10/Datasets/'\
                  'PRSA_Data_Aotizhongxin_20130301-20170228.csv')
```

4. Read the remaining 11 CSV files:

```
chan = pd.read_csv('https://raw.githubusercontent.com/'\
                   'PacktWorkshops/'\
                   'The-Data-Analysis-Workshop/master/'\
                   'Chapter10/Datasets/'\
                   'PRSA_Data_Changping_20130301-20170228.csv')

ding = pd.read_csv('https://raw.githubusercontent.com/'\
                   'PacktWorkshops/'\
                   'The-Data-Analysis-Workshop/master/'\
                   'Chapter10/Datasets/'\
                   'PRSA_Data_Dingling_20130301-20170228.csv')

dong = pd.read_csv('https://raw.githubusercontent.com/'\
                   'PacktWorkshops/'\
                   'The-Data-Analysis-Workshop/master/'\
                   'Chapter10/Datasets/'\
```

```
                        'PRSA_Data_Dongsi_20130301-20170228.csv')

    guan = pd.read_csv('https://raw.githubusercontent.com/'\
                        'PacktWorkshops/'\
                        'The-Data-Analysis-Workshop/master/'\
                        'Chapter10/Datasets/'\
                        'PRSA_Data_Guanyuan_20130301-20170228.csv')

    guch = pd.read_csv('https://raw.githubusercontent.com/'\
                        'PacktWorkshops/'\
                        'The-Data-Analysis-Workshop/master/'\
                        'Chapter10/Datasets/'\
                        'PRSA_Data_Gucheng_20130301-20170228.csv')

    hua = pd.read_csv('https://raw.githubusercontent.com/'\
                        'PacktWorkshops/'\
                        'The-Data-Analysis-Workshop/master/'\
                        'Chapter10/Datasets/'\
                        'PRSA_Data_Huairou_20130301-20170228.csv')

    nong = pd.read_csv('https://raw.githubusercontent.com/'\
                        'PacktWorkshops/'\
                        'The-Data-Analysis-Workshop/master/'\
                        'Chapter10/Datasets/'\
                        'PRSA_Data_Nongzhanguan_20130301-20170228.csv')

    shu = pd.read_csv('https://raw.githubusercontent.com/'\
                        'PacktWorkshops/'\
                        'The-Data-Analysis-Workshop/master/'\
                        'Chapter10/Datasets/'\
                        'PRSA_Data_Shunyi_20130301-20170228.csv')

    tian = pd.read_csv('https://raw.githubusercontent.com/'\
                        'PacktWorkshops/'\
                        'The-Data-Analysis-Workshop/master/'\
                        'Chapter10/Datasets/'\
                        'PRSA_Data_Tiantan_20130301-20170228.csv')

    wan = pd.read_csv('https://raw.githubusercontent.com/'\
                        'PacktWorkshops/'\
```

```
                    'The-Data-Analysis-Workshop/master/'\
                    'Chapter10/Datasets/'\
                    'PRSA_Data_Wanliu_20130301-20170228.csv')

    wans = pd.read_csv('https://raw.githubusercontent.com/'\
                    'PacktWorkshops/'\
                    'The-Data-Analysis-Workshop/master/'\
                    'Chapter10/Datasets/'\
                    'PRSA_Data_Wanshouxigong_20130301-20170228.csv')
```

5. Create a list called **dfs** that contains all of the previously created DataFrames:

```
    dfs = [aot, chan, ding, dong, guan, guch, hua, nong, shu, \
           tian, wan, wans]
```

6. Use the **.concat()** function to join all the DataFrames in **dfs** together vertically. Name this concatenated DataFrame **air**:

```
    air = pd.concat(dfs)
```

7. Reset the index of the **air** DataFrame:

```
    air.reset_index(drop = True, inplace = True)
```

Each DataFrame that we have concatenated to form the **air** DataFrame has its own index. This index starts from **0** and goes to **35064** because each CSV file has **35065** entries. However, our **air** DataFrame shouldn't be indexed this way because then there will be 12 instances of indices ranging from 0 to 35064. Therefore, we reset the index.

8. Print the first five rows of **air** using the **.head()** function:

```
    air.head()
```

The expected output is as follows:

	No	year	month	day	hour	PM2.5	PM10	SO2	NO2	CO	O3	TEMP	PRES	DEWP	RAIN	wd	WSPM	station
0	1	2013	3	1	0	4.0	4.0	4.0	7.0	300.0	77.0	-0.7	1023.0	-18.8	0.0	NNW	4.4	Aotizhongxin
1	2	2013	3	1	1	8.0	8.0	4.0	7.0	300.0	77.0	-1.1	1023.2	-18.2	0.0	N	4.7	Aotizhongxin
2	3	2013	3	1	2	7.0	7.0	5.0	10.0	300.0	73.0	-1.1	1023.5	-18.2	0.0	NNW	5.6	Aotizhongxin
3	4	2013	3	1	3	6.0	6.0	11.0	11.0	300.0	72.0	-1.4	1024.5	-19.4	0.0	NW	3.1	Aotizhongxin
4	5	2013	3	1	4	3.0	3.0	12.0	12.0	300.0	72.0	-2.0	1025.2	-19.5	0.0	N	2.0	Aotizhongxin

Figure 10.1: The first five rows of the air DataFrame

9. Print the last five rows of **air** using the **.tail()** function so that we can see that the DataFrame contains data from different stations:

```
air.tail()
```

The expected output is as follows:

	No	year	month	day	hour	PM2.5	PM10	SO2	NO2	CO	O3	TEMP	PRES	DEWP	RAIN	wd	WSPM	station
420763	35060	2017	2	28	19	11.0	32.0	3.0	24.0	400.0	72.0	12.5	1013.5	-16.2	0.0	NW	2.4	Wanshouxigong
420764	35061	2017	2	28	20	13.0	32.0	3.0	41.0	500.0	50.0	11.6	1013.6	-15.1	0.0	WNW	0.9	Wanshouxigong
420765	35062	2017	2	28	21	14.0	28.0	4.0	38.0	500.0	54.0	10.8	1014.2	-13.3	0.0	NW	1.1	Wanshouxigong
420766	35063	2017	2	28	22	12.0	23.0	4.0	30.0	400.0	59.0	10.5	1014.4	-12.9	0.0	NNW	1.2	Wanshouxigong
420767	35064	2017	2	28	23	13.0	19.0	4.0	38.0	600.0	49.0	8.6	1014.1	-15.9	0.0	NNE	1.3	Wanshouxigong

Figure 10.2: The last five rows of the air DataFrame

As you can see, the station name is that of our last CSV file, which means all 12 CSV files have been concatenated into this one DataFrame. Additionally, the index numbers go up to 420767. If we had not re-indexed the DataFrame, then this would've just been up to 35064, and the index values 0 to 35064 would have repeated themselves 12 times—once for each station.

10. View the statistical information of **air** using the **.describe()** function:

```
air.describe()
```

Part of the output is shown below:

	No	year	month	day	hour	PM2.5	PM10	SO2	NO2	
count	420768.000000	420768.000000	420768.000000	420768.000000	420768.000000	412029.000000	414319.000000	411747.000000	408852.000000	400067.(
mean	17532.500000	2014.662560	6.522930	15.729637	11.500000	79.793428	104.602618	15.830835	50.638586	1230.7
std	10122.116943	1.177198	3.448707	8.800102	6.922195	80.822391	91.772426	21.650603	35.127912	1160.
min	1.000000	2013.000000	1.000000	1.000000	0.000000	2.000000	2.000000	0.285600	1.026500	100.(
25%	8766.750000	2014.000000	4.000000	8.000000	5.750000	20.000000	36.000000	3.000000	23.000000	500.(
50%	17532.500000	2015.000000	7.000000	16.000000	11.500000	55.000000	82.000000	7.000000	43.000000	900.(
75%	26298.250000	2016.000000	10.000000	23.000000	17.250000	111.000000	145.000000	20.000000	71.000000	1500.(
max	35064.000000	2017.000000	12.000000	31.000000	23.000000	999.000000	999.000000	500.000000	290.000000	10000.(

Figure 10.3: Statistical information of the air DataFrame

As you can see, there are 16 numerical columns in **air**. They capture data about the following:

Column	Description
No	Serial number of the instance
year	Year the data was captured
month	Month the data was captured
day	Day of the month the data was captured
hour	Hour of the day the data was captured
PM2.5	Concentration of fine particles in microgram/meter^3 (particles from vehicles' exhausts, operations such as burning fuels)
PM10	Concentration of particles with a diameter of 10 micrometers or less, in microgram/meter^3
SO2	Concentration of sulphur dioxide in microgram/meter^3
NO2	Concentration of nitrogen dioxide in microgram/meter^3
CO	Concentration of carbon monoxide in microgram/meter^3
O3	Concentration of ozone in microgram/meter^3
TEMP	Temperature in degrees Celsius
PRES	Atmospheric pressure in hPa
DEWP	Dew point temperature in degree Celsius
RAIN	Amount of precipitation in mm
WSPM	Wind speed in meters/second

Figure 10.4: Column description

If you examine the previous outputs, you can see two categorical columns as well—**station** and **wd**. **station** is the name of the weather station/area from where the data has been collected, and **wd** is the direction of the wind. So, overall, we have 18 features. However, the **No** column seems unnecessary since our DataFrame is already indexed, so let's drop that.

11. Drop the **No** column from air using the **.drop()** function:

```
air = air.drop(['No'], axis = 1)
```

12. Rename the **PM2.5** column to **PM25** so that there are no errors when referring to it when carrying out operations on the column:

```
air.rename(index = str, columns = {'PM2.5' : 'PM25',}, \
          inplace = True)
```

13. Check for missing values using **.isnull()** and **sum()**:

```
air.isnull().sum()
```

The expected output is as follows:

```
No                   0
year                 0
month                0
day                  0
hour                 0
PM25              8739
PM10              6449
SO2               9021
NO2              12116
CO               20701
O3               13277
TEMP               398
PRES               393
DEWP               403
RAIN               390
wd                1822
WSPM               318
station              0
dtype: int64
```

Figure 10.5: The number of missing values per column in the air DataFrame

This output shows us that all columns except for the **date** and **time** columns and the **station** column have missing values. Let's check the percentage of missing values for the entire dataset.

14. Calculate the percentage of missing values. Round the percentage up to **4** characters:

```
round(air.isnull().sum()/len(air.index), 4)*100
```

The expected output is as follows:

```
No            0.00
year          0.00
month         0.00
day           0.00
hour          0.00
PM25          2.08
PM10          1.53
SO2           2.14
NO2           2.88
CO            4.92
O3            3.16
TEMP          0.09
PRES          0.09
DEWP          0.10
RAIN          0.09
wd            0.43
WSPM          0.08
station       0.00
dtype: float64
```

Figure 10.6: The percentage of missing values per feature in air

The percentage of missing values is quite low, and so removing the instances with missing values shouldn't impact the data too much. But let's decide whether we want to delete the instances or impute them with other values in a bit, after we've checked for outliers.

15. Print the first five rows of **air** to see what our current DataFrame looks like:

```
air.head()
```

The expected output is as follows:

	year	month	day	hour	PM25	PM10	SO2	NO2	CO	O3	TEMP	PRES	DEWP	RAIN	wd	WSPM	station
0	2013	3	1	0	4.0	4.0	4.0	7.0	300.0	77.0	-0.7	1023.0	-18.8	0.0	NNW	4.4	Aotizhongxin
1	2013	3	1	1	8.0	8.0	4.0	7.0	300.0	77.0	-1.1	1023.2	-18.2	0.0	N	4.7	Aotizhongxin
2	2013	3	1	2	7.0	7.0	5.0	10.0	300.0	73.0	-1.1	1023.5	-18.2	0.0	NNW	5.6	Aotizhongxin
3	2013	3	1	3	6.0	6.0	11.0	11.0	300.0	72.0	-1.4	1024.5	-19.4	0.0	NW	3.1	Aotizhongxin
4	2013	3	1	4	3.0	3.0	12.0	12.0	300.0	72.0	-2.0	1025.2	-19.5	0.0	N	2.0	Aotizhongxin

Figure 10.7: The first five rows of our updated air DataFrame

> **NOTE**
>
> To access the source code for this specific section, please refer to https://packt.live/2YKCOdk.
>
> You can also run this example online at https://packt.live/2YGwSSX. You must execute the entire Notebook in order to get the desired result.

In this exercise, we have successfully loaded and joined all 12 CSV files into one DataFrame and checked for missing values.

OUTLIERS

You should recall that an outlier is a data point that is different from the majority of data points. When visualized, this data point is far away from the rest—hence, the name outlier. For example, if you have a set of 12 numbers, of which 11 are between 1 and 6 and 1 has the value of 37, that data point will be an outlier because it is extremely different and far away from the rest of the data points.

Boxplots are a type of visualization that are great for visualizing outliers. They provide us with a lot of information about our data, such as the median, the first quartile, the third quartile, the minimum and maximum values, as well as the existence of outliers.

Let's do a quick exercise based on the example of 12 numbers to understand how to spot an outlier from a boxplot.

EXERCISE 10.02: IDENTIFYING OUTLIERS

In this exercise, you will create a small DataFrame with only 12 rows, each consisting of a random number. You will then plot this column of the DataFrame as a boxplot to see how to recognize an outlier.

1. Open a new Jupyter notebook and import the required packages:

```
import pandas as pd
import seaborn as sns
import matplotlib.pyplot as plt
```

2. Create a list called **a**, consisting of 12 data points in total – 11 should be between **1** and **6**, and 1 should be the value of **37**:

```
a = [1, 3, 4, 2, 1, 4, 6, 5, 1, 3, 2, 37]
```

3. Convert this list into a DataFrame using the **pd.DataFrame** function. Call this DataFrame **df**:

```
df = pd.DataFrame(a)
```

4. Print the first five rows of the DataFrame using the **.head()** function:

```
df.head()
```

The expected output is as follows:

	0
0	1
1	3
2	4
3	2
4	1

Figure 10.8: The first five rows of df

5. Rename the column heading **nums** using the **.rename()** function. Keep the index as **str** and the **inplace** parameter should be **True**:

```
df.rename(index = str, columns = {0 : 'nums', }, \
          inplace = True)
```

6. Create a boxplot called **box_nums**. From seaborn, use the **.boxplot()** method and feed it the **nums** column from **df** as data:

```
box_nums = sns.boxplot(df['nums'])
```

The expected output is as follows:

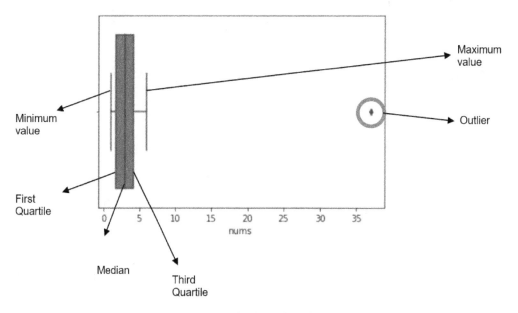

Figure 10.9: The boxplot of nums

7. Print the statistical information about **df** using the **.describe()** method:

```
df.describe()
```

The expected output is as follows:

	nums
count	12.000000
mean	5.750000
std	9.973829
min	1.000000
25%	1.750000
50%	3.000000
75%	4.250000
max	37.000000

Figure 10.10: The statistical information of df

NOTE

To access the source code for this specific section, please refer to https://packt.live/2URrN92.

You can also run this example online at https://packt.live/30Vw1k5. You must execute the entire Notebook in order to get the desired result.

We can observe from the boxplot and the statistical information of **df** that most of the values in this DataFrame lie between 1 and 6. However, one value is on the extreme right of the boxplot (circled in red). This data point is an outlier.

In the following activity, you will use the skills learned in this exercise to identify outliers in the actual dataset.

ACTIVITY 10.01: CHECKING FOR OUTLIERS

In this activity, you will visualize the features using boxplots to check the distribution of the data and identify outliers. Judging from *Figure 10.8*, there are definitely outliers present in almost all the pollutant features. You can say this with confidence by looking at the mean, median, and maximum values of each of these columns.

The maximum value for features such as **PM25**, **PM10**, and the gases are all quite extreme in comparison to the mean and median values. This implies that there are several values that are too high.

The following steps will help you to complete the activity:

1. Plot a boxplot for the **PM25** feature using seaborn.

    The expected output is as follows:

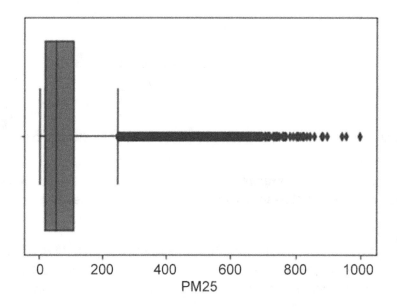

Figure 10.11: The boxplot of PM25

This boxplot shows us that there are several outliers with values above the range of 230–250. Let's say that 250 is our upper limit and check how many data points are outliers (that is, they have a value above 250).

2. Check how many instances contain values of **PM25** higher than **250**.

The expected output is as follows:

```
18668
```

There are quite a few outliers in PM25.

3. Store all the instances from *Step 2* in a DataFrame called **pm25** and print the first five rows of the DataFrame:

The output will be as follows:

	year	month	day	hour	PM25	PM10	SO2	NO2	CO	O3	TEMP	PRES	DEWP	RAIN	wd	WSPM	station
120	2013	3	6	0	284.0	315.0	133.0	174.0	4000.0	28.0	4.9	1008.5	-6.4	0.0	NE	1.2	Aotizhongxin
121	2013	3	6	1	272.0	300.0	131.0	166.0	4000.0	22.0	4.8	1008.3	-5.9	0.0	NE	1.5	Aotizhongxin
140	2013	3	6	20	254.0	396.0	107.0	154.0	4200.0	17.0	4.4	1008.2	-2.5	0.0	SSW	1.1	Aotizhongxin
141	2013	3	6	21	266.0	380.0	117.0	159.0	3799.0	17.0	3.8	1007.7	-2.2	0.0	WSW	1.9	Aotizhongxin
142	2013	3	6	22	254.0	335.0	111.0	148.0	4099.0	17.0	2.4	1007.3	-2.5	0.0	WSW	1.2	Aotizhongxin

Figure 10.12: First five rows of pm25

4. Print the station names of the instances in **PM25** to ensure that all the instances are not just from one station, but from multiple stations. This reduces the chances of them being incorrectly stored values.

The expected output is as follows:

```
array(['Aotizhongxin', 'Changping', 'Dingling', 'Dongsi', \
       'Guanyuan', 'Gucheng', 'Huairou', 'Nongzhanguan', \
       'Shunyi', 'Tiantan', 'Wanliu', 'Wanshouxigong'], \
      dtype=object)
```

5. Now, plot a boxplot for **PM10**.

The expected output is as follows:

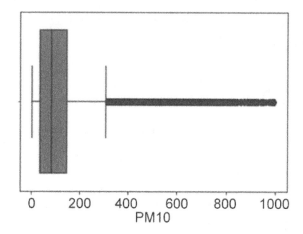

Figure 10.13: The boxplot of PM10

Once again, there seem to be many outliers with values above 300. Let's set an upper limit of 320 to be on the safe side.

6. Store all the instances from **PM10** in a DataFrame called **pm10** and print the first five rows.

The output will be as follows:

	year	month	day	hour	PM25	PM10	SO2	NO2	CO	O3	TEMP
139	2013	3	6	19	242.0	338.0	124.0	164.0	3700.0	17.0	5.1
140	2013	3	6	20	254.0	396.0	107.0	154.0	4200.0	17.0	4.4
141	2013	3	6	21	266.0	380.0	117.0	159.0	3799.0	17.0	3.8
142	2013	3	6	22	254.0	335.0	111.0	148.0	4099.0	17.0	2.4
143	2013	3	6	23	260.0	360.0	119.0	145.0	4000.0	17.0	2.3

Figure 10.14: First five rows for PM10

7. Calculate the number of instances that have a value of **PM10** that's above **320**.

    The expected output is as follows:

    ```
    12865
    ```

    This is less than those in **PM25**, but it's still quite large.

8. Calculate the number of instances that possess outlying values of both **PM25** and **PM10**.

    The expected output is as follows:

    ```
    10047
    ```

    This number implies that a majority of the instances with outliers possess outlying values in both **PM25** and **PM10** together, which means they could be related.

9. The **air** DataFrame can be displayed as follows:

    ```
    air.describe()
    ```

    The output will be as follows:

	year	month	day	hour	PM25	PM10
count	420768.000000	420768.000000	420768.000000	420768.000000	412029.000000	414319.000000
mean	2014.662560	6.522930	15.729637	11.500000	79.793428	104.602618
std	1.177198	3.448707	8.800102	6.922195	80.822391	91.772426
min	2013.000000	1.000000	1.000000	0.000000	2.000000	2.000000
25%	2014.000000	4.000000	8.000000	5.750000	20.000000	36.000000
50%	2015.000000	7.000000	16.000000	11.500000	55.000000	82.000000
75%	2016.000000	10.000000	23.000000	17.250000	111.000000	145.000000
max	2017.000000	12.000000	31.000000	23.000000	999.000000	999.000000

Figure 10.15: Description of the air DataFrame

10. Plot a boxplot for the SO2 column.

The expected output is as follows:

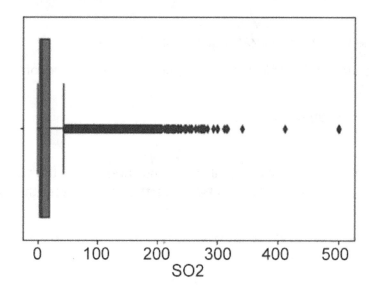

Figure 10.16: Boxplot for SO2

There seem to be a lot of outliers here too, above the value of approximately **70**.

11. Check how many instances have values above **70**.

The expected output is as follows:

```
14571
```

12. Calculate the number of instances that possess outlying values of **PM25**, **PM10**, and **SO2**.

13. Next, check how many instances contain values of **SO2** higher than **300**.

14. Now, plot a boxplot for **NO2**.

The boxplot will be as follows:

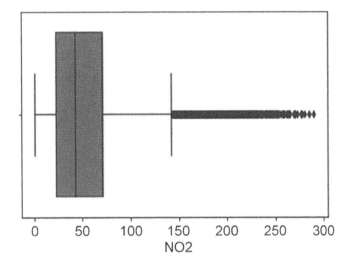

Figure 10.17: Boxplot for NO2

15. Similarly, check how many instances contain values of **NO2** higher than **150**.

16. Calculate the number of instances that possess outlying values of **PM25**, **PM10**, **SO2**, and **NO2**.

17. Similarly, we will be plotting a boxplot for **CO**. The plot will be as follows:

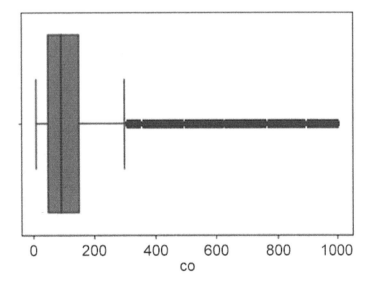

Figure 10.18: Boxplot of CO

18. Check how many instances contain values of **CO** higher than **3000**.

19. In a similar fashion, we plot a boxplot for **O3**:

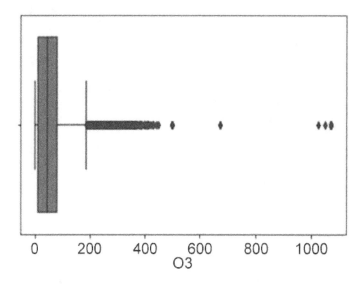

Figure 10.19: Boxplot of O3

20. Check how many instances contain values of **O3** higher than **200**.

21. Check how many instances contain values of **O3** higher than **470**.

22. Next, we plot a boxplot for **rain**. The plot will be as follows:

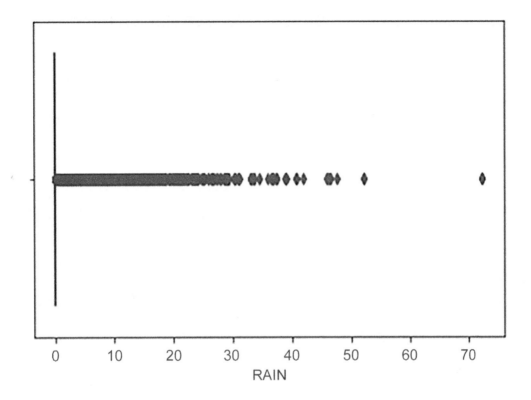

Figure 10.20: The boxplot of rain

Now that we've identified the outliers present in each feature for all the stations, let's take a look at how the values for each feature are distributed in each station.

23. Create a list of the following colors: **windows blue, amber, faded green,** and **dusty purple** and set the parameters for the plots as follows: **Figsize** as **20, 10**; **Titlesize** as **18**; **Labelsize** as **12**; **Xtick labelsize** as **14**; **Ytick labelsize** as **14**.

24. Plot a boxplot with the **x** axis as **station** and the **y** axis as **PM25**. Set the data parameter as the **air** DataFrame, but with the missing values dropped.

The expected output is as follows:

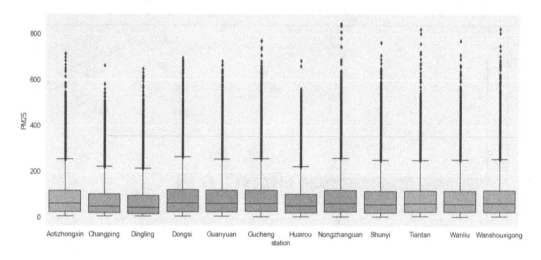

Figure 10.21: Boxplots for PM25 for each station

As you can see, the values of the outlying instances seem to be within a similar range at each station. Thus, the distribution of the data seems consistent.

25. Similarly, plot a boxplot with the 'x' axis as **station** and the 'y' axis as **PM10**. Set the data parameter as the **air** DataFrame, but with the missing values dropped.

The expected output is as follows:

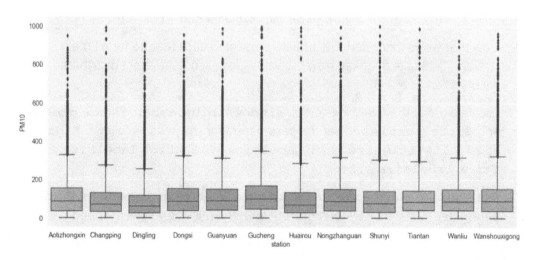

Figure 10.22: Boxplots for PM10

26. Next, plot a boxplot with the **x** axis as **station** and the **y** axis as **SO2**. Set the data parameter as the **air** DataFrame, but with the missing values dropped.

    The expected output is as follows:

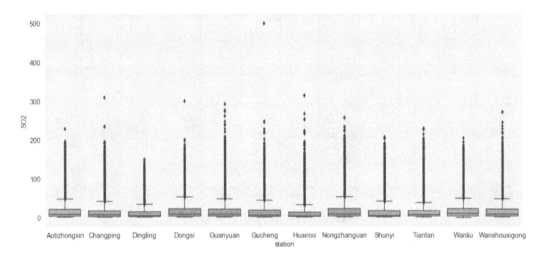

Figure 10.23: Boxplots for SO2

These look slightly more skewed. There are definite extreme outliers here, especially in the data for **Gucheng**. Even **Changping**, **Dongsi**, and **Huairou** have **SO2** values that don't seem normal and are quite distant from the rest of the values.

27. Plot a boxplot with the **x** axis as **station** and the **y** axis as **NO2**. Set the data parameter as the **air** DataFrame, but with the missing values dropped.

The output will be as follows:

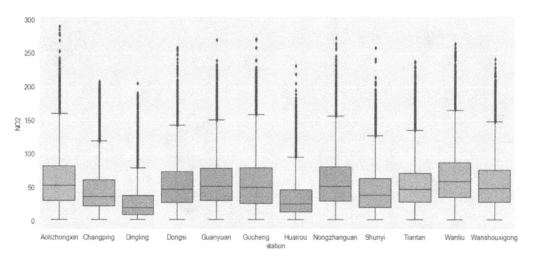

Figure 10.24: Boxplots for NO2

The values for **NO2** seem to differ more between stations, with those in **Aotizhongxin** being the highest, and those in **Dingling** being the lowest. There do seem to be some extreme outlying values here as well above **250**.

28. Plot a boxplot with the **x** axis as **station** and the **y** axis as **CO**. Set the data parameter as the **air** DataFrame, but with the missing values dropped.

The output will be as follows:

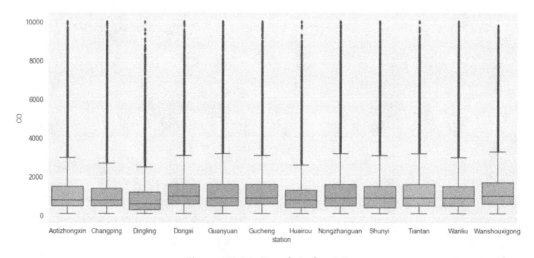

Figure 10.25: Boxplots for CO

The outliers for **CO** seem pretty consistent across all the stations, with each station having at least one value close to or equivalent to **1000**.

29. Also, plot a boxplot with the **x** axis as **station** and the **y** axis as **O3**. Set the data parameter as the **air** DataFrame, but with the missing values dropped.

The output will be as follows:

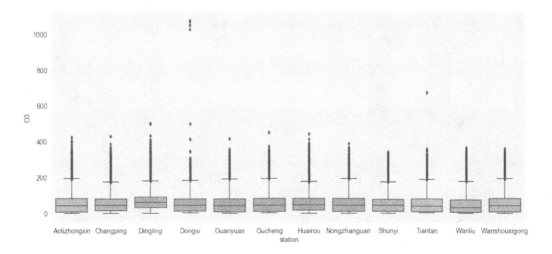

Figure 10.26: Boxplots for O3

There are extreme outliers in the case of **O3**, and these outliers should be genuine outliers (mistakes in capturing data) because such high levels of ozone in the air are harmful.

30. Plot a boxplot with the **x** axis as **station** and the **y** axis as **RAIN**. Set the data parameter as the **air** DataFrame, but with the missing values dropped.

The output will be as follows:

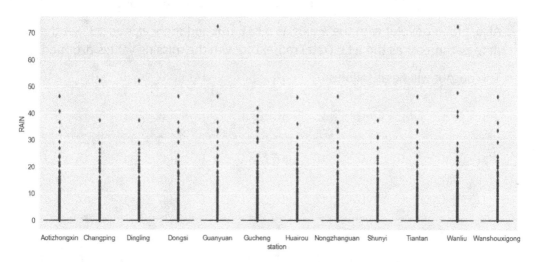

Figure 10.27: Boxplot for RAIN

You can see the outliers for **RAIN** in the output plot. In this activity, we have successfully analyzed the distribution of data for several features with respect to the entire dataset, as well as with respect to each individual station. Through the plotting of boxplots, we have identified the pattern of outliers for each feature.

However, we are not going to delete or tamper with these outliers, since we are just analyzing the data and not actually feeding it into a machine learning model. If we were feeding it into a model, it would be wise to either delete the outlier instances or impute them with new values since the model would learn incorrect patterns and trends.

> **NOTE**
>
> The solution to the activity can be found on page 571.

MISSING VALUES

Most real-world datasets have instances with values that are NaN or blank. These are missing values. The significance of missing values depends on multiple factors: the number of missing values, the number of features that have missing values, the tasks that are going to be carried out on data, and so on.

If the data is going to be fed into a machine learning model, then missing values should be dealt with. While some algorithms are capable of learning and predicting from data with missing values, it obviously makes more sense to train a model on data without missing values. This ensures that the model will learn relationships and patterns accurately.

Additionally, if there are many missing values or missing values in significant features of a dataset, they should also be dealt with.

There are two main ways to deal with missing values: deleting the instances or columns that have them (if they aren't significant), or imputing them with other values.

Imputation can occur in different ways. Missing values from numerical features can be imputed with the mean or median of the feature, or values can be calculated using a linear regression model. In the case of categorical features, missing values can be imputed with the mode of the feature, or classes can be predicted by a logistic regression model.

If the number of missing values isn't too large, then imputation with mean, median, or mode is a good way to go. Determining whether to choose the mean or the median as an imputation value in the case of numerical features depends on the number of outliers. If there are many outliers in a feature, then it is recommended to impute the missing values of that feature with the median.

In the following exercise, we will impute the missing values with the median.

EXERCISE 10.03: DEALING WITH MISSING VALUES

In *Activity 10.01,Checking for Outliers*, you identified several features with outlying values, and when there are that many outliers, the missing values should be imputed with the median of each feature. In this exercise, you will deal with the missing values in the air DataFrame by imputing values:

1. Create a copy of the **air** DataFrame and call it **new_air**:

```
new_air = air
```

2. Print the number of missing values per feature, using `.isnull()` and `.sum()`:

```
new_air.isnull().sum()
```

The expected output is as follows:

```
year                0
month               0
day                 0
hour                0
PM25             8739
PM10             6449
SO2              9021
NO2             12116
CO              20701
O3              13277
TEMP              398
PRES              393
DEWP              403
RAIN              390
wd               1822
WSPM              318
station             0
dtype: int64
```

Figure 10.28: The number of missing values per feature in new_air

3. Use the `.fillna()` function on the **PM25** column and fill the NaN values with the median of the **PM25** column:

```
new_air['PM25'].fillna(new_air['PM25'].median(), inplace=True)
```

4. Use the `.fillna()` function for the **PM10, SO2, NO2, CO, O3, TEMP, PRES, DEWP, RAIN,** and **WSPM** columns and fill the NaN values with the median of the respective parameters:

```
new_air['PM10'].fillna(new_air['PM10'].median(), inplace=True)
new_air['SO2'].fillna(new_air['SO2'].median(), inplace=True)
new_air['NO2'].fillna(new_air['NO2'].median(), inplace=True)
new_air['CO'].fillna(new_air['CO'].median(), inplace=True)
new_air['O3'].fillna(new_air['O3'].median(), inplace=True)
new_air['TEMP'].fillna(new_air['TEMP'].median(), inplace=True)
new_air['PRES'].fillna(new_air['PRES'].median(), inplace=True)
new_air['DEWP'].fillna(new_air['DEWP'].median(), inplace=True)
new_air['RAIN'].fillna(new_air['RAIN'].median(), inplace=True)
new_air['WSPM'].fillna(new_air['WSPM'].median(), inplace=True)
```

5. Now, recheck the missing values per feature using `.isnull()` and `.sum()`:

```
new_air.isnull().sum()
```

The expected output is as follows:

```
year             0
month            0
day              0
hour             0
PM25             0
PM10             0
SO2              0
NO2              0
CO               0
O3               0
TEMP             0
PRES             0
DEWP             0
RAIN             0
wd            1822
WSPM             0
station          0
dtype: int64
```

Figure 10.29: The number of missing values per feature in new_air post imputation with median values

wd still has some missing values. This is the wind direction column and is categorical. Therefore, we can't use the median for imputation. Instead, we'll use the mode—the set of data values that appears most often.

For instance, let's say you have the following array: **colors = ['yellow', 'blue', 'green', 'blue']**. The mode of this array is **blue**, because the mode is the most frequent value in a set of data.

6. Fill the missing values in **wd** with the mode of **wd**:

```
new_air = new_air.fillna(new_air['wd'].value_counts().index[0])
```

7. Now, recheck the missing values per feature using `.isnull()` and `.sum()`:

```
new_air.isnull().sum()
```

The expected output is as follows:

```
year          0
month         0
day           0
hour          0
PM25          0
PM10          0
SO2           0
NO2           0
CO            0
O3            0
TEMP          0
PRES          0
DEWP          0
RAIN          0
wd            0
WSPM          0
station       0
dtype: int64
```

Figure 10.30: No missing values are left post imputation

> **NOTE**
>
> To access the source code for this specific section, please refer to https://packt.live/2Y5PFYy.
>
> You can also run this example online at https://packt.live/3hzWJ7E. You must execute the entire Notebook in order to get the desired result.

As you can see, we now have a DataFrame that contains no missing values.

EXERCISE 10.04: OBSERVING THE CONCENTRATION OF PM25 AND PM10 PER YEAR

In this exercise, you will visualize various features of our **new_air** DataFrame to observe trends and patterns. We will do a few in this exercise, and the rest will be completed by you in the following activity.

Since we want to observe a trend between two of the pollutants and the year, we are going to create DataFrames wherein we have grouped the date by the pollutant column and the **year** column.

Perform the following steps to complete the exercise:

1. Create a DataFrame called **year_pm25** that will contain the average concentration of PM25 particles per year. To do this, select the **PM25**, **year**, and **station** columns from **new_air** and group it by **year**. For the average, calculate the median of each ear using the **.median()** function. Sort these values by the year column in descending order:

```
year_pm25 = new_air[['PM25','year','station']]\
            .groupby(["year"]).median().reset_index()\
            .sort_values(by = 'year', ascending = False)
```

2. Print the **year_pm25** DataFrame:

```
year_pm25
```

The expected output is as follows:

	year	PM25
4	2017	48.0
3	2016	50.0
2	2015	54.0
1	2014	60.0
0	2013	58.0

Figure 10.31: The median of PM25 particles per year

3. Create a point plot using seaborn of this DataFrame, with the **x** axis as **year** and the **y** axis as **PM25**:

```
sns.pointplot(x = 'year', y = 'PM25', data = year_pm25)
```

The expected output is as follows:

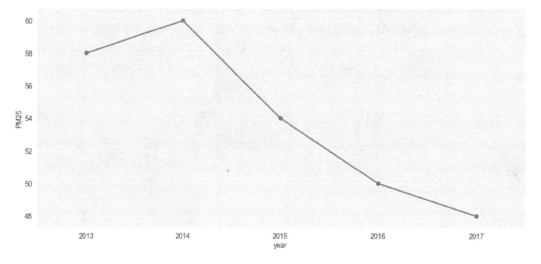

Figure 10.32: Point plot of PM25 per year

As you can see in the preceding graph, 2014 had the highest concentration of PM25 particles. After this, the concentration rapidly dropped by 10 micrograms/meter³ in 2017. However, an important thing to remember is that the dataset contains information from only the first 2 months of 2017—January and February. So, this may be a reason for the concentration being so low.

4. Create a DataFrame called **year_pm10** that will contain the average concentration of **PM10** particles per year. To do this, select the **PM10**, **year**, and **station** columns from **new_air** and group it by year. For the average, calculate the median of each year using the **.median()** function. Sort these values by the **year** column in descending order and print the DataFrame:

```
year_pm10 = new_air[['PM10','year','station']]\
            .groupby(["year"]).median().reset_index()\
            .sort_values(by = 'year', ascending = False)
year_pm10
```

The expected output is as follows:

	year	PM10
4	2017	71.0
3	2016	74.0
2	2015	79.0
1	2014	93.0
0	2013	86.0

Figure 10.33: Concentration of PM10 particles

5. Create a point plot of this DataFrame using seaborn. Make the **x** axis **year** and the **y** axis **PM10** using the **year_pm10** DataFrame:

```
sns.pointplot(x = 'year', y = 'PM10', data = year_pm10)
```

The expected output is as follows:

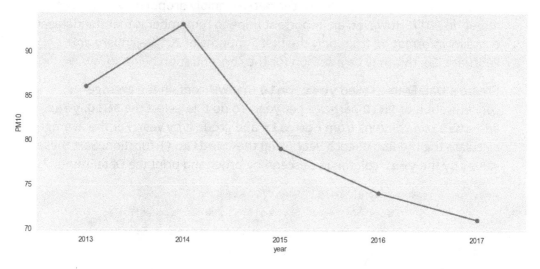

Figure 10.34: Point plot for the PM10 column

> **NOTE**
>
> To access the source code for this specific section, please refer to https://packt.live/37J97ha.
>
> You can also run this example online at https://packt.live/3dfwDna. You must execute the entire Notebook in order to get the desired result.

The preceding graph displays a similar trend as that of *Figure 10.32*, which means that there is a relationship between PM25 and PM10 particles. They were both at their peak concentration in 2014, after which their concentration dropped and reached its lowest in 2017.

We have now successfully observed the trends of PM25 and PM10 particles per year by plotting line graphs. In the following activities, you are going to repeat these steps to observe the trends between the remaining pollutants and year and month.

ACTIVITY 10.02: OBSERVING THE POLLUTANT CONCENTRATION PER YEAR

In this activity, you are going to visualize more features within the **new_air** DataFrame using the skills you have learned so far.

The following steps will help you to complete this activity:

1. Create a DataFrame called **year_so2** that contains the median of **SO2** concentration per year.

2. Print **year_so2**.

3. Create a point plot for **year_so2**.

4. Repeat the same process for the **NO2**, **CO**, and **O3** columns.

    The expected output of a DataFrame for **year_so2** is as follows:

	year	SO2
4	2017	12.0000
3	2016	4.0000
2	2015	6.0000
1	2014	9.0000
0	2013	10.8528

Figure 10.35: The year_so2 DataFrame

The expected output of the point plot for **year_so2** is as follows:

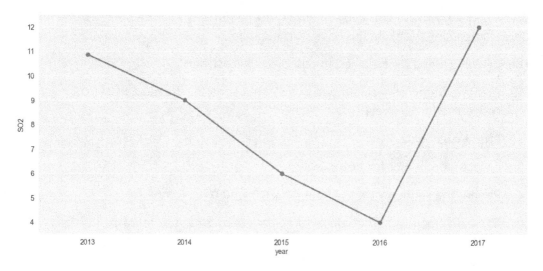

Figure 10.36: The median SO2 concentration per year

The expected output of a DataFrame for **year_no2** is as follows:

	year	NO2
4	2017	50.0
3	2016	39.0
2	2015	41.0
1	2014	45.0
0	2013	46.0

Figure 10.37: The year_no2 DataFrame

The expected output of the point plot for **year_no2** is as follows:

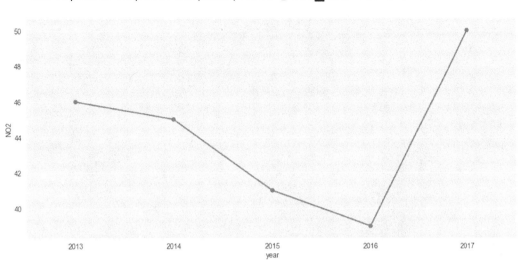

Figure 10.38: The median NO2 concentration per year

The concentration of **NO2** has also decreased, like that of **SO2**; however, unlike **SO2**, the decrease has been smaller. It dropped the most from 2014 to 2015.

The expected output of a DataFrame for **year_co** is as follows:

	year	CO
4	2017	900.0
3	2016	800.0
2	2015	900.0
1	2014	900.0
0	2013	900.0

Figure 10.39: The average concentration of CO per year

The expected output of the point plot for **year_co2** is as follows:

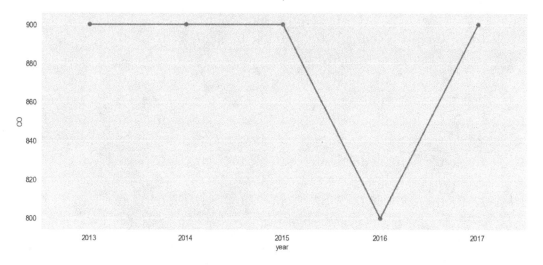

Figure 10.40: The median concentration of CO per year

The concentration of **CO** was constant for 3 years, and then dropped by 100 in 2016. Maybe if data for the remaining months of 2017 had also been collected, the median concentration for 2017 would also be 800 or lower.

The expected output of a DataFrame for **year_o3** is as follows:

	year	O3
4	2017	38.0
3	2016	45.0
2	2015	45.0
1	2014	45.0
0	2013	45.0

Figure 10.41: The year_o3 DataFrame

The expected output of the point plot for **year_o3** is as follows:

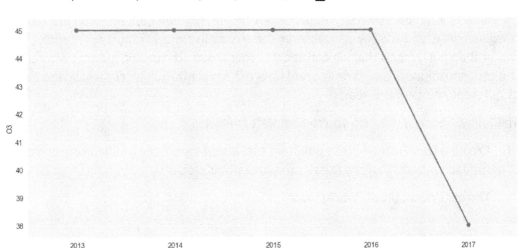

Figure 10.42: Point plot for average concentration of O3 per year

The amount of ozone appears to have remained constant during the first 4 years, before dropping in 2017. But once again, this could be because there was less data collected in 2017.

NOTE

The solution to the activity can be found on page 586.

In this activity, we have successfully observed how the concentrations of six pollutants have changed over the years by creating grouped DataFrames for each pollutant and plotting visualizations.

ACTIVITY 10.03: OBSERVING POLLUTANT CONCENTRATION PER MONTH

This activity is similar to *Activity 10.02, Observing the Pollutant Concentration per Year*; however, here, you are going to observe the trends in concentration per month rather than per year so that we can see whether there are specific months wherein the concentrations are high or low and how the concentration increases or decreases at different points of the year.

The following steps will help you to complete the activity:

1. Create a DataFrame for the pollutant **PM25** that stores the median concentration for each month. Plot the DataFrame on a point plot.

    The expected output is as follows:

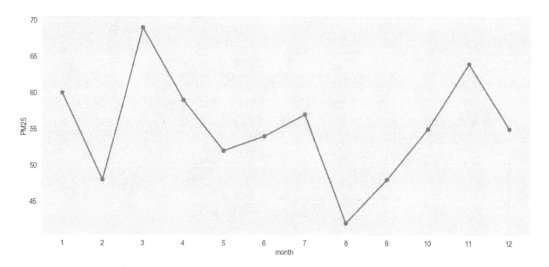

Figure 10.43: The average PM25 concentration per month

The PM25 concentration varies considerably from month to month, with many spikes visible in the graph.

2. Create a DataFrame for the pollutant **PM10** that stores the median concentration for each month. Plot the DataFrame as a point plot.

The expected output is as follows:

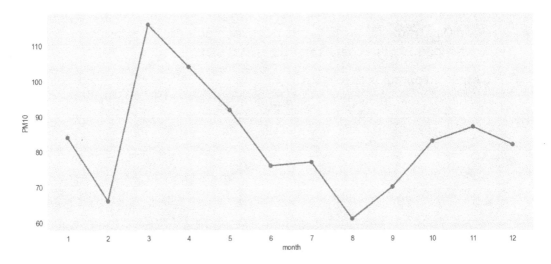

Figure 10.44: The average PM10 particles per month

The PM10 concentration sees a large spike from month 2 to month 3. It then drops considerably, decreasing until month 8, when it begins to rise again.

3. Create a DataFrame for the pollutant **SO2** that stores the median concentration for each month. Plot the DataFrame as a point plot.

The output will be as follows:

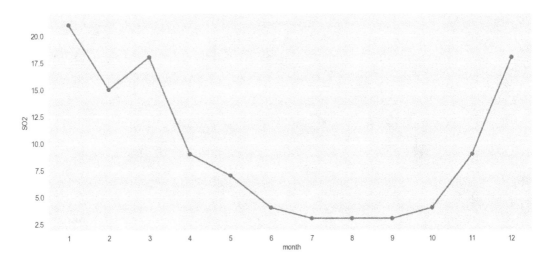

Figure 10.45: The average SO2 concentration per month

There is a large decrease in SO2 from month 3, which levels out between months 7 and 9, before increasing again.

4. Create a DataFrame for the pollutant **NO2** that stores the median concentration for each month. Plot the DataFrame as a point plot.

The expected output is as follows:

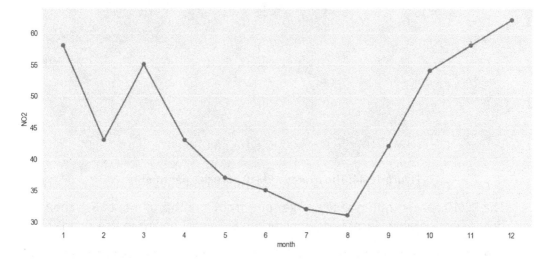

Figure 10.46: The concentration of NO2 per month

The NO2 pattern is similar to that of SO2. It decreases continually from month 3 to month 8, when it begins to increase sharply.

5. Create a DataFrame for the pollutant **CO** that stores the median concentration for each month. Plot the DataFrame as a point plot.

    The expected output is as follows:

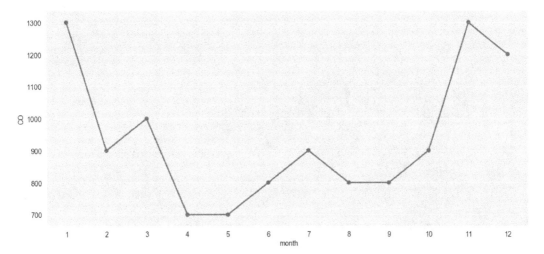

Figure 10.47: The concentration of CO per month

There is some variation in the CO concentration over time. There are peaks in month 1 and month 11, with smaller spikes in months 3 and 7.

6. Create a DataFrame for the pollutant **O3** that stores the median concentration for each month. Plot the DataFrame as a point plot.

The expected output is as follows:

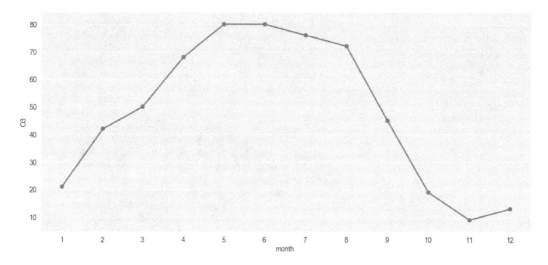

Figure 10.48: The median concentration of O3 per month

The concentration of **O3** rises in the first 5 months, remains constant in June, and then slowly begins to drop. There is a rapid decrease between August and October. In December, it begins to rise again.

> **NOTE**
>
> The solution to the activity can be found on page 593.

In this activity, we have successfully observed the relationship between months and the concentration of pollutants.

> **NOTE**
>
> For further practice and analysis, you can repeat the steps of *Activity 10.03, Observing Pollutant Concentration per Month* for the **hour** column as well. Additionally, you can convert the **day**, **month**, and **year** columns into a **date** column, and then break that into a **day_week** column that will tell you the day of the week. Then, you can repeat *Activity 10.03, Observing Pollutant Concentration per Month* on this column to observe the trends in the concentration of the pollutants per day of the week.

You might be wondering why we can't just plot all the pollutants on the same graph. The reason we can't do this is because their axes are quite different. If we were to plot them on the same graph, the axes would be very large and, hence, the plots would be extremely spread out, prohibiting us from understanding the relationships between the concentrations and the time period (year and month). To accurately observe relationships between the pollutants, we will plot a heatmap in the next exercise.

HEATMAPS

Heatmaps are a type of visualization that display correlations between different features of a dataset. Correlations can be positive or negative, and strong or weak.

The features are set as rows and columns, and the cells are color-coded based on their correlation value. Features with a high positive number are strongly positively correlated.

EXERCISE 10.05: CHECKING FOR CORRELATIONS BETWEEN FEATURES

In this exercise, you will plot a heatmap to observe whether there are any correlations between features of the **new_air** DataFrame:

1. Import **numpy** as **np**:

```
import numpy as np
```

2. Create a variable called **corr** that will store the correlations between the features of **new_air**. Calculate these correlations by applying the **.corr()** function on **new_air**:

```
corr = new_air.corr()
```

3. Mask the zero values using the **zeros_like()** function, with **corr** as the correlations to check, and set **dtype** as **np.bool**:

```
mask = np.zeros_like(corr, dtype=np.bool)
mask[np.triu_indices_from(mask)] = True
```

4. Plot a heatmap with seaborn, using **corr**. Set the number of decimal points as **2** and **mask** as **mask**:

```
sns.heatmap(corr, annot=True, fmt=".2f" , mask=mask)
```

5. Set the **x** and **y** tick labels as the columns of **corr**:

```
plt.xticks(range(len(corr.columns)), corr.columns)
plt.yticks(range(len(corr.columns)), corr.columns)
```

6. Display the heatmap:

```
plt.show()
```

The expected output is as follows:

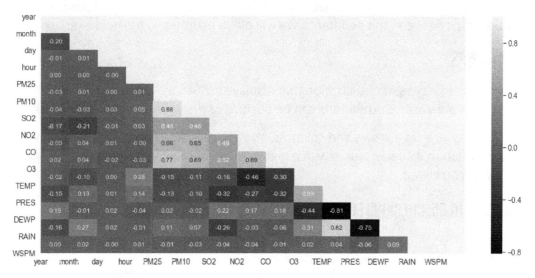

Figure 10.49: Correlations between the features of new_air

The pollutants seem to have a positive correlation in relation to one another. However, there isn't a strong correlation observed between any other features.

> **NOTE**
>
> To access the source code for this specific section, please refer to https://packt.live/37Cmuzv.
>
> You can also run this example online at https://packt.live/3daPFuP. You must execute the entire Notebook in order to get the desired result.

In this exercise, we have successfully observed correlations between the pollutants.

Through this analysis, we can conclude that the concentration of pollutants across all 12 localities in Beijing has generally decreased from 2013 to 2016. Along with this, we also observed the trends between the concentration of pollutants and the month of the year, as well as the concentration of each pollutant in each of the 12 localities. We observed that the concentrations were mostly the same in each locality.

SUMMARY

In this chapter, we played around with data pertaining to the quality of air in multiple localities of Beijing, China. We observed trends over different measures of time to see how the concentration of various pollutants differed.

In this book, we looked at several data cleaning, preparation, analysis, and visualization techniques and applied them to a diverse range of datasets from a variety of domains. We made informed decisions to delete or impute instances based on the data available, and tweaked existing features to create new ones by converting them into different formats and breaking them down into several features.

These processes helped us to derive additional insights from our data. Additionally, we learned to ensure that we ask our data the right questions and understand what information it can and cannot provide us with. It is important not to have unreasonable expectations from your data.

You are now equipped with the tools and knowledge required to analyze any data out there!

APPENDIX

CHAPTER 01: BIKE SHARING ANALYSIS

ACTIVITY 1.01: INVESTIGATING THE IMPACT OF WEATHER CONDITIONS ON RIDES

1. Import the required libraries and the initial **hour** data:

```
# import libraries
import pandas as pd
import matplotlib.pyplot as plt
import seaborn as sns
from scipy.stats import pearsonr
%matplotlib inline
# load hourly data
data = pd.read_csv('https://raw.githubusercontent.com/'\
                   'PacktWorkshops/'\
                   'The-Data-Analysis-Workshop/master/'\
                   'Chapter01/data/hour.csv')
```

2. Create a new column in which **weathersit** is mapped to the four categorical values specified in *Exercise 1.01, Preprocessing Temporal and Weather Features* (**clear**, **cloudy**, **light_rain_snow**, and **heavy_rain_snow**):

```
# create new column by encoding the weathersit one
weather_mapping = {1: 'clear', 2: 'cloudy', \
                   3: 'light_rain_snow', 4: 'heavy_rain_snow'}
data['weather'] = data['weathersit']\
                  .apply(lambda x: weather_mapping[x])
```

3. Define a Python function that accepts as input the hour data, a column name, and a weather condition, and then returns a seaborn **regplot** in which regression plots are produced between the provided column name and the registered and casual rides for the specified weather condition:

```
"""
define a function for creating a regression plot for a specified
weather
condition
"""

def create_regression_plot(data, col, weather_cond):
```

```
    # extract data for the specific weather condition
    plot_data = data[data['weather'] == weather_cond]
    # create regplot for registered users
    ax = sns.regplot(x=col, y="registered", data=plot_data, \
                    scatter_kws={"alpha":0.05})
    # create regplot for casual users
    ax = sns.regplot(x=col, y="casual", data=plot_data, \
                    scatter_kws={"alpha":0.05})
    ax.set_xlabel("")
    ax.set_ylabel("")
    ax.set_title(f"{col} | {weather_cond}")
    return ax
```

4. Produce a 4 x 4 plot in which each column represents a specific weather condition (**clear**, **cloudy**, **light_rain_snow**, and **heavy_rain_snow**), and each row of the specified four columns (**temp**, **atemp**, **hum**, and **windspeed**):

```
weather_conditions = data.weather.unique()
columns = ["temp", "atemp", "hum", "windspeed"]
plt.figure(figsize=(20,30))
for col_index, col in enumerate(columns):
    for row_index, weather_cond in enumerate(weather_conditions):
        plot_number = row_index + col_index*4 + 1
        plt.subplot(4,4,plot_number)
        create_regression_plot(data, col, weather_cond)
```

5. Define a second function that accepts as input the hour data, a column name, and a specific weather condition, and then prints the Pearson's correlation and p-value between the registered and casual rides and the provided column, for the specified weather condition (once correlation is computed between the registered rides and the specified column, and once between the casual rides and the specified column):

```
# create function for computing pearson correlation
def print_correlations(data, col, weather_cond):
    # extract data for the specific weather condition
    corr_data = data[data['weather'] == weather_cond]
```

```
    # compute pearson correlation between col and registered rides
    pearson_corr_r = pearsonr(corr_data[col], \
                              corr_data["registered"])

    # compute pearson correlation between col and registered rides
    pearson_corr_c = pearsonr(corr_data[col], corr_data["casual"])

    # print correlations
    print(f"Pearson correlation (registered, {col}): \
corr={pearson_corr_r[0]:.03f}, pval={pearson_corr_r[1]:.03f}")
    print(f"Pearson correlation (casual, {col}): \
corr={pearson_corr_c[0]:.03f}, pval={pearson_corr_c[1]:.03f}")
```

6. Iterating over the four columns (**temp**, **atemp**, **hum**, and **windspeed**) and four weather conditions (**clear**, **cloudy**, **light_rain_snow**, and **heavy_rain_snow**), print the correlation for each column and each weather condition by using the function defined in *Step 5*:

```
"""
print correlations for temp, atemp, hum and windspeed columns
with registered and casual rides
"""
weather_conditions = data.weather.unique()
columns = ["temp", "atemp", "hum", "windspeed"]
for col in columns:
    for weather_cond in weather_conditions:
        print_correlations(data, col, weather_cond)
```

The output should be as follows:

```
Pearson correlation (registered, temp): corr=0.340, pval=0.000
Pearson correlation (casual, temp): corr=0.459, pval=0.000
Pearson correlation (registered, temp): corr=0.285, pval=0.000
Pearson correlation (casual, temp): corr=0.437, pval=0.000
Pearson correlation (registered, temp): corr=0.356, pval=0.000
Pearson correlation (casual, temp): corr=0.433, pval=0.000
Pearson correlation (registered, temp): corr=0.360, pval=0.766
Pearson correlation (casual, temp): corr=0.277, pval=0.821
Pearson correlation (registered, atemp): corr=0.334, pval=0.000
Pearson correlation (casual, atemp): corr=0.451, pval=0.000
Pearson correlation (registered, atemp): corr=0.285, pval=0.000
Pearson correlation (casual, atemp): corr=0.434, pval=0.000
Pearson correlation (registered, atemp): corr=0.366, pval=0.000
Pearson correlation (casual, atemp): corr=0.445, pval=0.000
Pearson correlation (registered, atemp): corr=0.810, pval=0.399
Pearson correlation (casual, atemp): corr=0.756, pval=0.454
Pearson correlation (registered, hum): corr=-0.282, pval=0.000
Pearson correlation (casual, hum): corr=-0.331, pval=0.000
Pearson correlation (registered, hum): corr=-0.156, pval=0.000
Pearson correlation (casual, hum): corr=-0.289, pval=0.000
Pearson correlation (registered, hum): corr=-0.229, pval=0.000
Pearson correlation (casual, hum): corr=-0.243, pval=0.000
Pearson correlation (registered, hum): corr=-0.423, pval=0.722
Pearson correlation (casual, hum): corr=-0.500, pval=0.667
Pearson correlation (registered, windspeed): corr=0.113, pval=0.000
Pearson correlation (casual, windspeed): corr=0.111, pval=0.000
Pearson correlation (registered, windspeed): corr=0.048, pval=0.001
Pearson correlation (casual, windspeed): corr=0.063, pval=0.000
Pearson correlation (registered, windspeed): corr=-0.005, pval=0.842
Pearson correlation (casual, windspeed): corr=0.054, pval=0.042
Pearson correlation (registered, windspeed): corr=-0.776, pval=0.435
Pearson correlation (casual, windspeed): corr=-0.828, pval=0.379
```

Figure 1.52: Correlation between weather and the registered/casual rides

NOTE

To access the source code for this specific section, please refer to https://packt.live/3foIRv4.

You can also run this example online at https://packt.live/37AkAQ1. You must execute the entire Notebook in order to get the desired result.

CHAPTER 02: ABSENTEEISM AT WORK

ACTIVITY 2.01: ANALYZING THE SERVICE TIME AND SON COLUMNS

1. First, let's import the data and the necessary libraries:

```
# perform statistical test for avg duration difference
import pandas as pd
import seaborn as sns
import matplotlib.pyplot as plt

%matplotlib inline

# import data from the github page of the book
data = pd.read_csv('https://raw.githubusercontent.com/'\
                   'PacktWorkshops/'\
                   'The-Data-Analysis-Workshop/master/'\
                   'Chapter02/data/Absenteeism_at_work.csv', \
                   sep=";")
```

2. Now, create a kernel density estimation plot of the **Service time** column:

```
# create KDE plot of the Service time column
plt.figure()
ax = sns.kdeplot(data["Service time"])
ax.set_xlabel("Service time")
plt.savefig('figs/assignment_kde_plot.png', \
            format='png', dpi=300)
```

The output will be as follows:

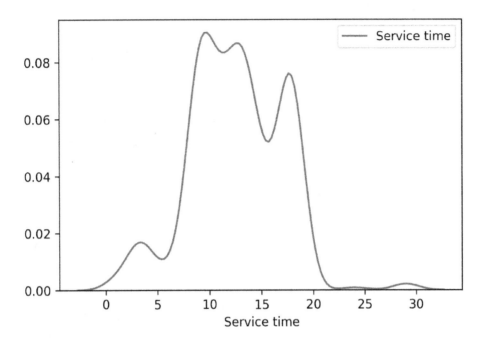

Figure 2.62: KDE plot for service time

3. Test the distribution for normality via the Kolmogorov-Smirnov test:

```
# test distribution for Normality
from scipy.stats import kstest
ks_res = kstest(data["Service time"], "norm")
print(f"Kolmogorov-Smirnov test for normality \
pvalue: {ks_res[1]:.03f}")
```

The output will be as follows:

```
Kolmogorov-Smirnov test for normality pvalue: 0.000
```

From the resulting value of the test, we can reject the null hypothesis that the **Service time** column has a normal distribution.

4. Create a violin plot of the **Service time** column against the **Reason for absence** column:

```
"""
create violin plot for the Service time, against Reason for absence
"""
plt.figure(figsize=(12,5))
sns.violinplot(x="Reason for absence", \
               y="Service time",data=data)
plt.savefig('figs/assignment_service_time_vs_absence.png', \
            format='png', dpi=300)
```

The output will be as follows:

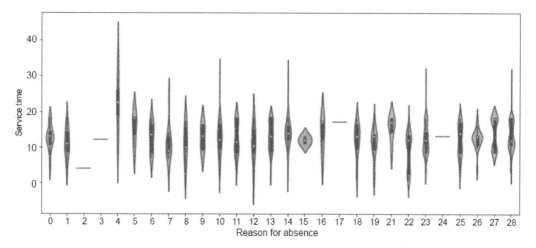

Figure 2.63: Violin plot for the Service time column

5. Create a correlation plot between the **Service time** and **Absenteeism time in hours** columns:

```
"""
plot for the Service time, against Reason for absence
produce correlation plot between Service time and Absenteeism time in
hours
"""
from scipy.stats import yeojohnson
plt.figure(figsize=(10, 6))
service_time = data["Service time"]
```

```
absenteeism_time = yeojohnson(data["Absenteeism time in hours"]\
                         .apply(float))[0]
ax = sns.jointplot(x=service_time, y=absenteeism_time, \
               kind="reg")
ax.set_axis_labels("Service time", \
               "Transformed absenteeism time in hours")
plt.savefig('figs/assignment_jointplot.png', \
         format='png', dpi=300)
```

The output will be as follows:

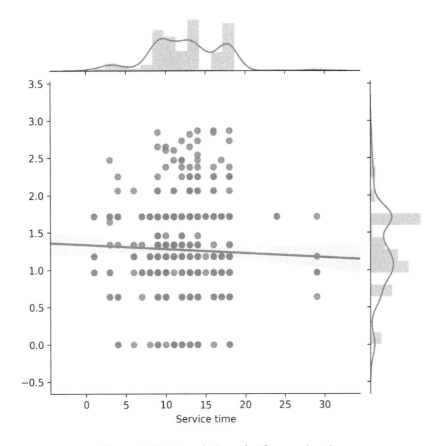

Figure 2.64: Correlation plot for service time

6. Finally, to analyze the distributions of **Absenteeism time in hours** for employees with a different number of children, create a violin plot in which the *x*-axis contains the **Son** column and the *y*-axis contains the **Absenteeism time in hours** column, as follows:

```
"""
analyze distribution of Absenteeism time in hours, per number of
children
"""
plt.figure(figsize=(10, 6))
ax = sns.violinplot(x = "Son", y="Service time", data=data)
plt.savefig('figs/assignment_hours_vs_son.png', \
                format='png', dpi=300)
```

The output will be as follows:

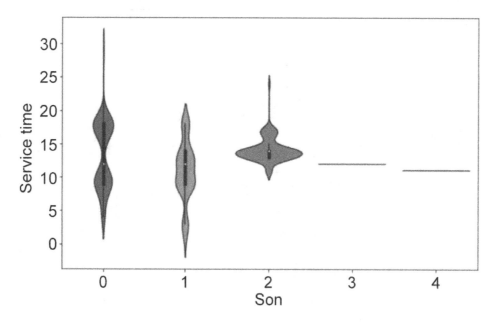

Figure 2.65: Distribution of absent time for employees with a different number of children

> **NOTE**
>
> To access the source code for this specific section, please refer to https://packt.live/2AAdFKJ.
>
> You can also run this example online at https://packt.live/2N6PZ3a. You must execute the entire Notebook in order to get the desired result.

CHAPTER 03: ANALYZING BANK MARKETING CAMPAIGN DATA

ACTIVITY 3.01: CREATING A LEANER LOGISTIC REGRESSION MODEL

1. Start by importing the necessary Python packages:

```
# import necessary libraries
import pandas as pd
import numpy as np
import statsmodels.api as sm
```

2. Load the data from GitHub:

```
# pull data from github
bank_data = pd.read_csv("https://raw.githubusercontent.com/"\
                "PacktWorkshops/"\
                "The-Data-Analysis-Workshop/master/"\
                "Chapter03/data/bank-additional/"\
                "bank-additional-full.csv", sep=";")
```

3. Now, create the feature matrix to be fed into the logistic regression model. Here, we'll use the **duration, campaign, pdays, cons.price.idx, cons.conf.idx**, and **euribor3m** columns. You will also need to add a constant term:

```
# create a feature matrix
columns = ["duration", "campaign", "pdays", "cons.price.idx", \
           "cons.conf.idx", "euribor3m"]
X = bank_data[columns]
X = sm.add_constant(X)

X.head()
```

The output of the preceding code is as follows:

	const	duration	campaign	pdays	cons.price.idx	cons.conf.idx	euribor3m
0	1.0	261	1	999	93.994	-36.4	4.857
1	1.0	149	1	999	93.994	-36.4	4.857
2	1.0	226	1	999	93.994	-36.4	4.857
3	1.0	151	1	999	93.994	-36.4	4.857
4	1.0	307	1	999	93.994	-36.4	4.857

Figure 3.46: Feature matrix to be used in the logistic regression model

4. You also need to transform the target variable into numerical values (as the logistic regression algorithm expects numerical target values):

```
# transform target variable
y = np.where(bank_data["y"] == "yes", 1, 0)
```

5. Define the logistic regression model and fit the data:

```
# define and fit model
logistic_regression_model = sm.Logit(y, X)
result = logistic_regression_model.fit()
print(result.summary())
```

The output of the preceding code is as follows:

```
                          Logit Regression Results
===============================================================================
Dep. Variable:                       y    No. Observations:              41188
Model:                           Logit    Df Residuals:                  41181
Method:                            MLE    Df Model:                          6
Date:                 Wed, 12 Feb 2020    Pseudo R-squ.:                0.3690
Time:                         19:53:11    Log-Likelihood:              -9149.5
converged:                        True    LL-Null:                     -14499.
Covariance Type:             nonrobust    LLR p-value:                   0.000
===============================================================================
                   coef     std err          z      P>|z|      [0.025      0.975]
-------------------------------------------------------------------------------
const          -43.1379       3.524    -12.240      0.000     -50.046     -36.230
duration         0.0045     7.11e-05     63.505      0.000       0.004       0.005
campaign        -0.0495       0.011     -4.331      0.000      -0.072      -0.027
pdays           -0.0016     6.81e-05    -22.928      0.000      -0.002      -0.001
cons.price.idx   0.4921       0.038     12.877      0.000       0.417       0.567
cons.conf.idx    0.0699       0.003     20.137      0.000       0.063       0.077
euribor3m       -0.7200       0.015    -47.462      0.000      -0.750      -0.690
===============================================================================
```

Figure 3.47: Results from the logistic regression model

6. You can use the coefficients from *Figure 3.41* in order to write the equations for the probabilities **Pr(y=yes)** and **Pr(y=no)**. By denoting the **duration, campaign, pdays, cons.price.idx, cons.conf.idx** and **euribor3m** columns with $x_1,...,x_6$ the following equations should be derived:

$$Pr(y=yes)$$
$$= \frac{exp(-43.1379+0.0045.x_1-0.0495.x_2-0.0016.x_3+0.4921.x_4+0.0699.x_5-0.72.x_6)}{1+exp(-43.1379+0.0045.x_1-0.0495.x_2-0.0016.x_3+0.4921.x_4+0.0699.x_5-0.72.x_6)}$$

$$Pr(y=no)$$
$$= \frac{1}{1+exp(-43.1379+0.0045.x_1-0.0495.x_2-0.0016.x_3+0.4921.x_4+0.0699.x_5-0.72.x_6)}$$

Figure 3.48: Estimations of the probabilities according to the coefficients that were obtained by the logistic regression model

7. Note that you managed to create a model with way higher pseudo R-square metric (**0.369**) with respect to the one in *Figure 3.33* (0.233, respectively) by keeping the number of features low.

> **NOTE**
>
> To access the source code for this specific section, please refer to https://packt.live/30Pt9Fl.
>
> You can also run this example online at https://packt.live/2AGw3Bm. You must execute the entire Notebook in order to get the desired result.

CHAPTER 04: TACKLING COMPANY BANKRUPTCY

ACTIVITY 4.01: FEATURE SELECTION WITH LASSO

1. Import **Lasso** from the sklearn.linear_model package:

```
from sklearn.linear_model import Lasso
from sklearn.feature_selection import SelectFromModel
```

2. Fit the independent and dependent variables with lasso regularization for the **mean_imputed_df4** DataFrame:

```
features_names=X6.columns.tolist()
lasso = Lasso(alpha=0.01 ,positive=True)
lasso.fit(X6,y6)
```

3. Print the coefficients of lasso regularization:

```
coef_list=sorted(zip(map(lambda x: round(x,4), \
                    lasso.coef_.reshape(-1)),\
                    features_names), reverse=True)
coef_list [0:5]
```

The output will be as follows:

```
[(0.0009, 'X21'), (0.0002, 'X2'), (0.0001, 'X42'),
 (0.0, 'X9'), (0.0, 'X8')]
```

4. Get the significant features and write down the variable's description from the data dictionary.

By performing lasso regularization, we end up with only 3 significant features out of 64. The columns that are significant are as follows:

X21: Sales (n)/sales (n-1)

X2: Total liabilities/total assets

X42: Profit on operating activities/sales

5. Perform the preceding steps for **mean_imputed_df5** as well:

```
features_names=X7.columns.tolist()
lasso = Lasso(alpha=0.01 ,positive=True)
lasso.fit(X7,y7)
coef_list=sorted(zip(map(lambda x: round(x,4),\
                lasso.coef_.reshape(-1)),\
                features_names),reverse=True)
coef_list [0:10]
```

The output will be as follows:

```
[(0.0216, 'X51'),
 (0.0015, 'X2'),
 (0.001, 'X9'),
 (0.001, 'X36'),
 (0.0003, 'X59'),
 (0.0003, 'X52'),
 (0.0001, 'X61'),
 (0.0001, 'X31'),
 (0.0001, 'X30'),
 (0.0001, 'X20')]
```

The columns that are significant are as follows:

X51: Short-term liabilities/total assets

X2: Total liabilities/total assets

X9: Sales/total assets X36-total sales/total assets

X59: Long-term liabilities/equity

X52: (short-term liabilities * 365)/cost of products sold)

X61: Sales/receivables X31 - (gross profit + interest)/sales

X30: (total liabilities - cash)/sales

X20: (inventory * 365)/sales

6. Next, perform the same steps for **iterative_imputed_df4**:

```
features_names=X8.columns.tolist()
lasso = Lasso(alpha=0.01 ,positive=True)
lasso.fit(X8,y8)
coef_list=sorted(zip(map(lambda x: round(x,4), \
                        lasso.coef_.reshape(-1)),\
                        features_names),reverse=True)
coef_list [0:5]
```

The output will be as follows:

```
[(0.0009, 'X21'), (0.0002, 'X2'), (0.0001, 'X42'),
 (0.0, 'X9'), (0.0, 'X8')]
```

The columns that are significant are as follows:

X21: Sales (n)/sales (n-1)

X2: Total liabilities/total assets

X42: Profit on operating activities/sales

7. Perform the same steps for **iterative_imputed_df5**:

```
features_names=X9.columns.tolist()
lasso = Lasso(alpha=0.01,positive=True)
lasso.fit(X9,y9)
coef_list=sorted(zip(map(lambda x: round(x,4),\
                        lasso.coef_.reshape(-1)),\
                        features_names),reverse=True)
coef_list [0:10]
```

The output will be as follows:

```
[(0.0213, 'X51'),
 (0.0015, 'X2'),
 (0.0012, 'X9'),
 (0.0009, 'X36'),
 (0.0003, 'X59'),
 (0.0003, 'X52'),
 (0.0001, 'X61'),
 (0.0001, 'X31'),
 (0.0001, 'X30'),
 (0.0001, 'X20')]
```

NOTE

To access the source code for this specific section, please refer to https://packt.live/2ABdSgG.

You can also run this example online at https://packt.live/37zH9Ei. You must execute the entire Notebook in order to get the desired result.

CHAPTER 05: ANALYZING THE ONLINE SHOPPER'S PURCHASING INTENTION

ACTIVITY 5.01: PERFORMING K-MEANS CLUSTERING FOR ADMINISTRATIVE DURATION VERSUS BOUNCE RATE AND ADMINISTRATIVE DURATION VERSUS EXIT RATE

1. Select the **Administrative Duration** and **Bounce Rate** columns. Assign the column to a variable called **x**:

```
x = df.iloc[:, [1, 6]].values
x.shape
```

2. Initialize the k-means algorithm:

```
wcss = []
for i in range(1, 11):
    km = KMeans(n_clusters = i, init = 'k-means++', \
                max_iter = 300, n_init = 10, random_state = 0, \
                algorithm = 'elkan', tol = 0.001)
```

3. For the different values of **K**, compute the **Kmeans** inertia and store it in a variable called **wcss**:

```
    km.fit(x)
    labels = km.labels_
    wcss.append(km.inertia_)
```

4. Plot a graph between **wcss** and the corresponding **k** value:

```
plt.rcParams['figure.figsize'] = (15, 7)
plt.plot(range(1, 11), wcss)
plt.grid()
plt.tight_layout()
plt.title('The Elbow Method', fontsize = 20)
plt.xlabel('No. of Clusters')
plt.ylabel('wcss')
plt.show()
```

Once the graph has been plotted, find the optimum value of **K**. The optimum value of **K** is a point where there is a bend in the graph. The elbow graph will be as follows:

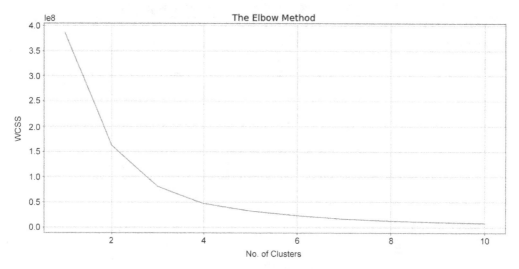

Figure 5.43: Elbow graph for administrative duration versus bounce rate

From the preceding graph, we can see that the bend is present for **k=2**, which is the optimum value.

5. Perform k-means clustering between **Administrative duration vs Bounce Rate** with **k=2**. By performing k-means clustering, we get centroids of both the clusters:

```
km = KMeans(n_clusters = 2, init = 'k-means++', \
            max_iter = 300, n_init = 10, random_state = 0)
y_means = km.fit_predict(x)
```

6. Assign the color **pink** for uninterested customers and the color **cyan** for our target customer:

```
plt.scatter(x[y_means == 0, 0], x[y_means == 0, 1], s = 100, \
            c = 'pink', label = 'Un-interested Customers')
plt.scatter(x[y_means == 1, 0], x[y_means == 1, 1], s = 100, \
            c = 'cyan', label = 'Target Customers')
```

7. Use the color **blue** to denote the centroid of the cluster, which can be obtained from the cluster:

```
plt.scatter(km.cluster_centers_[:,0], km.cluster_centers_[:, 1], \
            s = 50, c = 'blue' , label = 'centeroid')
```

8. Plot a scatter plot between **Administrative Duration vs Bounce Rate**:

```
plt.title('Administrative Duration vs Bounce Rate', fontsize = 20)
plt.grid()
plt.xlabel('Administrative Duration')
plt.ylabel('Bounce Rates')
plt.legend()
plt.show()
```

The output will be as follows:

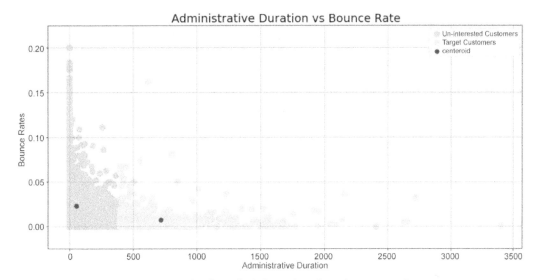

Figure 5.44: Scatterplot for administrative duration versus bounce rate

From the preceding graph, we can infer that the uninterested customer spends much less time in administrative pages compared with target customers, who spend around 750 seconds on the administrative page before bouncing back.

Similarly, perform k-means clustering for **Administrative Duration vs Exit Rate**.

9. Select the **Administrative Duration** and **Bounce Rate** columns. Assign the column to a variable called **x**:

```
x = df.iloc[:, [1, 7]].values
```

10. Initialize the k-means algorithm:

```
wcss = []
for i in range(1, 11):
    km = KMeans(n_clusters = i, init = 'k-means++', \
                max_iter = 300, n_init = 10, \
                random_state = 0, algorithm = 'elkan', tol = 0.001)
```

11. For the different values of **K**, compute the **Kmeans** inertia and store it in a variable called **wcss**:

```
    km.fit(x)
    labels = km.labels_
    wcss.append(km.inertia_)
```

12. Plot a graph between **wcss** and the corresponding **k** value:

```
plt.rcParams['figure.figsize'] = (15, 7)
plt.plot(range(1, 11), wcss)
plt.grid()
plt.tight_layout()
plt.title('The Elbow Method', fontsize = 20)
plt.xlabel('No. of Clusters')
plt.ylabel('wcss')
plt.show()
```

Once the graph has been plotted, find the optimum value of **K**. The optimum value of **K** is a point where there is a bend in the graph. The elbow graph is as follows:

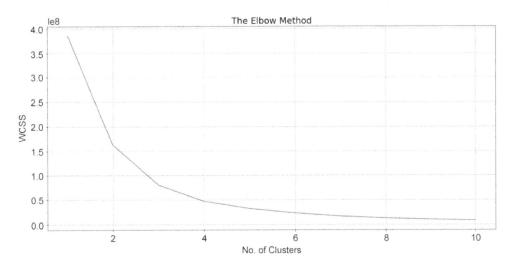

Figure 5.47: Elbow method for administrative duration versus exit rate

From the preceding graph, we can see that the bend is present for **k=2**, which is the optimum value.

13. Perform k-means clustering between **Administrative duration vs Exit Rate** with **k=2**. By performing k-means clustering, we get the centroids of both clusters:

```
km = KMeans(n_clusters = 2, init = 'k-means++', \
            max_iter = 300, n_init = 10, random_state = 0)
y_means = km.fit_predict(x)
```

14. Assign the color **pink** for uninterested customers and the color **yellow** for our target customer:

```
plt.scatter(x[y_means == 0, 0], x[y_means == 0, 1], s = 100, \
            c = 'pink', label = 'Un-interested Customers')
plt.scatter(x[y_means == 1, 0], x[y_means == 1, 1], s = 100, \
            c = 'yellow', label = 'Target Customers')
```

15. Use the color **blue** to denote the centroid of the cluster, which can be obtained from the cluster:

```
plt.scatter(km.cluster_centers_[:,0], km.cluster_centers_[:, 1], \
            s = 50, c = 'blue' , label = 'centeroid')
```

16. Plot a scatter plot between **Administrative Duration vs Bounce Rate**:

```
plt.title('Administrative Duration vs Exit Rates', fontsize = 20)
plt.grid()
plt.xlabel('Administrative Duration')
plt.ylabel('Exit Rates')
plt.legend()
plt.show()
```

The output will be as follows:

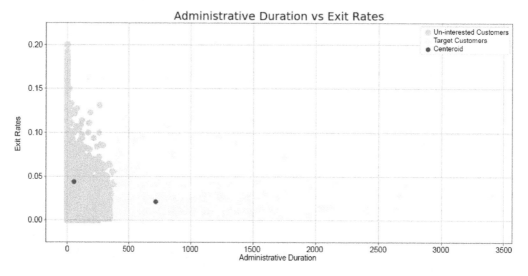

Figure 5.46: Scatterplot for administrative duration versus exit rate

---

NOTE

To access the source code for this specific section, please refer to https://packt.live/2YGDPmR.

You can also run this example online at https://packt.live/2BjRsAf. You must execute the entire Notebook in order to get the desired result.

CHAPTER 06: ANALYSIS OF CREDIT CARD DEFAULTERS

ACTIVITY 6.01: EVALUATING THE CORRELATION BETWEEN COLUMNS USING A HEATMAP

1. Plot the heatmap for all the columns in the DataFrame (other than the **ID** column) by using **sns.heatmap** and keep the figure size as **30,10** for better visibility:

```
sns.set(rc={'figure.figsize':(30,10)})
sns.set_context("talk", font_scale=0.7)
```

2. Use **Spearman** as the method parameter to compute Spearman's rank correlation coefficient:

```
sns.heatmap(df.iloc[:,1:].corr(method='spearman'), \
            cmap='rainbow_r', annot=True)
```

The output of the heatmap is as follows:

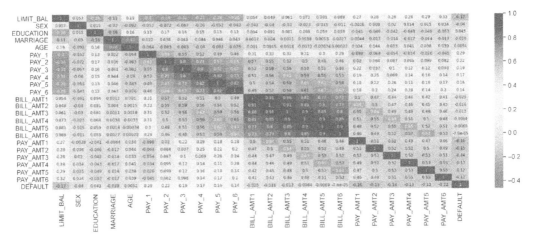

Figure 6.28: Heatmap for Spearman's rank correlation

3. In order to get the exact correlation coefficients of each column with the **DEFAULT** column, apply the `.corr()` function on each column with respect to the **DEFAULT** column:

```
df.drop("DEFAULT", axis=1)\
.apply(lambda x: x.corr(df.DEFAULT,method='spearman'))
```

The output will be as follows:

```
ID             -0.013952
LIMIT_BAL      -0.169586
SEX            -0.039961
EDUCATION       0.043425
MARRIAGE       -0.028174
AGE             0.005149
PAY_1           0.292213
PAY_2           0.216919
PAY_3           0.194771
PAY_4           0.173690
PAY_5           0.159043
PAY_6           0.142523
BILL_AMT1      -0.025327
BILL_AMT2      -0.015554
BILL_AMT3      -0.012670
BILL_AMT4      -0.008357
BILL_AMT5      -0.006851
BILL_AMT6      -0.000076
PAY_AMT1       -0.160493
PAY_AMT2       -0.150977
PAY_AMT3       -0.139388
PAY_AMT4       -0.127979
PAY_AMT5       -0.116587
PAY_AMT6       -0.121444
dtype: float64
```

Figure 6.29: Output for the correlation function

NOTE

To access the source code for this specific section, please refer to https://packt.live/37DXOGI.

You can also run this example online at https://packt.live/2UTtvXs. You must execute the entire Notebook in order to get the desired result.

CHAPTER 07: ANALYZING THE HEART DISEASE DATASET

ACTIVITY 7.01: CHECKING FOR OUTLIERS

1. Plot a box plot using **sns.boxplot** for the **st_depr** column:

```
sd = sns.boxplot(df['st_depr'])
plt.show()
```

The output will be as follows:

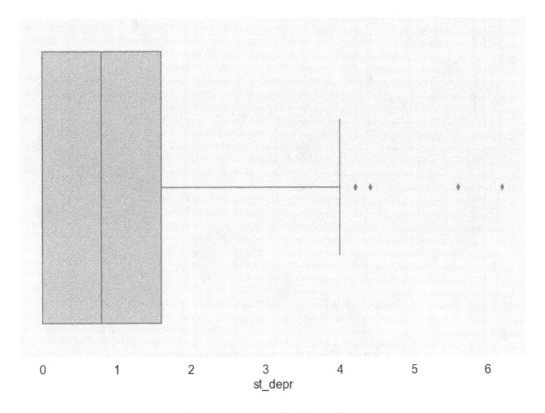

Figure 7.22: Box plot for st_depr

2. Plot a box plot using **sns.boxplot** for the **colored_vessels** column:

```
cv = sns.boxplot(df['colored_vessels'])
plt.show()
```

The output will be as follows:

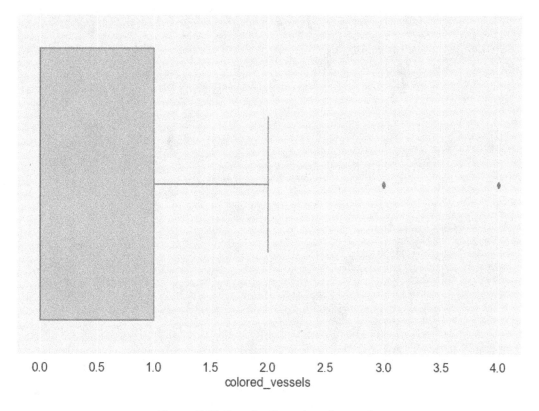

Figure 7.23: Boxplot for colored_vessels

3. Plot a box plot using **sns.boxplot** for the **thalassemia** column:

```
t = sns.boxplot(df['thalassemia'])
plt.show()
```

The output will be as follows:

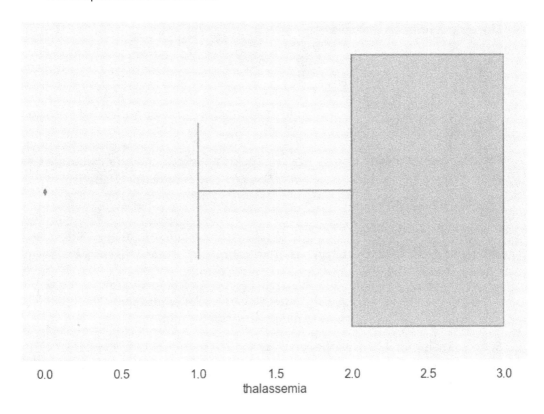

Figure 7.24: Boxplot for thalassemia

> **NOTE**
>
> To access the source code for this specific section, please refer to https://packt.live/2N4I0DF.
>
> You can also run this example online at https://packt.live/2BiGv2c. You must execute the entire Notebook in order to get the desired result.

ACTIVITY 7.02: PLOTTING DISTRIBUTIONS AND RELATIONSHIPS BETWEEN COLUMNS WITH RESPECT TO THE TARGET COLUMN

1. Print the total number of patients with each type of chest pain:

```
df.chest_pain.value_counts()
```

The output will be as follows:

```
0    143
2     87
1     50
3     23
Name: chest_pain, dtype: int64
```

2. Create a countplot with **chest_pain** as **x**, **data** as **df**, and **hue** as **target**. First, create a legend for the plot with **Absent** and **Present** as labels:

```
c = sns.countplot(x = 'chest_pain', data = df, hue = 'target')
plt.legend(['Absent', 'Present'])
```

3. Set the title to **Distribution of Presence of Heart Disease by Chest Pain Type**:

```
c.set_title('Distribution of Presence of Heart Disease '\
            'by Chest Pain Type')
```

4. Set the labels of the bars as the four types of chest pain, that is, **Typical Anginal**, **Atypical Anginal**, **Non-anginal Pain**, and **Asymptomatic**:

```
c.set_xticklabels(['Typical Angina', 'Atypical Angina', \
                   'Non-anginal Pain', 'Asymptomatic'])
plt.show()
```

The plot will be as follows:

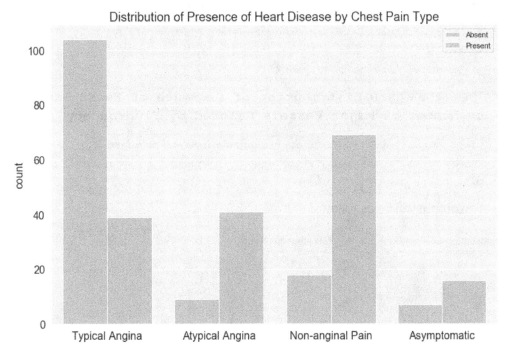

Figure 7.25: Distribution of Presence of Heart Disease by Chest Pain Type

5. Print the total number of patients with each number of colored vessels:

```
df.colored_vessels.value_counts()
```

The output will be as follows:

```
0    175
1     65
2     38
3     20
4      5
Name: colored_vessels, dtype: int64
```

6. Create a countplot with **colored_vessels** as **x**, **data** as **df**, and **hue** as **target**. First, create a legend for the plot with **Absent** and **Present** as labels:

```
d = sns.countplot(x = 'colored_vessels', data = df, \
                   hue = 'target')
plt.legend(['Absent', 'Present'])
```

7. Then, set the title to **Distribution of Presence of Heart Disease by Number of Major Vessels Colored by Fluoroscopy**:

```
d.set_title('Distribution of Presence of Heart Disease by '\
             'Number of Major Vessels Coloured by Fluoroscopy')
plt.show()
```

The output will be as follows:

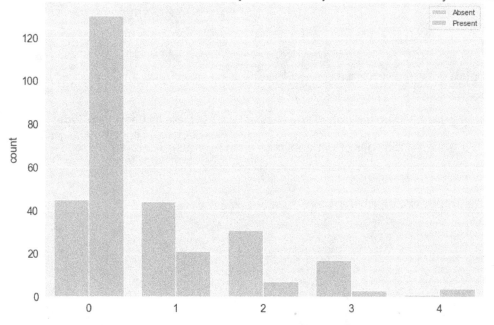

Figure 7.26: Distribution of Presence of Heart Disease by Number of Major Vessels Colored by Fluoroscopy

8. Print the total number of patients with each type of slope:

```
df.slope.value_counts()
```

The output will be as follows:

```
2    142
1    140
0     21
Name: slope, dtype: int64
```

9. Create a countplot with **slope** as **x**, **data** as **df**, and **hue** as **target**. First, create a legend for the plot with **Absent** and **Present** as labels:

```
f = sns.countplot(x = 'slope', data = df, hue = 'target')
plt.legend(['Absent', 'Present'])
```

10. Then, set the title to **Distribution of Presence of Heart Disease by Slope**:

```
f.set_title('Distribution of Presence of Heart Disease by Slope')
```

11. Lastly, set the labels of the bars as the three types of slope, that is, **Upsloping**, **Flat**, and **Downsloping**:

```
f.set_xticklabels(['Upsloping', 'Flat', 'Downsloping'])
plt.show()
```

The output will be as follows:

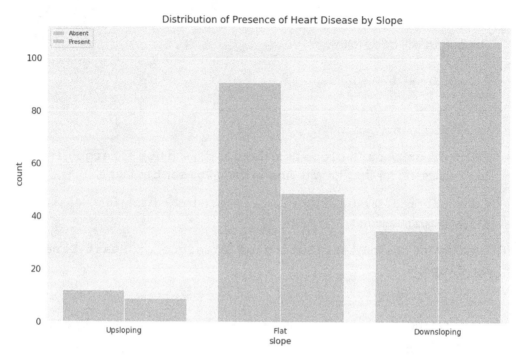

Figure 7.27: Distribution of Presence of Heart Disease by Slope

NOTE

To access the source code for this specific section, please refer
to https://packt.live/3e93Ph7.

You can also run this example online at https://packt.live/30Pky5u. You must
execute the entire Notebook in order to get the desired result.

ACTIVITY 7.03: PLOTTING THE RELATIONSHIP BETWEEN THE PRESENCE OF HEART DISEASE AND THE CHOLESTEROL COLUMN

1. Create a scatter plot with **x** as **age**, **y** as **chol**, both **hue** and **style** as **target**, and **df** as **age**:

```
g= sns.scatterplot(x = 'age', y = 'chol', hue = 'target', \
                   style = 'target', data = df)
```

2. Set the title to **Presence of Heart Disease based on Age and Cholesterol**:

```
g.set_title('Presence of Heart Disease based on '\
            'Age and Cholesterol')
```

3. Set **xlabel** as **Age** and **ylabel** as **Cholesterol**:

```
plt.xlabel('Age')
plt.ylabel('Cholesterol')
```

The output will be as follows:

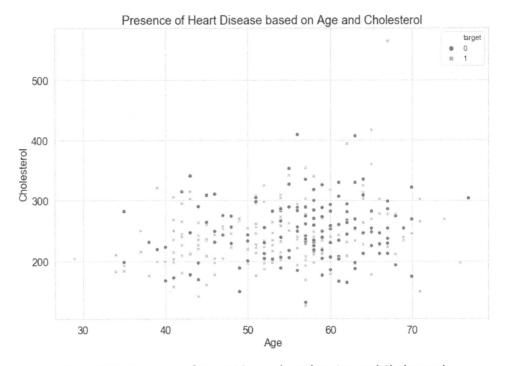

Figure 7.28: Presence of Heart Disease based on Age and Cholesterol

4. Create a new column called **chol_cat** with bins starting at **120** and ending at **380** with intervals of **20**:

```
df['chol_cat'] = pd.cut(df.chol, \
                        bins = list(np.arange(120, 380, 20)))
```

5. Create two subplots—one for patients with heart disease and one for patients without. Group the **target** column by the **chol_cat** column and count the number of instances in the groups. Plot a bar graph for each. Set the titles for the two as **'Present'** and **'Absent'**, respectively, with the x axis as **'Cholesterol Groups'** and the y axis as **Count**:

```
df['chol_cat'] = pd.cut(df.chol, \
                        bins = list(np.arange(120, 380, 20)))

plt.subplot(121)
df[df.target == 1].groupby('chol_cat')['chol']\
.count().plot(kind = 'bar')
plt.title('Present')
plt.xlabel('Cholesterol Group')
plt.ylabel('Count')

plt.subplot(122)
df[df.target == 0].groupby('chol_cat')['chol']\
.count().plot(kind = 'bar')
plt.title('Absent')
plt.xlabel('Cholesterol Group')
plt.ylabel('Count')
```

The output will be as follows:

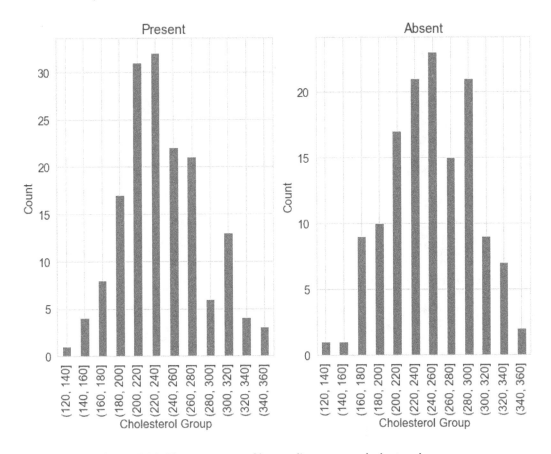

Figure 7.29: The presence of heart disease per cholesterol group

> **NOTE**
>
> To access the source code for this specific section, please refer
> to https://packt.live/3eatYfx.
>
> You can also run this example online at https://packt.live/30PkGlu. You must
> execute the entire Notebook in order to get the desired result.

CHAPTER 08: ANALYZING ONLINE RETAIL II DATASET

ACTIVITY 8.01: PERFORMING DATA ANALYSIS ON THE ONLINE RETAIL II DATASET

1. Import the required packages:

```
import pandas as pd
import numpy as np
import seaborn as sns
import matplotlib.pyplot as plt
```

In a Jupyter notebook, install **plotly** using the following command:

```
!pip install plotly
```

Import **plotly.express** from the installed package:

```
import plotly.express as px
```

2. Store each of the CSV files in two different DataFrames:

```
r09 = pd.read_csv('https://raw.githubusercontent.com/'\
                  'PacktWorkshops/'\
                  'The-Data-Analysis-Workshop/master/'\
                  'Chapter08/Datasets/online_retail_II.csv')
r09.head()
```

The output will be as follows:

	Invoice	StockCode	Description	Quantity	InvoiceDate	Price	Customer ID	Country
0	489434	85048	15CM CHRISTMAS GLASS BALL 20 LIGHTS	12	01/12/2009 07:45	6.95	13085.0	United Kingdom
1	489434	79323P	PINK CHERRY LIGHTS	12	01/12/2009 07:45	6.75	13085.0	United Kingdom
2	489434	79323W	WHITE CHERRY LIGHTS	12	01/12/2009 07:45	6.75	13085.0	United Kingdom
3	489434	22041	RECORD FRAME 7" SINGLE SIZE	48	01/12/2009 07:45	2.10	13085.0	United Kingdom
4	489434	21232	STRAWBERRY CERAMIC TRINKET BOX	24	01/12/2009 07:45	1.25	13085.0	United Kingdom

Figure 8.44: Top rows for DataFrame r09

Similarly, create the second DataFrame:

```
r10 = pd.read_csv('https://raw.githubusercontent.com/'\
                  'PacktWorkshops/'\
                  'The-Data-Analysis-Workshop/master/'\
                  'Chapter08/Datasets/online_retail_II2.csv')
r10.head()
```

The output will be as follows:

	Invoice	StockCode	Description	Quantity	InvoiceDate	Price	Customer ID	Country
0	536365	85123A	WHITE HANGING HEART T-LIGHT HOLDER	6	01/12/2010 08:26	2.55	17850.0	United Kingdom
1	536365	71053	WHITE METAL LANTERN	6	01/12/2010 08:26	3.39	17850.0	United Kingdom
2	536365	84406B	CREAM CUPID HEARTS COAT HANGER	8	01/12/2010 08:26	2.75	17850.0	United Kingdom
3	536365	84029G	KNITTED UNION FLAG HOT WATER BOTTLE	6	01/12/2010 08:26	3.39	17850.0	United Kingdom
4	536365	84029E	RED WOOLLY HOTTIE WHITE HEART.	6	01/12/2010 08:26	3.39	17850.0	United Kingdom

Figure 8.45: Top rows for DataFrame r10

3. Concatenate the two DataFrames into one called **retail** using the **.concat()** function and add the keys **09-10** and **10-11**:

```
dfs = [r09, r10]
retail = pd.concat(dfs, keys = ['09-10', '10-11'])
retail
```

The output will be as follows:

		Invoice	StockCode	Description	Quantity	InvoiceDate	Price	Customer ID	Country
	0	489434	85048	15CM CHRISTMAS GLASS BALL 20 LIGHTS	12	01/12/2009 07:45	6.95	13085.0	United Kingdom
	1	489434	79323P	PINK CHERRY LIGHTS	12	01/12/2009 07:45	6.75	13085.0	United Kingdom
09-10	2	489434	79323W	WHITE CHERRY LIGHTS	12	01/12/2009 07:45	6.75	13085.0	United Kingdom
	3	489434	22041	RECORD FRAME 7" SINGLE SIZE	48	01/12/2009 07:45	2.10	13085.0	United Kingdom
	4	489434	21232	STRAWBERRY CERAMIC TRINKET BOX	24	01/12/2009 07:45	1.25	13085.0	United Kingdom
...	...	...	...	...	...	...	...	...	...
	541905	581587	22899	CHILDREN'S APRON DOLLY GIRL	6	09/12/2011 12:50	2.10	12680.0	France
	541906	581587	23254	CHILDRENS CUTLERY DOLLY GIRL	4	09/12/2011 12:50	4.15	12680.0	France
10-11	541907	581587	23255	CHILDRENS CUTLERY CIRCUS PARADE	4	09/12/2011 12:50	4.15	12680.0	France
	541908	581587	22138	BAKING SET 9 PIECE RETROSPOT	3	09/12/2011 12:50	4.95	12680.0	France
	541909	581587	POST	POSTAGE	1	09/12/2011 12:50	18.00	12680.0	France

1067371 rows × 8 columns

Figure 8.46: Result of concatenation

4. Rename the columns as we did in *Exercise 8.01, Loading and Cleaning Our Data*:

```
retail.rename(index = str, \
              columns = {'Invoice' : 'invoice', \
                         'StockCode' : 'stock_code', \
                         'Quantity' : 'quantity', \
                         'InvoiceDate' : 'date', \
                         'Price' : 'unit_price', \
                         'Country' : 'country', \
                         'Description' : 'desc', \
                         'Customer ID' : 'cust_id'}, inplace = True)

retail.head()
```

The output will be as follows:

	invoice	stock_code	desc	quantity	date	unit_price	cust_id	country
0	489434	85048	15CM CHRISTMAS GLASS BALL 20 LIGHTS	12	01/12/2009 07:45	6.95	13085.0	United Kingdom
1	489434	79323P	PINK CHERRY LIGHTS	12	01/12/2009 07:45	6.75	13085.0	United Kingdom
2	489434	79323W	WHITE CHERRY LIGHTS	12	01/12/2009 07:45	6.75	13085.0	United Kingdom
3	489434	22041	RECORD FRAME 7" SINGLE SIZE	48	01/12/2009 07:45	2.10	13085.0	United Kingdom
4	489434	21232	STRAWBERRY CERAMIC TRINKET BOX	24	01/12/2009 07:45	1.25	13085.0	United Kingdom

Figure 8.47: The first five rows of the concatenated DataFrame

5. Check the statistical information for **retail**:

```
retail.isnull().sum().sort_values(ascending = False)
```

The output will be as follows:

```
cust_id       243007
desc            4382
country            0
unit_price         0
date               0
quantity           0
stock_code         0
invoice            0
dtype: int64
```

Figure 8.5: Ascending arrangement of statistics

You can fetch the details of the DataFrame by using the `.describe()` function.

```
retail.describe()
```

The output will be as follows:

	quantity	unit_price	cust_id
count	1.067371e+06	1.067371e+06	824364.000000
mean	9.938898e+00	4.649388e+00	15324.638504
std	1.727058e+02	1.235531e+02	1697.464450
min	-8.099500e+04	-5.359436e+04	12346.000000
25%	1.000000e+00	1.250000e+00	13975.000000
50%	3.000000e+00	2.100000e+00	15255.000000
75%	1.000000e+01	4.150000e+00	16797.000000
max	8.099500e+04	3.897000e+04	18287.000000

Figure 8.48: Statistical information about retail

6. Use the `.loc()` function to determine how many instances in **retail** have **38970.0** as their **unit_price** value:

```
retail.loc[retail['unit_price'] == 38970.0]
```

The output will be as follows:

	invoice	stock_code	desc	quantity	date	unit_price	cust_id	country
10-11	222681	C556445	M Manual	-1	10/06/2011 15:31	38970.0	15098.0	United Kingdom

Figure 8.49: Using the .loc function

7. Use the `.loc()` function again to determine how many instances in retail have **-53594.360000** as their **unit_price** value:

```
retail.loc[retail['unit_price'] == -53594.360000]
```

The output will be as follows:

	invoice	stock_code	desc	quantity	date	unit_price	cust_id	country
09-10	179403	A506401	B Adjust bad debt	1	29/04/2010 13:36	-53594.36	NaN	United Kingdom

Figure 8.50: Using the .loc function

8. Calculate how many negative values of **unit_price** and **quantity** are present in **retail**. If they are only a small percentage of the total number of instances, then remove them from **retail**:

```
(retail['unit_price'] <= 0).sum()
```

The output will be as follows:

```
6207
```

Similarly, find out the number of negative values of **quantity**:

```
(retail['quantity'] <= 0).sum()
```

The output will be as follows:

```
22950
```

9. Display the total number of negative instances for the **unit_price** and **quantity** columns:

```
retail[(retail['unit_price'] <= 0) & (retail['quantity'] <= 0) \
        & (retail['cust_id'].isnull())]
```

The output will be as follows:

	invoice	stock_code	desc	quantity	date	unit_price	cust_id	country
263	489464	21733	85123a mixed	-96	01/12/2009 10:52	0.0	NaN	United Kingdom
283	489463	71477	short	-240	01/12/2009 10:52	0.0	NaN	United Kingdom
09-10 284	489467	85123A	21733 mixed	-192	01/12/2009 10:53	0.0	NaN	United Kingdom
470	489521	21646	NaN	-50	01/12/2009 11:44	0.0	NaN	United Kingdom
3114	489655	20683	NaN	-44	01/12/2009 17:26	0.0	NaN	United Kingdom
...	...	...	...	...	...	...	...	...
535333	581210	23395	check	-26	07/12/2011 18:36	0.0	NaN	United Kingdom
535335	581212	22578	lost	-1050	07/12/2011 18:38	0.0	NaN	United Kingdom
10-11 535336	581213	22576	check	-30	07/12/2011 18:38	0.0	NaN	United Kingdom
536910	581226	23090	missing	-338	08/12/2011 09:56	0.0	NaN	United Kingdom
538925	581422	23169	smashed	-235	08/12/2011 15:24	0.0	NaN	United Kingdom

3457 rows × 8 columns

Figure 8.51: Total number of negative values for unit_price and quantity

10. Store the instances with missing values in another DataFrame:

```
null_retail = retail[retail.isnull().any(axis=1)]
null_retail
```

The output will be as follows:

		invoice	stock_code	desc	quantity	date	unit_price	cust_id	country
	263	489464	21733	85123a mixed	-96	01/12/2009 10:52	0.00	NaN	United Kingdom
	283	489463	71477	short	-240	01/12/2009 10:52	0.00	NaN	United Kingdom
09-10	284	489467	85123A	21733 mixed	-192	01/12/2009 10:53	0.00	NaN	United Kingdom
	470	489521	21646	NaN	-50	01/12/2009 11:44	0.00	NaN	United Kingdom
	577	489525	85226C	BLUE PULL BACK RACING CAR	1	01/12/2009 11:49	0.55	NaN	United Kingdom
...	...	...	...	...	...	...	...	...	...
	541536	581498	85099B	JUMBO BAG RED RETROSPOT	5	09/12/2011 10:26	4.13	NaN	United Kingdom
	541537	581498	85099C	JUMBO BAG BAROQUE BLACK WHITE	4	09/12/2011 10:26	4.13	NaN	United Kingdom
10-11	541538	581498	85150	LADIES & GENTLEMEN METAL SIGN	1	09/12/2011 10:26	4.96	NaN	United Kingdom
	541539	581498	85174	S/4 CACTI CANDLES	1	09/12/2011 10:26	10.79	NaN	United Kingdom
	541540	581498	DOT	DOTCOM POSTAGE	1	09/12/2011 10:26	1714.17	NaN	United Kingdom

243007 rows × 8 columns

Figure 8.52: The null_retail DataFrame

11. Delete the instances with missing values from **retail**:

```
new_retail = retail[(retail['unit_price'] > 0) \
                & (retail['quantity'] > 0)]
new_retail.describe()
```

The output will be as follows:

	quantity	unit_price	cust_id
count	1.041671e+06	1.041671e+06	805549.000000
mean	1.096345e+01	4.077038e+00	15331.954970
std	1.265149e+02	5.144898e+01	1696.737039
min	1.000000e+00	1.000000e-03	12346.000000
25%	1.000000e+00	1.250000e+00	13982.000000
50%	3.000000e+00	2.100000e+00	15271.000000
75%	1.000000e+01	4.130000e+00	16805.000000
max	8.099500e+04	2.511109e+04	18287.000000

Figure 8.53: The statistical information about new_retail

12. Plot a boxplot for **unit_price** to see if there are any outliers. If there are, remove those instances:

```
plt.subplots(figsize = (12, 6))
up = sns.boxplot(new_retail.unit_price)
```

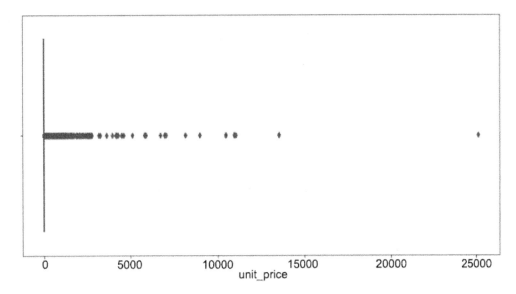

Figure 8.54: The boxplot for unit_price displaying outliers

13. Similarly, plot the **unit_price** boxplot for the modified values:

```
new_retail = new_retail[new_retail.unit_price < 15000]
new_retail.describe()
```

The output will be as follows:

	quantity	unit_price	cust_id
count	1.041670e+06	1.041670e+06	805549.000000
mean	1.096346e+01	4.052935e+00	15331.954970
std	1.265150e+02	4.518687e+01	1696.737039
min	1.000000e+00	1.000000e-03	12346.000000
25%	1.000000e+00	1.250000e+00	13982.000000
50%	3.000000e+00	2.100000e+00	15271.000000
75%	1.000000e+01	4.130000e+00	16805.000000
max	8.099500e+04	1.354133e+04	18287.000000

Figure 8.55: DataFrame with modified values

14. Plot a boxplot for the **unit_price** of the **new_retail** DataFrame.

```
up_new = sns.boxplot(new_retail.unit_price)
```

The output will be as follows:

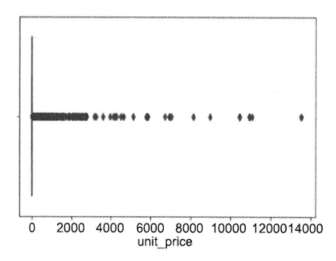

Figure 8.56: The boxplot for the modified unit_price column

15. Plot a boxplot for **quantity** to see if there are any outliers. If there are, remove those instances:

```
plt.subplots(figsize = (12, 6))
q = sns.boxplot(new_retail.quantity)
```

The output will be as follows:

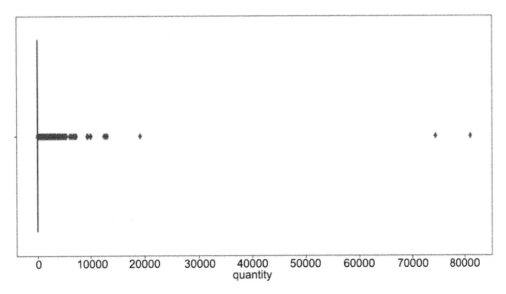

Figure 8.57: The boxplot for quantity displaying outliers

16. Plot the boxplot for **quantity** without outliers:

```
new_retail = new_retail[new_retail.quantity < 25000]
new_retail.describe()
```

The output will be as follows:

	quantity	unit_price	cust_id
count	1.041668e+06	1.041668e+06	805547.000000
mean	1.081448e+01	4.052940e+00	15331.957294
std	6.651307e+01	4.518691e+01	1696.735430
min	1.000000e+00	1.000000e-03	12346.000000
25%	1.000000e+00	1.250000e+00	13982.000000
50%	3.000000e+00	2.100000e+00	15271.000000
75%	1.000000e+01	4.130000e+00	16805.000000
max	1.915200e+04	1.354133e+04	18287.000000

Figure 8.58: New DataFrame details

17. Plot a boxplot for the **quantity** column of the **new_retail** DataFrame.

```
q_new = sns.boxplot(new_retail.quantity)
```

The output will be as follows:

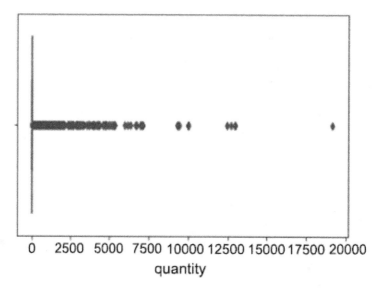

Figure 8.59: The boxplot for quantity without outliers

18. Use the following code to get some details about the **new_retail** DataFrame:

```
new_retail[(new_retail.desc.isnull()) \
        & (new_retail.cust_id.isnull())]
```

The output will be as follows:

	invoice	stock_code	desc	quantity	date	unit_price	cust_id	country

Figure 8.60: The new_retail DataFrame

19. Fetch the details of the DataFrame using the **.info()** function:

```
new_retail.info()
```

The output will be as follOws:

```
<class 'pandas.core.frame.DataFrame'>
MultiIndex: 1041668 entries, (09-10, 0) to (10
-11, 541909)
Data columns (total 8 columns):
invoice        1041668 non-null object
stock_code     1041668 non-null object
desc           1041668 non-null object
quantity       1041668 non-null int64
date           1041668 non-null object
unit_price     1041668 non-null float64
cust_id        805547 non-null float64
country        1041668 non-null object
dtypes: float64(2), int64(1), object(5)
memory usage: 72.7+ MB
```

Figure 8.61: Details for the new_retail DataFrame

20. Drop all the null values in the new DataFrame:

```
new_retail = new_retail.dropna()
new_retail.info()
```

The new DataFrame details will be as follows:

```
<class 'pandas.core.frame.DataFrame'>
MultiIndex: 805547 entries, (09-10, 0) to (10-
11, 541909)
Data columns (total 8 columns):
invoice       805547 non-null object
stock_code    805547 non-null object
desc          805547 non-null object
quantity      805547 non-null int64
date          805547 non-null object
unit_price    805547 non-null float64
cust_id       805547 non-null float64
country       805547 non-null object
dtypes: float64(2), int64(1), object(5)
memory usage: 57.1+ MB
```

Figure 8.62: Details of the new DataFrame

21. Move the values to a new DataFrame to avoid confusion:

```
retail = new_retail
retail.head()
```

The output will be as follows:

		invoice	stock_code	desc	quantity	date	unit_price	cust_id	country
	0	489434	85048	15CM CHRISTMAS GLASS BALL 20 LIGHTS	12	01/12/2009 07:45	6.95	13085.0	United Kingdom
	1	489434	79323P	PINK CHERRY LIGHTS	12	01/12/2009 07:45	6.75	13085.0	United Kingdom
09-10	2	489434	79323W	WHITE CHERRY LIGHTS	12	01/12/2009 07:45	6.75	13085.0	United Kingdom
	3	489434	22041	RECORD FRAME 7" SINGLE SIZE	48	01/12/2009 07:45	2.10	13085.0	United Kingdom
	4	489434	21232	STRAWBERRY CERAMIC TRINKET BOX	24	01/12/2009 07:45	1.25	13085.0	United Kingdom

Figure 8.63: DataFrame without null values

22. Convert the text in the **desc** column to lowercase:

```
retail.desc = retail.desc.str.lower()
retail.head()
```

The output will be as follows:

		invoice	stock_code	desc	quantity	date	unit_price	cust_id	country
	0	489434	85048	15cm christmas glass ball 20 lights	12	01/12/2009 07:45	6.95	13085.0	United Kingdom
	1	489434	79323P	pink cherry lights	12	01/12/2009 07:45	6.75	13085.0	United Kingdom
09-10	2	489434	79323W	white cherry lights	12	01/12/2009 07:45	6.75	13085.0	United Kingdom
	3	489434	22041	record frame 7" single size	48	01/12/2009 07:45	2.10	13085.0	United Kingdom
	4	489434	21232	strawberry ceramic trinket box	24	01/12/2009 07:45	1.25	13085.0	United Kingdom

Figure 8.64: Converting text into lowercase

23. Convert the **date** column into datetime format:

```
retail['date'] = pd.to_datetime(retail.date, \
                                format = '%d/%m/%Y %H:%M')
retail.head()
```

The output will be as follows:

		invoice	stock_code	desc	quantity	date	unit_price	cust_id	country
	0	489434	85048	15cm christmas glass ball 20 lights	12	2009-12-01 07:45:00	6.95	13085.0	United Kingdom
	1	489434	79323P	pink cherry lights	12	2009-12-01 07:45:00	6.75	13085.0	United Kingdom
09-10	2	489434	79323W	white cherry lights	12	2009-12-01 07:45:00	6.75	13085.0	United Kingdom
	3	489434	22041	record frame 7" single size	48	2009-12-01 07:45:00	2.10	13085.0	United Kingdom
	4	489434	21232	strawberry ceramic trinket box	24	2009-12-01 07:45:00	1.25	13085.0	United Kingdom

Figure 8.65: Converting date into datetime format

24. Add six new columns with the following names: **year_month**, **year**, **month**, **day**, **day_of_week**, and **hour**:

```
retail.insert(loc = 4, column = 'year_month', \
              value = retail.date.map(lambda x: 100 \
                                      * x.year + x.month))
retail.insert(loc = 5, column = 'year', \
              value = retail.date.dt.year)
retail.insert(loc = 6, column = 'month', \
              value = retail.date.dt.month)
retail.insert(loc = 7, column = 'day', \
              value = retail.date.dt.day)
retail.insert(loc = 8, column ='hour', \
              value = retail.date.dt.hour)
retail.insert(loc = 9, column='day_of_week', \
              value=(retail.date.dt.dayofweek)+1)
retail.head()
```

The output will be as follows:

	invoice	stock_code	desc	quantity	year_month	year	month	day	hour	day_of_week	date	unit_price
0	489434	85048	15cm christmas glass ball 20 lights	12	200912	2009	12	1	7	2	2009-12-01 07:45:00	6.95
1	489434	79323P	pink cherry lights	12	200912	2009	12	1	7	2	2009-12-01 07:45:00	6.75
2	489434	79323W	white cherry lights	12	200912	2009	12	1	7	2	2009-12-01 07:45:00	6.75
3	489434	22041	record frame 7" single size	48	200912	2009	12	1	7	2	2009-12-01 07:45:00	2.10
4	489434	21232	strawberry ceramic trinket box	24	200912	2009	12	1	7	2	2009-12-01 07:45:00	1.25

Figure 8.66: Adding new columns

25. Add a column called **spent**, which is the **quantity** multiplied by the **unit_price**:

```
retail.insert(loc = 11, column = 'spent', \
              value = (retail['quantity'] * retail['unit_price']))
retail.head()
```

The output will be as follows:

	invoice	stock_code	desc	quantity	year_month	year	month	day	hour	day_of_week	date	spent
0	489434	85048	15cm christmas glass ball 20 lights	12	200912	2009	12	1	7	2	2009-12-01 07:45:00	83.4
1	489434	79323P	pink cherry lights	12	200912	2009	12	1	7	2	2009-12-01 07:45:00	81.0
2	489434	79323W	white cherry lights	12	200912	2009	12	1	7	2	2009-12-01 07:45:00	81.0
3	489434	22041	record frame 7" single size	48	200912	2009	12	1	7	2	2009-12-01 07:45:00	100.8
4	489434	21232	strawberry ceramic trinket box	24	200912	2009	12	1	7	2	2009-12-01 07:45:00	30.0

Figure 8.67: Adding the spent column

26. Rearrange the columns as we did in *Exercise 8.02: Preparing Our Data*:

```
retail = retail[['invoice', 'country', 'cust_id', 'stock_code', \
                 'desc','quantity', 'unit_price', 'date', \
                 'spent', 'year_month', 'year', 'month', 'day', \
                 'day_of_week', 'hour']]
retail.head()
```

The output will be as follows:

	invoice	country	cust_id	stock_code	desc	quantity	unit_price	date	spent	year_month	year
0	489434	United Kingdom	13085.0	85048	15cm christmas glass ball 20 lights	12	6.95	2009-12-01 07:45:00	83.4	200912	2009
1	489434	United Kingdom	13085.0	79323P	pink cherry lights	12	6.75	2009-12-01 07:45:00	81.0	200912	2009
2	489434	United Kingdom	13085.0	79323W	white cherry lights	12	6.75	2009-12-01 07:45:00	81.0	200912	2009
3	489434	United Kingdom	13085.0	22041	record frame 7" single size	48	2.10	2009-12-01 07:45:00	100.8	200912	2009
4	489434	United Kingdom	13085.0	21232	strawberry ceramic trinket box	24	1.25	2009-12-01 07:45:00	30.0	200912	2009

Figure 8.68: The first five rows of the modified retail DataFrame

27. Determine which customers placed the most and fewest orders:

```
ord_cust = retail.groupby(by = ['cust_id', 'country'], \
                          as_index = False)['invoice'].count()
ord_cust.head(10)
```

The output will be as follows:

	cust_id	country	invoice
0	12346.0	United Kingdom	33
1	12347.0	Iceland	253
2	12348.0	Finland	51
3	12349.0	Italy	175
4	12350.0	Norway	17
5	12351.0	Unspecified	21
6	12352.0	Norway	103
7	12353.0	Bahrain	24
8	12354.0	Spain	58
9	12355.0	Bahrain	35

Figure 8.69: Orders made by customers in each country

28. Plot the graph for visualizing the preceding information:

```
plt.subplots(figsize = (15, 6))
oc = plt.plot(ord_cust.cust_id, ord_cust.invoice)
plt.xlabel('Customer ID')
plt.ylabel('Number of Orders')
plt.title('Number of Orders made by Customers')
plt.show()
```

The output will be as follows:

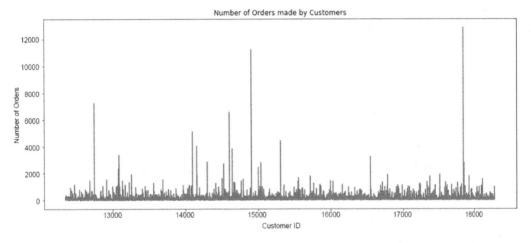

Figure 8.70: The top number of orders per customer

29. Find details about the orders per customer:

```
ord_cust.describe()
```

The output will be as follows:

	cust_id	invoice
count	5891.000000	5891.000000
mean	15309.025632	136.741979
std	1718.894226	353.448622
min	12346.000000	1.000000
25%	13823.500000	21.000000
50%	15308.000000	53.000000
75%	16794.500000	142.000000
max	18287.000000	12890.000000

Figure 8.71: Describing the customer orders

30. Determine which country has the customers that have spent the most money on orders:

```
ord_cust.sort_values(by = 'invoice', ascending = False).head()
```

The output will be as follows:

	cust_id	country	invoice
5446	17841.0	United Kingdom	12890
2551	14911.0	EIRE	11245
413	12748.0	United Kingdom	7228
2250	14606.0	United Kingdom	6566
1744	14096.0	United Kingdom	5111

Figure 8.72: The top five customers

31. Find the amount spent by customers:

```
spent_cust = retail.groupby(by = ['cust_id', 'country'], \
                            as_index = False)['spent'].sum()
spent_cust.head()
```

The output will be as follows:

	cust_id	country	spent
0	12346.0	United Kingdom	372.86
1	12347.0	Iceland	5633.32
2	12348.0	Finland	2019.40
3	12349.0	Italy	4428.69
4	12350.0	Norway	334.40

Figure 8.73: Amount of money spent

32. Plot a graph for the amount of money spent by the customers:

```
plt.subplots(figsize = (15, 6))
sc = plt.plot(spent_cust.cust_id, spent_cust.spent)
plt.xlabel('Customer ID')
plt.ylabel('Total Amount Spent')
plt.title('Amount Spent by Customers')
plt.show()
```

The output will be as follows:

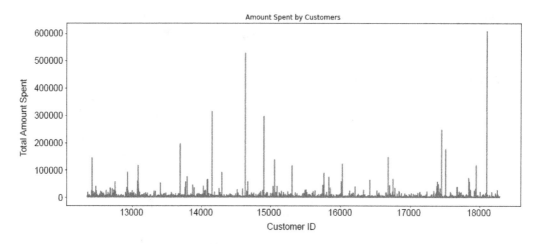

Figure 8.74: The amount spent by customers

33. Arrange the values in ascending order to get a clear picture:

```
spent_cust.sort_values(by = 'spent', ascending = False).head()
```

The output will be as follows:

	cust_id	country	spent
5705	18102.0	United Kingdom	608821.65
2290	14646.0	Netherlands	528602.52
1802	14156.0	EIRE	313946.37
2551	14911.0	EIRE	295972.63
5063	17450.0	United Kingdom	246973.09

Figure 8.75: The five customers who spent the most money

Thus, you can now tell that the customer with ID 18102 has spent the most money.

34. Get more details about the new DataFrame:

```
retail.tail()
retail.head()
```

The output for **retail.tail()** will be as follows:

	invoice	country	cust_id	stock_code	desc	quantity	unit_price	date	spent	year_month	year
541905	581587	France	12680.0	22899	children's apron dolly girl	6	2.10	2011-12-09 12:50:00	12.60	201112	2011
541906	581587	France	12680.0	23254	childrens cutlery dolly girl	4	4.15	2011-12-09 12:50:00	16.60	201112	2011
10-11 541907	581587	France	12680.0	23255	childrens cutlery circus parade	4	4.15	2011-12-09 12:50:00	16.60	201112	2011
541908	581587	France	12680.0	22138	baking set 9 piece retrospot	3	4.95	2011-12-09 12:50:00	14.85	201112	2011
541909	581587	France	12680.0	POST	postage	1	18.00	2011-12-09 12:50:00	18.00	201112	2011

Figure 8.76: Output for retail.tail()

The output for **retail.head()** will be as follows:

	invoice	country	cust_id	stock_code	desc	quantity	unit_price	date	spent	year_month	year	month
0	489434	United Kingdom	13085.0	85048	15cm christmas glass ball 20 lights	12	6.95	2009-12-01 07:45:00	83.4	200912	2009	12
1	489434	United Kingdom	13085.0	79323P	pink cherry lights	12	6.75	2009-12-01 07:45:00	81.0	200912	2009	12
09-10 2	489434	United Kingdom	13085.0	79323W	white cherry lights	12	6.75	2009-12-01 07:45:00	81.0	200912	2009	12
3	489434	United Kingdom	13085.0	22041	record frame 7" single size	48	2.10	2009-12-01 07:45:00	100.8	200912	2009	12
4	489434	United Kingdom	13085.0	21232	strawberry ceramic trinket box	24	1.25	2009-12-01 07:45:00	30.0	200912	2009	12

Figure 8.77: Output for retail.head()

35. Determine which month had the most orders:

```
ord_month = retail.groupby(['invoice'])['year_month']\
            .unique().value_counts().sort_index()
ord_month
```

The output will be as follows:

```
[200912]    1512
[201001]    1011
[201002]    1104
[201003]    1524
[201004]    1329
[201005]    1377
[201006]    1497
[201007]    1381
[201008]    1293
[201009]    1689
[201010]    2133
[201011]    2587
[201012]    1400
[201101]     986
[201102]     997
[201103]    1321
[201104]    1149
[201105]    1555
[201106]    1393
[201107]    1331
[201108]    1280
[201109]    1755
[201110]    1929
[201111]    2657
[201112]     777
Name: year_month, dtype: int64
```

Figure 8.78: Finding the month with the most orders

36. Plot a graph to find which month had the most orders:

```
om = ord_month.plot(kind= 'bar', figsize = (15, 6))
om.set_xlabel('Month')
om.set_ylabel('Number of Orders')
om.set_title('Orders per Month')
om.set_xticklabels(('Dec 09', 'Jan 10', 'Feb 10', 'Mar 10', \
                    'Apr 10', 'May 10','Jun 10', 'Jul 10', \
                    'Aug 10', 'Sep 10', 'Oct 10', 'Nov 10', \
                    'Dec 10', 'Jan 11', 'Feb 11', 'Mar 11', \
                    'Apr 11', 'May 11', 'Jun 11', 'Jul 11', \
                    'Aug 11', 'Sep 11', 'Oct 11', 'Nov 11', \
                    'Dec 11'), rotation = 'horizontal')
plt.show()
```

The output will be as follows:

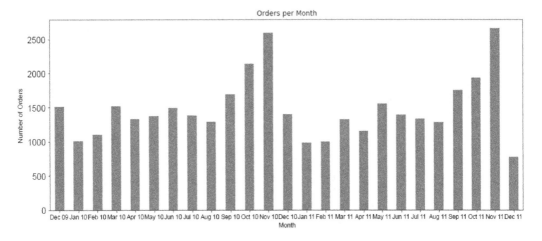

Figure 8.79: The orders per month

As you can see, the number of orders is the highest in the month of November.

37. Determine which day of the month had the most orders:

```
ord_day = retail.groupby('invoice')['day']\
        .unique().value_counts().sort_index()
ord_day
```

The output will be as follows:

```
[1]      1296
[2]      1172
[3]      1073
[4]      1224
[5]      1297
[6]      1279
[7]      1514
[8]      1487
[9]      1250
[10]     1235
[11]     1284
[12]     1083
[13]     1108
[14]     1304
[15]     1285
[16]     1267
[17]     1294
[18]     1258
[19]     1122
[20]     1167
[21]     1243
[22]     1200
[23]     1153
[24]     1185
[25]     1228
[26]     1118
[27]     1063
[28]     1295
[29]     1019
[30]      900
[31]      564
Name: day, dtype: int64
```

Figure 8.80: Finding the day of the month with maximum orders

38. Plot the graph to find the day of the month with the most orders:

```
od = ord_day.plot(kind='bar', figsize = (15, 6))
od.set_xlabel('Day of the Month')
od.set_ylabel('Number of Orders')
od.set_title('Orders per Day of the Month')
od.set_xticklabels(labels = [i for i in range (1, 32)], \
                   rotation = 'horizontal')
plt.show()
```

The output will be as follows:

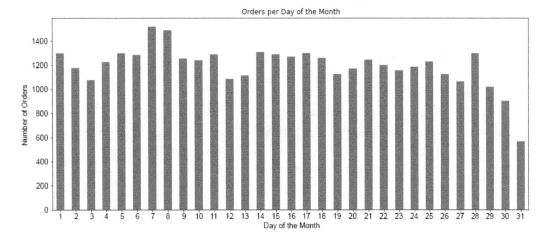

Figure 8.81: Orders per day of the month

From the preceding plot, you can see that the 7th and 8th are the days of the month when the most orders are received.

39. Determine which day of the week had the most orders:

```
ord_dayofweek = retail.groupby('invoice')['day_of_week']\
                    .unique().value_counts().sort_index()
ord_dayofweek
```

The output will be as follows:

```
[1]      5755
[2]      6626
[3]      6649
[4]      7773
[5]      5386
[6]        30
[7]      4748
Name: day_of_week, dtype: int64
```

Figure 8.82: Finding the day of the week with the most orders

40. Plot the graph to find the day of the week with the most orders:

```
odw = ord_dayofweek.plot(kind='bar', figsize = (15, 6))
odw.set_xlabel('Day of the Week')
odw.set_ylabel('Number of Orders')
odw.set_title('Orders per Day of the Week')
odw.set_xticklabels(labels = ['Mon', 'Tues', 'Wed', 'Thurs', \
                             'Fri', 'Sat', 'Sun'], \
                  rotation = 'horizontal')
plt.show()
```

The output will be as follows:

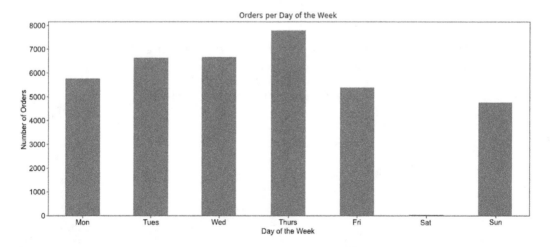

Figure 8.83: Orders per day of the week

As you can see in the preceding graph, Thursday is the day when the most orders are received.

41. Determine which customers spent the most money on one item:

```
q_item = retail.groupby(by = ['desc'], \
                        as_index = False)['quantity'].sum()
q_item.head()
```

The output will be as follows:

	desc	quantity
0	doormat union jack guns and roses	169
1	3 stripey mice feltcraft	663
2	4 purple flock dinner candles	340
3	50's christmas gift bag large	1885
4	animal stickers	385

Figure 8.84: Customers that spend the most money on one item

42. Sort the values in the **quantity** column in ascending order:

```
q_item.sort_values(by = 'quantity', ascending = False).head()
```

The output will be as follows:

	desc	quantity
5167	world war 2 gliders asstd designs	109169
5046	white hanging heart t-light holder	93640
295	assorted colour bird ornament	79913
2392	jumbo bag red retrospot	75759
752	brocade ring purse	71129

Figure 8.85: Top five most ordered items

43. Sort the quantity of items sold per month in descending order from the **retail** DataFrame:

```
item_month = retail.groupby(by = ['desc', 'year_month'], \
                            as_index = False)['quantity'].sum()
item_month.sort_values(by = 'quantity', ascending = False).head()
```

The output will be as follows:

	desc	year_month	quantity
5516	black and white paisley flower mug	201002	19248
8835	brocade ring purse	201009	13853
50510	set/6 woodland paper plates	201003	13099
50502	set/6 woodland paper cups	201003	13062
50468	set/6 strawberry paper cups	201003	13009

Figure 8.86: Finding out which item is the most sold item in the year

44. Similarly, sort the most sold items of the week in descending order from the **retail** DataFrame:

```
item_dayofweek = retail.groupby(by = ['desc', 'day_of_week'], \
                                as_index = False)\
                                ['quantity'].sum()
item_dayofweek.sort_values(by = 'quantity', \
                           ascending = False).head()
```

The output will be as follows:

	desc	day_of_week	quantity
27691	world war 2 gliders asstd designs	4	33334
1596	assorted colour bird ornament	4	22480
27048	white hanging heart t-light holder	2	20900
27050	white hanging heart t-light holder	4	20373
3966	brocade ring purse	5	19842

Figure 8.87: Finding out which item is the most sold item in the week

```
item_coun = retail.groupby(by = ['desc', 'country'], \
                           as_index = False)['quantity'].sum()
item_coun.sort_values(by = 'quantity', ascending = False).head()
```

The output will be as follows:

	desc	country	quantity
28897	world war 2 gliders asstd designs	United Kingdom	100720
28184	white hanging heart t-light holder	United Kingdom	86327
1637	assorted colour bird ornament	United Kingdom	74256
3800	brocade ring purse	United Kingdom	70725
12697	jumbo bag red retrospot	United Kingdom	69011

Figure 8.88: Finding out which item is the most sold item across all countries

45. Now, sort the items based on customer ID, stock code, and date:

```
retail_sort = retail.sort_values(['cust_id', \
                                  'stock_code', 'date'])
retail_sort_shift1 = retail_sort.shift(1)
retail_sort_reorder = retail_sort.copy()

retail_sort_reorder['reorder'] = np.where(retail_sort\
                                  ['stock_code'] \
                                  == retail_sort_shift1\
                                  ['stock_code'], 1, 0)
retail_sort_reorder.head()
```

The output will be as follows:

	invoice	country	cust_id	stock_code	desc	quantity	unit_price	date	spent	year_month	year
107803	499763	United Kingdom	12346.0	15056BL	edwardian parasol black	1	5.95	2010-03-02 13:08:00	5.95	201003	2010
107802	499763	United Kingdom	12346.0	15056N	edwardian parasol natural	1	5.95	2010-03-02 13:08:00	5.95	201003	2010
09-10	107804 499763	United Kingdom	12346.0	15056P	edwardian parasol pink	1	5.95	2010-03-02 13:08:00	5.95	201003	2010
107801	499763	United Kingdom	12346.0	20679	edwardian parasol red	1	5.95	2010-03-02 13:08:00	5.95	201003	2010
107800	499763	United Kingdom	12346.0	20682	red spotty childs umbrella	1	3.25	2010-03-02 13:08:00	3.25	201003	2010

Figure 8.89: Using the sort function to reorder

46. Create a new DataFrame for the reordered items:

```
rsr = pd.DataFrame((retail_sort_reorder\
                   .groupby('desc')['reorder'].sum()))\
                   .sort_values('reorder', ascending = False)
rsr.head()
```

The output will be as follows:

	reorder
desc	
white hanging heart t-light holder	3691
jumbo bag red retrospot	2120
regency cakestand 3 tier	2114
assorted colour bird ornament	1767
postage	1434

Figure 8.90: Finding out the most reordered items

47. Sort the reordered items in descending order of **quantity**:

```
q_up = retail.groupby(by = ['unit_price'], \
                as_index = False)['quantity'].sum()
q_up.sort_values('quantity', ascending = False).head(10)
```

The output will be as follows:

	unit_price	quantity
93	1.25	1038743
37	0.42	975149
116	1.65	785515
67	0.85	727418
101	1.45	469900
169	2.55	394637
185	2.95	337905
82	1.06	333979
142	2.10	325789
44	0.55	309178

Figure 8.91: Sorting the reordered items by quantity

48. Form an array to display the correlation coefficients for **unit_price** and **quantity** columns:

```
up_arr = np.array(retail.unit_price)
q_arr = np.array(retail.quantity)
np.corrcoef(up_arr, q_arr)
```

The output will be as follows:

```
array([[ 1.        ,  -0.00923511],
       [-0.00923511,  1.        ]])
```

49. Determine which countries the customers who placed the minimum number of orders are from:

```
ord_coun = retail.groupby(['country'])['invoice']\
            .count().sort_values()
ord_coun.head()
```

The output will be as follows:

```
country
Saudi Arabia        9
Czech Republic     25
Nigeria            30
Lebanon            45
Korea              53
Name: invoice, dtype: int64
```

Figure 8.97: Countries that placed the fewest orders

50. Plot the graph to visualize the preceding output:

```
ocoun = ord_coun.plot(kind='barh', figsize = (15, 6))
ocoun.set_xlabel('Number of Orders')
ocoun.set_ylabel('Country')
ocoun.set_title('Orders per Country')
plt.show()
```

The output will be as follows:

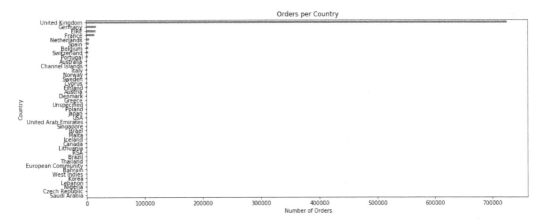

Figure 8.92: Distribution of orders by country

51. Delete the count of orders from **United Kingdom** as follows:

```
del ord_coun['United Kingdom']
```

Now plot the graph again:

```
ocoun2 = ord_coun.plot(kind='barh', figsize = (15, 6))
ocoun2.set_xlabel('Number of Orders')
ocoun2.set_ylabel('Country')
ocoun2.set_title('Orders per Country')
plt.show()
```

The output will be as follows:

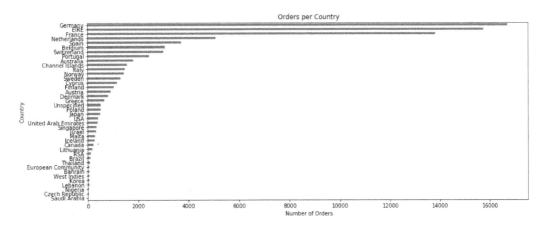

Figure 8.93: Number of orders per country

As you can see, Germany is the country with the highest number of orders.

52. Let's find out the country with the most money spent on orders:

```
coun_spent = retail.groupby('country')['spent']\
             .sum().sort_values()
cs = coun_spent.plot(kind='barh', figsize = (15, 6))
cs.set_xlabel('Amount Spent')
cs.set_ylabel('Country')
cs.set_title('Amount Spent per Country')
plt.show()
```

The output will be as follows:

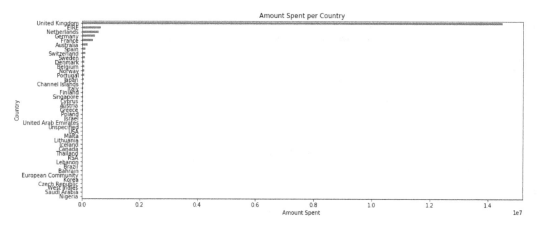

Figure 8.94: Country with the most money spent on orders

53. Delete the values for **United Kingdom** in the DataFrame and visualize the output in a graph:

```
del coun_spent['United Kingdom']
cs2 = coun_spent.plot(kind='barh', figsize = (15, 6))
cs2.set_xlabel('Amount Spent')
cs2.set_ylabel('Country')
cs2.set_title('Amount Spent per Country')
plt.show()
```

The output will be as follows:

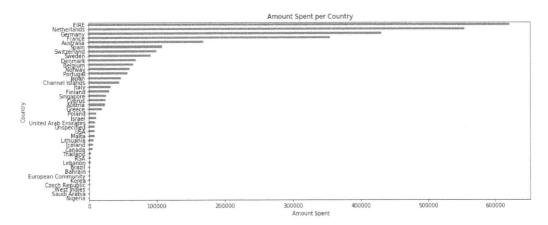

Figure 8.95: The amount spent per country excluding the United Kingdom

> **NOTE**
>
> To access the source code for this specific section, please refer to https://packt.live/2CfhOnl.
>
> You can also run this example online at https://packt.live/3e945N7. You must execute the entire Notebook in order to get the desired result.

As you can see, the Ireland is the country that has the customers who spent the most money on orders.

CHAPTER 09: ANALYSIS OF THE ENERGY CONSUMED BY APPLIANCES

ACTIVITY 9.01: ANALYZING THE APPLIANCES ENERGY CONSUMPTION

1. Using seaborn, plot a boxplot for the **a_energy** column:

```
app_box = sns.boxplot(new_data.a_energy)
```

The output will be as follows:

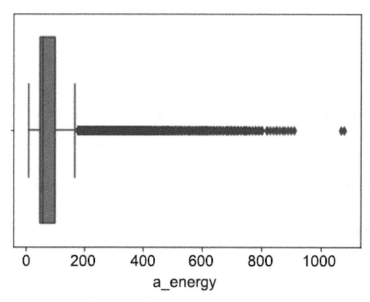

Figure 9.28: Box plot of a_energy

2. Use **.sum()** to determine the total number of instances wherein the value of the energy consumed by appliances is above 200 Wh:

```
out = (new_data['a_energy'] > 200).sum()
out
```

The output will be as follows:

```
1916
```

3. Calculate the percentage of the number of instances wherein the value of the energy consumed by appliances is above 200 Wh:

```
(out/19735) * 100
```

The output will be as follows:

```
9.708639473017481
```

4. Use `.sum()` to check the total number of instances wherein the value of the energy consumed by appliances is above 950 Wh:

```
out_e = (new_data['a_energy'] > 950).sum()
out_e
```

The output will be as follows:

```
2
```

5. Calculate the percentage of the number of instances wherein the value of the energy consumed by appliances is above 950 Wh:

```
(out_e/19735) * 100
```

6. Create a new DataFrame called **energy**, that is, **new_data** without the instances where **a_energy** is above 200 Wh:

```
energy = new_data[(new_data['a_energy'] <= 200)]
```

7. Print the statistical information of **energy** using `.describe()`:

```
energy.describe()
```

The output will be as follows:

	a_energy	kitchen_temp	kitchen_hum	liv_temp	liv_hum	laun_temp
count	17819.000000	17819.000000	17819.000000	17819.000000	17819.000000	17819.000000
mean	68.728324	21.687676	40.158323	20.294921	40.470961	22.230049
std	31.378141	1.605252	3.933742	2.172435	4.062130	1.971209
min	10.000000	16.790000	27.023333	16.100000	20.463333	17.200000
25%	50.000000	20.760000	37.260000	18.790000	37.930000	20.790000
50%	60.000000	21.600000	39.560000	19.926667	40.560000	22.100000
75%	80.000000	22.600000	42.900000	21.472333	43.326667	23.290000
max	200.000000	26.200000	59.633333	29.856667	56.026667	29.200000

Figure 9.29: The first five rows of energy

> **NOTE**
>
> To access the source code for this specific section, please refer to https://packt.live/3eg8Bty.
>
> You can also run this example online at https://packt.live/2V7lTQr. You must execute the entire Notebook in order to get the desired result.

ACTIVITY 9.02: OBSERVING THE TREND BETWEEN A_ENERGY AND DAY

1. Create a table called **app_day** that stores the total energy consumed by appliances per day of the week. To do this, use **.groupby()** on **day** in **new_en** and **.sum()** on **a_energy**:

```
app_day = new_en.groupby(by = ['day'], \
                         as_index = False)['a_energy'].sum()
```

2. Print **app_day**:

```
app_day
```

The output will be as follows:

	day	a_energy
0	1	161190
1	2	175930
2	3	191700
3	4	177830
4	5	161170
5	6	173640
6	7	183210

Figure 9.30: The total energy consumed by appliances per day of the week

3. Sort **app_day** in descending order to find out which day of the week the appliances consumed the most amount of energy:

```
app_day.sort_values(by = 'a_energy', ascending = False)
```

The output will be as follows:

	day	a_energy
2	3	191700
6	7	183210
3	4	177830
1	2	175930
5	6	173640
0	1	161190
4	5	161170

Figure 9.31: The total energy consumed by appliances on different days of the week

4. Set the figure size as **15, 6**:

```
plt.subplots(figsize = (15, 6))
```

5. Using seaborn, create a bar plot for the **day** and **a_energy** columns in **app_day**:

```
ad = sns.barplot(app_day.day, app_day.a_energy)
```

6. Set the **x**-axis label as **Day of the Week**, the **y**-axis label as **Energy Consumed by Appliances**, and the title as **Total Energy Consumed by Appliances**:

```
plt.xlabel('Day of the Week')
plt.ylabel('Energy Consumed by Appliances')
plt.title('Total Energy Consumed by Appliances')
```

7. Display the plot using **.show()**:

```
plt.show()
```

The output will be as follows:

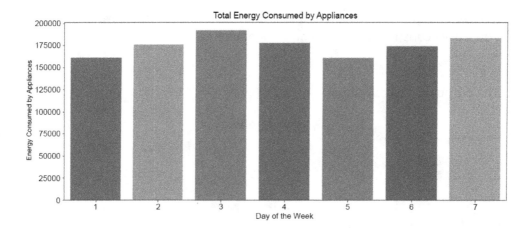

Figure 9.32: The total energy consumed by appliances each day of the week

> **NOTE**
>
> To access the source code for this specific section, please refer to https://packt.live/2YGGFIC.
>
> You can also run this example online at https://packt.live/2Y5S99k. You must execute the entire Notebook in order to get the desired result.

ACTIVITY 9.03: PLOTTING DISTRIBUTIONS OF THE HUMIDITY COLUMNS

1. Create a list called **col_hum** consisting of the humidity columns from **new_en**:

```
col_hum = ['kitchen_hum', 'liv_hum', 'laun_hum', 'off_hum', \
           'bath_hum', 'out_b_hum', 'iron_hum', 'teen_hum', \
           'par_hum']
```

2. Create a DataFrame called **hum**, containing data from the columns mentioned in **col_hum**:

```
hum = new_en[col_hum]
```

3. Print the first five rows of **hum**:

```
hum.head()
```

The output will be as follows:

	kitchen_hum	liv_hum	laun_hum	off_hum	bath_hum	out_b_hum	iron_hum	teen_hum
0	47.596667	44.790000	44.730000	45.566667	55.20	84.256667	41.626667	48.900000
1	46.693333	44.722500	44.790000	45.992500	55.20	84.063333	41.560000	48.863333
2	46.300000	44.626667	44.933333	45.890000	55.09	83.156667	41.433333	48.730000
3	46.066667	44.590000	45.000000	45.723333	55.09	83.423333	41.290000	48.590000
4	46.333333	44.530000	45.000000	45.530000	55.09	84.893333	41.230000	48.590000

Figure 9.33: The hum DataFrame

4. Plot a histogram for each of these variables with 15 bins each:

```
hum.hist(bins = 15, figsize = (12, 16))
```

The output will be as follows:

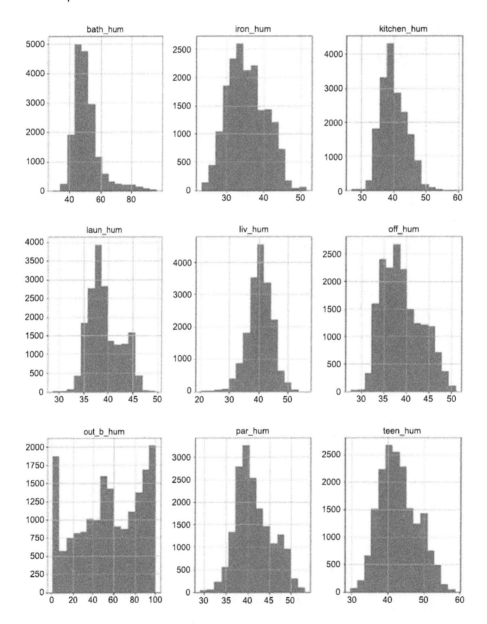

Figure 9.34: The distributions of the humidity variables

5. Create a list called **col_weather**, consisting of the remaining columns from **new_en**:

```
col_weather = ["out_temp", "dew_point", "out_hum", "out_press", \
               "wind", "visibility"]
```

6. Create a DataFrame called **weath** containing data from the columns mentioned in **col_weather**:

```
weath = new_en[col_weather]
```

7. Print the first five rows of **weath**:

```
weath.head()
```

The output will be as follows:

	out_temp	dew_point	out_hum	out_press	wind	visibility
0	6.600000	5.3	92.0	733.5	7.000000	63.000000
1	6.483333	5.2	92.0	733.6	6.666667	59.166667
2	6.366667	5.1	92.0	733.7	6.333333	55.333333
3	6.250000	5.0	92.0	733.8	6.000000	51.500000
4	6.133333	4.9	92.0	733.9	5.666667	47.666667

Figure 9.35: The weath DataFrame

8. Plot a histogram for each of these variables with 15 bins each:

```
weath.hist(bins = 15, figsize = (12, 16))
```

The output will be as follows:

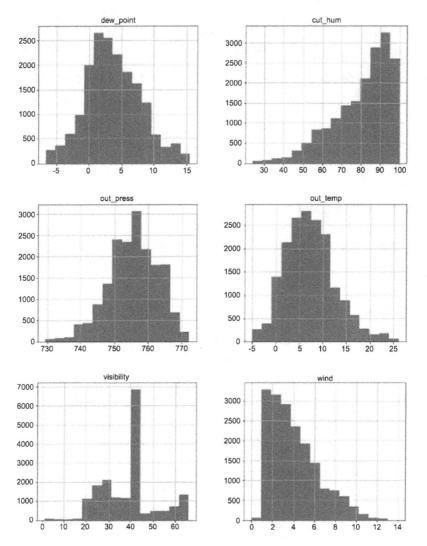

Figure 9.36: The distributions of the weather variables

> **NOTE**
>
> To access the source code for this specific section, please refer to https://packt.live/30Npqb4.
>
> You can also run this example online at https://packt.live/2YInxtF. You must execute the entire Notebook in order to get the desired result.

CHAPTER 10: ANALYZING AIR QUALITY

ACTIVITY 10.01: CHECKING FOR OUTLIERS

1. Plot a boxplot for the **PM25** feature using seaborn:

```
pm_25 = sns.boxplot(air['PM25'])
```

The output will be as follows:

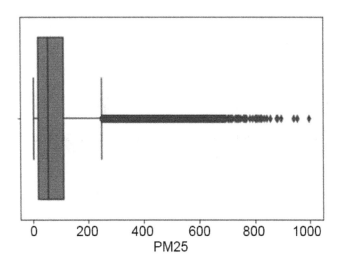

Figure 10.50: Boxplot for PM25

2. Check how many instances contain values of **PM25** higher than **250**:

```
(air['PM25'] >= 250).sum()
```

The output will be as follows:

```
18668
```

3. Store all the instances from *Step 2* in a DataFrame called **pm25** and print the first five rows:

```
pm25 = air.loc[air['PM25'] >= 250]
pm25.head()
```

The output will be as follows:

	year	month	day	hour	PM25	PM10	SO2	NO2	CO	O3	TEMP	PRES	DEWP	RAIN	wd	WSPM	station
120	2013	3	6	0	284.0	315.0	133.0	174.0	4000.0	28.0	4.9	1008.5	-6.4	0.0	NE	1.2	Aotizhongxin
121	2013	3	6	1	272.0	300.0	131.0	166.0	4000.0	22.0	4.8	1008.3	-5.9	0.0	NE	1.5	Aotizhongxin
140	2013	3	6	20	254.0	396.0	107.0	154.0	4200.0	17.0	4.4	1008.2	-2.5	0.0	SSW	1.1	Aotizhongxin
141	2013	3	6	21	266.0	380.0	117.0	159.0	3799.0	17.0	3.8	1007.7	-2.2	0.0	WSW	1.9	Aotizhongxin
142	2013	3	6	22	254.0	335.0	111.0	148.0	4099.0	17.0	2.4	1007.3	-2.5	0.0	WSW	1.2	Aotizhongxin

Figure 10.51: First five rows of pm25

4. Print the station names of the instances in **PM25** to ensure all the instances are not just from one station, but from multiple stations. This reduces the chances of them being incorrectly stored values:

```
pm25.station.unique()
```

The output will be as follows:

```
array(['Aotizhongxin', 'Changping', 'Dingling', 'Dongsi',
       'Guanyuan','Gucheng', 'Huairou', 'Nongzhanguan', 'Shunyi',
       'Tiantan', 'Wanliu', 'Wanshouxigong'], dtype=object)
```

5. Now, plot a boxplot for **PM10**:

```
pm_10 = sns.boxplot(air.PM10)
```

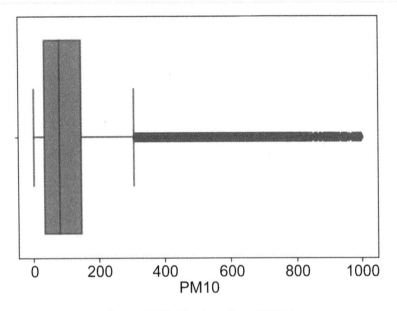

Figure 10.52: The boxplot of PM10

6. Store all the instances from **PM10** in a DataFrame called **pm10** and print the first five rows:

```
pm10 = air.loc[air['PM10'] >= 320]
pm10.head()
```

	year	month	day	hour	PM25	PM10	SO2	NO2	CO	O3	TEMP
139	2013	3	6	19	242.0	338.0	124.0	164.0	3700.0	17.0	5.1
140	2013	3	6	20	254.0	396.0	107.0	154.0	4200.0	17.0	4.4
141	2013	3	6	21	266.0	380.0	117.0	159.0	3799.0	17.0	3.8
142	2013	3	6	22	254.0	335.0	111.0	148.0	4099.0	17.0	2.4
143	2013	3	6	23	260.0	360.0	119.0	145.0	4000.0	17.0	2.3

Figure 10.53: First five rows for PM10

7. Check how many instances contain values of **PM10** higher than **320**:

```
(air['PM10'] >= 320).sum()
```

The output will be as follows:

```
12865
```

8. Calculate the number of instances that possess outlying values of both **PM25** and **PM10**:

```
air.loc[(air['PM25'] >= 250) & (air['PM10'] >= 320)]
```

The output will be as follows:

	year	month	day	hour	PM25	PM10	SO2	NO2	CO	O3	TEMP	PRES	DEWP	RAIN	wd	WSPM	station
140	2013	3	6	20	254.0	396.0	107.0	154.0	4200.0	17.0	4.4	1008.2	-2.5	0.0	SSW	1.1	Aotizhongxin
141	2013	3	6	21	266.0	380.0	117.0	159.0	3799.0	17.0	3.8	1007.7	-2.2	0.0	WSW	1.9	Aotizhongxin
142	2013	3	6	22	254.0	335.0	111.0	148.0	4099.0	17.0	2.4	1007.3	-2.5	0.0	WSW	1.2	Aotizhongxin
143	2013	3	6	23	260.0	360.0	119.0	145.0	4000.0	17.0	2.3	1007.2	-2.4	0.0	NNE	1.3	Aotizhongxin
149	2013	3	7	5	275.0	337.0	46.0	103.0	5599.0	17.0	1.6	1006.7	-1.5	0.0	NNE	1.7	Aotizhongxin
...	...	...	...	...	...	...	...	...	...	...	...	...	...	...	...	...	...
420187	2017	2	4	19	409.0	409.0	56.0	159.0	400.0	10.0	7.1	1013.5	-8.1	0.0	WNW	2.4	Wanshouxigong
420188	2017	2	4	20	389.0	389.0	42.0	153.0	400.0	7.0	7.7	1014.1	-10.2	0.0	NW	3.0	Wanshouxigong
420358	2017	2	11	22	259.0	369.0	75.0	108.0	1500.0	76.0	-1.7	1023.6	-13.9	0.0	ENE	0.9	Wanshouxigong
420359	2017	2	11	23	303.0	410.0	92.0	109.0	1700.0	2.0	-1.9	1023.5	-14.0	0.0	N	0.8	Wanshouxigong
420360	2017	2	12	0	350.0	388.0	96.0	106.0	2300.0	2.0	-3.2	1023.6	-12.9	0.0	NE	1.1	Wanshouxigong

10047 rows × 17 columns

Figure 10.54: Calculating outlying values of PM25 and PM10

9. Calculate the sum of values of **PM25** less than **250** and values of **PM10** less than **320**:

```
((air['PM25'] >= 250) & (air['PM10'] >= 320)).sum()
```

The output will be as follows:

```
10047
```

10. The **air** DataFrame can be displayed as follows:

```
air.describe()
```

The output will be as follows:

	year	month	day	hour	PM25
count	420768.000000	420768.000000	420768.000000	420768.000000	412029.000000
mean	2014.662560	6.522930	15.729637	11.500000	79.793428
std	1.177198	3.448707	8.800102	6.922195	80.822391
min	2013.000000	1.000000	1.000000	0.000000	2.000000
25%	2014.000000	4.000000	8.000000	5.750000	20.000000
50%	2015.000000	7.000000	16.000000	11.500000	55.000000
75%	2016.000000	10.000000	23.000000	17.250000	111.000000
max	2017.000000	12.000000	31.000000	23.000000	999.000000

Figure 10.55: The air DataFrame

11. Plot a boxplot for **so2**:

```
so2 = sns.boxplot(air.SO2)
```

The output will be as follows:

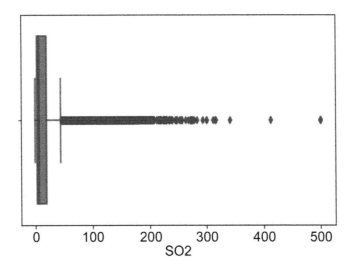

Figure 10.56: Boxplot for SO2

12. Check how many instances contain values of **SO2** higher than **70**:

```
(air['SO2'] >= 70).sum()
```

The output will be as follows:

```
14571
```

13. Calculate the number of instances that possess outlying values of **PM25**, **PM10**, and **SO2**:

```
((air['PM25'] >= 250) & (air['PM10'] >= 320) \
  & (air['SO2'] >= 70)).sum()
```

The output will be as follows:

```
2297
```

14. Next, check how many instances contain values of **SO2** higher than **300**:

```
(air['SO2'] >= 300).sum()
```

The output will be as follows:

```
9
```

15. Now, plot a boxplot for **NO2**:

```
no2 = sns.boxplot(air.NO2)
```

The output will be as follows:

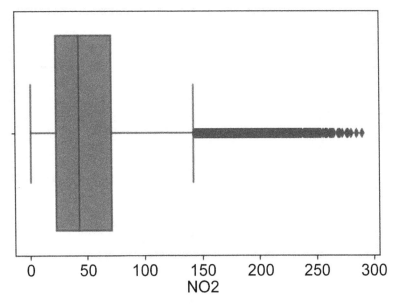

Figure 10.57: Boxplot for NO2

16. Similarly, check how many instances contain values of **NO2** higher than **150**:

```
(air['NO2'] >= 150).sum()
```

The output will be as follows:

```
5502
```

17. Calculate the number of instances that possess outlying values of **PM25**, **PM10**, **SO2**, and **NO2**:

```
((air['PM25'] >= 250) & (air['PM10'] >= 320) \
  & (air['SO2'] >= 200) & (air['NO2'] >= 150).sum()).sum()
```

The output is as follows:

```
0
```

18. Similarly, plot a boxplot for **CO**:

```
co = sns.boxplot(air.CO)
```

The output will be as follows:

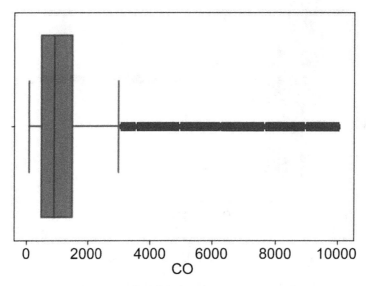

Figure 10.58: Boxplot for CO

19. Check how many instances contain values of **CO** higher than **3000**:

```
(air['CO'] >= 3000).sum()
```

The output will be as follows:

```
30355
```

20. In the similar fashion, plot a boxplot for **O3**.

```
o3 = sns.boxplot(air.O3)
```

The boxplot will be as follows:

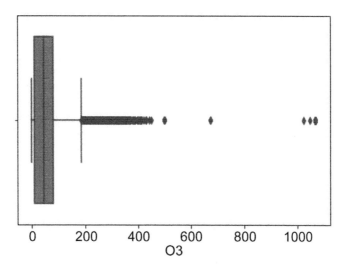

Figure 10.59: Boxplot for O3

21. Check how many instances contain values of **O3** higher than **200**:

```
(air['O3'] >= 200).sum()
```

The output will be as follows:

```
13358
```

22. Check how many instances contain values of **O3** higher than **470**:

```
(air['O3'] >= 470).sum()
```

The output is as follows:

```
24
```

23. Next, plot a boxplot for **RAIN**:

```
rain = sns.boxplot(air.RAIN)
```

The output is as follows:

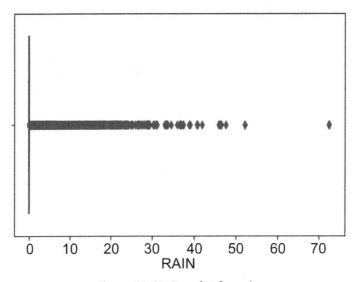

Figure 10.60: Boxplot for rain

24. Create a list of the following colors: **windows blue**, **amber**, **faded green**, and **dusty purple**, and set the parameters for the plots as follows: **Figsize** as **20, 10**; **Titlesize** as **18**; **Labelsize** as **12**; **Xtick labelsize** as **14**; **Ytick labelsize** as **14**:

```
colors = ["windows blue", "amber", "faded green", "dusty purple"]
sns.set(rc = {"figure.figsize": (18,8), \
            #"axes.titlesize" : 18, \
            "axes.labelsize" : 14, \
            "xtick.labelsize" : 14, "ytick.labelsize" : 14 })
```

25. Plot a boxplot with the **x** axis as **station** and the **y** axis as **PM25**. Set the data parameter as the **air** DataFrame, but with the missing values dropped:

```
sns.boxplot(x = 'station', y = 'PM25', \
            data = air.dropna(axis = 0).reset_index())
```

The plot will be as follows:

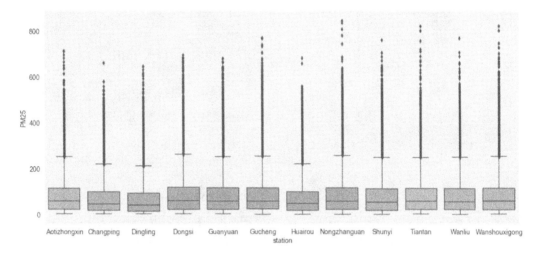

Figure 10.61: Boxplots for PM25 for each station

As you can see, the values of the outlying instances seem to be within a similar range at each station. Thus, the distribution of the data seems consistent.

26. Plot a boxplot with the **x** axis as **station** and the **y** axis as **PM10**. Set the data parameter as the **air** DataFrame, but with the missing values dropped:

```
sns.boxplot(x = 'station', y = 'PM10', \
            data = air.dropna(axis = 0).reset_index())
```

The plot will be as follows:

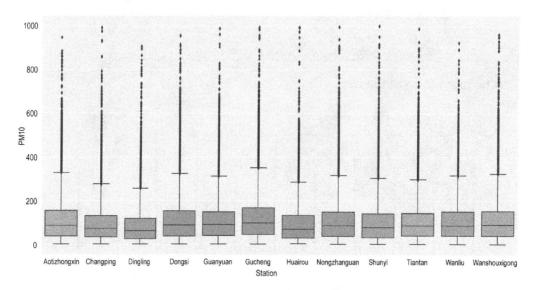

Figure 10.62: Boxplots for PM10

27. Plot a boxplot with the **x** axis as **station** and the **y** axis as **SO2**. Set the data parameter as the **air** DataFrame, but with the missing values dropped:

```
sns.boxplot(x = 'station', y = 'SO2', \
            data = air.dropna(axis = 0).reset_index())
```

The plot will be as follows:

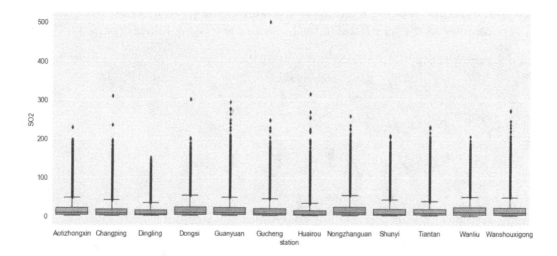

Figure 10.63: Boxplots for SO2

These look slightly more skewed. There are definite extreme outliers here, especially in the data for **Gucheng**. Even **Changping**, **Dongsi**, and **Huairou** have **SO2** values that don't seem normal and are quite distant from the rest of the values.

28. Plot a boxplot with the **x** axis as **station** and the **y** axis as **NO2**. Set the data parameter as the **air** DataFrame, but with the missing values dropped:

```
sns.boxplot(x = 'station', y = 'NO2', \
            data = air.dropna(axis = 0).reset_index())
```

The plot will be as follows:

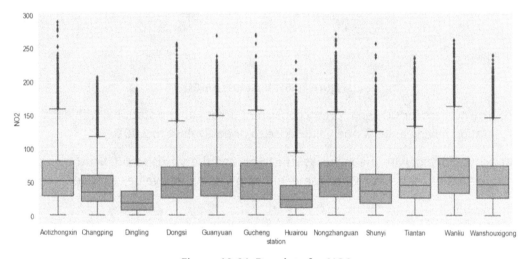

Figure 10.64: Boxplots for NO2

The values for **NO2** seem to differ more between stations, with those in **Aotizhongxin** being the highest, and those in **Dingling** being the lowest. There do seem to be some extreme outlying values here as well above **250**.

29. Plot a boxplot with the **x** axis as **station** and the **y** axis as **CO**. Set the data parameter as the **air** DataFrame, but with the missing values dropped:

```
sns.boxplot(x = 'station', y = 'CO', \
            data = air.dropna(axis = 0).reset_index())
```

The plot will be as follows:

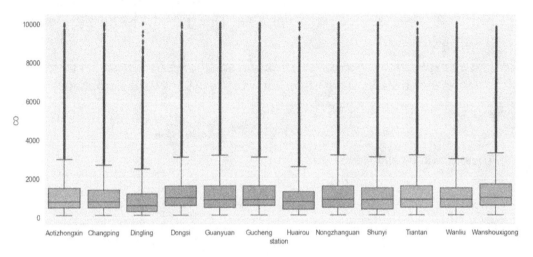

Figure 10.65: Boxplots for CO

The outliers for **CO** seem pretty consistent across all the stations, with each station having at least one value close to or equivalent to **1000**.

30. Plot a boxplot with the **x** axis as **station** and the **y** axis as **O3**. Set the data parameter as the **air** DataFrame, but with the missing values dropped:

```
sns.boxplot(x = 'station', y = 'O3', \
            data = air.dropna(axis = 0).reset_index())
```

The plot will be as follows:

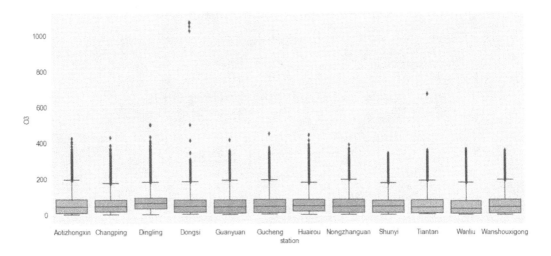

Figure 10.66: Boxplots for O3

There are extreme outliers in the case of **O3**, and these outliers will be genuine outliers (mistakes in capturing data) because such high levels of ozone in the air are harmful.

31. Plot a boxplot with the **x** axis as **station** and the **y** axis as **RAIN**. Set the data parameter as the **air** DataFrame, but with the missing values dropped:

```
sns.boxplot(x = 'station', y = 'RAIN', \
            data = air.dropna(axis = 0).reset_index())
```

The plot will be as follows:

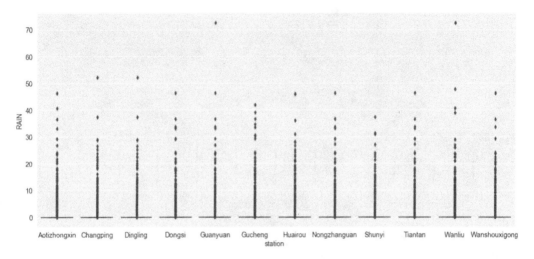

Figure 10.67: Boxplots for RAIN

> **NOTE**
>
> To access the source code for this specific section, please refer to https://packt.live/3fziK4q.
>
> You can also run this example online at https://packt.live/2UPloLA. You must execute the entire Notebook in order to get the desired result.

As you can see, there are extreme outliers in the case of **RAIN** as well, with **Guanyuan** and **Wanliu** having almost the same values.

ACTIVITY 10.02: OBSERVING THE POLLUTANT CONCENTRATION PER YEAR

1. Create a DataFrame called **year_so2** that contains the median of the **SO2** concentration per year:

```
year_so2 = new_air[['SO2','year','station']]\
        .groupby(["year"]).median().reset_index()\
        .sort_values(by = 'year', ascending = False)
```

2. Print **year_so2**:

```
year_so2
```

The expected output of a DataFrame for **year_so2** is as follows:

	year	SO2
4	2017	12.0000
3	2016	4.0000
2	2015	6.0000
1	2014	9.0000
0	2013	10.8528

Figure 10.68: The year_so2 DataFrame

3. Create a point plot for **year_so2**:

```
sns.pointplot(x = 'year', y = 'SO2', data = year_so2)
```

The expected output of the point plot for **year_so2** is as follows:

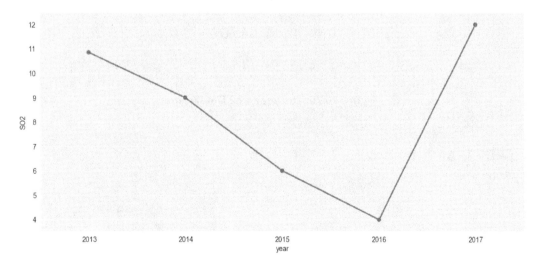

Figure 10.69: The median SO2 concentration per year

The preceding graph depicts a steady decrease in the concentration of **SO2** from 2013 to 2016, which is when it was at its lowest. It jumps up, however, in 2017. Once again, this could be due to the fact that 2017 only contains data for 2 months.

4. Create a DataFrame called **year_no2** that contains the median of the **NO2** concentration per year:

```
year_no2 = new_air[['NO2','year','station']]\
        .groupby(["year"]).median().reset_index()\
        .sort_values(by = 'year', ascending = False)
```

5. Print **year_no2**:

```
year_no2
```

The expected output of a DataFrame for **year_no2** is as follows:

	year	NO2
4	2017	50.0
3	2016	39.0
2	2015	41.0
1	2014	45.0
0	2013	46.0

Figure 10.70: The year_no2 DataFrame

6. Create a point plot for **year_no2**:

```
sns.pointplot(x = 'year', y = 'NO2', data = year_no2)
```

The expected output of the point plot for **year_no2** is as follows:

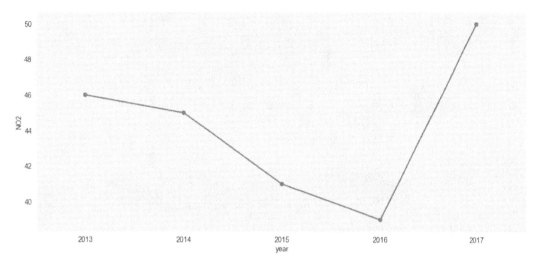

Figure 10.71: The median NO2 concentration per year

The concentration of **NO2** has also decreased like that of **SO2**; however, unlike that of **SO2**, the decrease has been smaller. It dropped the most from 2014 to 2015.

7. Create a DataFrame called **year_co** that contains the median of the **CO** concentration per year:

```
year_co = new_air[['CO','year','station']]\
        .groupby(["year"]).median().reset_index()\
        .sort_values(by = 'year', ascending = False)
```

8. Print **year_co**:

```
year_co.head()
```

The expected output of a DataFrame for **year_co** is as follows:

	year	CO
4	2017	900.0
3	2016	800.0
2	2015	900.0
1	2014	900.0
0	2013	900.0

Figure 10.72: The average concentration of CO per year

9. Create a point plot for **year_co**:

```
sns.pointplot(x = 'year', y = 'CO', data = year_co)
```

The expected output of the point plot for **year_co** is as follows:

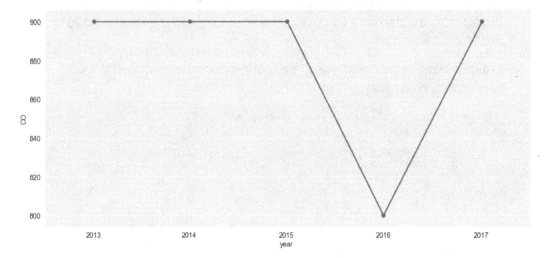

Figure 10.73: The median concentration of CO per year

The concentration of CO was constant for 3 years, and then dropped by 100 in 2016. Maybe if data for the remaining months of 2017 had also been collected, the median concentration for 2017 would also be 800 or lower.

10. Create a DataFrame called **year_o3** that contains the median of the **O3** concentration per year:

```
year_o3 = new_air[['O3','year','station']]\
          .groupby(["year"]).median().reset_index()\
          .sort_values(by = 'year', ascending = False)
```

11. Print **year_o3**:

```
year_o3.head()
```

The expected output of a DataFrame for **year_o3** is as follows:

	year	O3
4	2017	38.0
3	2016	45.0
2	2015	45.0
1	2014	45.0
0	2013	45.0

Figure 10.74: The year_o3 DataFrame

12. Create a point plot for **year_o3**:

```
sns.pointplot(x = 'year', y = 'O3', data = year_o3)
```

The expected output of the point plot for **year_o3** is the following:

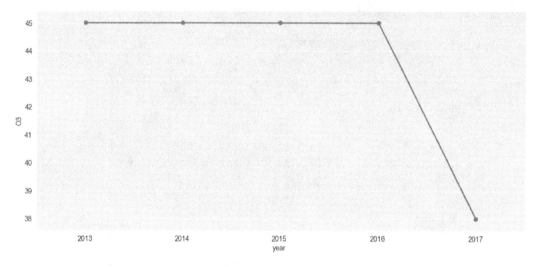

Figure 10.75: Point plot for average concentration of O3 per year

> **NOTE**
>
> To access the source code for this specific section, please refer to https://packt.live/3ecl7c4.
>
> You can also run this example online at https://packt.live/2ALcE2d. You must execute the entire Notebook in order to get the desired result.

ACTIVITY 10.03: OBSERVING POLLUTANT CONCENTRATION PER MONTH

13. Create a DataFrame for the pollutant **PM2.5** that stores the median concentration for each month. Plot the DataFrame as a point plot:

```
mpm25 = new_air[['PM25','month','station']]\
        .groupby(["month"]).median().reset_index()\
        .sort_values(by = 'month',ascending = False)
sns.pointplot(x = 'month', y = 'PM25', data = mpm25)
```

The expected output is as follows:

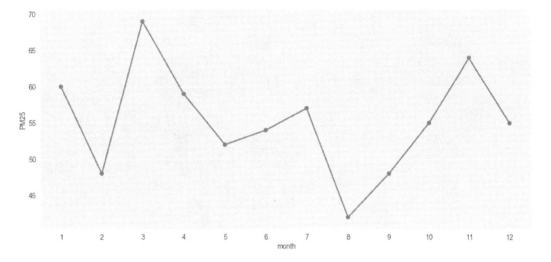

Figure 10.76: The average PM25 per month

The preceding graph displays quite an erratic trend in the median concentration of PM25 particles per month. The concentration is at its lowest in the month of August and at its highest in March.

14. Create a DataFrame for the pollutant **PM10** that stores the median concentration for each month. Plot the DataFrame as a point plot:

```
mpm10 = new_air[['PM10','month','station']]\
        .groupby(["month"]).median().reset_index()\
        .sort_values(by = 'month',ascending = False)
sns.pointplot(x = 'month', y = 'PM10', data = mpm10)
```

The expected output is as follows:

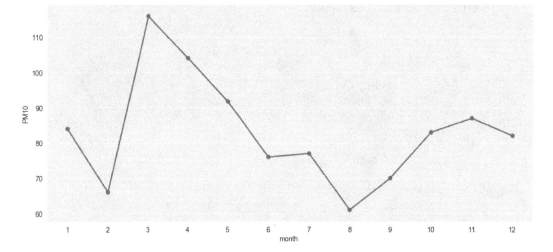

Figure 10.77: The average PM10 particles per month

Once again, the plots of PM25 and PM10 particles are quite similar, with the highest concentration of both being observed in March, and the lowest in August.

15. Create a DataFrame for the pollutant **SO2** that stores the median concentration for each month. Plot the DataFrame as a point plot:

```
mso2 = new_air[['SO2','month','station']]\
        .groupby(["month"]).median().reset_index()\
        .sort_values(by = 'month',ascending = False)
sns.pointplot(x = 'month', y = 'SO2', data = mso2)
```

The output will be as follows:

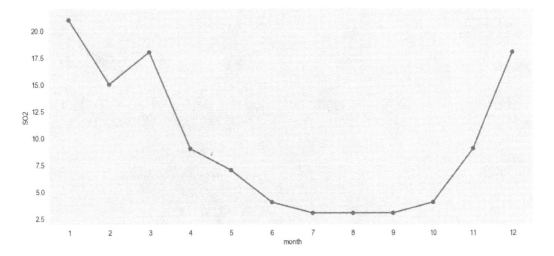

Figure 10.78: The average SO2 concentration per month

The concentration of **SO2** in general goes down between January and September, but begins to rise in October, increasing rapidly in November and December.

16. Create a DataFrame for the pollutant **NO2** that stores the median concentration for each month. Plot the DataFrame as a point plot:

```
mno2 = new_air[['NO2','month','station']]\
        .groupby(["month"]).median().reset_index()\
        .sort_values(by = 'month',ascending = False)
sns.pointplot(x = 'month', y = 'NO2', data = mno2)
```

The expected output is as follows:

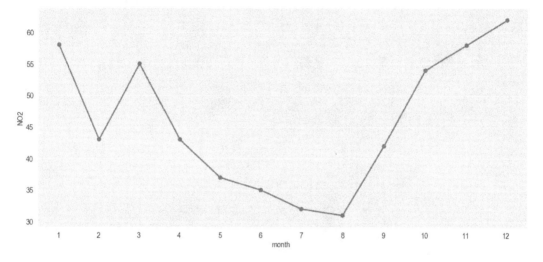

Figure 10.79: The concentration of NO2 per month

In general, the concentration of **NO2** appears to drop between March and August, but then increases rapidly in September and October before increasing slowly in November and December.

17. Now, create a DataFrame for the pollutant **CO** that stores the median concentration for each month. Plot the DataFrame as a point plot:

```
mco = new_air[['CO','month','station']]\
    .groupby(["month"]).median().reset_index()\
    .sort_values(by = 'month',ascending = False)
sns.pointplot(x = 'month', y = 'CO', data = mco)
```

The expected output is as follows:

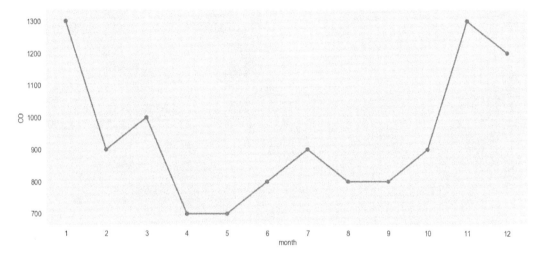

Figure 10.80: The concentration of CO per month

The concentration of **CO** also seems to follow an erratic trend, with it being highest in January, November, and December. The months between January and November have a comparatively low concentration of **CO**, with April and May having the lowest.

18. Now, create a DataFrame for the pollutant **O3** that stores the median concentration for each month. Plot the DataFrame as a point plot:

```
mo3 = new_air[['O3','month','station']]\
      .groupby(["month"]).median().reset_index()\
      .sort_values(by = 'month',ascending = False)
sns.pointplot(x = 'month', y = 'O3', data = mo3)
```

The expected output is as follows:

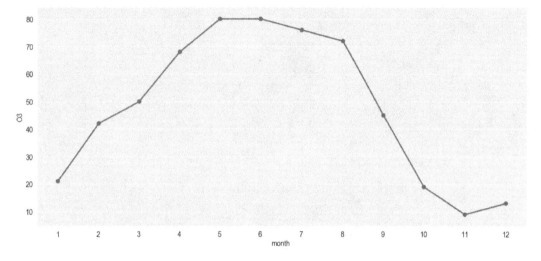

Figure 10.81: The median concentration of O3 per month

> **NOTE**
>
> To access the source code for this specific section, please refer to https://packt.live/37C9CJG.
>
> You can also run this example online at https://packt.live/37FDp4q. You must execute the entire Notebook in order to get the desired result.

INDEX

Y

Z

CPSIA information can be obtained
at www.ICGtesting.com
Printed in the USA
LVHW101535220920
666798LV00006B/151